Systemic Risk in the Financial Sector

Centre for International
Governance Innovation

Systemic Risk in the Financial Sector

Ten Years after the Great Crash

EDITORS

DOUGLAS W. ARNER

EMILIOS AVGOULEAS

DANNY BUSCH

STEVEN L. SCHWARCZ

ISBN 978-1-928096-88-7 (cloth)
ISBN 978-1-928096-89-4 (paper)
ISBN 978-1-928096-90-0 (ePUB)
ISBN 978-1-928096-91-7 (ePDF)

Library and Archives Canada Cataloguing in Publication

Title: Systemic risk in the financial sector : ten years after the great crash / editors: Douglas W. Arner ; Emilios Avgouleas ; Danny Busch ; Steven L. Schwarcz.

Names: Arner, Douglas W., editor. | Avgouleas, Emilios, 1968- editor. | Busch, Danny, editor. | Schwarcz, Steven L., editor. | Centre for International Governance Innovation, issuing body.

Description: Includes bibliographical references.

Identifiers: Canadiana (print) 20190137479 | Canadiana (ebook) 20190143738 | ISBN 9781928096887 (cloth) | ISBN 9781928096894 (paper) | ISBN 9781928096900 (ePUB) | ISBN 9781928096917 (ePDF)

Subjects: LCSH: Global Financial Crisis, 2008-2009. | LCSH: Monetary policy. | LCSH: Economic policy.

Classification: LCC HB3722 .S97 2019 | DDC 339.5—dc23

Published by the Centre for International Governance Innovation (CIGI).

Cover design by Brigitte Binet. Page design by Brooklynn Schwartz.

Printed and bound in Canada.

Centre for International
Governance Innovation

Centre for International Governance Innovation
67 Erb Street West
Waterloo, ON Canada N2L 6C2

www.cigionline.org

Contents

Abbreviations and Acronyms

ABCP	asset-backed commercial paper
ABMI	ASEAN+3 Bond Market Initiative
AFC	Asian financial crisis
AIFs	alternative investment funds
AIFMD	Alternative Investment Fund Managers Directive
AIG	American International Group
AI/ML	artificial intelligence and machine learning
AMCs	asset management companies
AMRO	ASEAN+3 Macroeconomic Research Office

ASEAN	Association of Southeast Asian Nations
ASEAN+3	Association of Southeast Asian Nations Plus Three
AT1	Additional Tier 1
ATB	Alberta Treasury Branches
BCBS	Basel Committee on Banking Supervision
BIS	Bank for International Settlements
BoC	Bank of Canada
BRRD	Bank Recovery and Resolution Directive
CBBA	Central Bank as Banking Authority index
CBI	central bank independence
CBSS	Central Bank Supervisor Share index
CCMRS	cooperative capital markets regulatory system
CCPs	central counterparty clearing houses
CDIC	Canada Deposit Insurance Corporation
CDSs	credit default swaps
CEPR	Centre for Economic Policy Research
CEPS	Centre for European Policy Studies
CET1	common equity tier one
CFTC	Commodity Futures Trading Commission
CIBC	Canadian Imperial Bank of Canada
CIGI	Centre for International Governance Innovation
CISS	coincident index of systemic stress
CJEU	Court of Justice of the European Union
CMHC	Canada Mortgage and Housing Corporation
CMI	Chiang Mai Initiative
CMIM	Chiang Mai Initiative Multilateralization Agreement
CMRA	Capital Markets Regulatory Authority

CMSA	Capital Markets Stability Act
CMU	Capital Markets Union
CoCos	contingent convertible bonds
CRAs	credit rating agencies
CREF	College Retirement Equities Fund
CSA	Canadian Securities Administrators
CSRI	cyclical systemic risk indicator
CTRO	chief technology risk officer
DGS	Deposit Guarantee Scheme
DoF	Department of Finance
D-SIBs	domestic systemically important banks
DTI	debt to income
EBA	European Banking Authority
EBU	European Banking Union
ECB	European Central Bank
ECGI	European Corporate Governance Institute
EIOPA	European Insurance and Occupational Pensions Authority
EMIR	European Market Infrastructure Regulation
EMU	Economic and Monetary Union
ESAs	European Supervisory Authorities
ESM	European Stability Mechanism
ESMA	European Securities and Markets Authority
ESRB	European Systemic Risk Board
FCAC	Financial Consumer Agency of Canada
FDIC	Federal Deposit Insurance Corporation
FIBO	Financial Industry Business Ontology
FICO	minimum credit score

fintech	financial technology
FISC	Financial Institutions Supervisory Committee
FMIs	financial market infrastructures
FPC	Financial Policy Committee
FRB	Federal Reserve Board
FRS	Federal Reserve System
FRBKC	Federal Reserve Bank of Kansas City
FRBNY	Federal Reserve Bank of New York
FRFIs	federally regulated financial institutions
FSB	Financial Stability Board
FSHH	Financial Supervision Herfindahl Hirschman Index
FSOC	Financial Stability Oversight Council
FSRI	financial stability risk index
G7	Group of Seven
G20	Group of Twenty
GFC	global financial crisis
GLEIF	Global Legal Entity Identifier Foundation
GMT	Grilli, Masciandaro and Tabellini Index
GMU	George Mason University
G-SIB	global systemically important bank
G-SIFI	global systemically important financial institution
G-SIIs	global systemically important insurers
HAMP	Home Affordable Modifications Program
HKU	University of Hong Kong
HM	Her Majesty's (Treasury)
HoA	Heads of Agencies Committee
IAIS	International Association of Insurance Supervisors

ICOs	initial coin offerings
IIROC	Investment Industry Regulatory Organization of Canada
IMF	International Monetary Fund
IOSCO	International Organization of Securities Commissions
IT	information technology
LAW	Leaning Against the Wind
LEI	Legal Entity Identifier
LoLR	lender of last resort
LTV	loan to value
MAPP	macroprudential policy index
MBS	mortgage-backed securities
M-M	Modigliani-Miller
MMMFs	money market mutual funds
MoF	Ministry of Finance
MPS	Monte dei Paschi di Sienna
MREL	Minimum Requirements for Own Funds and Eligible Liabilities
NBER	National Bureau of Economic Research
NBNI	non-bank, non-insurer
NCWO	no creditor worse off
NPEs	non-performing bank exposures
NPLs	non-performing loans
OECD	Organisation for Economic Co-operation and Development
OFR	Office of Financial Research
OLA	Orderly Liquidation Authority
OSC	Ontario Securities Commission
OSFI	Office of the Superintendent of Financial Institutions
OTC	over-the-counter

OTD	originate to distribute
PEPP	Pan-European Personal Pension Product
PSI	private sector involvement
regtech	regulatory technology
repo	repurchase agreement
RMBSs	residential mortgage-backed securities
ROE	return on equity
SAC	Senior Advisory Committee
SCAP	Supervisory Capital Assessment Program
SDRs	swap data repositories
SEC	US Securities and Exchange Commission
SIFIs	systemically important financial institutions
SRB	Single Resolution Board
SRC	Systemic Risk Charge
SRF	Single Resolution Fund
SRM	Single Resolution Mechanism
SSM	Single Supervisory Mechanism
STS	simple, transparent and standardized
T2	Tier 2
TBTF	too big to fail
TCTF	too connected to fail
techfin	technology finance
TFEU	Treaty on the Functioning of the European Union
TLAC	total loss-absorbing capacity
TRs	trade repositories
UCITS	Undertakings for the Collective Investment in Transferable Securities
VaR	value at risk
VMGH	variation margin gains haircut

Introduction: Thinking Hard about Systemic Risk

HOWELL E. JACKSON

As we pass the tenth anniversary of the apex of the financial crisis in the fall of 2008, the contributors to this volume are focused admirably and with considerable insight on the phenomenon at the core of the crisis: the manifestations of extreme systemic risks to the financial system starting in the summer of 2007 and continuing through 2009 and beyond. The breadth of coverage is impressive, exploring the centrality of leverage (John Geanakoplos) and inadequate capital requirements (Anat R. Admati and Martin F. Hellwig); the systemic risks associated with clearing houses (Paolo Saguato and Guido Ferrarini); the role of macroeconomic policies in precipitating the crisis (Donato Masciandaro); the risks associated with new financial technologies (Douglas W. Arner, Ross P. Buckley and Dirk Zetzsche); the challenges of shadow banking (Danny Busch and Mirik van Rijn); the coherence of resolution strategies that have been adopted in response to the crisis (Tobias H. Tröger and also Emilios Avgouleas and Charles Goodhart), as well as the potential risks associated with moving toward an overly harmonized international system of systemic risk regulation (Roberta Romano); the value of data standardization (Richard Berner and Kathryn Judge); and the merits of entity versus activities regulation (Jeremy C. Kress, Patricia A. McCoy and Daniel Schwarcz). Several of the contributors attempt more holistic assessments of the problem of systemic risk in the financial system — one chapter taking a comparative perspective between US and EU regulation (Ron Feldman and Paul Hiebert); another chapter comparing Canadian experiences with systemic risks (Anita Anand and Maziar Peihani); yet another extending the analysis to earlier financial crises (Ross P. Buckley, Emilios Avgouleas and Douglas W. Arner); and capped off with a concluding chapter offering a more comprehensive and theoretical presentation of the subject (Steven L. Schwarcz).

It should come as no surprise that scholars of this calibre are still working through their understanding of systemic risks in financial regulation a full decade after the financial crisis. After all, it was not until 30 years after the Great Depression that Milton Friedman and Anna Schwartz published *A Monetary History of the United States* in 1963, with its now canonical critique of Federal Reserve Board policy in the 1930s; arguably, scholars still have not universally accepted a shared understanding as to whether the Glass-Steagall Act of 1933 or some modern update thereon constitutes sound public policy. So, on the time scale needed to fully absorb the significance of major financial disasters, we are in the early days and should not expect to reach immediate consensus on either diagnoses or prognoses. Still, we should be striving to understand the financial crisis and its implications. To this end, this volume makes many helpful and original contributions. It also affords me the opportunity in this introduction to refine my own understanding of systemic risk in the aftermath of the financial crisis, a perspective that is highly sympathetic to many of the contributions in this volume, but one that may offer readers a framework that illuminates various facets of systemic risk that are explored in the volume as well as highlighting several areas where the views of some of the contributors might be seen to be in tension with each other.[1]

Defining the Concept of Systemic Risk

A prerequisite to any discussion of systemic risk is a workable definition of that term. Perhaps surprisingly, policy analysts discussing systemic risks can be frustratingly opaque in defining the concept, and one observes many different formulations in the literature. Some definitions focus solely on macroeconomic consequences. The European Central Bank (ECB), for example, has defined systemic risk as a risk of financial instability "so widespread that it impairs the functioning of a financial system to the point where economic growth and welfare suffer materially."[2] In some instances, the scope of systemic risks is pushed even farther to encompass "any set of circumstances that threatens the stability of or public confidence in the financial system," potentially extending to climate change or rogue asteroids.[3]

Others have focused on more specific factors, including imbalances, correlated exposures, spillovers to the real economy, information disruptions, feedback behaviour, asset bubbles

1 At the outset, I should note that elements of what follows build off of work that I have done with my two co-authors, Michael Barr and Margaret Tahyar, in *Financial Regulation: Law and Policy* (Foundation Press, 2016). In the first edition, we infused discussion of illustrations of systemic risk in dozens of chapters throughout the text, and then in the second edition added in a more holistic treatment of systemic risk in a new chapter, presenting a conceptual framework of systemic risk, upon which I draw and expand in this introduction. See Michael S Barr, Howell E Jackson & Margaret E Tahyar, *Financial Regulation: Law and Policy*, 2nd ed (Foundation Press, 2018) at 737–46.

2 See ECB, "Macro-Prudential Policy Objectives and Tools" (2010) Financial Stability Rev 129 at 129.

3 Monica Billio et al, "Econometric measures of connectedness and systemic risk in the finance and insurance sectors" (2012) 104:3 J Financial Economics 535 at 537.

and contagion.[4] The Office of Financial Research has followed a similarly spirited approach and grouped threats to financial stability into six categories of risk: macroeconomic, market, credit, solvency and leverage, funding and liquidity, and contagion.[5] Paul Tucker, former deputy governor of the Bank of England, offers yet another perspective, focusing on risks that threaten the provision of core financial services, but linking the severity of those risks to contemporaneous macroeconomic conditions.[6]

My own preference is to amalgamate these and other approaches, and to link the definition of systemic risk to the paths through which exogenous shocks to specific areas of the financial services industry are magnified to produce substantial, negative consequences for the provision of core financial services to the broader economy. Conceptually, this definition of systemic risk offers a potentially helpful distinction between microprudential risks, which principally affect those directly exposed to a failing firm or disrupted transaction, and systemic risks, which spread beyond those in direct privity with distressed firms or transactions and threaten the broader economy. This definition also suggests the need to pay close attention to the channels through which the failure of individual firms or the disruption of specific financial transactions might give rise to economic injuries to parties that are not directly exposed to troubled firms or failed transactions. It also invites analysts to distinguish between the channels of transmission for systemic risk and economic or market conditions that exacerbate the potential severity with which these transmission mechanisms disrupt the provision of core financial services.[7]

To flesh out this approach to systemic risk and integrate it into the chapters that follow, I begin with some preliminary words about exogenous shocks and then offer a taxonomy of four principal channels of transmission for systemic risk, plus a handful of exacerbating factors. I then discuss a number of tensions that arise in developing effective regulatory responses to systemic risks — tensions that are well illustrated in the chapters of this volume.

Surprise as a Precursor of Systemic Risk

One of the common themes of the chapters that follow is the proposition that systemic risk has its origins in the unexpected: "a little bit of 'scary news' [that] can trigger a great crash" (Geanakoplos) or "[s]udden financial market changes cause an 'information overload'...sparking a panic" (Schwarcz) or a "localized shock...with repercussions [for] the broader economy" (Busch and van Rijn). Throughout this volume, the authors speak in terms of surprise as a

4 See Dimitrios Bisias et al, "A Survey of Systemic Risk Analytics" (2012) 4 Annual Rev Financial Economics 255 at 256.

5 Office of Financial Research, *Financial Stability Report* (2017) at 29.

6 See Paul Tucker, "The Design and Governance of Financial Stability Regimes" CIGI, Essays on International Finance, September 2016 at 3–4:

> The purpose of a regime for financial system stability is to maintain the supply of core financial services, and the objective is the degree of resilience desired in the system as a whole given society's tolerance for crisis and the costs, if any, of making the system more robust. Seen thus, the core of a regime for stability is a standard of resilience and mechanisms for maintaining it in the face of endemic regulatory arbitrage, technical innovation and evolving demands from users and customers. But how resilient the financial system needs to be is affected by the problem of missing regimes for [national balance sheet] management and external macroeconomic balance, since real economy inefficiencies and international imbalances make the world a riskier place.

7 My definition is consonant with the Federal Reserve Board's recent formulation of the concept of financial stability: "A stable financial system, when hit by adverse events, or 'shocks,' continues to meet the demands of households and businesses for financial services, such as credit provision and payment services. In contrast, in an unstable system, these same shocks are likely to have much larger effects, disrupting the flow of credit and leading to declines in employment and economic activity." See Federal Reserve Board, *Financial Stability Report* (2018) at 3.

trigger: a sudden loss of confidence in financial markets, an unexpected movement in exchange rates or a surprise cyber attack. Clearly these and other exogenous shocks can impose substantial and unanticipated losses on financial firms and market participants. But beyond these direct injuries, the kinds of surprises that give rise to systemic risks are those that generate far-reaching uncertainty. In the formulation of Berner and Judge, "Financial crises are informational events. Many of the classic forms of market dysfunction, from runs by short-term creditors (such as depositors) to liquidity providers refusing to continue playing that role, are, at least in part, the by-product of incomplete or asymmetric information about events or changes in circumstances." In the early stages of many financial crises, market participants scrambled to update their prior assumptions regarding asset values and solvency in light of new and unexpected "informational events," with potentially devastating consequences for the broader economy, which finds itself cut off from key financial services as the financial sector sorts out what Schwarcz nicely denominates a "mutual misinformation problem."

Of course, one of the goals of the post-financial-crisis reforms discussed in this volume is the effort on the part of regulators to reduce the likelihood and significance of future surprises. Stress testing and counter-cyclical capital buffers are examples of such reforms, as is the sort of scenario planning that is supposed to go into the design of resolution and recovery plans. But the limitations of the human mind to anticipate the future, as well as its proven capacity to repeat mistakes of the past, leave most experts wary that the years ahead will see their share of exogenous shocks and, so, we must attend to their potential systemic consequences or suffer from our failure to do so.

Four Channels of Transmission

Exogenous shocks are amplified into systemic events through four principal channels of transmission, all of which are discussed with considerable insight and colour in the pages that follow.

The Loss of Essential and Non-substitutable Financial Functions

Perhaps the most obvious channel of transmission is the sudden loss of financial function that is both essential and not readily substitutable. One example would be a failure of a major financial institution — perhaps UBS in Switzerland or Fannie Mae in the United States — that plays such an important role in a country's economy that the economy would suffer significant hardship if the firm were to disappear suddenly. This is the classic "too-big-to-fail" problem, much discussed and much decried. But large banks are not the only providers of essential and non-substitutable financial functions. As Anand and Peihani discuss in the case of Canadian asset-backed commercial paper, the sudden disruption of a segment of the capital markets can also interfere with a core financial function with severe economic consequences. Moreover, as recounted in Saguato and Ferrarini, centralized clearing houses established in the wake of the financial crisis may also now be essential and non-substitutable, should they become insolvent in the face of a future economic shock. With the growth of marketplace lending and new forms of structured finance in the decade since the crisis, the extent of essential and non-substitutable financial functions performed outside of the traditional banking sector can only have increased, and many of the chapters in this volume appropriately focus on the rise of shadow banking.

Knock-on Effects from Direct Failures

Even if the failure of a large firm does not, in and of itself, generate systemic risk concerns, losses from that firm's failure can be passed on to the firm's creditors and thereby create disruptions. As Feldman and Hiebert point out, "The TBTF problem arises when the largest and most systemically important banks fail and impose their losses onto other banks. The spread of these losses fuels contagion as turmoil spreads throughout financial markets and into the rest of the economy." Back in the 1980s, fears of knock-on effects of this sort led federal authorities to prop up Continental Illinois and its substantial correspondent relationships with smaller banks across the Midwest; similarly spirited concerns led the Federal Reserve to intervene in support of American International Group (AIG) in September 2008. Again, many of the reforms of recent years — from limitations on counterparty risk to restraints on intra-day exposures in the payment system — are intended to guard against cascading failures of this sort, but the problem is endemic in a modern financial system. Interestingly, Avgouleas and Goodhart see the potential for such knock-on effects were authorities to implement plans to bail-in external creditors holding convertible debt instruments. So knock-on effects remain an important transmission mechanism for systemic risks.

Contagion through Runs in Short-term Credit

No doubt the classic mechanism for the transmission of systemic risk is contagion. Traditionally, this is evidenced in the form of a bank run, but it is now also observed in the drying up of capital market sources of financing, such as auction-rate preferred stock or a host of securitization vehicles that disappeared in the depths of the financial crisis. I place contagion third on my list of transmission mechanisms — not as a measure of its importance, but only because contagion is typically preceded by the discovery of problems in an isolated group of firms or the unexpected devaluation of an important class of assets.[8] Tröger's chapter nicely summarizes this too-familiar pattern of an idiosyncratic failure leading to knock-on effects and fire sales of assets followed by contagion: "The failure of a systemically important financial institution can affect other financial institutions because it is a counterparty for many other market participants; it is forced to fire-sell assets, which leads to depressed prices for assets that other institutions use as collateral (demand for higher margins), and its default sparks a panic that spreads to other institutions. These consequences, in turn, carry over to the real economy." Contagion is also an excellent illustration of the consequences of the uncertainty that exogenous shocks and resulting information gaps can create. For both individual firms and capital markets, contagion destroys liquidity and, left unchecked, can lead a modern economy into a death spiral.

Disruptions through Complex Interconnections

Distinct from contagion, but related, is the transmission of systemic risk as a result of complex financial networks. The failure of foreign exchange clearing systems transmitted a systemic shock in this way back in 1974 and gave rise to the term "Herstatt risk." Problems associated with clearing and settling over-the-counter (OTC) derivatives were perceived to be a major concern

8 That contagion is not the only transmission mechanism on my list puts me in opposition to those who claim that "[f]inancial crises are everywhere and always due to problems of short-term debt." See John H Cochrane, "Toward a Run-free Financial System" in Martin Neil Baily & John B Taylor, eds, *Across the Great Divide: New Perspectives on the Financial Crisis* (Stanford, CA: Hoover Institution Press, 2014) 197 at 197 (quoting a famous aphorism of Doug Diamond from 2008). See also Hal S Scott, *Connectedness and Contagion* (Cambridge, MA: MIT Press, 2016).

to regulatory authorities in the financial crisis. In times of financial stress and uncertainty, the opacity of these interconnected obligations complicates valuations and exacerbates contagion. Even if the underlying transactions might ultimately be unwound without extensive losses, uncertainty about their disposition exacerbates panics and accelerates contagion, a point explored in Schwarcz's chapter with respect to securitizations based on subprime assets in the financial crisis. As Saguato and Ferrarini explain, the justification for creating centralized clearing houses for derivatives was to increase transparency and reduce uncertainty in these markets during periods of financial distress, albeit (as mentioned earlier) at the risk of creating a new systemically important financial institution.

Exacerbating Factors

Within the basic structure of these four transmission mechanisms, much of the analysis in the chapters that follow focuses on factors (and regulatory responses) that can exacerbate the transmission of systemic risk.

Excessive Leverage and Illiquidity

As a number of the volume's authors document, much of the regulatory response to the financial crisis has been focused on increasing the resilience of the financial system to withstand future shocks. As much as anyone, Admati and Hellwig have championed the case for higher capital requirements and argued, as they summarize in their chapter here, that capital requirements are still not high enough. Geanakoplos adds to this debate by exploring the role of inflated collateral values in leading capital reserves to be overstated in boom years preceding a financial crisis. And part of the justification for a centralized clearing house for OTC derivatives explored in Saguato and Ferrarini's chapter is based on the assumption that standardized margin requirements and joint obligations of clearing house members will help withstand exogenous shocks to the value of derivative contracts in the same way that higher capital requirements help financial firms absorb unexpected losses on their balance sheets. Similarly, increases in liquidity requirements that have taken place since the financial crisis are intended to help firms withstand the initial stages of contagion, reducing the need to dispose of assets at distressed prices and giving central banks time to implement emergency lending measures. Beyond providing institutions resilience in the face of exogenous shocks, these measures add a degree of salutary market discipline from both investors and managers as the costs of financial crises — at least in the initial stages — are more directly imposed on private parties, creating the incentive to more carefully monitor the accumulation of risks. In the absence of adequate capital and sufficient liquidity reserves, moral hazard problems are compounded, increasing the likelihood of exogenous shocks.

Common Models and Funding Strategies

Perhaps less well understood before the financial crisis, but extensively documented in this volume, is the extent to which common models and funding strategies can exacerbate the likelihood of financial crises. Just as an economy can face a financial crisis if too large a share of its credit comes from a single financial firm, systemic risk concerns can arise when common funding strategies are sourced through the capital markets. Anand and Peihani show how this happened with the Canadian asset-backed commercial paper market, and Buckley, Avgouleas and Arner also document its occurrence in the earlier Asian financial crisis. Similarly, one of the problems encountered with subprime asset securitization in the United States was an overreliance on the same flawed credit rating agency models for mortgage-backed securities. Once the market lost confidence in that rating system — a major exogenous shock — there was substantial uncertainty as to the true value of a wide range of assets across the financial services industry, prompting panic and a near complete loss of liquidity. To the extent that contagion is driven by market inferences about the implications of an exogenous shock to one firm or market segment, the higher the degree of commonality in modelling and funding strategies, the more extensive the inferences are likely to be. By reducing the use of private credit ratings in regulatory requirements in the United States, the Dodd-Frank Act addressed, in part, this exacerbating factor, but the analysis presented in this volume shows that reliance on common models and funding strategies is widespread in modern financial markets and a persistent accelerant of systemic risks. And, as Arner, Buckley and Zetzsche outline in their chapter on fintech and regtech, it is quite likely that technological innovations will move us toward an even greater degree of common business models and commonalities across risk management systems.

Incomplete Supervisory Oversight

Another recurring theme in this volume is the incompleteness of supervisory oversight as an accelerant of systemic risk. One good illustration is Berner and Judge's chapter on data standardization, focusing on the need for regulatory authorities to define and collect standardized data on financial transactions. Information of this sort allows supervisors to anticipate how inter-firm exposures may be accumulating over time — necessary to police in order to prevent knock-on effects in times of crisis — but also essential for understanding complex interconnections when problems do arise. Another category of supervisory incompleteness concerns limitations on the scope of macroprudential authorities over shadow banking activities in capital markets of the sort that led to systemic risk concerns in the financial crisis. As Busch and van Rijn explain, that crisis "shows that systemic risk can occur in different sectors, or indeed across different sectors, and have a variety of distinct characteristics....It is therefore of great importance for jurisdictions to have a broad monitoring system in place, capable of identifying systemic risk throughout the entire financial sector." This theme re-emerges in numerous chapters, including Anand and Peihani's discussion of Canadian supervision as well as the Kress, McCoy and Schwarcz exploration of entity versus activities restrictions. In addition to addressing the major lesson of the financial crisis — that systemic risks arise throughout the financial system — the creation of uniform macroprudential supervision across the financial system reduces what would otherwise be strong incentives for financial activities to move into the least-regulated sector of the industry, with limited transparency and no publicly mandated requirements designed to provide resilience in times of financial stress.

Misaligned Government Policies

The role of government policies in compounding the transmission of systemic risks is another theme in several of the chapters. As several authors note, misguided macroeconomic policies — such as government programs promoting excessive leverage in real estate markets, or the failure of regulatory authorities to prevent widespread consumer abuse in consumer credit markets — can contribute to asset bubbles or abrupt adjustments of foreign exchange rates, which may then precipitate financial crises. Of course, the challenge comes in designing regulatory agencies that are simultaneously effective, responsive and not inadvertently pro-cyclical. For example, demanding higher capital requirements in advance of a financial crisis may alleviate systemic risks, whereas requiring higher capital in the midst of a crisis can be an accelerant. As Masciandaro demonstrates in his chapter on central banks as macroprudential authorities, the design challenges here are formidable — especially for central bankers required to balance monetary policy goals with financial stability. As Anand and Peihani suggest, however, as greater amounts of financial activity shift into capital markets, our financial systems may become more susceptible to sudden changes in macroeconomic policy than was the case in the past when more intermediation was done on the balance sheets of banks and other financial firms.

Tensions in Regulatory Strategies

One of the advantages of a multi-authored collection of essays is that it allows the reader the opportunity to experience well-reasoned arguments that, at various points, come into tension with each other. This volume contains several examples, not the least of which is an alternative taxonomy for approaching the topic of systemic risk contained in Schwarcz's concluding chapter.[9] I conclude by commenting upon several of these tensions.

Ex Ante versus *Ex Post*

In approaching problems of systemic risk, policy analysts tend to stress two different areas of intervention: *ex ante* approaches, such as capital requirements or activities restriction intended to prevent exogenous shocks from escalating into financial crises; and *ex post* responses, such as lender-of-last-resort functions and *in extremis* public support for financial markets and firms. Resolution strategies occupy something of a hybrid position in that they need to be established *ex ante*, but are intended to operate *ex post* by recapitalizing failed institutions with private resources and without triggering contagion of short-term creditors. Sometimes these two approaches come into tension. As Saguato and Ferrarini explore, the benefits that centralized clearing houses provide in terms of building resilience in derivatives markets *ex ante* can produce a systemically important financial failure if losses prove to be overwhelming in the midst of a financial crisis. Tröger and also Avgouleas and Goodhart make similar points about resolution planning. While there are undoubtedly benefits *ex ante* of requiring financial firms to have substantial amounts of loss-absorbing capital *ex ante*, there are potential systemic risks of demanding that those creditors be bailed in at the height of a financial crisis because of the potential for knock-on effects leading to contagion. For precisely this reason, many seasoned regulators are diehard supporters of *ex ante* solutions in ordinary times, but open to *ex post* interventions and even public bailouts when serious financial crises arise. Janus-faced perhaps, but also pragmatic.

Activities versus Entities

A final tension concerns the question of how best to provide consistent oversight of systemic risks in capital markets as well as financial firms. As mentioned earlier, incomplete supervisory systems can exacerbate systemic risks, but it is not always clear how best to achieve consistency

9 In contrast to my schema emphasizing exogenous shocks, four principal mechanisms of transmission and a number of exacerbating factors, Schwarcz analyzes systemic risk in terms of three types of shocks that can trigger collapse, plus five market failures that can cause those shocks. In addition, he identifies three mechanisms of transmission: interconnectedness, size and non-substitutability. Clearly, we are dealing with many of the same concepts, but organized in slightly different ways.

across legal structures that provide similar financial functions but in different ways. Capital markets regulation in the United States offers a prime case in point. As originally envisioned, the Dodd-Frank Act contemplated the extension of bank-like prudential regulation into major asset managers and other systemically important firms operating in the capital markets. But difficulties in defining the regulatory boundaries for this extension of supervision, as well as concerns that bank-like regulation may not be appropriate for capital market activities, have led US authorities to rely more on supervision of capital market activities than on supervision of major entities engaged in those activities. Kress, McCoy and Schwarcz challenge the wisdom of this change in policy, arguing that while systemic risks may now originate in capital markets, those risks accumulate and are magnified on the balance sheets of legal entities, thus making entity-based regulation an essential component of any fully developed system of systemic risk oversight. This is a major policy dispute on which leading authorities have dramatically different views.

The Challenges and Pitfalls of Coordination and Consistency

A final tension concerns the often unexplored downside of regulatory coordination and consistency. Many authors in this volume speak to the importance of consistent and comprehensive systems of supervisory oversight. And, in many areas, the case for such coordination is compelling — as in Berner and Judge's discussion of data standardization and the several chapters that speak to the desirability of resolution planning systems that are consistent and coordinated across national boundaries. Yet, the Romano chapter on the pitfalls of global harmonization offers a cautionary tale. Consistent with much of her prior work, Romano notes the dangers of coordination and consistency in the face of continuing financial innovation. Just as common models within the financial services industry can exacerbate systemic risk, international convergence on a single set of regulatory standards can constrain the supervisory tool kit over time and leave regulators incapable of responding to unanticipated market developments. The trick, of course, is to balance the values of coordination and consistency with the need to maintain a dynamic and forward-looking global regulatory system.

Resolving these and other tensions in the oversight of systemic risk remains an important and necessary challenge.

1

Regulating Systemic Risk in Canada

ANITA ANAND AND MAZIAR PEIHANI

The effects of the global financial crisis (GFC) were profound: stock prices plummeted, investors tried to liquidate their holdings, financial institutions teetered on the brink of bankruptcy and credit markets froze as liquidity vanished from financial markets. Systemic risk that may have seemed obvious to market observers was realized when Lehman Brothers filed for bankruptcy on September 15, 2008. Just prior to this filing, the Dow Jones Index suffered the largest loss since September 11, 2001, plummeting more than 500 points. With this decline, US$700 billion in value vanished from retirement plans, government pension funds and other investment portfolios.[1] World markets only started to stabilize after the announcement of the US$700-billion Troubled Asset Relief Program and similar massive bailouts by governments around the world.[2]

1 Financial Crisis Inquiry Commission, *The Financial Crisis Inquiry Report: Final Report of the National Commission on the Causes of the Financial and Economic Crisis in the United States* (January 2011) at 356, online: <www.gpo.gov/fdsys/pkg/GPO-FCIC/pdf/GPO-FCIC.pdf>.

2 George Walker, "Credit Contraction, Financial Collapse and Global Recession: pt 1" (2009) 1 JIBFL 5; A Cohen, "Global Financial Crisis – Timeline" (2009) 1 JIBFL 10.

The GFC led to an unprecedented wave of structural and regulatory reforms internationally and within the Group of Twenty (G20) countries.[3] Building on existing literature regarding systemic risk and financial policy, this chapter examines the Canadian financial system and assesses the structural and regulatory reforms that have followed the GFC. The chapter analyzes the post-crisis regulatory regime based on its ability to detect, prevent and address sources of systemic risk in the financial system. We adopt a broad notion of systemic risk that goes beyond the commonly held view that systemic risk arises from the widespread distress caused by failure of individual financial institutions, often referred to as the domino effect.[4] Rather than concentrating exclusively on contagion or chains of failures, we believe that systemic risk can also arise from the common exposure to macroeconomic factors across sectors and institutions in the financial markets.[5]

This chapter acknowledges that a multiplicity of factors contributes to the resiliency of a financial system. In Canada's case, for example, these factors include stronger bank capital ratios, stricter mortgage underwriting requirements, law reforms and new resolution tools. We argue that heightened leverage in the financial system, which is reflected in high household debt and inflated house prices, remains an important source of vulnerability across Group of Seven (G7) economies and especially in Canada. We contend that Canadian regulators' ability to address systemic risk is limited by the structure of the regime, built on a sector-by-sector model, without any one institution responsible for comprehensively regulating the financial system. The regulatory regime is a partial consequence of the historical evolution of financial markets in Canada and their constitutional underpinnings.

As the Canadian case study reveals, diffusion of regulatory oversight can lead to failures in addressing system-wide issues, as well as poor communication and coordination among various bodies, all of which may fail to contain systemic risk. One possible solution, advocated in international assessments as well as academic literature on systemic risk, is to establish a macroprudential regulator to monitor the entire financial system.[6] As will be explained, whereas this approach has been adopted in other jurisdictions, such as the United States and the United Kingdom, it is unlikely to gain momentum in Canada, given the reality of path dependency in regulatory policy making.

3 See G20 Information Centre, "Global Plan for Recovery and Reform" (Statement issued by the G20 leaders, London, 2 April 2009), online: <www.g20.utoronto.ca/2009/2009communique0402.html>; G20 Information Centre, "Global Plan Annex: Declaration on Strengthening the Financial System" (Statement issued by the G20 leaders, London, 2 April 2009), online: <www.g20.utoronto.ca/2009/2009ifi.html>. L

4 For an example of this view, see Steven L. Schwarcz, "Systemic Risk" (2008) 97 Geo LJ 193, which focuses on "economic shock," "failure of a chain of markets or institutions" and "a chain of significant losses to financial institutions" as key concepts in defining systemic risk.

5 Claudio Borio, "Towards a macroprudential framework for financial supervision and regulation?" (2003) Bank for International Settlements (BIS) Working Paper No 128 at 5–7, online: <www.bis.org/publ/work128.pdf>; see also Anita Anand, Michael Trebilcock & Michael Rosenstock, "Institutional Design and the New Systemic Risk in Banking Crises" in Anita Anand, ed, *Systemic Risk and Institutional Design* (Oxford, UK: Oxford University Press, 2016) [Anand, *Systemic Risk*].

6 As we will discuss later in this chapter, both the International Monetary Fund (IMF) and the Financial Stability Board (FSB) have made such a recommendation to policy makers. For notable examples in the literature that are in line with this view, see Paul Jenkins & David Longworth, "Securing Monetary and Financial Stability: Why Canada Needs a Macroprudential Policy Framework" (2015) CD Howe Institute Commentary No 429 at 10–11, online: <www.cdhowe.org/sites/default/files/attachments/research_papers/mixed/commentary_429.pdf>; Samuel Howorth et al, "Improving Canada's Financial Stability Governance Regime" CIGI, Special Report, 22 November 2016 at 6–7, online: <www.cigionline.org/publications/improving-canadas-financial-stability-governance-regime>; Paul Tucker, "The Design and Governance of Financial Stability Regimes" CIGI, Essays on International Finance, vol 3, September 2016, online: <www.cigionline.org/sites/default/files/financial_essay_vol.3_web.pdf>.

The absence of a formal macroprudential regulator does not prevent Canadian regulators from working collaboratively toward more effective management of systemic risk. This goal can be achieved by establishing financial stability as an overriding priority for inter-agency regulatory groups. These bodies should extend their membership to include all key federal and provincial regulators and establish a robust working plan for monitoring system-wide vulnerabilities, which would ensure timely attention and action on problems by competent authorities. This chapter offers specific recommendations to enhance coordination among different policy-making bodies in the financial markets.

We begin by discussing the modern financial and regulatory landscape in Canada and then examine the structural and regulatory reforms that were undertaken after the GFC. We focus on three areas of reform, namely: bank regulatory reforms; housing market measures; and securities law reforms, in particular the recently proposed Capital Markets Stability Act. The chapter then assesses the challenges of systemic risk oversight followed by reform suggestions that can help to establish a more integrated framework for systemic risk oversight.

The Canadian Financial Landscape

Canada has a sophisticated financial system that provides liquidity for participants alongside prudential oversight and stability for depositors. With more than 10 years having passed since the GFC, it is appropriate to examine the current state of Canada's financial system in order to assess its ability to respond to systemic risks. This section highlights the core characteristics of Canada's financial system and provides an overview of its regulatory framework.

Canada's financial system is dominated by a handful of key players in most financial subsectors. Cumulatively, their assets total approximately 500 percent of Canada's GDP.[7] Three particular market constituent groups — banks, insurance companies and pension funds — wield significant market influence, given their assets and market functions.

The country's banking sector is highly concentrated, with the six federally chartered banks — the Royal Bank of Canada, Toronto Dominion, Bank of Nova Scotia, Canadian Imperial Bank of Canada (CIBC), Bank of Montreal and National Bank of Canada — holding 93 percent of the country's total bank assets in aggregate.[8] These banks primarily engage in household lending, corporate lending, wealth management and trading.

As of February 2018, Canada's total household credit stood at $2.1 trillion,[9] of which 71 percent comprised residential mortgages and 28 percent comprised consumer credit such as personal lines of credit and credit cards.[10] Chartered banks account for 77 percent and non-bank firms, such as trust and loan companies and credit unions, account for 19 percent of Canada's total household credit.[11] Particularly problematic in this debt-heavy environment is the existence of the shadow

7 IMF, *Canada: Financial Sector Stability Assessment* (2014) IMF Country Report No 14/29 [IMF, *FSSA*] at 8, online: <www.imf.org/external/pubs/cat/longres.aspx?sk=41299.0>.

8 *Ibid* at 11.

9 All dollar figures in Canadian dollars unless otherwise noted.

10 BoC, "Household Credit: Overview of Total Household Credit" (2018), online: <https://credit.bankofcanada.ca/householdcredit#1>.

11 BoC, "Household Credit: Sources of Household Credit" (2018), online: <https://credit.bankofcanada.ca/householdcredit#1>.

banking industry, which consists chiefly of credit intermediation outside the traditional banking system.[12] The Bank of Canada (BoC) estimates that its credit value amounts to $1.1 trillion, roughly half of the $2.1 trillion of traditional bank liabilities.[13] The most important components of shadow banking are investment funds (46 percent) followed by repo (repurchase agreement) and securities lending transactions (29 percent). These figures are considerable, engaging the interests of diverse financial market participants, including individual investors, smaller lending operations, and the various intermediaries and counterparties relying on shadow banking activities for their business. These sizeable loans present systemic risk challenges by increasing consumer debt loads on those borrowers who may be more vulnerable to an increased interest rate.

The insurance sector forms the second of the three constituent groups, wielding significant influence on Canada's financial market. Indeed, Canada's insurance sector accounts for 16 percent of the country's financial sector assets. The industry is broadly divided in terms of life insurance and property and casualty insurance specializations. Three domestic firms (Sun Life Financial, Great-West Life and Manulife Financial) hold three-quarters of life and health insurance assets in Canada.[14] In contrast, the property and casualty insurance sector is highly competitive and includes a number of foreign-owned companies that collect more than half of the premiums earned in Canada.[15]

Beyond the two insurance lines, mortgage insurance forms a major portion of Canada's total insurance sector value. Mortgage insurance coverage is provided by the Canada Mortgage and Housing Corporation (CMHC), a federal Crown corporation, and two private insurance firms.[16] All federally regulated lenders must obtain mortgage default insurance for home buyers with less than a 20 percent down payment. As of March 2015, government-backed insurance covered 56 percent of all outstanding residential mortgages.[17]

Lastly, Canadian pension funds occupy a unique position as significant players in Canadian and global financial markets. Their investment capacity is broad, their influence is significant and their diverse asset classes offer enviable returns while mitigating risk. These funds hold approximately 15 percent of the country's total assets in the financial system. Of this 15 percent,

12 For the definition of shadow banking, see FSB, *Shadow Banking: Strengthening Oversight and Regulation – Recommendations of the Financial Stability Board* (FSB, 2011) at 3, online: <www.financialstabilityboard.org/wp-content/uploads/r_111027a.pdf>.

13 See Bo Young Chang et al, *Monitoring Shadow Banking in Canada: A Hybrid Approach* (BoC, 2016) at 28, online: <www.bankofcanada.ca/wp-content/uploads/2016/12/fsr-december-2016-chang.pdf>.

14 IMF, *FSSA*, *supra* note 7 at 58. See also Department of Finance Canada, *Supporting a Strong and Growing Economy: Positioning Canada's Financial Sector for the Future* (Department of Finance Canada, 2016) [Department of Finance Canada, *Supporting a Strong and Growing Economy*] at 13, online: <www.fin.gc.ca/activty/consult/ssge-sefc-eng.pdf>.

15 As of 2016, there were 74 foreign incorporated property and casualty insurers operating in Canada, with assets of $35 billion. See Department of Finance Canada, *Supporting a Strong and Growing Economy*, *supra* note 14 at 14; FSB, *Peer Review of Canada: Review Report* (FSB, 2012) at 9, online: <www.fsb.org/wp-content/uploads/r_120130.pdf>.

16 Namely Genworth MI Canada and Canada Guaranty. See Department of Finance Canada, "Overview: Lender Risk Sharing for Government-Backed Insured Mortgages" (21 October 2016), online: <www.fin.gc.ca/n16/data/16-136_1-eng.asp#_ftn1>.

17 *Ibid.* In the event a mortgage insurer is unable to make an insurance payout to the lender, the federal government backs 100 percent of the CMHC's liability as well as the private insurers' liability (subject to a 10 percent deductible). See Department of Finance Canada, *Supporting a Strong and Growing Economy*, *supra* note 14 at 15.

the eight largest public pension funds control two-thirds of this share, with more than $1 trillion in net assets under management.[18]

Canada's capital market activity is concentrated, with banks playing a dominant role through their subsidiaries. Indeed, the six largest securities dealers are owned by the big six Canadian banks. In 2015, bank subsidiaries underwrote 61 percent of all deals, accounting for 64 percent of the value of the issued securities.[19] The three most prominent exchanges in Canada are the Toronto Stock Exchange, the Bourse de Montréal and the TSX Venture Exchange. The clearing, settlement and recording of financial transactions are undertaken by financial market infrastructures, three of which have been designated as systemically important.[20] Given the integrated and concentrated financial system, it is unsurprising that Canadian financial markets can be exposed to systemic risks. The structure of a regime, in our view, is itself a vulnerability. We turn now to examine the regulatory characteristics of this regime in greater detail.

The Regulatory Regime of Canada's Financial Market

This section examines the composition of Canada's financial market in terms of regulators that have some role in managing or overseeing systemic risk. Fundamentally, Canada's regulatory system is based on a complex constitutional framework that divides the responsibility for supervision of the financial markets between federal and provincial governments and their designated agencies. The ramifications of this divided regulatory approach is that financial institutions are federally regulated while securities markets, including public companies, are regulated at the provincial level.[21] Firms in other sectors, such as insurance companies, trust and loan companies, credit unions and pension plans, can be incorporated and regulated at both the provincial and federal levels.[22]

Thirteen provincial and territorial regulatory authorities regulate the securities markets across Canada. The provinces of Alberta, British Columbia, Ontario and Quebec supervise about 95 percent of the country's capital markets.[23] While each regulator is operationally independent and administers a separate set of laws and regulations, they have experienced moderate success in harmonizing their policies and supervisory practices.[24] However, in certain areas involving new

18 These pension funds are the Canada Pension Plan, Caisse de dépôt et placement du Québec, the Ontario Teachers' Pension Plan, the Public Sector Pension Investment Board, the British Columbia Investment Management Corporation, the Alberta Investment Management Corporation, the Healthcare of Ontario Pension Plan and the Ontario Municipal Employees Retirement System.

19 See also IMF, *FSSA*, *supra* note 7 at 10.

20 *Ibid.* These are the Large Value Transfer System, CDX and Canadian Derivatives Clearing Service.

21 Office of the Superintendent of Financial Institutions (OSFI), *Supervisory Framework* (April 2014), online: <www.osfi-bsif.gc.ca/Eng/fi-if/rai-eri/sp-ps/Pages/sff.aspx>.

22 See OSFI, "Who We Regulate" (23 October 2014), online: <www.osfi-bsif.gc.ca/Eng/wt-ow/Pages/wwr-er.aspx?sc=1&gc=4#WWRLink14>; IMF, *FSSA*, *supra* note 7 at 21.

23 IMF, "Canada: Financial Sector Assessment Program: IOSCO Objectives and Principles of Securities Regulation – Detailed Assessment of Implementation" (March 2014), IMF Country Report No 14/73 [IMF Country Report] at 8, online: <www.imf.org/external/pubs/ft/scr/2014/cr1473.pdf>.

24 Harmonization has been facilitated by the Canadian Securities Administrators (CSA), the umbrella organization for provincial and territorial securities regulators that seeks to improve, coordinate and harmonize regulation of capital markets in Canada. See CSA, "Who We Are", online: <www.securities-administrators.ca/aboutcsa.aspx?id=77>. We discuss the role of the CSA in enacting securities regulatory reforms in more detail below.

financial developments such as fintech (for example, robo advisers) and cryptoassets, the non-centralized regulatory structure creates jurisdictional confusion for regulated parties, regulatory overlap and inefficient regulatory resource allocation.

The exclusively provincial and territorial nature of Canadian securities regulation has been confirmed in two landmark decisions handed down by the Supreme Court of Canada.[25] These cases upheld the constitutional division of powers in Canada's federal system, ultimately deferring to the status quo of provincial oversight of securities markets. They also recognized the federal government's jurisdiction on matters of genuine national importance and scope going to trade as a whole, including management of systemic risk and national data collection, as distinct from provincial concerns.[26]

Apart from the regulation of capital markets, the responsibility for financial market oversight is shared at the federal level among the Ministry of Finance (MoF), the BoC, the Office of the Superintendent of Financial Institutions (OSFI), the Canada Deposit Insurance Corporation (CDIC) and the Financial Consumer Agency of Canada (FCAC). The MoF is headed up by the elected member of Parliament who has been designated to be the minister of finance by the prime minister. This ministry oversees the federal regulators and is in charge of all matters relating to the financial affairs of Canada not assigned to the Treasury Board or another minister. The BoC derives its authority from the Bank of Canada Act and oversees Canada's payment, clearing and settlement systems. The BoC is also the lender of last resort and is in charge of price stability in the financial system. OSFI is governed by a number of legislative frameworks and serves as the prudential regulator. The CDIC provides insurance against the loss of deposits of member institutions. Lastly, the FCAC is responsible for protecting consumers and informing them of financial products and services.

In a discussion of systemic risk, OSFI's role deserves particular attention because its primary responsibility is the supervision of the domestic systemically important banks (D-SIBs), which dominate financial intermediation in the Canadian economy. OSFI's approach to supervision is aligned with international standards, in particular the Basel Core Principles of Supervision, which serve as a basic reference for banking supervisors around the world.[27]

OSFI's approach to regulatory supervision over federally regulated financial institutions (FRFIs) enables the office to enact meaningful policy initiatives aimed at mitigating systemic risk. In March 2013, OSFI designated Canada's six largest banks (Royal Bank of Canada, Toronto Dominion, Bank of Nova Scotia, CIBC, Bank of Montreal and National Bank of Canada) as D-SIBs.[28] This designation subjects these banks to continued intense supervision and requires them to comply with stricter capital and disclosure requirements.[29] Furthermore, the CDIC has been named as the resolution authority for D-SIBs and has begun recovery and resolution planning for them. Taken together, the additional layer of prudential oversight ensures continued

25 *Reference re Securities Act*, 2011 SCC 66; *Reference re PanCanadian Securities Regulation*, 2018 SCC 48 (CanLII).

26 *Ibid.*

27 OSFI, *Supervisory Framework* (Ottawa: OSFI, 2010) at 1, online: <www.osfi-bsif.gc.ca/Eng/fi-if/rai-eri/sp-ps/Pages/sff.aspx>. See also BIS, Basel Committee on Banking Supervision, *Core Principles for Effective Banking Supervision* (BIS, 2012), online: <www.bis.org/publ/bcbs230.htm>. See also Anita Anand & Andrew Green, "Regulating Financial Institutions: The Value of Opacity" (2012) 57:3 McGill LJ 399.

28 OSFI, "The OSFI Pillar" (Spring 2013) at 1, online: <www.osfi-bsif.gc.ca/Eng/Docs/op_2013_sp.pdf>.

29 OSFI, *OSFI Annual Report 2013-2014* at 10, online: <www.osfi-bsif.gc.ca/eng/docs/ar-ra/1314/eng/ar1314.pdf>.

regulatory awareness of the banks' approaches to mitigating systemic risks. This high degree of scrutiny is sensible, given Canada's market concentration and the corresponding influence of such significant market participants.

As outlined above, Canada's federal regulatory organizations each has a distinct legal mandate, yet together they seek to achieve cooperation and coordination through a number of fora, including:

- the Financial Institutions Supervisory Committee (FISC), the primary forum through which the Department of Finance (DoF), OSFI, the CDIC and the BoC exchange information on banks and coordinate intervention for troubled banks; [30]
- the Senior Advisory Committee (SAC), a forum with the same membership as FISC, through which these bodies deliberate on financial policy issues, including proposed legislation, financial stability and regulatory frameworks;[31] and
- the Heads of Agencies Committee (HoA), which serves as an informal forum for policy coordination among the securities regulators and federal agencies. It includes chairs of the four largest securities commissions in Canada, as well as the BoC governor, the superintendent of financial institutions and senior officials from the DoF.[32] Following the GFC, the HoA's work focused on implementing G20 commitments, in particular those with respect to systemic risk.[33]

Holistically, these fora offer general integration among the various regulatory and advisory bodies. This institutional integration is beneficial from a risk-management perspective in that specialized bodies can share information with their peers and coordinate with market participants such as banks and other FRFIs. To date, this framework succeeds in ensuring that Canadian financial institutions meet or surpass the various international financial metrics relating to liquidity, capital requirements and stress indicators. As argued below, these fora also offer an important venue for dialogue and leadership on surveillance of system-wide vulnerabilities that may not be otherwise captured under the sector-by-sector regulatory model. Nevertheless, the fragmentary nature of this structure may expose the markets to systemic risk, whatever measures may be taken toward coordination.

30 See Office of the Auditor General of Canada, *2010 Fall Report of the Auditor General of Canada* at para 5.16, online: <www.oag-bvg.gc.ca/internet/English/parl_oag_201010_05_e_34288.html>. The FISC's meetings are chaired by OSFI and held quarterly. See also OSFI, "Opening remarks by Assistant Superintendent Carolyn Rogers to the Standing Senate Committee on National Finance, Ottawa, Ontario, May 17, 2017" [Carolyn Rogers, "Opening Remarks"], online: <www.osfi-bsif.gc.ca/Eng/osfi-bsif/med/sp-ds/Pages/cr20170517.aspx>.

31 Office of the Auditor General of Canada, *supra* note 30 at para 5.17. The SAC is chaired by the deputy minister of finance. The meetings are held three to four times a year.

32 IMF Country Report, *supra* note 23 at 41.

33 Over-the-counter (OTC) derivatives, shadow banking, hedge funds and financial benchmarks were among the themes being considered: *ibid* at 42. While the HoA meets quarterly, there has not been any recent public update on its work agenda or priorities: see Carolyn Rogers, "Opening Remarks", *supra* note 30.

Structural and Regulatory Reforms Following the GFC

In the post-GFC financial market, policy makers and market participants are vigilant about understanding risk in all its permutations, especially as it affects the broader financial system. According to a survey of financial institutions in Canada by the Global Risk Institute, the most significant risk concerns today are increased frequency and sophistication of cyber attacks, over-heated housing markets, ever-rising consumer debt and mounting geopolitical uncertainties around the globe.[34] The GFC and its aftermath serve as a useful case study of potential regulatory responses to the contagion that spread after the market for collateralized debt obligations collapsed. This section focuses on those responses, including reforms that are important from a systemic risk perspective.

In the banking sector, Canadian policy makers have implemented the Basel III capital and liquidity reforms that represent a central part of the G20 post-crisis reform agenda.[35] Under the new regulations issued by OSFI, banks are required to hold common equity tier one (CET1) of at least seven percent and a total capital buffer of at least 10.5 percent against risk-weighted assets.[36] Canadian banks are also expected to meet a leverage ratio of at least three percent.[37] OSFI determines the leverage ratio for individual institutions on a bilateral basis, which remains confidential.[38] The six largest Canadian banks have also been named by OSFI as D-SIBs. This designation means that these institutions are subject to enhanced disclosure requirements and intense supervision and must hold an additional one percent of CET1 capital.[39]

Another important reform concerns systemically important financial institution resolutions. In line with the Financial Stability Board's (FSB's) key attributes, Canada has introduced important changes to its bank resolution regime.[40] The CDIC has been designated as the resolution authority for Canadian D-SIBs through its Complex Resolution Division, which develops and maintains resolution plans for D-SIBs.[41] In the event that a D-SIB becomes, or is about to become, unviable, the governor-in-council will appoint the CDIC as the receiver

34 Global Risk Institute, "2017-2018 Risk Outlook Survey Results" (2018) Global Risk Institute White Paper, online: <http://globalriskinstitute.org/publications/2017-2018-risk-outlook-survey-results/>.

35 An important example is the capital adequacy requirements guideline through which OSFI implements Basel III capital rules. See OSFI, *Capital Adequacy Requirements (CAR)* (Ottawa: OSFI, 2018), online: <www.osfi-bsif.gc.ca/Eng/fi-if/rg-ro/gdn-ort/gl-ld/Pages/CAR18_chpt1.aspx#1.2>.

36 *Ibid* at para 55.

37 OSFI, *Leverage Requirements Guideline* (Ottawa: OSFI, 2014), online: <www.osfi-bsif.gc.ca/Eng/fi-if/rg-ro/gdn-ort/gl-ld/Pages/LR.aspx>.

38 *Ibid.*

39 OSFI, *Domestic Systemic Importance and Capital Targets - DTIs* (Ottawa: OSFI, 2013). See also OSFI, *OSFI Annual Report 2016-2017* (Ottawa: OSFI, 2017) at 10, online: <www.osfi-bsif.gc.ca/Eng/Docs/ar-ra/1617/eng/ar1617.pdf>. In a related development, the FSB named the Royal Bank of Canada a global systemically important bank (G-SIB). The G-SIB designation also subjects banks to additional regulatory and supervisory requirements, although such requirements can even go beyond the D-SIB framework due to the risks that the firm can pose to *global* financial stability. See FSB, Press Release, 43/2017, "FSB publishes 2017 G-SIB list" (21 November 2017), online: <www.fsb.org/2017/11/fsb-publishes-2017-g-sib-list/>; OSFI, News Release, "OSFI confirms Royal Bank of Canada designation as a global systemically important bank" (21 November 2017), online: <www.osfi-bsif.gc.ca/Eng/osfi-bsif/med/Pages/nr20171121.aspx>.

40 FSB, "Key Attributes of Effective Resolution Regimes for Financial Institutions" (FSB, 2014), online: <www.financialstabilityboard.org/2014/10/r_141015> [FSB, *Key Attributes*].

41 See CDIC, "Resolution Division", online: <www.cdic.ca/en/about-cdic/organization/Pages/crd.aspx>.

and can carry out necessary transactions for restructuring the bank's business.[42] The CDIC has a vast resolution tool kit that includes far-reaching powers such as disposing the bank's shares and subordinated assets or amalgamating the failing bank with another solvent institution.[43] Furthermore, the CDIC can sell all or part of the bank's assets and liabilities or create a bridge bank to take on systemically important functions until a more permanent solution is found. If the closure of a failing bank is not desirable, but resolution tools such as forced sale or a bridge bank cannot be used, the CDIC can keep the bank open by providing financial assistance in the form of deposits, loans, advances and guarantees.[44]

Securities Law Reforms

The Canadian Securities Administrators (CSA) have played an important role in reforming Canadian securities law. Much like the many federal regulatory institutions coordinate their efforts through the fora listed above, the provincial securities regulators communicate and coordinate policy choices through the CSA.[45] This umbrella organization introduced changes to the regulation of the OTC derivatives market. The reform agenda, which is carried out by the CSA and coordinated through the HoA,[46] has primarily focused on central clearing of OTC derivatives, enhancing market transparency through trade repositories, and migration of standard transactions to exchanges and trading platforms. Similar to the banking sector reforms, these measures largely follow the work carried out by transnational bodies such as the FSB and the International Organization of Securities Commissions (IOSCO).[47]

Following the GFC, the CSA established a systemic risk subcommittee in 2009. The move was influenced by IOSCO's recommendation that a securities regulator "should have or contribute to a process to monitor, mitigate, and manage systemic risk, appropriate to its mandate."[48] Similarly, the Ontario Securities Commission (OSC) has established a new Risk Committee to strengthen its capability to detect and manage systemic risk. The Commission took on promoting financial stability as a new organizational role.[49] The mandate of the Ontario Securities Act was amended to include systemic risk as a focal point in addition to investor protection and market efficiency.[50]

42 See OSFI, *Guide to Intervention for Federally Regulated Deposit-Taking Institut*ions, online: <www.osfi-bsif.gc.ca/Eng/fi-if/rai-eri/sp-ps/Pages/gid.aspx?pedisable=true>; *Canada Deposit Insurance Corporation Act*, RSC 1985, c C-3, s 39.13-14 [*CDIC Act*].

43 *Ibid*, s 10.

44 *Ibid*, s 39.

45 See CSA, "Who We Are", *supra* note 24.

46 The HoA is a systemic oversight committee comprised of OSFI, the BoC, the DoF, the CSA chair and four provincial securities regulators. Its primary mandate is to exchange information among members and coordinate on issues of mutual importance. See IMF, *FSSA*, *supra* note 7 at 26.

47 FSB, *Review of OTC derivatives market reform: Effectiveness and broader effects of the reforms* (FSB, 2017), online: <www.fsb.org/2017/06/review-of-otc-derivatives-market-reform-effectiveness-and-broader-effects-of-the-reforms/>; IOSCO, *Report of the Basel Committee on Banking Supervision and the Board of IOSCO* (18 March 2015) [IOSCO, *Report*], online: <www.iosco.org/publications/?subsection=pr&id=480>.

48 IOSCO, *Report*, *supra* note 47, referencing Principle 6.

49 See Anita Anand, "Is systemic risk relevant to securities regulation?" (2010) 60:4 UTLJ 59; Anita Anand, ed, *Systemic Risk, Institutional Design, and the Regulation of Financial Markets* (Oxford, UK: Oxford University Press, 2016). See also Mary Condon, "Canada's Role in Expanded IOSCO Principles" (Address delivered at the Toronto Securities Leadership Seminar, 9 July 2012), online: <www.osc.gov.on.ca/en/NewsEvents_sp_20120709_canada-role-iosco-principles.htm>; Ontario Securities Commission (OSC), *Challenging the Status Quo: Annual Report 2017*, online: <www.osc.gov.on.ca/documents/en/Publications/Publications_rpt_2017_osc-annual-rpt_en.pdf>.

50 *Ontario Securities Act*, RSO 1990, c S.5, s 1.1.

The most ambitious institutional reform on systemic risk, however, came in August 2014 when the federal government proposed the Capital Markets Stability Act (CMSA).[51] The move came after an earlier failure to establish a national securities regulator. In *Reference Re Securities Act*, discussed above, the Supreme Court deemed the Canadian Securities Act to be outside the federal government's purview.[52] The court, however, recognized federal jurisdiction on matters of genuine national importance, including management of systemic risk and national data collection.[53] Following the Supreme Court's judgment, the federal government published a consultative draft of the CMSA that was subsequently revised in January 2016.[54]

The Capital Markets Regulatory Authority (CMRA) is the new body that would administer the new framework proposed in the CMSA. The CMRA would deal with systemic risk in the capital markets, defined as "a threat to the stability of Canada's financial system that originates in, is transmitted through or impairs capital markets and that has the potential to have a material adverse effect on the Canadian economy."[55] The CMRA can designate a product, service or benchmark as systemically important, although it does not have any entity-level designation powers. It can also issue regulations or orders on entities. However, all regulations are subject to agreement by the Council of Ministers, comprised of ministers of participating provinces responsible for the capital markets regulation as well as the federal minister of finance.[56] As these individuals are elected officials, the initiative is inevitably subject to the political process.[57] Taken together, this approach to securities market regulation bolsters the individual influence of securities regulators across provinces and territories, and emphasizes the importance of coordination among these regulatory bodies in anticipation of financial crises.

Household Debt: Mortgages and Market Stability

Beyond the regulation of capital markets, a number of measures have been taken to address increasing household debt and housing imbalances. These elements present another area of systemic risk that challenges the stability of Canada's financial market. Indeed, Canada has one of the highest levels of household debt among G7 countries, with the household debt-to-income ratio reaching almost 170 percent in 2017.[58] The bulk of household credit growth comes from mortgages and home equity lines of credit.[59] Housing prices continue to grow at a faster

51 See DoF, "Capital Markets Stability Act – Draft for Consultation" (2014), online: <www.fin.gc.ca/drleg-apl/2014/cmsa-lsmc-l-eng.asp>. See also Anita Anand, "After the Reference: Regulating Systemic Risk in Canadian Financial Markets" in Anita Anand, ed, *What's Next for Canada: Securities Regulation After the Reference* (Toronto: Irwin Law, 2012).

52 *Reference re Securities Act*, *supra* note 25.

53 *Ibid.*

54 See CCMRS, *Capital Markets Stability Act – Draft for Consultation* (January 2016), online: <http://ccmr-ocrmc.ca/wp-content/uploads/cmsa-consultation-draft-revised-en.pdf>.

55 *Ibid*, art 3.

56 *Ibid*, s 76; *Memorandum of Agreement Regarding the Cooperative Capital Markets Regulatory System*, art 3(iv), online: <http://dev.ccmr-ocrmc.ca/wp-content/uploads/MOA-English.pdf>.

57 Anita Anand, "What About the Investors?" (2017) Canadian Foundation for the Advancement of Investor Rights White Paper, online: <http://faircanada.ca/wp-content/uploads/2017/05/170505_FAIR-Anand-White-Paper-FINAL.pdf>.

58 IMF, "Canada – 2013 Article IV Consultation Concluding Statement of the Mission" [IMF, "Article IV Consultation"] at 3, online: <www.imf.org/en/News/Articles/2015/09/28/04/52/mcs112613>.

59 BoC, *Financial System Review* (November 2017) at 4, online: <www.bankofcanada.ca/wp-content/uploads/2017/11/fsr-november2017.pdf>.

pace than justified by fundamental economics, with Toronto and Vancouver dominating the housing price acceleration. For example, housing prices in Toronto surged by 32 percent from 2016 to 2017.[60] In Vancouver, housing prices grew by more than 50 percent from mid-2013 to mid-2016. While the slowdown of housing activity and the introduction of a 15 percent property tax on non-resident buyers caused a short pause to this trend, prices in Vancouver picked up shortly thereafter.[61]

Against this background, Canadian authorities have sought to enhance the resiliency of the banking system in the midst of a housing downturn and to enhance the rigour of mortgage underwriting practices. OSFI's Guideline B-20 requires that mortgage decisions be made based on an assessment of the borrower's background as well as their willingness and capacity to service debt.[62] The guideline advises banks to conduct in-person appraisal of the property and recommends those using third-party appraisal to ensure that appraisers operate "independent[ly] from the mortgage acquisition, loan processing and loan decision process."[63]

These provisions are complemented by Guideline B-21, which sets out further requirements regarding due diligence on lenders' underwriting practices, portfolio management and stress testing, and portfolio risk management and stress testing.[64] Since 2008, the federal government has also gradually tightened mortgage insurance rules, including reducing the maximum amortization period for insured mortgages from 40 to 25 years, introducing a minimum credit score of 620 as well as a minimum down payment of five percent for new mortgages,[65] and reducing the loan-to-value ratio for insured refinanced mortgages from 100 percent to 80 percent.[66]

The BoC has weighed in on the issue by noting that the Canadian housing market, with its debt ramifications, has market-wide problems. Indeed, Canada's housing market has often been described as overheated.[67] The increased cost of housing has coincided with a nearly decade-long period of cheap consumer credit. Consequently, Canadian households have become significantly indebted by borrowing against their home equity.

In particular, the BoC is concerned about Canadians using home equity lines of credit to increase their borrowing capacity to very risky levels. BoC Governor Stephen Poloz explicitly noted that 40 percent of all housing-backed loans are now blended home equity lines of credit, on which borrowers can choose to pay interest only and no principal. The risk of this high household debt

60 BoC, *Financial System Review* (June 2017) at 12, online: <www.bankofcanada.ca/wp-content/uploads/2017/06/fsr-june2017.pdf>.

61 *Ibid.*

62 See OSFI, "Guideline B-20: Residential Mortgage Underwriting Practices and Procedures", online: <www.osfi-bsif.gc.ca/Eng/fi-if/rg-ro/gdn-ort/gl-ld/Pages/b20_dft.aspx>.

63 *Ibid.*

64 OSFI, *Residential Mortgage Insurance Underwriting Practices and Procedures* (November 2014), online: <www.osfi-bsif.gc.ca/Eng/fi-if/rg-ro/gdn-ort/gl-ld/Pages/b21.aspx>.

65 If the purchase price exceeds $500,000, the minimum down payment for the portion of the house price over $500,000 will be 10 percent. See CMHC, "What are the General Requirements to Qualify for Homeowner Mortgage Loan Insurance?", online: <www.cmhc-schl.gc.ca/en/co/moloin/moloin_003.cfm>.

66 *Ibid.* See also IMF, "Article IV Consultation", *supra* note 58, Annex III.

67 "The end of Canada's housing boom?", Editorial, *The Economist* (18 May 2017), online: <www.economist.com/news/americas/21722249-american-protectionism-not-only-threat-economy-end-canadas-housing-boom>.

level makes Canadians more exposed to falling home prices and higher interest rates.[68] As a result of these risks, the BoC has consistently warned Parliament and the public about the risk of higher household debt levels.[69] While the housing market is cooling on a general level, the risk of high household debt coupled with likely increases in interest rates can exacerbate the stresses on systemic stability.

Limitations of a Sector-by-sector Regulatory Model

The GFC raised the persistent issue of how to ensure effective oversight of systemic risk in a financial system. As discussed above, Canada mainly follows an institutional approach to regulation whereby separate agencies are entrusted with regulating different institutions and functions. While OSFI regulates federally incorporated banks and insurance companies, securities regulators oversee issuers of securities and investment firms. As Anita Anand, Michael Trebilcock and Michael Rosenstock note, different regulatory objectives can also underpin each regulatory domain.[70] For example, whereas OSFI's primary goal is to promote solvency among financial institutions, the FCAC and securities regulators are particularly concerned with the conduct of business, aiming to protect investors and consumers in the marketplace. This type of regulation in "silos" can prove difficult in times of financial market crisis, where regulatory coordination is warranted.

The recent experience of Home Capital, an alternative mortgage lender that experienced financial distress following a mortgage fraud scandal, highlights the challenges that an institutional or sector-by-sector model faces in regulating today's interconnected markets. Although Home Capital had broken ties with brokers and underwriters involved in fraudulent mortgage practices, it was accused by the OSC of publicly hiding the incident and its impact on its mortgage business. Following escalating tension with the OSC, Home Capital issued subsequent statements to meet its disclosure obligations. However, these statements led to a significant loss of market confidence and raised uncertainty over the health of the broader housing market.[71] Following a press release on March 27, 2017, which acknowledged the mortgage fraud incident, Home Capital shares plunged by more than 75 percent from $27.72 on March 27 to $5.85 on May 5, and depositors withdrew more than $2 billion from the lender.[72] Faced by a significant liquidity crunch, Home Capital took on an emergency line of credit from a major Canadian pension fund, followed by additional equity financing and a

68 Poloz summarized these dangers in the following terms: "It's time to remind folks that prices of houses can go down as well as up" (*ibid*). See Janet McFarland & Justin Giovannetti, "BoC's Poloz issues warning about speculation in Toronto housing market", *The Globe and Mail* (12 April 2017), online: <www.theglobeandmail.com/real-estate/the-market/toronto-and-hamilton-home-prices-soar-to-march-record/article34679288/>.

69 David Cochrane, "Household debt, home prices biggest risk to Canadian economy, Bank of Canada says", *CBC News* (28 November 2017), online: <www.cbc.ca/news/politics/bank-of-canada-household-debt-1.4422623>.

70 Anita Anand, Michael Trebilcock & Michael Rosenstock, "Institutional Design and the New Systemic Risk in Banking Crises" in Anita Anand, ed, *Systemic Risk, Institutional Design, and the Regulation of Financial Markets* (Oxford, UK: Oxford University Press, 2017) 1 at 25.

71 Home Capital Group Inc., *2017 Annual Report* (2017) at 21, online: <www.homecapital.com/annual_reports/2017/HomeCapitalAnnualReport2017.pdf>; Home Capital Group Inc., *2017 Second Quarter Report* (2017) at 3, online: <www.homecapital.com/quarterly_reports.asp>.

72 Armina Ligaya & Barbara Shecter, "'Like the perfect storm': An FP Investigation into the events that took Home Capital to the brink", *Financial Post* (22 Sept 2017), online: <http://business.financialpost.com/news/inside-the-rise-and-fall-of-home-capital>.

$2-billion line of credit from Berkshire Hathaway. More recently, the firm managed to secure a smaller credit facility on more favourable terms from two Canadian banks.[73]

Although the Home Capital episode did not lead to significant financial market contagion, it nonetheless illustrates the challenges involved in coordinating regulatory oversight and enforcement. Whereas the mortgage fraud was initially seen as a disclosure failure within the OSC's jurisdiction, the OSC's enforcement came to bear upon the firm's solvency, an imperative beyond the OSC's mandate. Indeed, the firm's press releases, which came after significant pressure from the OSC, triggered a massive depositor run and undermined the market confidence in both Home Capital and even the broader alternate mortgage sector.[74] Arguably, the OSC's enforcement actions fell perfectly within its mandate. However, it is unclear whether the regulator sought to communicate and coordinate with OSFI before intervention. As the next section suggests, similar challenges also surfaced earlier in the asset-backed commercial paper (ABCP) crisis, although the implications were much larger this time.

The ABCP Crisis Revisited

Canada's institutional regulatory approach came under significant pressure in the ABCP crisis. Fears of contagion arising from potential exposure to US subprime mortgages, combined with uncertainty about the underlying assets and the associated leverage, led to a rush by investors to exit the market. At the centre of the crisis was $35 billion in non-bank, or third-party, sponsored ABCP that was frozen because of the inability of conduits to roll over the papers.[75] Due to different regulatory requirements for ABCP sponsorship, conduits sponsored by the Canadian banks were monitored by OSFI, whereas third-party conduits sponsored by foreign banks, such as Deutsche Bank, were regulated only by their home authorities. These banks, which did not have retail operations in Canada, refused to provide liquidity support for their conduits when the crisis unfolded. The conduits themselves were assumed to be governed by securities law. In a parliamentary hearing, Julie Dickson, then superintendent of OSFI, said: "People are covered. If you are an investor in a security in Canada, you are covered by the securities commissions. My job is to look after banks and bank depositors. If you're an investor, you're covered by securities commissions."[76]

However, third-party conduits were, in fact, exempted from prospectus requirements, as their debt notes had received gold-plated credit ratings; investors were not covered by securities regulators.[77] During this period, ABCP was distributed almost exclusively in the exempt market,

73 James Bradshaw, "Home Capital taps banks to replace Buffett credit line", *The Globe and Mail* (16 May 2018), online: <www.theglobeandmail.com/business/article-home-capital-secures-new-credit-line-to-replace-buffett-funding/>.

74 Daniel Tencer, "As Home Capital Crisis Deepens, Some Talk Openly of Canada-Wide 'Contagion'", *Huffington Post* (1 May 2017), online: <www.huffingtonpost.ca/2017/05/01/home-capital-contagion-financial-system-canada_n_16365938.html>.

75 IMF, *Canada: Financial Sector Assessment Program – Crisis Management and Bank Resolution Framework – Technical Note* (March 2014), IMF Country Report No 14/67 at 18, online: <www.imf.org/en/Publications/CR/Issues/2016/12/31/Canada-Financial-Sector-Assessment-Program-Crisis-Management-and-Bank-Resolution-Framework-41403>; see also John Chant, "The ABCP Crisis in Canada: The Implications for the Regulation of Financial Markets" (2008) Expert Panel on Securities Regulation.

76 House of Commons, Standing Committee on Finance, "Evidence", 39th Parl, 2nd Sess, No 50 (16 June 2008) (Julie Dickson), online: <www.ourcommons.ca/DocumentViewer/en/39-2/FINA/meeting-50/evidence>.

77 Paul Halpern et al, *Back from the Brink: Lessons from the Canadian Asset-Backed Commercial Paper Crisis* (Toronto: Rotman-UTP Publishing, 2016) at 23–24.

a market in which securities regulators permit issuers to distribute securities without a full-blown prospectus or, in the case of the short-term debt exemption that was used to distribute ABCP, any disclosure at all.

So, in the years preceding the crisis, the third-party ABCP market expanded aggressively on a fragile business model while the risks it posed to the broader financial system grew and were generally unmonitored by any of the regulators. Then, when the crisis finally hit, the federal and provincial governments ultimately provided a $14-billion liquidity facility to restore trust in the ABCP market and support restructuring of the papers.[78]

Five originating factors can help explain the magnitude of this crisis. First, ABCP issuers were exempt from securities law prospectus requirements, which would have mandated a certain level of disclosure with respect to the notes or commercial paper being issued.[79] As John Chant observes, the disclosure that accompanied ABCP failed to communicate the associated risks; for example, information relating to the quality, mix and weighting of the assets underlying the notes (including highly leveraged exposure to derivatives) or the contingency of liquidity provision agreements that would have been useful information for investors in these securities.[80]

Second, sponsors of ABCP issuers, or their activities in respect of them, were in many cases not subject to regulatory supervision. Banks treated their sponsorship of ABCP conduits as an off-balance-sheet activity, which allowed them to evade regulatory capital requirements and other prudential requirements.

Third, these domestic and foreign banks, as well as non-bank financial institutions, also acted as a source of liquidity for the ABCP conduits, providing them with standby lines of credit. Many such liquidity providers were not subject to capital requirements and were otherwise minimally regulated (i.e., if the provider was not a financial institution).

Fourth, the conduct of rating agencies (in this case the Dominion Bond Rating Service) was unregulated, yet these were the agencies that were endorsing the securities for distribution.[81] The use of the short-term debt exemption effectively delegated responsibility for oversight of the ABCP market from securities regulators to rating agencies.

Fifth, the risks borne by ABCP were passed on to the public by investment dealers and salespeople who are subject to "know your client" and "suitability" rules administered by the Investment Industry Regulatory Organization of Canada (IIROC), but not to any explicit fiduciary duty.[82] These salespeople did not understand the products they were selling,[83] and

78 IMF, "Canada: Financial System Stability Assessment – Update" (February 2008), IMF Country Report No 08/59 at 22, online: <www.imf.org/en/Publications/CR/Issues/2016/12/31/Canada-Financial-System-Stability-Assessment-Update-21710>.

79 Anita Anand, "Is Systemic Risk Relevant to Securities Regulation?" (2010) 60:4 UTLJ 941 at 954 (Anand, "Systemic Risk"). Our discussion of these factors builds on the work of Chant, *supra* note 75 at 9.

80 Chant, *supra* note 75 at 10–12, 23. See also Scott Hendry, Stéphane Lavoie & Carolyn Wilkins, *Securitized Products, Disclosure, and the Reduction of Systemic Risk* (BoC, 2010), online: <www.bankofcanada.ca/wp-content/uploads/2011/12/fsr-0610-hendry.pdf>.

81 OSC, *Designated Rating Organizations, Related Policies and Consequential Amendments*, OSC NI 25-101, online: <www.osc.gov.on.ca/en/28587.htm>.

82 Chant, *supra* note 75 at 15.

83 IIROC, *Regulatory Study, Review and Recommendations Concerning the Manufacture and Distribution by IIROC Member Firms of Third-Party Asset-Backed Commercial Paper in Canada* (October 2008) at 74.

dense disclosure meant that investors had little hope of understanding the securities they were purchasing, even if they tried.

Collectively, these factors suggested weaknesses in the fragmented regulatory regime. Regulatory authorities failed to act in a coordinated manner, which perhaps allowed the ABCP crisis to evolve more quickly and to reach greater proportions than if regulators had worked together to forestall it.[84] In other words, the diffusion of regulatory oversight (i.e., different bodies overseeing different aspects of the same market) reduced the ability of these bodies to appreciate the size and scope of the crisis and to act effectively *ex ante* to contain its effects.[85]

In the aftermath of the GFC, various regulatory initiatives sought to incorporate some of the lessons from the ABCP experience. Legislative changes recognized the capacity of systemic risk to negatively impact the broader economy. For instance, Ontario's Securities Act now contains an objective "to contribute to the stability of the financial system and the reduction of systemic risk."[86] Although not yet in force, the draft CMSA adopted as a core objective the "effective detection, prevention and management of systemic risk to Canada's financial system."[87]

Yet the CMSA embodies a sectoral approach to systemic risk: because of constitutional limitations, it is concerned only with capital markets rather than the entire financial system. Furthermore, the administration of the legislation has been assigned to the CMRA, which is not a stand-alone federal regulator but a cooperative body whose jurisdiction reaches only the participating provinces and territories.

In its recent decision on *Reference re Pan-Canadian Securities Regulation*, the Supreme Court upheld the constitutionality of the proposed cooperative capital markets regulatory system (CCMRS).[88] Nevertheless, the new national regulator will likely face challenges in securing necessary cooperation in data collection and systemic risk oversight from provinces, in particular Alberta and Quebec, which have refused to join the cooperative scheme.[89] A notable challenge will be the oversight of derivatives markets, which falls within the provinces' mandate of "day-to-day" regulation of securities markets. At the same time, derivatives trading constitutes a meaningful source of systemic risk.[90] To what extent the new national regulator could effectively oversee the developments in the derivatives markets, therefore, remains an important question.

84 Chant, *supra* note 75 at 40.

85 Although Chant does not explicitly advocate consolidation of financial regulation in Canada, he notes that "[w]ith consolidation, the regulator would be able to take a broad view and consider the overall effects of the measure and respond appropriately. The case for consolidation would be strengthened if there is evidence that communication between different parts of a single agency proves more effective than communication among agencies" (*ibid*).

86 *Securities Act (Ontario)*, RSO 1990, c S.5, s 1.1.

87 See the Preamble in CCMRS, *Capital Markets Stability Act – Draft for Consultation* (January 2016), online: <http://ccmr-ocrmc.ca/wp-content/uploads/cmsa-consultation-draft-revised-en.pdf>.

88 *Reference re Pan-Canadian Securities Regulation*, 2018 SCC 48 at paras 81–85.

89 See Harvey Naglie, "Not Ready for Prime Time: Canada's Proposed New Securities Regulator" (2017) CD Howe Institute Commentary No 489 at 18, online: <www.cdhowe.org/public-policy-research/not-ready-prime-time-canada percentE2 percent80 percent99s-proposed-new-securities-regulator>. Note that Alberta and Quebec have not joined the CMRA; see CCMRS, "The Cooperative Capital Markets Regulatory System" (2018), online: <http://ccmr-ocrmc.ca/>; Anita Anand, "Canada's new securities regulatory structure is a disservice to investors", *The Globe and Mail* (31 May 2017), online: <www.theglobeandmail.com/report-on-business/rob-commentary/new-securities-regulatory-structure-a-disservice-to-investors/article35167692/>.

90 *Reference re Securities Act*, *supra* note 25 at para 125; see also Anita Anand, "Supreme Court Opens the Door to a New Model of Securities Regulation", online: <www.cdhowe.org/intelligence-memos/anita-anand-supreme-court-opens-door-new-model-securities-regulation>.

Toward a More Integrated Approach to Systemic Risk

The absence of a macroprudential regulator may undermine efforts to monitor and take action on systemic risk. Both the IMF and the FSB have recommended assigning a macroprudential mandate to a single body that could take a "comprehensive view of systemic risk across all financial institutions and markets in Canada."[91] This recommendation is consistent with post-crisis reforms in other jurisdictions that have overhauled their institutional architecture to close regulatory gaps and facilitate financial sector-wide oversight of vulnerabilities. In the United States, for example, the Dodd-Frank Act has created the Financial Stability Oversight Council (FSOC), which is responsible for identifying systemic threats and recommending appropriate regulatory response.[92] The FSOC collects data on systemic risk through the Office of Financial Research, facilitates information sharing and cooperation among regulators, and can designate non-bank firms and financial market infrastructure as systemically important.[93]

In the United Kingdom, the Financial Services Act (2012) established a twin-peaks regime that moved the overall responsibility for financial stability to the Bank of England.[94] The Prudential Regulatory Authority, a subsidiary of the bank, regulates all systemically important financial institutions in banking, insurance and capital markets.[95] The bank's Financial Policy Committee (FPC) "identifies, monitors and takes action to remove or reduce systemic risks" with a comprehensive view of the UK financial system.[96] While the FPC does not have direct regulatory authority over financial institutions, it can issue directions and recommendations to the relevant authorities.[97] Finally, the European Union has established the European Systemic Risk Board (ESRB), which is tasked with macroprudential oversight of the financial system across the whole Union.[98] The ESRB can identify significant risks to financial stability and issue warnings and recommendations for remedial action.[99]

Canadian authorities, however, have indicated that they will not pursue the recommendation to establish a macroprudential regulator. Unless the CMRA is created under the CCMR, the responsibility for systemic risk will remain with the array of organizations discussed above, including OSFI, the BoC, and the provincial and territorial securities regulatory authorities.[100] The reluctance to establish a new macroprudential regulator can be explained by path dependency and an ongoing, unrelenting resistance of the existing regulatory regime to

---

91 See IMF, *FSSA*, *supra* note 7 at 25; FSB, *Peer Review of Canada: Review Report* (2012) at 36, online: <www.fsb.org/wp-content/uploads/r_120130.pdf>.

92 12 USC § 5323.

93 US Department of the Treasury, "Financial Stability Oversight Council", online: <www.treasury.gov/initiatives/fsoc/about/Pages/default.aspx>.

94 *Financial Services Act 2012* (UK), s 9.

95 *Ibid*, s 2(A)&(B).

96 *Ibid*, s 9(C).

97 *Ibid*, s 9(G)&(H).

98 *Regulation (EU) No 1092/2010 on European Union macro-prudential oversight of the financial system and establishing a European Systemic Risk Board* [2010] OJ, L 331, art 3(1).

99 *Ibid*, art 16(1).

100 IMF, *Canada: 2017 Article IV Consultation – Press Release and Staff Report* (Washington, DC: 2017) at 2, 13, 74, online: <www.imf.org/en/publications/cr/issues/2017/07/13/canada-2017-article-iv-consultation-press-release-and-staff-report-45074> [IMF, *2017 Article IV Consultation*].

transformative changes, given the costs and resources involved in such a transition.[101] Generally, path dependency can refer to decisions that may have been efficient *ex ante,* but that do not turn out to be efficient *ex post*. According to Stan Liebowitz and Stephen Margolis, an original decision and its consequences may have been an inferior option in hindsight; however, these qualities are unknowable at the time the decision is made.[102] At a later stage, it becomes clear that an alternative decision or path would have been more efficient, but the original decision is carried out due to continued commitment of resources. As they state, "there is a dependence on past conditions that leads to outcomes that are regrettable and costly to change."[103]

Institutional structures can be self-reinforcing, remaining on a given course in response to significant fixed costs associated with change, "learning effects" that reward knowledge of a particular practice, and expectations or preferences that solidify around the status quo.[104] The self-reinforcing tendency implies increasing returns to institutional structures, practices or norms, while switching costs associated with institutional reform can be expected to rise over time. Paul Pierson explains that increasing returns mean that small events at "critical junctures" can have significant long-term consequences.[105] Timing and political "inertia" are central, but change will usually be incremental.[106]

Anand, Trebilcock and Rosenstock have argued that while the GFC may have indicated that some type of reform to the complement of regulators governing Canada's financial system is necessary, arguments from path dependency suggest that "grand transformative changes are unlikely — or at least uncertain — and not necessarily a function of the severity of the GFC or the country at issue."[107] However, we maintain the possibility of incremental reforms, including changes to the legal mandates of existing regulatory institutions.[108] Similarly, while path dependency creates inertia against institutional change, Mariana Prado and Michael Trebilcock argue that path dependency can clarify what has happened in the past and also can be used to inform the feasibility of institutional reforms.[109]

Specific to the Canadian securities regulatory system, path dependency refers to the durability of the regime and the importance of history in fashioning a reform agenda. In particular, path dependency helps to explain the current structure of the regime that has resulted from the development of Canadian constitutional law and province-based institutions (for example, legislatures and securities commissions) that have charge over the development of securities legislation. Together, the jurisprudence and relevant institutions stand as historical constraints on the ability to achieve an efficient securities regulatory regime in this country.[110]

101 Anand, Trebilcock & Rosenstock in Anand, *Systemic Risk, supra* note 5.

102 Stan J Liebowitz & Stephen E Margolis, "The Fable of the Keys" (1990) 33:1 J L & Econ at 18.

103 *Ibid.*

104 *Ibid* at 351; see also Paul Pierson, "Increasing Returns, Path Dependence, and the Study of Politics" (2000) 94:2 Am Pol Sci Rev 251 at 254.

105 See Mariana Prado & Michael J Trebilcock, "Path Dependence, Development and the Dynamics of Institutional Reform" (2009) 59 UTLJ 342 at 357.

106 Paul Pierson, *Politics in Time* (Princeton, NJ: Princeton University Press, 2004) at 44, 153.

107 Anand, Trebilcock & Rosenstock in Anand, *Systemic Risk, supra* note 5.

108 *Ibid.*

109 Prado & Trebilcock, *supra* note 105 at 353.

110 See generally Anita Anand & Peter Klein, "Inefficiency and Path Dependency in Canada's Securities Regulatory System: Towards a Reform Agenda" (2005) 42:1 Can Bus LJ 41.

Nevertheless, whereas a complete institutional overhaul may never gather sufficient momentum in Canada, incremental reforms to achieve better regulatory outcomes are feasible. The absence of a formal macroprudential regulator does not prevent the existing authorities from working collectively to promote financial stability as a common good.[111] Indeed, most international bodies that have been leading post-crisis regulatory reforms, such as the Basel Committee on Banking Supervision or the FSB, operate outside the formal law-making processes.[112] These bodies are not the product of treaties and they lack any formal powers to impose rules on sovereign nations, but their standards have been enormously influential and have been largely followed by domestic jurisdictions.[113]

In a similar vein, Canadian regulators can seek to achieve communication and coordination through informal bodies, and the existing institutional flexibility can indeed facilitate regulatory experimentation in the face of complexity and the rapid pace of change in financial markets.[114] However, effective oversight of systemic risk requires establishing a robust agenda with clear goals and processes. First and foremost, a comprehensive picture of interlinkages and system-wide trends needs to be further developed. The BoC's *Financial System Review* can be an important stepping stone in this respect as it provides many important insights on systemic vulnerabilities. The BoC's analysis can be further complemented with input from the CMRA, which has both the authority and mandate to collect and analyze data on systemic risk in capital markets.

Conclusion

The GFC triggered an unprecedented wave of regulatory reforms that continue to unfold more than a decade later. While some substantive reforms, such as the Basel III requirements, have been relatively similar across jurisdictions, institutional and structural reforms remain widely uneven. Some jurisdictions have established new institutions with specific mandates for financial stability, however Canada continues to have a patchwork of regulators in charge of different segments of the financial system. The costs and resources involved in transformative changes, reinforced by the unique constitutional characteristics of Canada, can help to explain the inertia against institutional overhaul.

The fragmented nature of the existing regulatory model undermines systemic risk oversight and severely strains regulatory communication and coordination. Risky products and practices can build up outside the individual purview of regulators, such that their systemic implications go

111 On financial stability as a common good, see Tucker, *supra* note 6 at 21–22.

112 For further discussion on transnational regulatory networks and the rising prominence of soft law in global finance, see Anne-Marie Slaughter, *A New World Order* (Princeton, NJ: Princeton University Press, 2004) at 14; Anne-Marie Slaughter & David Zaring, "Networks Go International: An Update" (2006) 6:12 Ann Rev L & Soc Sci 215 at 215; Chris Brummer, *Soft Law and the Global Financial System: Rule Making in the 21st Century* (Cambridge, UK: Cambridge University Press, 2012) at 63–64.

113 See BIS, *Basel Committee Charter* (5 June 2018), art 3, online: <www.bis.org/bcbs/charter.htm>; FSB, *Charter of the Financial Stability Board*, art 23, online: <www.fsb.org/wp-content/uploads/FSB-Charter-with-revised-Annex-FINAL.pdf>; see also Joost Pauwelyn, Ramses A Wessel & Jan Wouters, "The Exercise of Public Authority through Informal International Lawmaking: An Accountability Issue?" (2011) Jean Monnet Working Paper 06/11, New York University School of Law at 13.

114 See Eilís Ferran & Kern Alexander, "Can Soft Law Bodies be Effective? Soft Systemic Risk Oversight Bodies and the Special Case of the European Systemic Risk Board" (2010) University of Cambridge Faculty of Law Research Paper No 36/2011, online: <https://papers.ssrn.com/sol3/papers.cfm?abstract_id=1676140>.

unaddressed. When this happens, it will only take an unpredictable trigger, such as refusal to extend liquidity to non-bank conduits in the ABCP episode, to cause a crisis to erupt. Regulators may then find that they have little choice but to bail out the failing institutions.

Since a complete institutional overhaul seems unfeasible, we argue for incremental reform and improvements to the existing institutions and cooperation channels for better oversight of systemic risk. In the absence of the CMRA taking shape, we recommend that high-level inter-agency groupings such as SAC take a leadership role on systemic risk management and mitigation. These institutions should establish a clear mission and agenda to promote financial stability, ensuring that system-wide vulnerabilities are detected and addressed in a timely and comprehensive fashion.

Further attention also needs to be paid to the connections between different policy domains and the vulnerabilities that can arise outside the traditional prudential domain. One important area is the interlinkage between monetary policy and financial stability. In the aftermath of the GFC and Canada's 2014 oil shock, interest rates have remained at historically low levels.[115] The prolonged low interest rates, which reflect the central bank's struggle to bring inflation back to target, have aimed to stimulate economic activity and growth.[116]

At the same time, however, loose monetary policy has led to the buildup of leverage in the financial system, which has translated in the Canadian context into increasing household debt and elevated housing prices.[117] As a result, both households and financial institutions are highly exposed to the risks of rising interest rates, income shocks and deflating asset prices.[118] It is therefore important not only to consider financial stability in the conduct of monetary policy but also to deploy macroprudential tools, such as a strong leverage ratio for financial institutions and loan-to-income ratios for households to limit leverage in the system.[119] Such measures could help to enhance resilience against the deflation of housing prices and insolvencies ensuing from fire sales that often accompany a "leverage cycle crash."[120]

Finally, monopolistic emphasis on D-SIBs' regulation is insufficient, as it excludes systemically important institutions that are chartered at the provincial level. Although some provinces, such as British Columbia and Quebec, have designated their large credit unions to be systemically

115 BIS, Committee on the Global Financial System, "Financial stability implications of a prolonged period of low interest rates" (2018) CGFS Papers No 61 at 1, online: <www.bis.org/publ/cgfs61.pdf>; for the historical trend of interest rates in Canada, see Trading Economics, "Canada Interest Rate" (2018), online: <https://tradingeconomics.com/canada/interest-rate>.

116 Timothy Lane, "Monetary Policy and Financial Stability – Looking for the Right Tools" (Remarks delivered at HEC Montreal, Montreal, 8 February 2016), online: <www.bankofcanada.ca/2016/02/monetary-policy-financial-stability-looking-right-tools/>.

117 *Ibid.*

118 In its economic outlook, the Organisation for Economic Co-operation and Development (OECD) notes that housing prices in Canada are both overvalued and rising, noting that the economy is vulnerable to both income shocks and higher borrowing costs. See OECD, "Focus on house prices" (2017), online: <www.oecd.org/eco/outlook/focusonhouseprices.htm>.

119 As John Geanakoplos notes, "The best way to stop a crash is to act long before it occurs, by restricting leverage in ebullient times." See John Geanakoplos, "The Leverage Cycle" (2010) Cowles Foundation Discussion Paper No 1715R at 4, online: <https://cowles.yale.edu/sites/default/files/files/pub/d17/d1715-r.pdf>; see also Emilios Avgouleas, "Bank Leverage Ratios and Financial Stability: A Micro- and Macroprudential Perspective" (2015) Levy Economics Institute of Bard College Working Paper No 849 at 23–24, online: <www.levyinstitute.org/pubs/wp_849.pdf>.

120 Ana Fostel & John Geanakoplos, "Reviewing the Leverage Cycle" (2013) Cowles Foundation Discussion Paper No 1918 at 28, online: <www.dallasfed.org/~/media/documents/research/events/2013/uncertaintygeanakoplos.pdf>.

important institutions,[121] others, such as Alberta, have not yet established a framework for enhanced regulation and supervision of their systemically important institutions.[122] This lack of multi-jurisdictional regulatory coordination creates regulatory gaps that threaten the stability of Canada's financial system.

Further effort is required to identify obstacles that hinder sharing data and communication among regulators, and to address them, whether through existing channels for cooperation or through legislative changes, if necessary. For example, the BoC's ability to build a comprehensive picture of the shadow banking system has been hindered by legal and logistical obstacles in sharing data among relevant authorities.[123]

At the heart of this chapter is a desire to enhance Canada's risk mitigation capacity by reflecting upon the lessons of the GFC. Canada may have fared well in the events of the GFC relative to most other economies. However, complacency in the face of systemic risks may undermine the country's prospective preparedness.

Authors' Note

We would like to thank Eric Wolfe and Robert Fay for their invaluable comments on this chapter.

121 Notable examples are Desjardins Group and Central 1 Credit Union, both of which have been designated as systemically important.

122 Specifically, Alberta Treasury Branches (ATB), a deposit-taking institution with more than $48 billion in assets and $33 billion in deposits, has not been designated as a systemically important institution. As a Crown corporation, the ATB enjoys full backing by the government and is directly connected to the province's financing. See ATB, "ATB 2017 Financial Report" (2017) at 35, online: <www.atb.com/SiteCollectionDocuments/About/annual_reports/atb_2017_annual_report.pdf>; Nicholas Le Pan, "Opportunities for Better Systemic Risk Management in Canada" (September 2017) CD Howe Institute Commentary No 490 at 12, online: <www.cdhowe.org/public-policy-research/opportunities-better-systemic-risk-management-canada>.

123 See Timothy Lane, "Shedding Light on Shadow Banking" (Remarks delivered at the CFA Society, Toronto, 26 June 2013), online: <www.bankofcanada.ca/2013/06/shedding-light-shadow-banking/>.

2

Bank Resolution a Decade after the Global Financial Crisis: A Systematic Reappraisal

EMILIOS AVGOULEAS AND CHARLES GOODHART

Following the collapse of Lehman Brothers, a number of large interconnected financial institutions had to be bailed out. Faced with a dual liquidity and confidence crisis, they were struggling to sustain solvency, but they could not be allowed to file for bankruptcy, as they were considered "too big to fail" (TBTF). The decision to bail out a number of major Western financial institutions was mainly taken over concerns about contagion in a disintegrating and highly vulnerable market, amidst a collapse of investor and user confidence, and because most jurisdictions did not have legal and regulatory regimes to deal with the special requirements of bank failures outside of corporate insolvency laws.

Since 2010, most Group of Twenty (G20) jurisdictions have introduced new recovery and resolution regimes to deal with bank failures (for example, the United Kingdom and the European Union) or have revised the scope and funding of pre-existing regimes (for example, the United States). Apart from the Financial Stability Board's (FSB's) Key Attributes,[1] which is a

1 FSB, *Key Attributes of Effective Resolution Regimes for Financial Institutions* (15 October 2014), online: <www.fsb.org/wp-content/uploads/r_141015.pdf>.

soft law document, resolution regimes worldwide have been enacted through legislation, namely in the European Union,[2] the United Kingdom and the United States.[3] The common objective of contemporary resolution regimes is, first, to facilitate the orderly failure of financial institutions in order to mitigate moral hazard and, second, to redirect the bulk of losses to the private sector, thereby eliminating the need for public bailouts. In contrast with corporate insolvency laws, which aim to maximize creditor satisfaction, the objectives of bank resolution regimes are to: secure operational continuity; stabilize the banking system by containing contagion through recapitalizing stressed institutions; and protect state funds by allocating losses to shareholders and debtholders, in the latter case through the use of debt-to-equity conversions or by writing off liabilities through the employment of the bail-in tool.[4] Stringent creditor monitoring of bank risk is presumed to constrain excessive leverage[5] because shareholders have strong incentives to increase leverage to maximize return on equity (ROE).[6] The threat of a creditor bail-in should eliminate the TBTF subsidy[7] that banks enjoy by raising the *ex ante* cost of bank funding. This, in principle, should also contain the governance costs that accompany excessive leverage in terms of pursuing highly risky strategies to maximize ROE[8] and managerial rents.[9]

Despite significant progress to meet resolution objectives, concerns remain as to whether the present arrangements will work effectively in the event of a systemic crisis. Requisite skepticism centres on three key issues. First, whether bailing in the creditors of a cross-border institution, including the conversion of pre-funded liabilities in the guise of total loss-absorbing capacity

2 EC, *Directive 2014/59/EU of the European Parliament and of the Council of 15 May 2014 establishing a framework for the recovery and resolution of credit institutions and investment firms*, [2014] OJ, L173/190 [*BRRD*].

3 *Title II of the Dodd-Frank Wall Street Reform and Consumer Protection Act of 2010*, Pub L No 111–203, HR 4173 [*Dodd-Frank Act*].

4 Emilios Avgouleas & Charles Goodhart, "A Critical Evaluation of Bail-Ins as Bank Recapitalisation Mechanisms" (2014) Centre for Economic Policy Research Discussion Paper No 10065, online: <http://ssrn.com/abstract=2478647>.

5 Emilios Avgouleas, "Bank Leverage Ratios and Financial Stability: A Micro- and Macroprudential Perspective" (2015) University of Edinburgh Working Paper.

6 AR Admati et al, "The Leverage Ratchet Effect" (2018) 73:1 J Finance 146 (first published as AR Admati et al, "The Leverage Ratchet Effect" [2013] Max Planck Institute for Research on Collective Goods Working Paper Series No 2013/13).

7 For an estimation of the potential impact that a creditor bail-in would have, see Frank Packer & Nikola Tarashev, "Rating Methodologies for Banks" (2011) BIS Q Rev 39; On the existence of the subsidy and calculations of its size and impact, see Kenichi Ueda & Beatrice Weder Di Mauro, "Quantifying the Value of the Subsidy for Systemically Important Financial Institutions" (2011) IMF Working Paper No 12/128; Reint Gropp, Hendrik Hakenes & Isabel Schnabel, "Competition, Risk-shifting, and Public Bail-Out Policies" (2011) 24:6 Rev Financial Studies 2084; Zan Li, Shinsheng Qu & Jing Zhang, "Quantifying the Value of Implicit Government Guarantees for Large Financial Institutions" (2011) Moody's Analytics Quantitative Research Group White Paper, online: <www.moodysanalytics.com/-/media/whitepaper/2011/2011-14-01-quantifying-the-value-of-implicit-government-guarantees-for-large-financial-institutions-20110114.pdf>; João AC Santos, "Evidence from the Bond Market on Banks' 'Too-Big-To-Fail' Subsidy" (2014) 20:2 Federal Reserve Bank of New York Economic Policy Review 29, online: <www.newyorkfed.org/medialibrary/media/research/epr/2014/EPRvol20no2.pdf>; Donald P Morgan & Kevin J Stiroh, "Too Big to Fail After All These Years" (2005) Federal Reserve Bank of New York Staff Reports No 220, online: <www.newyorkfed.org/medialibrary/media/research/staff_reports/sr220.pdf>; Zoe Tsesmelidakis & Robert C Merton, "The Value of Implicit Guarantees" (2012) Working Paper, online: <http://ssrn.com/abstract=2231317>.

8 See Admati, *supra* note 6; AR Admati et al, "Debt Overhang and Capital Regulation" (2012) Rock Center for Corporate Governance at Stanford University Working Paper No 114; Emilios Avgouleas & Jay Cullen, "Market Discipline and EU Corporate Governance Reform in the Banking Sector: Merits, Fallacies, and Cognitive Boundaries" (2014) 41:1 JL & Soc'y 28.

9 See Emilios Avgouleas & Jay Cullen, "Excessive Leverage and Bankers' Pay: Governance and Financial Stability Costs of a Symbiotic Relationship" (2014) 21:1 Colum J Eur L 1.

(TLAC)[10] or minimum requirement for own funds and eligible liabilities (MREL),[11] would prove sufficient to prevent the bailout of a global systemically important financial institution (G-SIFI). Second, there are possible undesirable consequences associated with bail-ins when the failure is systemic rather than idiosyncratic. These issues are discussed at great length in our earlier publications.[12] A third concern is whether there is sufficient liquidity to support a bank resolution. While this concern is pertinent to G-SIFI failures, the liquidity arrangements of domestic banks in resolution can also be unclear.

Other aspects of the resolution debate focus on the time horizon for the valuation of failing banks' losses[13] and the possibility of managerial and regulatory forbearance when there are fears that bailing-in bank creditors in an unstable market may heighten contagion. Another concern is the extent to which the reformed resolution regimes are sufficient to mitigate moral hazard, especially in the absence of an *ex post* penalty regime for bank managers.[14]

The last issue also relates to the question of whether current resolution regimes are premised on clear normative objectives. While the latter might sound more theoretical than practical, it is, in our view, a matter of cardinal importance. The normative values attached to any public policy regime are not merely expressed in its statutory objectives but also reflect and signal its implicit values, rationales and expected utilities. This lack of clarity and the overlapping and sometimes conflicting nature of resolution objectives under present frameworks are a key part of this chapter's analysis.

Accordingly, this chapter is divided into three sections following the present introduction. The second section unbundles the normative objectives of contemporary resolution regimes, highlighting inconsistencies and shortcomings. In this context, we advocate a more relaxed approach to the provision of liquidity in resolution to avoid fire sales or when relying on depressed valuations influenced by fire sales. The third section focuses on the implications of draconian creditor bail-in regimes and the timing of valuations. The fourth section concludes.

10 See FSB, "Total Loss-Absorbing Capacity Principles and Term Sheet" (9 November 2015), online: <www.fsb.org/2015/11/total-loss-absorbing-capacity-tlac-principles-and-term-sheet/>.

11 Under the Bank Recovery and Resolution Directive (BRRD) (art 45) and derivative legislation, EU banks must have a minimum cushion of regulatory capital and eligible liabilities expressed as a percentage of the total liabilities and own funds of the institution (MREL), which is the EU way of implementing the FSB TLAC standard. Doubts persist, however, as to whether MREL can cure the weaknesses of the EU resolution framework. See Emilios Avgouleas & Charles Goodhart, "An Anatomy of Bank Bail-ins: Why the Eurozone Needs a Fiscal Backstop for the Banking Sector" (2016) 2:2 Eur Economy 75, online: <http://european-economy.eu/2016-2/an-anatomy-of-bank-bail-ins-why-the-eurozone-needs-a-fiscal-backstop-for-the-banking-sector/>; Tobias H Tröger, "Too Complex to Work: A Critical Assessment of the Bail-in Tool under the European Bank Recovery and Resolution Regime" (2018) 4:1 J Financial Reg 35.

12 Emilios Avgouleas & Charles Goodhart, "Critical Reflections on Bank Bail-ins" (2015) 1:1 J Financial Reg 3.

13 Uncertainty concerning overall losses is associated with the timing and method of calculation of the value of bank assets with discrepancies between valuation when the bank enters resolution and at certain fixed points in future when the same assets might have recovered for some value. Thus, the timing of valuation is a matter of fundamental importance not just for the distribution of bank losses but also for observing the "no creditor worse off" (NCWO) principle.

14 See Steven L Schwarcz, "Too Big to Fool: Moral Hazard, Bailouts, and Corporate Responsibility" (2017) 102:2 Minn L Rev 761; Charles Nolan, Plutarchos Sakellaris & John D Tsoukalas, "Optimal Bailouts of Systemic Banks" (2017) Adam Smith Business School University of Glasgow Working Paper.

Express and Implicit Objectives of Bank Resolution Regimes: The State of Confusion

The Microprudential Dimension

Arguably the foremost objectives of bank resolution regimes are microprudential, regardless of the resolution technique that authorities choose to resolve a bank. The first microprudential goal is securing an orderly exit through an expedited legal process involving the restructuring, sale or liquidation of the affected institution and the utilization of pre-accumulated debt cushions (for example, contingent convertibles [CoCos], TLAC and MREL) that can be converted into equity to recapitalize the bank or written-off to absorb losses. The second microprudential objective of a bank resolution regime is the *ex ante* improvement of bank governance by augmenting risk controls and limiting leverage. This can be achieved by the close monitoring of creditors who want to avoid the cost of a bail-in. In addition, the risk of being bailed-in means that creditors ask a higher return for the money they lend to the bank, raising the cost of bank funding enough to eliminate the TBTF subsidy.[15] In contrast, inefficient bank resolution regimes can frustrate the impact of prudential rules that regulate capital and liquidity reserves, lending policies and large exposures, management quality and decision making, and systems and controls within going concern banks. A third microprudential objective is securing, where possible, bank recovery[16] to avoid moving the bank into disruptive resolution.

The Systemic/Macroprudential Dimension

Legal and regulatory regimes that mitigate contagion from bank failures inevitably have a systemic/macroprudential dimension. Peter Muelbert observes that resolution regimes have a macroprudential/systemic objective although they are not part of prudential regimes.[17] For this reason, the systemic dimension can often appear underdeveloped because resolution regimes tend to ignore the possible systemic dimensions of a crisis, and focus, instead, on private sector participation to ameliorate moral hazard. For this reason, insufficient attention has been given to interconnectedness risks in resolutions and the impact of resolution actions on investor, creditor and depositor confidence and the subsequent reactions of these constituencies, which can inadvertently propagate contagion. There are two reasons for this shortcoming. First, bank resolution techniques are exclusively microprudential with few exemptions due to systemic concerns.[18] Second, most regimes lack clear liquidity or "funding in resolution" arrangements,[19] although the provision of liquidity to prevent fire sales or valuations based on fire sales are

15 For a first study of creditor reaction to a reduction of the possibility of bailouts on creditor reaction, see Alexander Schäfer et al, "Bail-in expectations for European banks: Actions speak louder than words" (2016) European Systemic Risk Board Working Paper Series No 7.

16 Charles AE Goodhart & Miguel A Segoviano, "An approach for initiating interventions for bank recovery" (2017) 25:4 J Financial Ref & Compliance 360.

17 Peter O Muelbert, "Managing Risk in the Financial System" in Niamh Moloney, Eilís Ferran & Jennifer Payne, eds, *The Oxford Handbook of Financial Regulation* (Oxford, UK: Oxford University Press, 2015) 364 at 384.

18 For analysis of this point, see Steven L Schwarcz, "Beyond Bankruptcy: Resolution as a Macroprudential Regulatory Tool" (2019) 94:2 Notre Dame L Rev 709.

19 A shortcoming that is highlighted in the FSB reports on the implementation of the Key Attributes. See FSB, "Resilience through Resolvability — Moving from Policy Design to Implementation: Fifth Report to the G20 on Progress in Resolution" (2016) at 15, online: <www.fsb.org/wp-content/uploads/Resilience-through-resolvability—moving-from-policy-design-to-implementation.pdf>.

effective stabilizing measures. Conversely, frictions in the supply of liquidity could result in contagion from either counterparty defaults or fire sales.[20]

In this context, we regard the Bank of England's determination to provide sufficient liquidity during the resolution period, subject to the Her Majesty's (HM) Treasury indemnity, as appropriate.[21] However the United States, and more recently the European Union, have decided not to give central banks the power to supply resolution liquidity, opting instead for US Treasury and European Stability Mechanism (ESM) loans, which may be harder to obtain.

The Moral/Normative Dimension: A Political Economy Analysis

Resolution regimes have a number of explicit and implicit moral/normative goals that flow from or overlap with the aforementioned micro and macroprudential aspects of resolution regimes. The first is mitigating moral hazard, based on the desire to force banks to internalize operational costs by following the "polluter pays" principle, for example, curbing the TBTF subsidy and eliminating the possibility of public bailouts. The second moral/normative goal is to restore market discipline by restricting the funding of bailouts and other advantages pertaining to TBTF banks. From this stems a third moral facilitation of the Schumpeterian cycle. A properly calibrated resolution regime should ease the market exit of failing banks, while providing opportunities for new market entrants. The Schumpeterian cycle theorizes that underperformers would otherwise be sustained by public subsidies. Indeed, the expeditious and orderly exit of underperformers or restructuring in a controlled environment are important for overall economic efficiency, market competition characterized by a "level playing field" and the attainment of transparent capitalism.

The fourth apparent normative goal is the "punishment" of placid creditors. The implicit moral goals that flow from the microprudential and macroprudential aspects of the regime require interpretation, predominantly from a political economic analysis perspective. Thus, they are subject to dispute and none more than the apparent "punitive" nature of the regime.[22] If the goal of the regime is, however, the containment of moral hazard, a punitive aspect may be inevitable for deterrence purposes. But instead of merely relying on super-rational and expert creditors, who can play the role of effective bank management monitors — admittedly a minority among bank creditors — resolution regimes should target the two constituents: bank management and large shareholders whose opportunistic behaviour is the key source of moral hazard. Furthermore, the punitive aspects of the bail-in may prove counterproductive in the context of resolution frameworks that should primarily focus on orderly exit. They may incentivize bank management to delay the resolution process for as long as possible, if their views can influence regulators' decisions. In addition, the question remains as to who should be "punished": the incompetent, the unlucky, the rent-seekers or the risk-takers? Shifting the cost of bank failures from taxpayers to bank creditors via bail-ins, often means nothing other than a fundamental

20 See Emilios Avgouleas, "Fundamentals of Bank Supervision and the Lender of Last Resort in the Post-2008 Era: A Critical Appraisal and Forward Looking Recommendations" (2016) Edinburgh School of Law Research Paper No 2016.

21 See Bank of England, "The Bank of England's Approach to Resolution" (2017) at 22, box 2, online: <www.bankofengland.co.uk/-/media/boe/files/news/2017/october/the-bank-of-england-approach-to-resolution.pdf>.

22 *Cf* Tobias H Tröger, "Too Complex to Work: A Critical Assessment of the Bail-in Tool under the European Bank Recovery and Resolution Regime" (2018) 4:1 J Financial Reg 35. Tröger doubts the punitive dimension of creditor bail-in regimes.

shift of this cost from one social group to another.[23] The punitive approach would nonetheless be better defended if it was targeting bank management and large shareholders, even by means of *ex post* penalties.

Finally, the competitive pricing of banks' funding to reflect true levels of bank riskiness, since bail-in regimes remove the shield of bailouts from senior creditors, may have some impact on shareholder and management appetite for risk and leverage, which seem to be symbiotic.[24] Thus, it may reinforce market discipline and make banks safer. However, it may not prove as effective as anticipated unless complemented by a prudential regime that is geared toward boosting equity buffers.

Interest rates are critical for the level of risk assumed by banks and for attracting capital investment in the banks. A sustained period of very low interest rates typically leads to riskier lending with higher yields to keep the banks' ROE ratios from collapsing. This predictable lending behaviour also leads to the accumulation of concealed risks on banks' balance sheets. At the same time, a long period of ultra-low interest rates eats into banks' profitability and makes bank equity a less than attractive investment. In a crisis, low interest rates and relatively high costs of equity funding may prove more critical to banks' risk-taking behaviour and solvency than the TBTF subsidy.

Taxation regimes also impact on the cost of equity in a way that influences the mix of bank funding, capital structure and leverage even when the TBTF subsidy is diminished.[25] Moreover, operating efficiencies, technological advantages, investment in research and development, client networks, economies of scale and scope also create funding advantages. Similarly, the level of market dominance[26] is the result of a combination of factors as already mentioned and not just the result of the TBTF subsidy or of its absence.

23 Avgouleas & Goodhart, *supra* note 12.

24 Admati et al, *supra* note 6; Avgouleas & Cullen, *supra* note 9.

25 See AR Admati et al, "Fallacies, Irrelevant Facts, and Myths in the Discussion of Capital Regulation: Why Bank Equity Is Not Socially Expensive" (2013) Stanford Business School Working Paper 2013; AR Admati & Martin F Hellwig, *The Bankers' New Clothes: What's Wrong with Banking and What to Do About It* (Princeton, NJ: Princeton University Press, 2013).

26 Anthony Saunders & Ingo Walter, "Financial Architecture, Systemic Risk, and Universal Banking" (2012) 26:1 Financial Markets & Portfolio Management 39; Joseph P Hughes & Loretta J Mester, "Who Said Large Banks Don't Experience Scale Economies? Evidence from a Risk-Return-Driven Cost Function" (2013) 22:4 J Financial Intermediation 559; David C Wheelock & Paul W Wilson, "Do Large Banks Have Lower Costs? New Estimates of Returns to Scale for U.S. Banks" (2013) 44:1 J Money, Credit & Banking 171; Anna Kovner, James Vickery & Lily Zhou, "Do Big Banks Have Lower Operating Costs?" (2014) 20:2 Federal Reserve Bank of Economic Policy Review 1 ("quantitatively, a 10 percent increase in assets is associated with 0.3 to 0.6 percent decline in noninterest expense scaled by income or assets, depending on specification" at 2). For a critical review of these studies, see Emilios Avgouleas, "Large Systemic Banks and Fractional Reserve Banking: Intractable Dilemmas in Search of Effective Solutions" in Ross P Buckley, Emilios Avgouleas & Douglas W Arner, eds, *Reconceptualising Global Finance and Its Regulation* (Cambridge, UK: Cambridge University Press, 2016) 279.

The Bail-in Process: Moral Hazard, Post-resolution Challenges and Some Remedies

The goals of the bail-in process are different in each jurisdiction. In the United States, the process for a bail-in and conversion of creditor claims is embedded in the resolution regime for systemically important financial institutions (SIFIs), the so-called Orderly Liquidation Authority (OLA).[27] When a bail-in process is triggered under Title II of the Dodd-Frank Act, the aim is to provide sufficient capital buffers for a subsidiary company to continue operations following the liquidation of its holding company. Nonetheless, the feasibility of the OLA process has not been tested during a crisis.[28]

In the European Union, on the other hand, the "doom-loop" between bank instability and sovereign indebtedness has presented member state governments with a major problem. Despite the establishment of the ESM,[29] which could have offered a limited fiscal backstop to the European Banking Union (EBU), bank recapitalization in resolution relies on bailing-in bank liabilities. The EU resolution regime, based on the EU BRRD and the ESM statute,[30] requires bank creditors to cover the cost of a bank resolution up to eight percent of bank liabilities prior to any public contributions. This type of bail-in, with designated and general liabilities, is thought to be sufficient to cover the cost of bank failures and to sever the links between bank and sovereign indebtedness.

One of the biggest challenges facing modern resolution regimes is incentivizing regulators and management to act *ex ante* when confronting problematic assets, especially non-performing loans (NPLs). Experience shows that when banks face high levels of NPLs, for example, due to a preceding asset bubble (for example, Spain and Ireland) or because of adverse macroeconomic conditions (for example, Greece and Italy), regulators tend to act more expeditiously when the introduction of a fiscal backstop, normally in the form of a state-backed bad bank (for example, Sweden, Spain and Ireland) is being considered.[31] In contrast, an outright bail-in of creditors could raise concerns that could delay the triggering of resolution. The absence of punitive, *ex post* bank management sanctions, as suggested by Stephen L. Schwarcz and analytically discussed by Charles Nolan, Plutarchos Sakellaris and John D. Tsoukalas,[32] amounts to a major loophole. Resolution regimes, in their current form, do not address in full managerial incentives[33] resulting in a bail-in process that could propagate managerial forbearance. The most important problem in this context is not that management might conceal NPLs, since regulatory monitoring mechanisms are quite effective; it is the impact on regulatory decision making that management's unwillingness to reduce capital by excessively writing-off NPLs may have.

27 *Dodd-Frank Act*, *supra* note 3.

28 Paul Kupiec & Peter Wallison, "Can the 'Single Point of Entry' Strategy be used to Recapitalize a Failing Bank?" (2014) American Enterprise Institute Working Paper No 8.

29 *Intergovernmental Treaty Establishing the European Stability Mechanism*, Euro-area Member States, 2 February 2012, T/ESM 2012/en 2.

30 ESM, "By-Laws" (8 October 2012), online: <www.esm.europa.eu/sites/default/files/esm_by-laws.pdf>.

31 See Douglas W Arner, Emilios Avgouleas & Evan Gibson, "Overstating Moral Hazard: Lessons from Two Decades of Banking Crises" (2017) University of Hong Kong Faculty of Law Research Paper No 2017/003.

32 Schwarcz, *supra* note 14; Nolan, Sakellaris & Tsoukalas, *supra* note 14.

33 Nolan, Sakellaris & Tsoukalas, *supra* note 14.

An even bigger problem is a scenario where public authorities, fearing the systemic implications of a bail-in regime, opt for publicly funded solutions. An example is when, in an adverse macroeconomic environment, the accumulation of NPLs and other non-performing bank exposures (NPEs) arise from a combination of systemic (macroeconomic) and idiosyncratic factors. The fear that a bail-in could result in a loss of market confidence might force authorities to offer a reprieve to creditors of institutions where high accumulation of NPLs are mostly due to idiosyncratic factors, for example, when NPL levels in one bank are much higher than in other similar institutions. A good example here is the partial bailout of Monte dei Paschi di Sienna (MPS), which provided relief to retail creditors from a publicly funded "precautionary recapitalization" scheme to avoid triggering resolution under the BRRD (article 32[4][1][d]), which would have resulted in a mandatory eight percent minimum bail-in of the bank's liabilities.[34] The existence of a large number of retail bondholders, in part due to mis-selling,[35] was a very important factor looming large in the minds of lawmakers complicating decision-making even further, since the same bondholders also held an important chunk of Italian bank shares and comprised the bulk of bank depositors. Therefore, Italian authorities were faced with a very substantial risk of a systemic bank run for which the BRRD framework was affording no flexibility in the course of taking resolution (bail-in action).

The Banca d'Italia graph[36] (Figure 1) reveals that in the years leading up to the 2017 "early recapitalization," the accumulation of NPLs in MPS was twice the level of NPL growth in the total of the Italian banking sector. Thus, the bailout of MPS would have been hard to justify without reference to the effect that a bail-in of senior creditors would have had on the confidence of Italian bank shareholders.[37] Therefore, an inflexible bail-in process heightens rather than mitigates moral hazard. In fact, this is a situation that may be caused by rigid bail regimes, regardless of the composition of the bank creditor body. For example, whereas a retail bondholder run was delayed until the last minute, and eventually prevented in spite of the flaws of the MPS recapitalization process,[38] institutional holders of bail-inable debt would have run earlier and faster, creating a downward spiral for all Italian banks, if it had been they who held the bulk of Italian bank debt.

34 EC, "State Aid 47677: New aid and amended restructuring plan of Banca Monte dei Paschi di Siena" (2017) 4690 at 17.

35 See Stefano Micossi, "Testing the EU Framework for the Recovery and Resolution of Banks: the Italian Experience" (2019) LUISS SEP Policy Brief.

36 See Carmelo Barbagallo, *Banca Monte dei Paschi di Sienna* (Rome: Banking and Financial Supervision Department, Bank of Italy, 2017), online: <www.bancaditalia.it/pubblicazioni/interventi-vari/int-var-2017/Barbagallo-22112017.pdf>.

37 The subsequent performance of Italian banking stocks reinforces this view. As a relevant BIS study states: "Overall, the FTSE Italia All Share Banks index climbed by 10% from the beginning of June to the end of July, outperforming the STOXX Europe 600 Banks index, which returned nearly 5%." See Bilyana Bogdanova & Mathias Drehmann, "How did markets react to bank distress in Europe?" (2017) BIS Q Rev, online: <www.bis.org/publ/qtrpdf/r_qt1709u.htm>.

38 For excellent analysis of the problems raised by the relevant investor (bondholder) compensation arrangements, see Micossi, *supra* note 35 at 10–12.

Figure 1: Ratio between NPLs and Total Loans for MPS and the Total Italian Banking Sector, 2007–2016

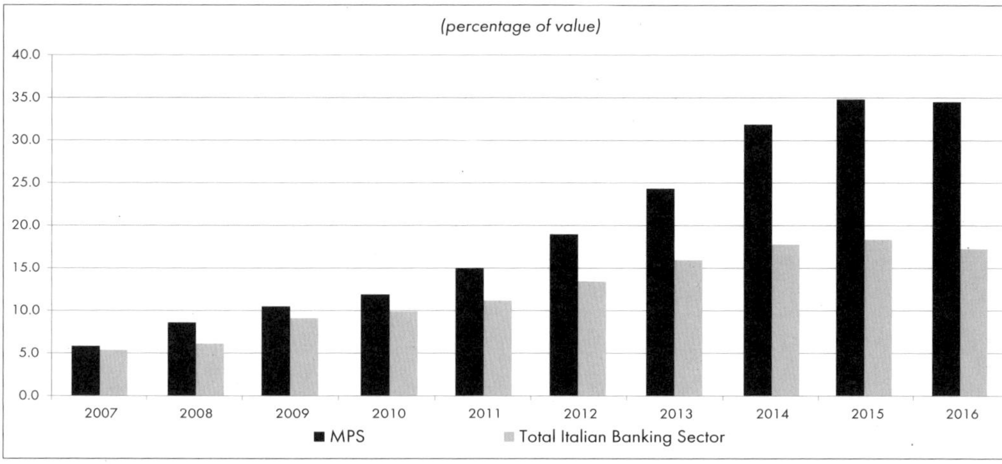

Source: Barbagallo, *supra* note 36 at 19.

Another good example is the winding down of the two Veneto banks in June 2017, as part of a wider rescue plan for the Italian banking sector. Veneto Banca (also associated with a mis-selling scandal) and Banca Popolare di Vicenza were wound down under controversial circumstances. The Single Resolution Board (SRB) held that the public interest test, when applying the BRRD regime,[39] was not satisfied.[40] In particular, the SRB held that: "[N]either of these banks provides critical functions, and their failure is not expected to have significant adverse impact on financial stability."[41] Both banks were wound down by applying insolvency proceedings under Italian bankruptcy law. The controversial injection of government money was approved by the European Commission on the basis of a private sector solution — selling the "good" parts of the insolvent banks to Intesa San Paolo, Italy's largest bank.[42] The senior bondholders of both banks were transferred to Intesa San Paolo and were not bailed in. A decision to wind up both banks independently of the EU resolution framework was criticized by the European Parliament.[43] But given the inflexibility of the BRRD's eight percent requirement, this was necessary to prevent the collapse of the Italian banking sector. Figure 2 is indicative of the stabilizing effect that the Italian plan had on stock prices and bond spreads.[44]

39 *BRRD*, *supra* note 2, art 32(1), (5); EC, *Regulation (EU) No 806/2014 of the European Parliament and of the Council of 15 July 2014 establishing uniform rules and a uniform procedure for the resolution of credit institutions and certain investment firms in the framework of a Single Resolution Mechanism and a Single Resolution Fund and amending Regulation (EU), [2015] No 1093/2010*, art 18(1), 9(c).

40 SRB, "Decision of the SRB concerning the assessment of the conditions for resolution in respect of Veneto Banca SpA" (2017) SRB/EES/2017/11, at 11–21; SRB, "Decision of the SRB concerning the assessment of the conditions for resolution in respect of Banca Popolare di Vicenza SpA" (2017) SRB/EES/2017/12 [SRB, "Decision of the SRB"].

41 SRB, "Decision of the SRB", *supra* note 40.

42 EC, "State Aid 45664: Orderly liquidation of Banca Popolare di Vicenza and Veneto Banca — Liquidation aid" (2017) 4501 final, at 20–24.

43 European Parliament, "The orderly liquidation of Veneto Banca and Banca Popolare di Vicenza" (2017) Economic Governance Support Unit Briefing No PE 602 094, online: <www.europarl.europa.eu/RegData/etudes/BRIE/2017/602094/IPOL_BRI(2017)602094_EN.pdf>.

44 Bogdanova & Drehmann, *supra* note 37.

Figure 2: No Contagion from Bank Failures in Europe

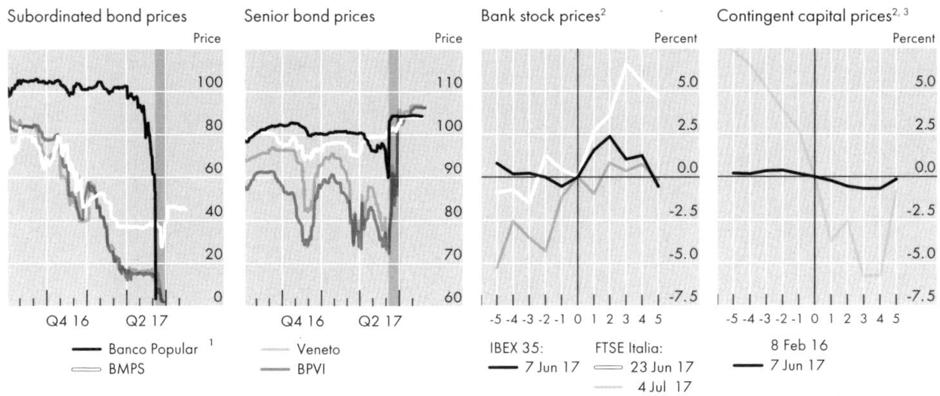

The shaded areas in the first two panels indicate the period 7 June to 4 July 2017.

1 For subordinated debt, AT1 contingent capital instrument. 2 Percentage changes over the stated window. Zero indicates the following event dates: 8 February 2016 (Deutsche Bank's statement on AT1 payments capacity), 7 June 2017 (the Single Resolution Board's (SRB's) endorsement of the resolution scheme for Banco Popular Español), 23 June 2017 (the SRB's resolution decision on Banca Popolare di Vicenza and Veneto Banca) and 4 July 2017 (the European Commission's approval of a precautionary recapitalization for Banca Monte dei Paschi di Siena. 3 Markit iBoxx USD liquid developed markets AT1 contingent capital index.

Source: Bogdanova & Drehmann, *supra* note 37.

At the same time, the NPL accumulation ratio for the two Veneto banks was substantially more than double that of the Italian banking sector as a whole (see Figure 3).[45]

Figure 3: Ratio between NPLs and Total Loans of the Veneto Banca, Popolare di Vicenza and the Total Italian Banking Sector, 2007–2016

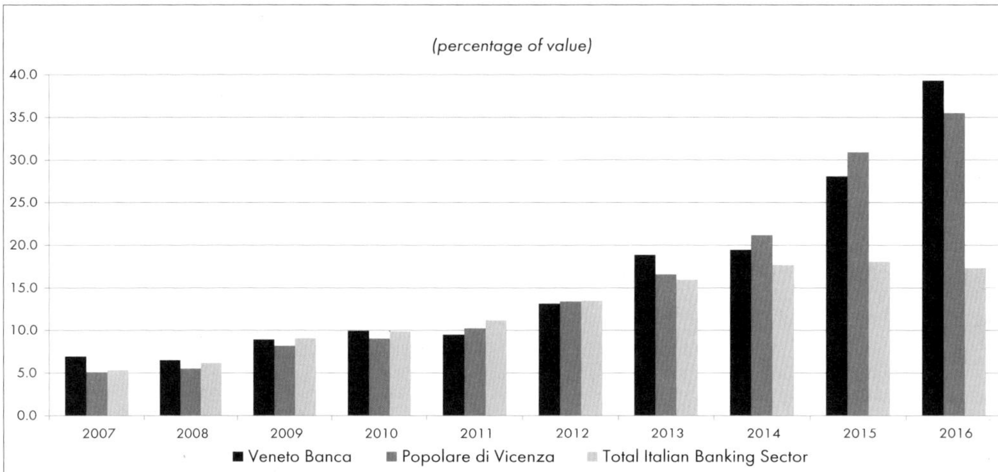

Source: Barbagallo, *supra* note 45.

45 Carmelo Barbagallo, *Veneto Banca e Banca Popolare di Vicenza* (Rome: Banking and Financial Supervision Department of the Bank of Italy, 2017) at 18, online: <www.bancaditalia.it/pubblicazioni/interventi-vari/int-var-2017/barbagallo-audizione-02112017.pdf>.

These examples, and especially the rescue of MPS, demonstrate that draconian bail-in regimes can have serious undesirable consequences that can weaken rather than strengthen market discipline.

Moreover, all forms of insurance raise the issue of moral hazard. The certainty that sufficient specially designated liabilities, such as CoCos (i.e., for a going-concern bank), TLAC and MREL, once resolution has been triggered, will be in place to provide adequate loss absorption is no exception. For example, convertible debt capital cushions proved insufficient to prevent the insolvency of the two Veneto banks, nor did they prevent Spain's Banco Popular from entering into resolution.[46] Specifically, in an effort to keep the two Veneto banks solvent, subordinated debt capital was converted in 2015 before the injection of public funds, and in 2017 prior to the banks being wound down. Then Banco Popular's supervisors forced the conversion of all Common Equity Tier 1 and Additional Tier 1 (AT1), including CoCos, in June 2017 to prevent the bank's collapse. This did not prevent a resolution action being instigated by the SRB as the bank had insufficient provisions for bad assets[47] and its capital buffers, including the convertible component, proved to be inadequate. So, a private sector sale was required to keep the bank from being liquidated. This prompted a groundswell of litigation from junior bondholders who were either written-off (AT1) or converted (Tier 2).[48] In all of these cases, no further creditor bail-in action was taken.

The Critical Matter of Asset Valuation in Resolution

The bail-in process cannot properly function unless bank losses are identified in a finite form. Bank losses, including unrealized future losses, must be accurately determined to avoid successive rounds of bail-in losses accruing to bank creditors. This can be challenging in practice. For example, bank losses have been consistently underestimated, both in the global financial crisis and subsequently in the European crisis. The valuation of assets is an inexact science and market cyclicality further complicates the appraisal task.[49] In the uncertain conditions when the market is experiencing generalized asset value declines, the new (incoming) accountants, employed by the resolution agency, are likely to take a bad or a worst-case scenario as their baseline for identifying losses. Previously, the accountants of the failing bank itself would have been encouraged (by management) to take a more positive view of the value of its assets. Thus, the transition from the bank's accountants to those of the resolution authority is likely to cause a huge discontinuity in the form of a massive drop in published accounting valuations. Furthermore, there is the issue of a potential rise in the valuation of bank assets once the first shock has subsided. This may also be found by factoring in the difference between the

46 See European Parliament, "The resolution of Banco Popular" (2017) Economic Governance Support Unit Briefing No PE 602.093.

47 *Ibid* at 2.

48 See Thomas Hale, "Investors sue Brussels over Banco Popular sale", *FT.com* (17 August 2017) ("International investors have launched legal action against the European authorities that oversaw the failure of Banco Popular, in the latest attempt to overturn the decisions that led to the bank's sale to Santander in June for €1"); Francesco Guarascio, "Investors file 51 lawsuits against EU for shutting Banco Popular", *Reuters.com* (30 August 2017) ("Disgruntled investors have filed 51 lawsuits against European Union regulators for shutting Spain's Banco Popular, marking one of the largest legal challenges yet to the EU and a fresh attack on the bloc's rules on bank rescues. The deluge of cases, filed with the European Union's General Court, are the first legal test of how the EU applies new bank rules aimed at forcing investors to bear the costs of rescuing a failing lender before taxpayer money is used").

49 Bank failures during boom conditions (resulting from fraud, such as Barings, for example) are easier to handle, with less risk of contagion.

current market value of the failing bank's assets and their long-term economic value, although, admittedly, the latter is a controversial concept.

The difference in valuations during different time periods is critical when it comes to assessing conformity with the NCWO principle. The reason for this is twofold. First, in an insolvency, creditors' losses are judged *ex post* once the firm has been liquidated or sold and the assets have been disposed of, whereas in a resolution, bank losses are determined either when the bank enters into resolution or shortly thereafter. Asset prices in resolution are normally marked against a depressed market, and both bank sales and asset sales are bound to attract a limited number of buyers, which compromises the concept of competitive market prices. The possibility of discrepancies in valuations upon entry into resolution and *ex post* valuations is also recognized by the European Banking Authority (EBA), which clarifies that the definitive valuation will be the *ex post* one where a definitive valuation upon entry to resolution is not possible.[50] The BRRD and EBA's technical standards recognize the *ex post* valuation approach is important when determining whether "shareholders and creditors do not receive worse treatment under resolution than they would have expected in a counterfactual liquidation under normal insolvency proceedings."[51] Martin Hellwig notes, in a recent study for the EU Parliament, that even this approach will not resolve the problem of attaching realistic calculations to an NCWO test.[52]

Beyond the application of the NCWO principle, there are other often neglected systemic implications attached to valuation in resolution. A pessimistic valuation will result in much deeper write-downs, write-offs or conversion haircuts, with the ensuing creditor losses being greater than previously anticipated based on the valuation assumptions of the pre-resolution auditors. This could lead investors to question the valuations of other banks, leading to a rapid deterioration in confidence and a contagious crisis.

One solution is to freeze payouts,[53] given that an additional backstop is provided by deposit insurance. A temporary moratorium of payments on asset disposals would require a robust

50 EBA, *Draft Handbook on Valuation for Purposes of Resolution* (2018), online: <https://eba.europa.eu/documents/10180/2120596/2018+11+12+-+Draft+Valuation+Handbook+-+clean.pdf> ("To enable the [Resolution Authority] to take action also in circumstances of urgency...the BRRD envisages the possibility for resolution action to be adopted also on the basis of a provisional valuation (Article 36(2) and (9))....Such valuation consists of two steps: the first requiring the subdivision of creditors into classes, the second establishing an estimate of the treatment that such classes would receive should the institution be put in insolvency...An ex-post definitive valuation is envisaged when the resolution decision has been informed on the basis of a provisional valuation (Article 36 (10) BRRD). The provisional and the ex-post definitive valuation...may yield different results, having regard to the higher granularity of the available information, the valuation approach adopted and the time available....The ex-post definitive valuation may rely on data and information not available to the valuer or the RA when performing the provisional valuation....In accordance with Article 6(e) of that Regulation, the valuation report should explain the differences between the methodologies and assumptions used in the provisional and in the ex-post definitive valuation" at 14–15).

51 The EBA Regulatory Technical Standards on valuations in resolution note: "[T]he assumptions governing the estimation of the treatment that shareholders or creditors would have received in insolvency are driven by the sole purpose of determining the appropriate discounted value of cash flows that could reasonably be expected under the relevant national insolvency procedures." EBA, "RTS on Valuation in Resolution, Final Draft: Regulatory Technical Standards on Valuation for the purposes of resolution and on valuation to determine difference in treatment following resolution under Directive 2014/59/EU on recovery and resolution of credit institutions and investment firms."

52 Martin F Hellwig, "Valuation reports in the context of banking resolution: What are the challenges? Banking Union Scrutiny" (2018) EP In-depth Analysis PE624.417, online: <www.europarl.europa.eu/RegData/etudes/IDAN/2018/624417/IPOL_IDA(2018)624417_EN.pdf> ("First, in a resolution procedure, one may never learn what investors' payouts in a counterfactual insolvency procedure would have been. Indeed, the very resolution decision that is taken may preclude the attainment of such information by anybody. For example, when the sale-of-business tool is used, the bank and its assets are likely to be integrated into the purchaser's business so that no additional information about the assets, let alone the proceeds of a potential liquidation is generated" at 13–14).

53 A temporary freeze on payments is discussed in the Bank of England's approach to resolution.

liquidity support mechanism to avoid severe side effects. These side effects include consequential defaults, for example, large corporations needing access to deposits, a panic or even a bank run.[54] With the BRRD and the SRM Regulation silent on resolution funding, the European Council recently gave the Single Resolution Fund (SRF) the power to borrow from the ESM (from 2024) to fund resolution actions.[55] This arrangement follows the Dodd-Frank Act resolution funding arrangements where the Federal Deposit Insurance Corporation can obtain resolution funding by borrowing from the US Treasury. Whether this decision offers an effective solution to the problem of "funding resolution" is doubtful, given the limited size of the fund and the conditions to mitigate moral hazard imposed by the ESM.[56]

Either way, subjectivity and arbitrariness when measuring risk and the illiquidity of non-tradable assets will remain, especially when assessing conditional probability distributions of future returns based on unreliable data. Markets may rebound following a downturn to provide reliable mark-to-market data, but in the absence of an arbitrary cut-off date, forbearance is no panacea.

Liquidity Support in Resolution

The EU approach to bail-ins increases the significance of liquidity support. The European Council decision to allow the ESM to lend money to the SRF to fund resolutions is important in acknowledging the existence of the problem. It is also a positive step that ESM provision of liquidity to the SRF will not be subject to ESM conditionality like sovereign funding. However, this facility will be limited by the size of the SRF reserves. We suggest that further liquidity could be provided by the ECB either to each legal entity, against the entity's collateral available to that entity, or channelled through a parent company. Typically, a G-SIFI is funded mostly through retail and other short-term deposits, which, in the event of a bail-in, could either dry up or even be withdrawn. Thus, a G-SIFI in resolution may require considerable official liquidity support. This should only be provided on a fully collateralized basis, with appropriate haircuts applied to the collateral, to reduce the risk of loss, but this depends on the adequacy of available collateral.

Lender of last resort (LoLR) liquidity is provided alongside other measures to stabilize a bank in crisis. These financial stability measures may not prevent the bank from entering resolution. The United Kingdom has a liquidity framework that allows HM Treasury to indemnify the central bank (Bank of England) when a loss is incurred from funding a bank in resolution (for

54 Hellwig, *supra* note 52 at 15.

55 The heads of state and government of the 19 euro-area countries endorsed a package of proposals on deepening the Economic and Monetary Union at the Euro Summit on December 14, 2018. Proposals included the introduction of the common backstop for the SRF provided by the ESM.

56 The size of the credit line will be aligned with the SRF funds, which by 2024 will be around €60 billion, or one percent of covered deposits in the Banking Union. If the credit line is used, the SRF will pay back the ESM loan with money from bank contributions within three years, although this period can be extended up to another two years. Disbursements under the common backstop will be approved by the ESM board of directors, consisting of high-level officials from the 19 euro-area finance ministries, by mutual agreement. Procedures will be in place so that such approval can be made swiftly and efficiently (in as little as 12 hours) in strict confidentiality because of the sensitive nature of the data. The council realized that the funding was inadequate, and the issue of "liquidity provision in resolution" will be discussed further in 2019.

example, a bridge bank).[57] If a central bank provides liquidity to fund a resolution, this may not qualify as LoLR finance but rather as state aid, which could require high-grade collateral. By this stage of the resolution process, some bank assets will be impaired, and the scope of central bank liquidity provided to a bank entering resolution would be uncertain, especially in the absence of a state indemnity facility.

The BRRD provides that resolution is primarily financed by national resolution funds that can also borrow from each other.[58] The Deposit Guarantee Scheme (DGS)[59] will have to contribute for the purpose of ensuring continuous access to covered deposits, and the requisite contributions will be in cash for an amount equivalent to the losses that the DGS would have had to bear in normal insolvency proceedings. Namely, the DGS contribution is made in cash in order to absorb the losses incurred from the covered deposits.[60] The DGS is solely liable for the protection afforded to covered depositors.[61] If following a contribution by the DGS, the institution under resolution fails at a later stage, and the DGS does not have sufficient funds to repay depositors, the DGS must have arrangements in place in order to raise the corresponding amounts expeditiously from its members. Otherwise, treating the DGS as an unsecured creditor in the event of a systemic crisis might raise doubts concerning the availability of sufficient funds.

At this stage of the resolution process, robust LoLR liquidity support would mitigate the risk of a fire sale and therefore it would contain systemic risk spillovers. Depressed market prices due to fire sales have an adverse effect on the value of the wider banking sector, especially in an environment where bank balance sheets are rather homogeneous. In our view, the United Kingdom's arrangements should also be followed in the EBU with an ESM backstop, in the form of a long-term indemnity, offered to the ECB to provide liquidity in resolution, whenever other arrangements for down-streaming liquidity come short.

Post Bail-in Bank Funding

Market confidence in the bailed-in institution would have to be quickly restored in order to preserve franchise value and reimburse official liquidity support.[62] This is mostly dependent on how fast the bank's capital structure will be rebuilt or the establishment of a strongly capitalized new bank in the event of a "closed" bank process. If an institution has entered into a death spiral and becomes subject to a run with customers, creditors and depositors all fast disappearing, reversing this trend would doubtlessly prove a daunting task.

Under the BRRD's open bank procedure, reliance on the creditor bail-in process to recapitalize banks can result in several funding rounds including post-resolution rounds. For example, a follow-up bail-in involving the Portuguese Novo Banco bank, which was the "good bank" that

57 See HM Treasury, "Banking Act 2009: Special Resolution Regime code of practice" (12 March 2015), online: <www.gov.uk/government/publications/banking-act-2009-revised-special-resolution-regime-code-of-practice>; EC, *Commission Delegated Regulation (EU) 2015/63 of 21 October 2014 supplementing Directive 2014/59/EU of the European Parliament and of the Council with regard to ex ante contributions to resolution financing arrangements,* [2015] OJ, L 11/44.

58 *BRRD*, *supra* note 2, arts 99ff.

59 *Ibid*, arts 45(6), 108(b), 109, recs 71, 110, 111.

60 *Ibid*, art 109(3).

61 *Ibid*, art 109(1).

62 See Joseph H Sommer, "Why Bail-In? And How!" (2014) 20:2 Federal Reserve Bank of New York Economic Policy Rev 207.

had been created following the resolution of the failed bank Espirito Santo.[63] Nonetheless, successive bail-in rounds can alarm investors when market funding is needed to restore the resolved bank, or its successors, to full financial health.

Policy makers tend to underestimate the dynamics of a bank run *ex post*, even where creditors face no potential losses in the aftermath of a resolution action. This is due, presumably, to reputation risks and the (possibly irrational) fear of future financial difficulties.[64] The dynamic is much greater when banks and creditors have experienced large losses from the triggering of, and subsequent, bail-in rounds.[65]

Resolution regimes that aim to restore systemic stability to serve their macroprudential objectives should also address the question of what happens when a bank exits the resolution stage, post-bail-in, and is returned to the regulator's custody, but market funding for it remains scarce.[66] While the aim of the bail-in is that the bank itself (in the EU framework) or its successor exit resolution as a going concern,[67] the possibility that the bank might face market reluctance to fund it, for example, due to reputation shocks and funders' behavioural constraints,[68] should not be discounted.

There are two possible approaches to post-resolution funding. The first would use the central bank to provide liquidity support as the LoLR. Arguably, liquidity support in this case could lead to avoidance of future bail-in rounds[69] and thus act as a solvency prop. In addition, LoLR funding at this early stage would come with a certain stigma attached. The second is funding the post-resolution bank through a pre-committed collateralized facility.

In the opinion of this chapter's first author, this could be done through fully collateralized bonds issued post-resolution to institutional investors that have committed to funding the facility *ex ante*.[70] Such a facility has the dual advantage of preventing any post-resolution creditor runs while substantially resolving the bank funding needs. The costs of such a funding scheme would depend on how successful the preceding resolution has been augmenting the incentives of the resolution authority and other relevant parties to handle resolutions with due concern to *ex post* market reactions. The second approach is also a fiscally neutral position, even though in the case of the EBU, the ESM could be used as a guarantor of the first tranche of such bonds, which, however, would inevitably result in over-collateralization.

63 For example, senior creditors of Novo Banco had to suffer further bail-in rounds despite the steep haircut applied to junior creditors who absorbed the losses of the bad bank. See Martin Arnold & Thomas Hale, "ECB under fire as Portugal hits Novo Banco bondholders", *FT.com* (7 January 2016); Christopher Whittall, "Investors File Suit Against Bank of Portugal Over Novo Banco", *WSJ.com* (5 April 2016).

64 See Mark Carlson & Jonathan Rose, "Can a Bank Run Be Stopped? Government Guarantees and the Run on Continental Illinois" (2016) BIS Working Papers No 554, online: <www.bis.org/publ/work554.pdf>.

65 Arnold & Hale, *supra* note 63; Whittall, *supra* note 63.

66 For a wider discussion, see Avgouleas, *supra* note 20.

67 *BRRD*, *supra* note 2, art 43(2)(a).

68 For insightful analysis of this problem, see Carlson & Rose, *supra* note 64.

69 Avgouleas, *supra* note 20.

70 This idea matured in the context of some intensive email exchanges between the first author and an esteemed colleague, Senior ESM Director Mike Hesketh, in the weeks preceding Mike's sudden death on May 2, 2019, and pays tribute to Mike's preliminary work on post-resolution bank funding.

Conclusion

This chapter has offered a systematic analysis of the reformed bank resolution regimes implemented during the post-GFC period. In this context, the chapter has considered the key objectives underpinning the new resolution regimes. Despite the progress made in key jurisdictions (for example, the United States, the United Kingdom and the European Union), problems with the application of contemporary resolution frameworks persist, especially in the European Union. The chapter has also highlighted the confusing nature of the explicit and implicit objectives pursued by reformed resolution regimes. Relevant analysis has particularly focused on the shortcomings of bail-in regimes in the pursuit of macroprudential objectives and the mitigation of moral hazard. Funding in resolution requires a more liberal liquidity regime to provide the desired stabilizing effect. However, resolution regimes per se cannot stabilize the banking system. Tax regime reforms, *ex post* penalties for bank management, increasing the liability of key shareholders and measuring more accurately the impact of very low interest rates on bank balance sheets are all equally important elements that need to be considered to ameliorate the TBTF effect and strengthen financial stability.

3

Three Major Financial Crises: What Have We Learned?

Ross P. Buckley, Emilios Avgouleas and Douglas W. Arner

Few experts predicted the Asian financial crisis (AFC), global financial crisis (GFC) or euro-zone debt crisis, and we certainly do not pretend to be able to predict the next one. Yet history teaches that fragility, which periodically erupts into a full-blown financial crisis, is an integral feature of market-based financial systems, in spite of the advent of sophisticated risk management tools and regulatory systems. If anything, the increased frequency of modern crises in the wake of financial globalization underscores how difficult it is to deal with systemic risk. We thus seek to compare these three major crises to distill the lessons to be learned and identify how to strengthen global financial systems.

The AFC

In 1997-1998, Asia experienced its worst financial crisis of the twentieth century. It started with Thailand. Over a period of years, foreign money flooded into the Thai economy, fuelling a massive current-account deficit combined with large-scale overborrowing from international markets and overlending.[1] Thailand was forced to allow its currency to float in July 1997, and the value of the baht plummeted as a result, highlighting huge mismatches between foreign currency borrowing and domestic currency sources of repayment.[2] Thailand's crisis raised questions vis-à-vis the health of other emerging markets with similar features, and contagion soon spread to Indonesia, Malaysia, the Philippines, South Korea and eventually Brazil, Russia and the United States via the near collapse of a large hedge fund, Long-Term Capital Management.[3]

Overview of the AFC

The AFC was not a conventional sovereign debt crisis. The indebtedness was that of the private sector, not the public or quasi-public sector, and it occurred within "a benign international environment with low interest rates and solid growth in output and exports."[4] Initially this was a series of currency crises that developed into more generalized financial and economic crises, at least for Indonesia, South Korea and Thailand, the three most severely affected countries. Currency devaluation made foreign currency debt repayments funded from domestic lending unmanageable, resulting in nationalization of financial sector liabilities in order to stem the resulting systemic financial crisis. Affected countries then found themselves facing unsustainable sovereign debt levels, which in turn required assistance from the International Monetary Fund (IMF) and others.

Causes of the AFC

The four principal causes of the AFC were the type and extent of indebtedness; financial sector weaknesses; fixed local exchange rates; and a region-wide loss of confidence that eventually spread to emerging market economies worldwide.

Type and Extent of Indebtedness

Short-term indebtedness increased significantly in 1995-1996 across the region.[5] The ratio of short-term to total debt in mid-1997 ranged from 67 percent in South Korea to 46 percent in Thailand and 19 percent in the Philippines.[6]

The primary problem with foreign investment in emerging markets' short-term debt is non-commitment.[7] Outflows may trigger a collapse in investor confidence. Volatility heightens when short-term debt is denominated in local currency, since a substantial devaluation will decimate a local currency portfolio.

1 Martin Feldstein, "A Self-Help Guide for Emerging Markets", *Foreign Affairs* (March/April 1999), online: <www.foreignaffairs.com/articles/1999-03-01/self-help-guide-emerging-markets>; Peter Passell, "For a new generation of Asian tigers, a harsh currency lesson", *The New York Times* (24 July 1997).

2 Ruse Arensman, "Economy stall in Thailand has a familiar look", *The Denver Post* (2 November 1997).

3 Paul Blustein, "Investors Reconsider Big Emerging-Markets Bets", *The Washington Post* (20 July 1997); "IMF happy with Malaysia, but says there is room for improvement", *The Australian* (29 April 1998).

4 World Bank, *Global Development Finance*, vol 1 (Washington, DC: World Bank, 1998) at 30 [World Bank, 1998], online: <http://documents.worldbank.org/curated/en/917631468138290229/pdf/multi-page.pdf>.

5 World Bank, *Global Development Finance*, vol 1 (Washington, DC: World Bank, 1997) at 16, online: <http://documents.worldbank.org/curated/en/978911468163455868/pdf/multi-page.pdf>.

6 *Ibid* at 35.

7 Alain Soulard, "The Role of Multilateral Financial Institutions in Bringing Developing Companies to U.S. Markets" (1994) 17:5 Fordham Intl LJ 145 at 147.

The extent of indebtedness in East Asia was the product, in part, of excess liquidity in the developed world in the two years prior to June 1997. East Asian stocks and bonds were acquired by US and European investors who had grown wary of low interest rates and feared that US stock markets had reached unsustainable heights.[8]

Financial Sector Weaknesses

Failure to Intermediate Capital Flows Effectively

Capital inflows often ended up in speculative property and stock market investments that could not generate the foreign currency reserves needed to repay foreign currency debt.[9]

Local banks borrowed short and lent long, mostly without hedging their foreign exchange exposures. Regulatory standards were inadequate.[10] Domestic banks were often controlled by people connected to the ruling political party and their conduct was influenced by the prospect of a bailout. Indiscriminate international borrowing and domestic lending meant that when the bubble burst, banks in Indonesia, South Korea and Thailand were in crisis.[11]

Premature Liberalization of Domestic Financial Markets

Prior to the AFC, foreign money had flooded into Thailand directly through institutional investors' portfolios in local stocks and bonds, and indirectly as Thai banks borrowed heavily from their foreign counterparts.[12] All three countries had opened their financial systems to international capital flows without reinforcing domestic stability.[13]

Fixed Exchange Rates

Prior to the AFC, fixed exchange rates appealed to developing countries because they appeared to offer lower credit costs[14] and inflation rates and discipline against government monetary or fiscal excesses.[15] However, when an economy with a fixed exchange rate is performing less strongly than the economy to whose currency its currency is fixed, adjustment is required. Otherwise, the fixed currency will become overvalued, as occurred in Mexico in 1993-1994, Thailand and Indonesia in 1996-1997, Russia in 1997-1998 and Argentina in 2000-2001.[16]

8 Blustein, *supra* note 3.

9 Shigemitsu Sugisaki, "Economic Crises in Asia" (Address delivered at the 1998 Harvard Asia Business Conference, Boston, 30 January 1998), online: <www.imf.org/en/News/Articles/2015/09/28/04/53/sp013098>.

10 World Bank, 1998, *supra* note 4 at 4.

11 Rudi Dornbusch, "A Bail-out Won't Do the Trick in Korea", *Business Week* (8 December 1997); Robert Garran, "Korea Crisis", *The Australian* (19 November 1997).

12 H Chow, "Crawling from the wreckage" (1997) 4 Emerging Markets Investor 15.

13 IMF, *World Economic Outlook* (Washington, DC: IMF, 1998) at 6, online: <www.imf.org/en/Publications/WEO/Issues/2016/12/31/Financial-Crises-Causes-and-Indicators>.

14 I Viscio, "The Recent Experience with Capital Flows to Emerging Market Economies" (1998) 65 OECD Economy Outlook 177; Pablo Bustelo, Clara Garcia & Iliana Olivié, "Global and Domestic Factors of Financial Crises in Emerging Economies: Lessons from the East Asian Episodes (1997–1999)" (Madrid: Instituto Complutense de Estudios Internacionales, 1999).

15 Feldstein, *supra* note 1; Barry Eichengreen & Ricardo Hausmann, "Exchange Rates and Financial Fragility" (1999) NBER Working Paper No 7418, online: <www.nber.org/papers/w7418>.

16 Alan S Blinder, "Eight Steps to a New Financial Order", *Foreign Affairs* (September/October 1999) at 50.

Fixed exchange rates also encourage excessive borrowing in foreign currency, which is high-risk if unhedged, and masks the real cost of borrowing. One of the strongest policy lessons of the AFC is that flexible exchange rates provide a real measure of protection against crises.[17]

Region-wide Loss of Confidence Triggers Contagion

The AFC saw the distinct economic troubles of five countries become a regional crisis[18] due to a region-wide loss of confidence that proved contagious.[19] It led to an outflow of capital that triggered currency depreciations. Thus, the massive foreign exchange exposures severely damaged the balance sheets of local corporations.[20]

Accumulation of Non-performing Loans

The AFC teaches some specific lessons about non-performing loans (NPLs). Pre-crisis weaknesses in loan underwriting and bank governance caused a surge in NPLs, which, combined with inadequate capital ratios, triggered insolvencies necessitating banking sector restructurings.[21]

The two countries most affected by the crisis, Thailand[22] and Indonesia,[23] had NPL ratios averaging more than 13 percent leading into the crisis. This high incidence of NPLs indicated inadequate prudential regulation and poor credit standards. Loans collateralized by property were common[24] and particularly vulnerable to falling values during the downward phase of the credit cycle. This can cause a sudden spike in banking sector NPLs, destabilizing balance sheets and therefore capital adequacy ratios that, in extreme cases, can lead to bank insolvency.

The capital adequacy ratios of the countries most affected by the crisis (while consistent with the Basel capital standards at the time) were insufficient, at eight to 10 percent, to absorb NPL charges.[25]

17 Laurence H Meyer, "Lessons from the Asian Crisis: A Central Banker's Perspective" (1999) Levy Economics Institute Working Paper No 276.

18 World Bank, 1998, *supra* note 4 at 30.

19 *Ibid* at 40.

20 *Ibid* at 5.

21 Ross P Buckley & Douglas W Arner, *From Crisis to Crisis: The Global Financial System and Regulatory Failure* (Alphen aan den Rijn, Netherlands: Kluwer Law International, 2011).

22 Narisa Laplamwanit, "A Good Look at the Thai Financial Crisis in 1997-98" (New York: Columbia University, 1999), online: <www.columbia.edu/cu/thai/html/financial97_98.html>; Craig C Julian, "The Impact of the Asian economic crisis in Thailand" (2000) 26 Managerial Finance 46, online: <https://epubs.scu.edu.au/cgi/viewcontent.cgi?article=1341&context=comm_pubs>.

23 Kenichi Takayasu & Yosie Yokoe, "Non-performing Loan Issue Crucial to Asia's Economic Resurgence" (1999) 44 Japan Research Institute, online: <www.jri.co.jp/english/periodical/rim/1999/RIMe199903npl/>.

24 Economics, Commerce and Industrial Relations Group, Current Issues Brief 23 1997-98, "Asian Financial Crisis" (29 June 1998), online: <www.aph.gov.au/About_Parliament/Parliamentary_Departments/Parliamentary_Library/Publications_Archive/CIB/CIB9798/98cib23>; Charles Collyns & Abdelhak Senhadji, "Lending Booms, Real Estate Bubbles and the Asian Crisis" (2002) IMF Working Paper No WP/02/20.

25 Masahiro Kawai, "Bank and Corporate Restructuring in Crisis-Affected East Asia: From Systemic Collapse to Reconstruction" in Gordon de Brouwer, ed, *Financial Markets and Policies in East Asia* (London, UK: Routledge, 2003) 82.

South Korea[26] and Malaysia[27] fared better than Thailand[28] and Indonesia[29] by implementing structured resolution plans that focused on recapitalizing banks and managing NPLs through asset management companies (AMCs).[30]

Analysis of Policy Responses

As confidence evaporated, there was a pro-cyclical effect characterized by mass bank closures. Paradoxically, these closures were a condition of the IMF's support programs.[31]

Thailand[32] and Indonesia[33] had the most closures, the deepest disruptions to financial stability and the largest expenditures of public funds to bail out their banking sectors. NPL ratios and bank closures peaked simultaneously in those jurisdictions.[34]

To manage the large volumes of NPLs, AMCs were created in Indonesia, Malaysia and Thailand (South Korea already had an AMC). These were largely effective in cleansing bank balance sheets of NPLs, strengthening capital ratios, stabilizing banking sectors and aiding economic recovery.[35]

26 The Korea Asset Management Corporation created an NPL resolution fund: Kim Kihwan, "The 1997-98 Korean Financial Crisis: Causes, Policy Response, and Lessons" (Presentation delivered at the High-Level Seminar on Crisis Prevention in Emerging Markets, Singapore, 10-11 July 2006), online: <www.imf.org/external/np/seminars/eng/2006/cpem/pdf/kihwan.pdf>.

27 Fumitaka Furuoka et al, "Economic Crisis and Response: Case Study of Malaysia's Response to Asian Financial Crisis" (2012) 11:1 J Contemporary Eastern Asia 49.

28 Laplamwanit, *supra* note 22; Kuejai Jungjaturapit, "Has Thailand Learned from the Asian Crisis of 1997?" (2008) Major Themes in Economics 35, online: <https://pdfs.semanticscholar.org/5ab1/73978125823231e6dc6b171feaf05ea44af6.pdf>. For Thailand's reforms, see Andrew Berg, "The Asian Crisis: Causes, Policy Responses, and Outcomes" (1999) IMF Working Paper No WP/99/138.

29 Foreign Affairs, Defence and Trade Group, Current Issues Brief 13 1997-98, "Crisis in Indonesia: Economy, Society and Politics" (8 April 1998), online: <www.aph.gov.au/About_Parliament/Parliamentary_Departments/Parliamentary_Library/Publications_Archive/CIB/CIB9798/98cib13>; Paula Ranta, *Malaysia's and Indonesia's Recovery from the Asian Financial Crisis: Comparison and Causes behind the Recovery* (Bachelor of Business Thesis, Helsinki Metropolia University of Applied Sciences, 2017), online: <www.theseus.fi/bitstream/handle/10024/130639/Ranta_Paula.pdf>.

30 Douglas W Arner, Emilios Avgouleas & Ewan Gibson, "Overstating Moral Hazard: Lessons from Two Decades of Banking Crises" (2017) University of Hong Kong Faculty of Law Research Paper No 2017/003.

31 IMF Staff, *Recovery from the Asian Crisis and the Role of the IMF* (Washington, DC: IMF, 2000), online: <www.imf.org/external/np/exr/ib/2000/062300.htm>; Stanley Fischer, "The Asian Crisis: A View from the IMF" (Address delivered at the Midwinter Conference of the Bankers' Association for Foreign Trade, Washington, DC, 22 January 1988), online: <www.imf.org/en/News/Articles/2015/09/28/04/53/sp012298>.

32 Thailand closed 56 bankrupt finance companies in 1997: Kawai, *supra* note 25. Korea closed only 14 banks: see RYC Wong et al, *Asian Financial Crisis: Causes and Development* (Hong Kong: Hong Kong Institute of Economics and Business Strategy, University of Hong Kong, 2000).

33 Indonesia closed 16 banks in 1997: see IMF Staff, *supra* note 31.

34 At the end of 1997, Thailand's NPL/total loans ratio was 22.6 percent and Indonesia's was 7.2 percent: see Kawai, *supra* note 25. Maria Socorro Gochoco-Bautista, Soo-Nam Oh & S Ghon Rhee, "In the Eye of the Asian Financial Maelstrom: Banking Sector Reforms in the Asia-Pacific Region" in Asian Development Bank, ed, *Rising to the Challenge in Asia: A Study of Financial Markets* (Manila: Asian Development Bank, 1999).

35 N Noerlina & Sylvia Cinthya Dewi, "Asian Financial Crisis: Overview of Asian Crisis and Recovery Progress" (2003) 4:1 The Winners 13.

Lessons Learned from the AFC

There are at least six enduring lessons from the AFC:

- Loss of confidence can facilitate the cross-border propagation of financial stability risks, exacerbating domestic vulnerabilities.
- Fixed exchange rates are high risk and floating exchange rates are generally preferable.
- The denomination of most of an economy's foreign debt in foreign currency is risky, in particular in the absence of hedging markets.
- Much of the debt needs of emerging markets should be funded with long-term local-currency-denominated instruments, complemented by equity markets featuring strong regulatory frameworks, in order to reduce currency risks.
- The infrastructure and regulation of local capital markets — both equity and debt — should provide alternatives to bank lending.
- Capital tends to flow recklessly to emerging markets in times of surplus liquidity in the developed world.

Cross-border Contagion

Restrictions on short-term capital flows aside, well-regulated financial systems with adequately capitalized financial institutions and adequate foreign currency reserves are the best protection against cross-border contagion. East Asia has bolstered its regional resilience through the Chiang Mai Initiative (CMI),[36] its multilateralization agreement (CMIM)[37] and the associated Association of Southeast Asian Nations Plus Three (ASEAN+3) Macroeconomic Research Office (AMRO).[38] In addition, emerging markets worldwide have improved financial regulation and developed substantial foreign exchange reserves as a means of self-insurance, although arguably to levels that had a role in the excess liquidity underlying the buildup of excesses prior to 2007.

Benefits of Floating Exchange Rates

Overvalued fixed exchange rates are often politically difficult to correct through devaluation. This can lead to burgeoning current account deficits, capital flight and currency crises.[39] Given

36 The CMI was set up in 2000: Barry Eichengreen, "What to Do with the Chiang Mai Initiative" (2003) 2:1 Asian Economic Papers 1.

37 The CMIM Agreement is a multilateral currency swap agreement among ASEAN+3 countries. ASEAN+3 Macroeconomic Research Office, *ASEAN+3 Regional Economic Outlook 2017 – ASEAN+3 Region: 20 Years after the Asian Financial Crisis* (Singapore: AMRO, 2007), online: <www.amro-asia.org/wp-content/uploads/2017/04/AREO2017_Full-Text.pdf>.

38 In May 2011, AMRO was founded as the regional surveillance unit of ASEAN+3, responsible for regional economic surveillance and overseeing the CMIM Agreement: see Pradumna Bickram Rana, Wai-Mun Chia & Yothin Jinjarak, "Monetary Integration in ASEAN+3: A Perception Survey of Opinion Leaders" (2012) 23:1 J Asian Economics 1.

39 Maurice Obstfeld & Kenneth Rogoff, "The Mirage of Fixed Exchange Rates" (1995) 9:4 J Economic Perspectives 79; John H Welch & Darryl McLeod, "The Costs and Benefits of Fixed Dollar Exchange Rates in Latin America" (1993) 3 Q Rev Economics & Finance 101.

the volumes of global currency flows,[40] floating exchange rates, coupled with strong foreign exchange reserves and liquidity arrangements, better enable nations to weather periodic international volatility. Across Asia, with the exception of China, countries have adopted floating exchange rates.

High Risks of Foreign Currency Borrowing

During the AFC, large-scale hedging of foreign currency exposures was extremely expensive and rare. If the currency risk is with the borrower, due to the denomination of the debt, in times of trouble it is transferred to the lender by the borrower's incapacity to service the debt. There is thus the clear need to develop local-currency-denominated financing channels and markets for hedging foreign currency exposures. There has been significant success across East Asia in developing local currency bond markets and regional debt markets, such that this debt has now become a significant asset class for international investors. Likewise, hedging markets and tools have developed for many of the more significant currencies.

Need for Long-term Local Currency Capital

The principal source of local currency capital has been domestic banks.[41] Long-term local currency capital markets allow emerging market debtors to raise capital with the currency risk on the investors and a repayment profile well adapted to avert crises. China, Indonesia and South Korea have, with regional support through the ASEAN+3 Bond Market Initiative (ABMI),[42] done well in the past two decades in developing their local currency sovereign bond markets.

In emerging market economies, banks are often pressured to make finance available to certain debtors for non-commercial reasons.[43] Crony capitalism was a major cause of the AFC.[44] This has been a focus for both individual economies and the Association of Southeast Asian Nations

40 Bank for International Settlements (BIS), "Triennial Central Bank Survey of foreign exchange and OTC derivatives markets in 2016" (11 December 2016), online: <www.bis.org/publ/rpfx16.htm>.

41 For a breakdown of debt structure in the ASEAN+3 countries, see Weiping Liu, "Short-Term Foreign Funds, a Comparative Study between China and Victim Countries of 1997 Asian Financial Crisis" (2007) 1:1 Global J Finance & Banking Issues; Glenn Stevens, "The Asian Crisis: A Retrospective" (Speech delivered at the Anika Foundation Luncheon, Reserve Bank of Australia, Sydney, 18 July 2007), online: <www.rba.gov.au/speeches/2007/sp-gov-180707.html>.

42 The ABMI created a regional bond guarantee system and regional settlement and clearance infrastructure. Mangal Goswami & Sunil Sharma, "The Development of Local Debt Markets in Asia" (2011) IMF Working Paper No WP/11/132.

43 Alison Harwood, Michael Pomerleano & Robert E Litan, *The Crisis in Emerging Financial Markets: A World Bank Group-Brookings Conference Report* (Washington, DC: Brookings Institution, 1999), online: <www.brookings.edu/research/the-crisis-in-emerging-financial-markets-a-world-bank-group-brookings-conference-report/>.

44 Eddy Lee, "The Debate on the Causes of the Asian Crisis: Crony Capitalism Versus International System Failure" (1999) 2 Internationale Politik und Gesellschaft 162; Ajit Singh & Ann Zammit, "Corporate Governance, Crony Capitalism and Economics: Should the US Business Model Replace the Asian Way of 'Doing Business?'" (2006) 14:4 Corporate Governance: An International Review 220; Raghuram G Rajan & Luigi Zingales, "Which Capitalism? Lessons from the East Asian Crisis" (1998) 11:3 J Applied Corporate Finance 40.

(ASEAN),[45] in particular through the ABMI and ASEAN Capital Markets Forum[46] and its implementation plan.[47]

International Capital Flows and Trade Imbalances

Most developing market crises, prior to the AFC, were preceded by a period of high liquidity in the developed world that funded large capital flows to developing countries. The AFC was not an exception, since the banks of the countries embroiled in it had borrowed excessively abroad. The primary task of bank regulators — maintaining the safety of their domestic financial systems — requires vigilance over the amount being lent to and invested in emerging market economies. Trade imbalances generating financial flows from the developing world are now a concern for developed economies and were a major element underlying the GFC.[48]

The GFC

The GFC began as a domestic mortgage crisis in the United States and rapidly spread throughout the world after the failure of Lehman Brothers and American International Group (AIG). Financial institutions lost confidence in dealing with one another and funding markets (including repo markets) froze, causing a widespread liquidity shock that, coupled with fears about the solvency of the world's largest financial institutions, led to the biggest financial crisis the world had seen up to that point. This section will provide an overview of the crisis and consider the causes, an analysis of policy responses and the lessons learned.

Causes of the GFC

The five principal causes of the GFC were excessive leverage; poorly functioning credit markets; a disconnect between regulatory structures and the financial system; misaligned incentives; and interconnectedness that facilitated the global transmission of systemic risk.[49] Each of these causes was underpinned by an excessive reliance on quantitative risk management mechanisms.

---

45 Reserve Bank of Australia, "Bond Market Development in East Asia" (2003) Reserve Bank of Australia Bull, online: <www.rba.gov.au/publications/bulletin/2003/dec/1.html>; BIS, "Weathering financial crises: bond markets in Asia and the Pacific" (2011) BIS Papers No 63, online: <www.bis.org/publ/bppdf/bispap63.pdf>; Cyn-Young Park, "Developing Local Currency Bond Markets in Asia" (2016) ADB Economics Working Paper No 495 at 4.

46 The Asian Bond Market Forum supports regulatory harmonization concerning cross-border bond transactions and market practices; see Goswami & Sharma, *supra* note 42 at 11.

47 Launched in 2015, the "Implementation Plan to Promote the Development of an Integrated Capital Market to achieve the objectives of the AEC Blueprint 2015" focused on adopting international standards, progressive liberalization and sequencing regional initiatives. Thirachai Phuvanatnaranubala, "Implementation Plan for ASEAN Capital Markets Integration" (Speech delivered at the second OECD Southeast Asian Regional Forum, Bangkok, 27 April 2009), online: <www.sec.or.th/TH/Documents/Information/speeches/speech270452.pdf>.

48 Ricardo J Caballero & Arvind Krishnamurthy, "Global Imbalances and Financial Fragility" (2009) National Bureau of Economic Research Working Paper No 14688; Ben Bernanke, "The Global Savings Glut and the U.S. Current Account Deficit" (Remarks delivered at the Sandridge Lecture, Virginia Association of Economists, Richmond, 14 April 2005).

49 See Emilios Avgouleas, *Governance of Global Financial Markets* (Cambridge, MA: Cambridge University Press, 2012) ch 2 [Avgouleas, *Governance*].

Excessive Leverage

Excessive leverage became a destabilizing factor as defaults started appearing[50] followed by fire sales, accentuating the importance of the leverage cycle in causing financial instability.[51]

Excessive lending was particularly concentrated in real estate markets catering to US borrowers of lesser credit quality.[52] The false perception that credit risk could be perfectly hedged on a portfolio basis allowed banks to accelerate mortgage lending, regardless of risk.[53] When subprime mortgagors began defaulting in large numbers, the US government-sponsored enterprises Fannie Mae and Freddie Mac were unable to honour their guarantees and faced bankruptcy.[54] The re-nationalization of these institutions averted their default and a systemic crisis, yet eroded market confidence.[55]

Excessive lending and leverage were not limited to real estate. Advisers such as credit rating agencies (CRAs) were more than willing participants in their pursuit of fees,[56] and investors followed their advice, either due to heuristics or rational herding.[57]

Malfunctioning Credit Markets

One of the key causes of the GFC was the liquidity crunch, which, given excessive use of short-term funding markets in the preceding period,[58] meant that large volumes of short-term funding could not be rolled over.[59] Another manifestation of the crunch was the market for asset-backed securities, whereby assets (for example, mortgages) could be repackaged and sold to investors, with the proceeds funding the origination of further assets to repeat the cycle.[60]

Misaligned incentives led to excessive risk-taking.[61] Securitization markets lacked transparency, obscuring the underlying risks.[62] Poor loan origination practices and unregulated non-banks were at the heart of the subprime mortgage crisis.[63]

---

50 For a summary of the "financial instability hypothesis," see Hyman P Minsky, "The Financial Instability Hypothesis" (1992) Jerome Levy Economics Institute of Bard College Working Paper No 74.

51 John Geanakoplos, "Solving the Present Crisis and Managing the Leverage Cycle" (2010) Federal Reserve Bank of New York Economic Policy Rev 101.

52 Douglas Arner, "The Global Credit Crisis of 2008: Causes, Consequences and Implications for International Finance" (2009) 43:1 Intl Lawyer 19 [Arner, "Global Credit Crisis"].

53 *Ibid.*

54 *Ibid* at 27.

55 *Ibid* at 28.

56 *Ibid* at 19.

57 Emilios Avgouleas, "The Global Financial Crisis, Behavioural Finance and Financial Regulation: In Search of a New Orthodoxy" (2009) 9:1 J Corporate L Stud 23.

58 Gary B Gorton & Andrew Metrick, "Securitized Banking and the Run on Repo" (2009) National Bureau of Economic Research Working Paper No 15223.

59 Markus K Brunnermeier, "Deciphering the Liquidity and Credit Crunch 2007–2008" (2009) 23:1 J Economic Perspectives 77; Markus K Brunnermeier & Lasse Heje Pedersen, "Market Liquidity and Funding Liquidity" (2009) 22:6 Rev Financial Stud 2201.

60 Arner, "Global Credit Crisis", *supra* note 52 at 16; Steven L Schwarcz, "Understanding the 'Subprime' Financial Crisis" (2009) 60:3 SCL Rev 549.

61 Avgouleas, *Governance*, *supra* note 49, ch 2, 3; Steven L Schwarcz, "Conflicts and Financial Collapse: The Problem of Secondary-Management Agency Costs" (2009) 26:2 Yale J Reg 457.

62 Steven L Schwarcz, "Disclosure's Failure in the Subprime Mortgage Crisis" (2008) Utah L Rev 1109.

63 Miguel Segoviano et al, "Securitization: Lessons Learned and the Road Ahead" (2013) IMF Working Paper No WP/13/255 at 15.

Over-the-counter (OTC) derivatives were designed to reduce the risk of the underlying asset (for example, subprime mortgages). The Basel II framework incentivized the increased use of credit derivatives to mitigate risks, which resulted in heightened counterparty risk among financial institutions (for example, banks) and major dealers (for example, Lehman Brothers, AIG).[64]

Prior to the GFC, OTC derivatives markets were generally unregulated and lacked transparency. Regulators failed to identify Bear Stearns's or AIG's unhedged bets in the subprime market.[65]

When AIG — the largest issuer of credit default swaps — became unable to honour its commitments, securitization structures unwound rapidly and reconcentrated credit risk into the vulnerable banks.[66] Moreover, the large degrees of interconnectedness that had been built through these instruments across the financial system intensified uncertainty about the solvency of major players.

CRAs supported the securitization structure by rating the securities that were sold to investors based on a tranche of mortgages' cash flows and risk profiles. Since the client paying for the rating was the issuer, "ratings shopping" may have resulted in upwardly biased ratings.[67] Prior to the GFC, CRAs were subject only to general terms of the International Organization of Securities Commissions (IOSCO) Code of Conduct.[68]

Disconnect between Regulatory Structures and the Financial System

Regulatory gaps and arbitrage played a central role in the GFC.[69] Regulatory structures did not reflect the structure of the financial system. This was most evident in blurred regulatory demarcations, the procyclical nature of capital regulations and the lack of macroprudential supervision.[70]

Macroprudential Supervisory Failure

Before the GFC, regulators ensured the stability of the financial system by ensuring the safety of institutions within it (microprudential regulation). This neglected potential interactions between those institutions[71] (so-called endogenous risk), between the financial system and the macroeconomic cycle, and between credit supply and asset bubbles. Guarding against risks arising in this context came to be known as macroprudential regulation.[72] If asset bubbles and

---

64 Arner, "Global Credit Crisis", *supra* note 52 at 24–25.

65 Frederic S Mishkin, "Over the Cliff: From the Subprime to the Global Financial Crisis" (2010) National Bureau of Economic Research Working Paper No 16609.

66 Avgouleas, *Governance*, *supra* note 49, ch 2.

67 Sergio Masciantonio & Andrea Tiseno, "The Rise and Fall of Universal Banking: Ups and Downs of a Sample of Large and Complex Financial Institutions Since the Late '90s" (Montreal: International Atlantic Economic Conference, 2012) at 14 (Figure 6).

68 Arner, "Global Credit Crisis", *supra* note 52 at 21.

69 Douglas W Arner, "Adaptation and Resilience in Global Financial Regulation" (2011) 89 NCL Rev 101 at 136 [Arner, "Adaptation"].

70 Rolf Weber et al, "Addressing Systemic Risk: Financial Regulatory Design" (2014) 49:149 Tex Intl LJ 149.

71 Markus Brunnermeier et al, *The Fundamental Principles of Financial Regulation* (Geneva: International Center for Monetary and Banking Studies, 2009).

72 Samuel G Hanson, Anil K Kashyap & Jeremy C Stein, "A Macroprudential Approach to Financial Regulation" (2011) 25:1 J Economic Perspectives 3; Xavier Freixas, Luc Laeven & José-Luis Peydró, *Systemic Risk, Crises, and Macroprudential Regulation* (Boston: MIT Press, 2015).

other forms of macroeconomic volatility can be identified sufficiently early, then corrective measures may be taken.[73]

The neglect of macroprudential linkages can be seen in the US regulators' decision to allow Lehman Brothers to fail, in the flawed belief it did not pose a systemic risk.

Blurred Regulatory Demarcations and Interconnectedness

In the United States, commercial and investment banks had been legislatively separated since the 1930s. Deregulation in the late 1990s fuelled the rise of universal banking (for example, Citigroup).[74] When the GFC unfolded, universal banks had large exposures to a range of toxic assets, notably through securitization. Faced with a liquidity crunch, coupled with insufficient capital buffers, many US and EU institutions required government recapitalizations,[75] reinforcing the too-big-to-fail (TBTF) phenomenon.[76] Securitization created linkages with non-bank financial institutions, namely investment banks (for example, Lehman Brothers and Bear Stearns) and insurance companies (for example, AIG). When securitization structures unwound, this resulted in the widespread failure of bank and non-bank financial institutions.

Procyclical Regulation

Basel II's adoption of quantitative risk modelling for risk management (i.e., capital held against market risk) proved inadequate in circumstances of extreme market stress. Reliance on credit ratings in determining bank capital enhanced the procyclicality of capital regulation because aggressive downgrading of credit ratings led to higher capital requirements.[77]

Market-to-market accounting standards during the GFC had a procyclical effect, as financial institutions had to continually revalue assets downward as more institutions deleveraged, thereby creating more solvency-threatening losses.[78]

Global Transmission of Systemic Risk

TBTF

Lehman Brothers was allowed to fail because it was presumed the failure of a medium-sized investment bank did not pose a systemic threat. However, unwinding the firm's position in markets globally dramatically increased uncertainty, shattered confidence among market participants and spread contagion across major investment and credit markets.

Derivatives were instrumental in the near collapse of AIG.[79] If AIG had been allowed to default on its derivatives exposures, the resultant systemic risk would probably have caused

73 Ross Cranston et al, *Principles of Banking Law,* 3rd ed (Oxford, UK: Oxford University Press, 2018) ch 2.

74 Emilios Avgouleas, "Large Systemic Banks and Fractional Reserve Banking" in Ross P Buckley, Emilios Avgouleas & Douglas W Arner, eds, *Reconceptualising Global Finance and Its Regulation* (Cambridge, UK: Cambridge University Press, 2016) ch 14.

75 Masciantonio & Tiseno, *supra* note 67 at 3–4.

76 Emilios Avgouleas, *The Reform of 'Too-Big-To-Fail' Bank: A New Regulatory Model for the Institutional Separation of 'Casino' from 'Utility' Banking* (Amsterdam: University of Amsterdam, 2010).

77 Arner, "Adaptation", *supra* note 69 at 24.

78 *Ibid* at 125; "Mark it and weep: Mark-to-market accounting hurts, but there is no better way", Editorial, *The Economist* (6 March 2008) 14; Office of the Chief Accountant, *Report and Recommendations Pursuant to Section 133 of the Emergency Economic Stabilization Act of 2008: Study on Mark-to-Market Accounting* (New York: United States Securities and Exchange Commission, 2008).

79 Arner, "Adaptation", *supra* note 69 at 123.

the insolvency of many of the world's largest financial institutions.[80] Nonetheless, the losses resulting from the demise of Lehman Brothers, combined with generalized loss of confidence in wholesale markets, caused a breakdown of the global financial system.

Domestic Regulators in a Global Financial System

The nature of the crisis required international coordination. Information gaps regarding cross-border institutions and their supervision were exposed, since the bodies setting global standards lacked any supervisory capacity and other cross-border crisis management systems were non-existent.[81] International and domestic regulatory structures lacked appropriate arrangements to manage the failure of complex global financial conglomerates.[82]

Financial Funding Market Failures

Reliance on short-term interbank, money market and capital market funding caused severe financial system liquidity strains when these markets became dysfunctional. Northern Rock in the United Kingdom and Bear Stearns in the United States had been unable to fund their business models, eventually requiring resolution through government intervention. Following the collapse of Lehman Brothers, financial funding market illiquidity became central to the systemic phase of the crisis.[83]

Analysis of Policy Responses

Despite central bank actions to bolster short-term liquidity markets to avoid a collapse of the financial system, initial regulatory approaches were calibrated far too narrowly, since they pursued two conflicting objectives: to stabilize the system and punish reckless bankers. Delays in calibrating the appropriate liquidity mechanisms were partially responsible for the credit crisis becoming a systemic crisis.[84]

Approaches differed between jurisdictions, but the underlying premise was to strengthen balance sheets and stabilize financial systems. The use of AMCs and/or guarantees was preferred. No bailout approach proved superior, as the choice depended on the market conditions.

From 2008 onward, the Group of Twenty (G20) led coordinated post-GFC reforms, which have resulted in domestic implementation of internationally agreed approaches.[85] International cooperation, setting financial standards and monitoring implementation were assigned to the Financial Stability Board (FSB).[86]

The G20 and FSB established the core elements of a new regulatory framework: building high-quality capital and liquidity standards and mitigating procyclicality; addressing systemically important financial institutions (SIFIs) through structural reform and resolution regimes; improving OTC derivatives markets through centralization of trading and clearing and a new

80 Arner, "Global Credit Crisis", *supra* note 52 at 29.

81 Douglas W Arner & Ross P Buckley, "Redesigning the Architecture of the Global Financial System" (2010) 11:2 Melbourne J Intl L 185; Avgouleas, *Governance*, *supra* note 49, ch 4, 5.

82 Arner, "Adaptation", *supra* note 69 at 144.

83 *Ibid* at 142.

84 *Ibid* at 31.

85 *Ibid* at 108.

86 See Douglas W Arner & Michael Taylor, "The Global Financial Crisis and the Financial Stability Board: Hardening the Soft Law of International Financial Regulation?" (2009) UNSWLJ 488.

risk management framework; strengthening accounting standards, especially vis-à-vis calculation of capital and risk and forward-looking provisions for new lending; strengthening adherence to international regulatory standards through regular peer reviews; reforming management compensation practices to redress perverse incentives; developing macroprudential tools; and refining the regulatory perimeter.[87]

Lessons Learned from the GFC

Setting aside highly significant systemic and microprudential concerns relating to bankers' incentives and financial sector culture, which are outside the scope of this chapter, five main lessons can be drawn from the GFC:

- Securitization cannot mitigate market risks in the absence of regulation correcting incentive mismatches.
- Comprehensive regulation of the financial system from both a macroprudential and microprudential standpoint is needed to support its resilience.
- Regulations should guard against moral hazard, especially regarding TBTF institutions, and should not be procyclical.
- Systemic risks need to be detected and mitigated but, as this may be difficult, a prophylactic approach that leads to *ex ante* building of adequate capital and liquidity buffers is probably the best regulatory strategy.
- A flexible and comprehensive framework is needed to resolve failing financial institutions.

Securitization Regulation Should Mitigate Market Risks

Prior to the GFC, securitization obscured inherent risks. Securitization should lead to simple structures that promote disclosure, and CRAs should be regulated to avoid conflicts of interest when assigning ratings.[88] The highly complex structures (for example, collateralized debt obligations) common before 2007 should be avoided.

Comprehensive Regulation of the Financial System Is Needed

Regulatory gaps, overlaps and divisions in a number of jurisdictions presented opportunities for regulatory avoidance. Regulatory arbitrage should be discouraged. Regulation and supervision must be suitably flexible to address financial activity emanating from any institution. This is a particular challenge in the context of technology and finance (i.e., fintech) to avoid regulatory arbitrage, ensure a level playing field and protect against risks from new participants. Many jurisdictions — in particular the European Union, United Kingdom and United States — have undertaken programs to reform regulatory structures, often building twin-peak regulatory systems and designing clear structures to address systemic risk.

87 Arner, "Adaptation", *supra* note 69 at 117.

88 Arner, "Global Credit Crisis", *supra* note 52 at 22.

Designing Regulations that Are Not Procyclical in Crisis Conditions

Basel II regulations and "mark-to-market" accounting standards proved to be procyclical under crisis conditions. Procyclicality was exacerbated when assets and credit ratings were devalued and downgraded. To strengthen balance sheets in crisis conditions, the robustness of capital, liquidity and leverage requirements should be tested *ex ante* and risk management must be improved. Adopting forward-looking accounting standards on top of these requirements will further mitigate procyclicality.[89] Counter-cyclical requirements and capital requirements calibrated for SIFIs should be built over time to buttress balance sheets against credit-rating downgrades or asset value write-offs. Basel III has addressed some of these issues, although concerns remain.

Effective Detection and Mitigation of Systemic Risk

Regulation of Market Infrastructure

Financial instruments that have the propensity to become systemic risk conduits (for example, OTC derivatives) require regulation that facilitates transparency and financial market infrastructure that can interrupt the transmission of systemic risk (for example, central counterparty clearing houses [CCPs]). This has been one of the major focuses post-crisis.[90] In CCPs, central counterparties maintain a member's guaranty fund, mandatory margins on open positions, and other funded and unfunded commitments by the CCP members. The existence of pre-committed resources acts as a counter-cyclical, macroprudential buffer to absorb the risk of counterparty default in OTC markets. Yet centralization of OTC clearing and settlement has also brought its own set of risks, given the massive concentration of counterparty risk within CCPs. The failure of one big CCP, an unlikely but not impossible event, could itself be systemic.

Macroprudential Supervision

Effective macroprudential supervision is critical. Supervisors must be equipped with the tools to assess and manage risks.[91] A number of new measures, such as leverage ratios, counter-cyclical capital requirements and lending controls (such as loan-to-value and loan-to-income ratios), have both a microprudential (institutional stability) and macroprudential (systemic stability) effect.[92] Reporting requirements and the resultant data sets available to regulators offer opportunities for regulatory technology (regtech) analytical approaches, including big data and artificial intelligence. This has been one of the most active areas of regulatory reform, with nearly 100 jurisdictions having made regulatory changes to create clear systems for addressing systemic risk.

---

89 Alicia Novoa, Jodi Scarlata & Juan Solé, "Procyclicality and Fair Value Accounting" (2009) IMF Working Paper No WP/09/39.

90 See e.g. *Dodd-Frank Wall Street Reform and Consumer Protection Act*, Pub L No 111–203, HR 4173, tit VII, tit VIII [*Dodd-Frank Act*]; EC, *Regulation (EU) No 648/2012 of 4 July 2012 on OTC derivatives, central counterparties and trade repositories*, [2012] OJ, L 201/1.

91 Michael W Taylor, Douglas W Arner & Evan C Gibson, "Central Banks' New Financial Stability Consensus" in David G Mayes, Pierre Siklos & Jan-Egbert Sturm, eds, *The Oxford Handbook of the Economics of Central Banking* (Oxford, UK: 2019).

92 Avgouleas, *Governance*, *supra* note 49, ch 2.

Framework for Resolving SIFIs

Domestic Arrangements and Powers

The absence of an effective SIFI resolution mechanism was key to the systemic phase of the GFC. This involves assessing the risks posed by interactions and interconnections. The primary lesson from the GFC is to have arrangements in place to either prevent or manage a failure. This requires a supervisor being equipped with a range of resolution powers.[93] This is broadly the approach now adopted by the FSB, US and EU frameworks.[94] While the FSB focuses primarily on global SIFIs, both the GFC and AFC highlight the necessity of individual jurisdictions developing contingency plans and resolution systems, in particular for domestic SIFIs. Discussions are also necessary at the regional level (in particular for regional SIFIs), a major issue in the euro-zone crisis and for ASEAN in the context of the ASEAN Banking Integration Framework.

Reinforcing International Cooperation

Reinforcing international cooperation is particularly pertinent for the resolution of SIFIs with cross-border operations. Problematically, financial crisis management is biased toward domestic concerns. The best approach is to formulate a predetermined contingency plan that accounts for cross-border risks and is constantly revised to keep up-to-date with market developments and constant supervisory monitoring.[95] This approach has been endorsed by the G20, IMF, the Basel Committee on Banking Supervision, the International Association of Insurance Supervisors and IOSCO.[96] Similar approaches need to be a focus as Asia seeks to liberalize cross-border financial institution operations in the ASEAN Banking Integration Framework.

The Euro-zone Crisis

Close on the heels of the GFC came the euro-zone debt crisis. Despite decades of effort to build a single financial market, almost all EU jurisdictions lacked proper (and especially cross-border) crisis resolution mechanisms. This led to a threat of widespread bank failures in EU countries and the near collapse of their financial systems. The banking crisis eventually morphed into a sovereign debt crisis due to "doom loop" dynamics, especially in countries such as Cyprus, Ireland and Spain, where banks had overextended themselves with reckless lending. At the same time, markets declined to roll over Greek debt, and the spreads on Irish, Italian, Portuguese and Spanish debt widened dangerously. This necessitated placing Cyprus, Greece, Ireland and Portugal under IMF and EU rescue programs. While in some cases these failed to achieve their macroeconomic objectives (for example, Greece), they were adequate to stem the fear of sovereign bankruptcies. Today, in the wake of the crisis and the 2016 Brexit vote, the European Union is at a critical crossroads: it must decide whether to take a path of closer integration of financial policies or of fragmentation with a gradual return to the pursuit of narrow national

---

93 FSB, *Key Attributes of Effective Resolution Regimes for Financial Institutions* (October 2011) at 7–8.

94 Title II of the *Dodd-Frank Act*, *supra* note 90; EC, *Directive 2014/59/EU establishing a framework for the recovery and resolution of credit institutions and investment firms* [2014] OJ, L 173/190.

95 See Rolf H Weber et al, "Addressing Systemic Risk: Financial Regulatory Design" (2014) 49:149 Tex Intl LJ.

96 FSB, *Reducing the moral hazard posed by systemically important financial institutions* (October 2010).

interests.[97] This section will traverse how the crisis should be conceptualized, its primary causes and the lessons it teaches.

Causes of the Euro-zone Crisis

Conceptualizing the Crisis

The euro-zone crisis should be seen as a sequence of four interlocking crises resulting from imbalanced monetary integration. As recycled surpluses were invested in the bonds of countries with intra-EU trade deficits (for example, Greece and Italy) and the banking systems of the euro-zone periphery (for example, Ireland and Spain), they financed massive real estate bubbles and accumulated unsustainable levels of public and private debt.[98]

The euro-zone crisis would have been less severe if members had delinked bank debt from sovereign indebtedness. The fact that many EU banks had invested in EU member state bonds, and were affected by the continuous recession, only made things worse. Since its establishment, the European Economic and Monetary Union (EMU) lacked crucial supporting institutions,[99] such as institutions that could absorb liquidity shocks, and cross-border supervisory and resolution structures to deal with cross-border spillover effects of a bank collapse.

Inadequacy of the Regulatory Architecture

The so-called financial stability trilemma holds[100] that the three objectives of financial stability, financial integration and national financial policies cannot be pursued successfully simultaneously. In spite of assertions to the contrary,[101] the euro-zone crisis has proven a common currency area or currency union is not viable without building transnational supervisory structures. This lesson has been well learned in Asia, where calls for a single regional currency have abated since the onset of the euro-zone crisis in 2010.

Institutional design is critical for the prevention and resolution of major financial crises. Prevention is managed through a framework of systemic risk controls and prudential regulations. Crisis management and resolution, on the other hand, require the establishment of supervisory and resolution structures with a cross-border remit, in order to override the principle of home-country control.[102]

Essential features to support financial stability were either not in place or insufficiently robust, in particular regarding the supervision and resolution of cross-border financial institutions, the single deposit guarantee and fiscal arrangements.

97 Emilios Avgouleas & Douglas Arner, "The Eurozone debt crisis and the European banking union: 'Hard choices', 'intolerable dilemmas' and the question of sovereignty" (2017) 50:1 International Lawyer 29.

98 Emilios Avgouleas, "Eurozone crisis and sovereign debt restructuring: intellectual fallacies and new lines of research" (Paper delivered at the Society of International Economic Law, Third Biennial Global Conference, Centre for International Law and Faculty of Law, National University of Singapore, July 2012).

99 C Fred Bergsten & Jacob Funk Kirkegaard, *The Coming Resolution of the European Crisis* (New York: Columbia International Affairs, 2012), online: <https://piie.com/publications/policy-briefs/coming-resolution-european-crisis>.

100 Dirk Schoenmaker, "The financial trilemma" (2011) 111 Economic Letters 57; Niels Thygesen, "Comments on the Political Economy of Financial Harmonisation in Europe" in Jeroen JM Kremers, Dirk Schoenmaker & Peter J Wierts, eds, *Financial Supervision in Europe* (Cheltenham, UK: Edward Elgar, 2003).

101 Tommaso Padoa-Schioppa, *The Road to Monetary Union in Europe: The Emperor, the Kings, and the Genies* (Oxford, UK: Oxford University Press, 2000).

102 Luis Garicano & Rosa M Lastra, "Towards a New Architecture for Financial Stability: Seven Principles" (2010) 13:3 J Intl Econ L 597.

The political economy of most other regions (including Asia) makes institutional centralization not feasible, but the euro-zone crisis has made the issues arising during the design phase of an integrated regional financial market clearer.

Home-country Control and Minimum Harmonization

The principles of home-country control and minimum harmonization left the European Union with an incomplete regulatory framework, since, in many cases, it merely augmented rather than replaced pre-existing national laws.[103]

The euro-zone crisis has shown that financial integration leads financial institutions to become tightly interconnected. This allows shocks in one market to be transmitted widely and quickly across other parts, such as the failure of Icelandic banks, the threat of collapse of the financial systems of Ireland and Spain, and the possibility of Greece's sovereign default.

In the European Union, the diversity of economies and issues arising out of inherent contradictions between national policy priorities meant reduced responsiveness to crisis. Lack of common deposit insurance in a well-integrated banking market at a time of cross-border crisis led to several conflicting policy choices and responses in an effort by states to protect their own citizens, which may not have been in conformity with single market policies, with Iceland's banking crisis and the fracture of Fortis being leading examples.[104]

From the standpoint of other regions, such risks must be considered at the outset of any regional financial process to minimize the chances of crisis.

Policy Responses to the Euro-zone Crisis

It was not until the 2008 GFC and the outbreak of the euro-zone crisis in 2010 that the need to enrich existing financial market integration models with structures that underpin financial stability and economic growth came to the attention of EU policy makers.

When the GFC broke out, European financial stability was hampered by colossal public and private debt, a flawed macroeconomic framework and an absence of institutions to handle a cross-border banking crisis. The euro zone's framework assumed any macroeconomic or banking system stability shocks could be dealt with nationally, due to the no-bailout clause in the EMU Treaty (article 123). The crisis meant the European Union had to enter the most transformative phase of its history.

The European Union had to devise mechanisms to prevent an immediate meltdown of its banking sector and reform its flawed institutions to prevent the euro-zone architecture from collapsing. This led to the establishment of the European Financial Stability Facility, now superseded by the European Stability Mechanism (ESM).

Since 2011, the European Union embarked on a number of initiatives to build an integrated surveillance framework regarding the implementation of fiscal policies under the Stability and

103 Emilios Avgouleas, "The Harmonisation of Rules of Conduct in EU Financial Markets: Economic Analysis, Subsidiarity and Investor Protection" (2000) 6 Eur LJ 72.

104 Emilios Avgouleas, Douglas W Arner & Uzma Ashraff, "Regional Financial Arrangements: Lessons from the Eurozone Crisis for East Asia" in Iwan J Azis & Hyun Song Shin, eds, *Global Shock, Risks, and Asian Financial Reform* (Cheltenham, UK: Edward Elgar, 2014) 377.

Growth Pact to strengthen economic governance and ensure budgetary discipline and structural reforms. The European Parliament and Council further adopted a set of new statutes aimed at strengthening the euro zone's economic governance by reducing deficits through tighter control of national finances.[105] This legislative package comprised concrete and decisive steps toward ensuring fiscal discipline to stabilize the EU economy and avert future crises. Further, the implementation of mandatory bail-ins aims to contain the impact of the banking crisis on sovereigns, although the restraining impact the threat of a bail-in has on regulators and bank management can also lead to forbearance, unless regulators deal with a bank failure that is due to idiosyncratic causes.[106] EU members need to complete the adjustment of internal and external imbalances, repair financial sectors and achieve sustainable public finances.[107] Piling up debt in their effort to bail out Europe's ailing banks only makes things worse by raising the cost of borrowing for euro-zone members to unsustainable levels. Such bailouts are unpopular with the citizens of lender countries[108] and borrowing countries, which tend to resent the accompanying austerity measures.

From the standpoint of other regional arrangements, perhaps the central consideration is how to avoid entanglement of domestic fiscal arrangements in a potential future crisis.

Three EU regulatory reforms stand out. First, the establishment of a European Banking Union (EBU) for euro-zone members under which the Single Supervisory Mechanism[109] (an offshoot of the ECB) is vested with supervisory powers and the Single Resolution Mechanism[110] is aimed at safeguarding the continuity of essential banking operations, protecting depositors, client assets and public funds, and minimizing risks to financial stability. Second, member states' resolution laws were harmonized and common EU rule books for the single market were developed by the European Supervisory Agencies (ESAs). Third, the ESM can alleviate member states' liquidity problems, subject to strict macroeconomic conditionality.[111]

While the centralization being pursued in the EBU is not politically feasible for many regions, three important considerations that emerge are harmonization of domestic regulatory systems, supervision of cross-border financial institutions and arrangements to address cross-border financial institution failures.

105 The set of reforms comprised five regulations and one directive.

106 Emilios Avgouleas & Charles Goodhart, "An Anatomy of Bank Bail-ins: Why the Eurozone Needs a Fiscal Backstop for the Banking Sector" (2016) 2 European Economy 75, online: <http://european-economy.eu/2016-2/an-anatomy-of-bank-bail-ins-why-the-eurozone-needs-a-fiscal-backstop-for-the-banking-sector/>.

107 European Commission, *European Economic Forecast* (Brussels: European Union, Spring 2012), online: <http://ec.europa.eu/economy_finance/publications/european_economy/2012/pdf/ee-2012-1_en.pdf>.

108 *Ibid.*

109 Council of the European Union, *Council Regulation (EU) No 1024/2013 of 15 October 2013 conferring specific tasks on the European Central Bank concerning policies relating to the prudential supervision of credit institutions* [2013] OJ, L 287/63.

110 European Commission, *Regulation (EU) No 806/2014 of the European Parliament and of the Council of 15 July 2014 establishing uniform rules and a uniform procedure for the resolution of credit institutions and certain investment firms in the framework of a Single Resolution Mechanism and a Single Resolution Fund and amending Regulation (EU) No 1093/2010* [2014] OJ, L 225/1.

111 *Treaty Establishing the European Stability Mechanism*, 2 February 2012 (entered into force 27 September 2012), online: <www.esm.europa.eu/sites/default/files/20150203_-_esm_treaty_-_en.pdf>.

Lessons Learned from the Euro-zone Crisis

The EU crisis response has emphasized the need to improve international and regional coordination on fiscal, monetary and financial policies affecting other states.

Financial Stability and Market Integration

Financial stability risks are magnified within integrated cross-border markets. Thus, it should not be seen as controversial that financial integration is not always beneficial. Despite the increased importance of enhanced regionalism and integration, policy formulation must be balanced.

Stable Currency Unions Presuppose Centralization of Bank Supervision

The European experience has demonstrated that centralization of bank supervision and resolution within a single currency zone is essential. Domestic policies are no substitute for regional commitments. The integration framework should facilitate the growth of regional economies while allowing the market to work freely.

Centralization Entails Critical Sovereignty Trade-offs

The European Union today faces a number of hard choices, including the intractable trade-off between national sovereignty and collective financial stability. The establishment of the EBU within the euro zone has clearly tilted the balance toward centralization. However, as the EBU remains incomplete, with no pan-European deposit guarantee scheme (due to German objections) the relationship between national economic sovereignty and collective financial stability remains undefined. Brexit-related discussions highlight the sovereignty concessions necessary to support an effective single market. In the process, a fiscal union to smooth out trade imbalances and contain shocks seems essential.[112]

But the level of sovereignty sacrifices required may be beyond the capacity of most national polities, as made clear by the Brexit vote and the troubles the European Union is facing with the new Italian government.

Looking Forward

The differences between the three crises may be greater than their similarities, which suggests that the next crisis will be different in its causes and consequences. Nevertheless, three important lessons stand out.

First, in an increasingly globalized world, formal international cooperation in financial stability and cross-border bank supervision and resolution may be necessary whenever national financial markets are closely integrated.[113] However, tensions regarding sovereignty make this unlikely outside of the European Union prior to the next crisis.

112 Agnès Bénassy-Quérré, Xavier Ragot & Guntram B Wolff, *Which fiscal union for the euro area?* (Brussels: Bruegel, 2016), online: <http://bruegel.org/2016/02/which-fiscal-union-for-the-euro-area/>.

113 For an example of such a model, see Avgouleas, *Governance, supra* note 49, ch 9.

While regional blocs are unlikely to accept the sovereignty sacrifice necessary for a single regional financial market based on a regional currency, economic and financial cooperation and coordination remain essential. Such efforts are reflected by ASEAN, ASEAN+3 and the Executives' Meeting of East Asia-Pacific Central Banks, as a result of the AFC. As integration continues, it is essential for parallel discussions to take place regarding both liberalization and crisis preparation through further development of the various regional fora of the international standard-setting bodies, such as the FSB Asia Regional Consultative Group, as well as international financial architecture.

Second, the only working assumption about which any regulator can be confident is that there will be another financial crisis in the future. Building robust crisis management, early intervention and resolution frameworks should be paramount. Individual countries need to design their own mechanisms for national and cross-border liquidity relief. Liquidity is fleeting and can easily disappear when the economy is exposed to short-term shocks or emerging structural weaknesses, or in a crisis of confidence. Regulators should remain watchful of interconnectedness risks and the possibility of contagion from the shadow banking sector that may quickly undermine stability.

While Asia focused on improving regulation in the aftermath of the AFC, with very good results during the GFC, it has made relatively less progress in the context of resolution mechanisms. As such, emphasis on improving regulation and financial safety nets, including resolution frameworks, needs to continue. At the same time, as China's financial system continues to become more integrated internationally and regionally, new risks are arising. A framework to deal with potential crises of the major forms (currency, banking/financial, current account/competitiveness and sovereign debt) is needed.

The best approaches to crisis prevention vary. For currency crises, a flexible exchange rate backed by reasonably large foreign exchange reserves is probably the best starting point, supplemented by bilateral and regional support arrangements. For banking and financial crises, the starting point is regulation, with a focus on participation in international standard-setting processes, and development of regional implementations and domestic arrangements. For current account/competitiveness crises, at the regional level, AMRO offers a macroeconomic monitoring arrangement to supplement the IMF's international monitoring. In addition, development of domestic and regional financial systems to support local currency financing and risk management is important.

Third, if a full-blown financial crisis develops, the speed of the policy response and the decisiveness of public institutions, especially regarding central bank liquidity tools to alleviate immediate refinancing pressures, matter greatly for the restoration of confidence. Tested remedies, such as the use of AMCs, ought not to be discarded on the grounds of moral hazard and bailout subsidies. Affected countries should instead build a transparent framework that distributes losses equitably and targets rapid restoration of confidence.

The expansion of regulation post-GFC has been well adapted to prevent another GFC, but loopholes remain, especially regarding the regulatory perimeter and shadow banks. If anything, these issues are greater across most of Asia than in Europe and North America. As fintech continues to transform financial systems across the world, the appropriate treatment of new technologies and participants becomes even more important. Improving the abilities of regulators through regtech must be a major focus.

Today there is a globalized financial system that is far different from the series of lightly interconnected national systems envisaged by John Maynard Keynes and Harry Dexter White. Based on the lessons of the AFC, individual countries and regions must take steps to secure their own successes and protect themselves from financial crises. Yet, deeper integration should not be expected in the absence of substantial political will, which normally only arises in the aftermath of a major disaster. In fact, the AFC caused the strong focus on financial stability and step-by-step integration across the region, including the regional preference for foreign exchange reserve accumulation. Those efforts served the region very well in the GFC, with many of the Asian post-AFC measures being adopted globally post-GFC.

While the new crisis may develop in emerging market currencies and debt, following turbulence in Turkey and elsewhere, the most likely source of a major transformative event in our view will be how such turbulence impacts Asia's large economies: China and India. Most Asian currencies are already more directly impacted by the yuan than the dollar. In some ways, a regional currency is emerging. Renminbi internationalization for the region is already a reality. Likewise, as China's financial system and capital account are gradually liberalized and Chinese financial institutions expand across the region, China will assume a greater role as a regional economic hegemon, especially if weaknesses in its own economy, such as a developing housing bubble and the large shadow banking sector, are reined in.

The outsize dominance of many developing country and emerging market financial systems by foreign institutions will require careful consideration to manage integration with China and eventually India. Arguably, China's rise may serve to incentivize regional integration, much as the postwar rise of the United States did for the evolution of the European Union.

The first step in any crisis management approach is prevention, but this should also be combined with management and resolution. Cooperation in cross-border and cross-sectoral systemic risk monitoring through supervisory colleges should be strengthened by establishing a coherent structure for microprudential supervision cooperation. This should be followed with a crisis management structure, and knowledgeable regulators with a role in standard setting. Crisis management arrangements need to focus on liquidity at the regional, international and bilateral levels, as liquidity in major currencies is only available in unlimited volumes from the central bank responsible for that currency. Such arrangements must be partnered with macroeconomic monitoring arrangements, in particular at the regional and international levels (through the IMF).

In addition to liquidity and macroeconomic surveillance, the GFC and euro-zone crises have highlighted the importance of financial stability arrangements, in particular from the macroprudential/counter-cyclical standpoint.

Regions should consider having a regional systemic risk board supported by country central banks in the mode of the European Systemic Risk Board. The responsibilities of "regional SRBs" would fit very well in regional frameworks for systemic risk detection, including serving warning and signalling functions, but they will still require regional central banks to participate and share data. Initially, this would be an arrangement that would not entail any loss of sovereignty but only the sharing of confidential information and the issuance of warnings to members.

Such regional systemic risk bodies would be particularly timely, given the challenge of the rise of fintech and the expansion of e-commerce and social media firms such as Alibaba and Facebook into finance (the so-called techfins).[114] The associated cyber security risks have been demonstrated most pointedly by the Bangladesh central bank robbery.[115]

Furthermore, given shadow banking's importance and cross-border links (including via fintechs and techfins), future regional systemic risk bodies would have a valuable role as systemic risk data consolidators and impartial monitors. When a crisis hits, regional bodies for systemic risk monitoring can prove valuable, especially in offering authoritative guidance on coordinated bank rescues or resolutions. Naturally, it will not involve any burden sharing, but could evolve as a trusted venue for information sharing and rescue/resolution cooperation. A regional body could become the principal forum for consultation and coordination of policy responses to Basel and the FSB.

In terms of domestic implementation of international and regional financial regulatory standards, international and regional development banks would be the lead in supporting reform processes. Further, the multilateral development banks and the IMF must become agents of change in bank corporate governance cultures around the world, augmenting bank management accountability.

As regards resolution, TBTF avoidance of bail-ins on a systemic basis breeds moral hazard. If circumstances dictate, this does not mean that creditors (with the exception of depositors) should escape lightly. Individual jurisdictions in ASEAN+3 and around the globe desperately need to upgrade bank resolution regimes before the next crisis and not rely overly on bailouts.

Finally, a culture of transparency, openness and cooperation ought to be pursued in all future integration initiatives. Since the risks are increasingly regional and global, purely country-based responses may prove largely obsolete. Recognizing that financial stability on a regional or even global level can easily fall victim to "tragedy of the commons" behaviour is an important first step. Like trade and environmental protection, regional financial stability binds closely together the prosperity of individual nations. Therefore, it offers fertile ground for interaction between national regulatory authorities, central banks and governments, giving rise to a wider economic cooperation impetus for the benefit of all.

Authors' Note

The authors gratefully acknowledge the financial support of the Hong Kong Research Grants Council Theme-based Research Scheme (Enhancing Hong Kong's Future as a Leading International Financial Centre), the Asian Development Bank and King & Wood Mallesons, and the invaluable research assistance of Jessica Chapman, Evan Gibson, Rohan Balani, Michael Squires and Sarah Webster. All responsibility is the authors'.

114 Dirk A Zetzsche et al, "From FinTech to TechFin: The Regulatory Challenges of Data-Driven Finance" NYU J L & Bus, online: <https://papers.ssrn.com/sol3/papers.cfm?abstract_id=2959925>.

115 Kim Zetter, "That Insane $81M Bangladesh Bank Heist? Here's What We Know", *Wired* (17 May 2016), online: <www.wired.com/2016/05/insane-81m-bangladesh-bank-heist-heres-know/>.

4

Fintech, Regtech and Systemic Risk:
The Rise of Global Technology Risk

DOUGLAS W. ARNER, ROSS P. BUCKLEY
AND DIRK ZETZSCHE

This chapter analyzes the impact of financial and regulatory technologies on systemic risk. Following the 2008 global financial crisis (GFC), there is a general consensus that systemic risk is usually the result of the financial intermediary's size (too big to fail [TBTF]) or of interrelationships between intermediaries (too connected to fail [TCTF]). Both TBTF and TCTF are now seen as core aspects of financial stability regulation, from both a microprudential (TBTF) and macroprudential (TCTF) standpoint. Traditionally, issues relating to technology have been included in the context of operational risk, recognized as one key form of financial risk, along with credit risk, market risk and legal risk.[1] As a result of the emergence of digitization and datafication, we suggest that technology risks (including cyber security and data protection) should be seen as a separate form of risk, beyond the traditional operational risk categorization. Technology risks can arise in the context of individual institutions, but also in the context of the interconnections of institutions. More fundamentally, however, technology risks have the potential to impact financial sector confidence and stability directly.

1 See Basel Committee on Banking Supervision (BCBS), *Basel III: A global regulatory framework for more resilient banking systems* (2017), online: <www.bis.org/publ/bcbs189.pdf>.

Regarding TBTF, we will highlight the rapid buildup of size, drawing on the example of techfins (data giants such as Amazon and Alibaba, moving into financial services). Techfins are firms that enjoy access to abundant data who may: serve as the source of the data, either raw or analyzed, that banks use to refine their risk assessments and product offerings to customers; serve as the conduit through which banks can access and interact with customers (for instance, banking on and through Facebook); or provide financial services directly to customers using their data advantage.[2] Large tech and e-commerce firms that have access to such data are increasingly moving into finance, in ways different from financial technology firms (fintechs), as they often benefit from regulatory gaps and/or disparities in treatment with traditional financial institutions, economies of scope and scale, and network effects (i.e., a tendency toward concentration in both data and finance). This combination suggests that techfins may in fact potentially increase TBTF risks, in addition to raising concerns about competition and data protection.

Regarding TCTF, we argue that in a world of digitized finance, all is connected via the data feed, and such connectivity creates systemic risk. In particular, traditional bank-owned and bank-run infrastructure is replaced by new, systemically important infrastructure owned by someone else and that someone else is potentially not a financial intermediary in the traditional sense (i.e., not regulated at all and not subject to measures we associate with systemic risk, such as bail-in/bailout, segregation of critical infrastructure, and so forth). Examples include market concentration in data feeds, cloud services (non-financial firm providing data and hosting services for financial firms and regulators), and others. In addition, cyber security risks arise dramatically across all aspects of finance.

As for cyber security and technology risk, we argue that in terms of importance this type of risk now comprises another major form of risk, alongside the other main traditional categories of financial risk. Digitization/datafication, cyber security and TBTF/TCTF considerations together create a world where the financial system is more vulnerable than before. Where technology risks are new drivers of instability, regulators are well advised to focus on these new forms of risk, both in terms of their connection to other forms of risk as well as independently.

To conclude, we present some basic principles of how cyber security and technology risks can be regulated and monitored, but also outline the deficiencies of existing or traditional approaches. The deficiencies in the regulatory system with regard to technology risks are similar to those that we experienced with respect to macroprudential risks prior to the 2008 GFC. Those deficiencies include lack of understanding, deficiencies in mandates, loopholes in regulation, lack of coordination among regulators, information asymmetries, lack of expertise on the part of financial intermediaries and regulators, and so forth. We encourage a new risk agenda that responds to technology risks proactively.

The chapter is structured as follows. To set the stage, the chapter first presents a brief summary of existing understanding of sources of systemic risk. Next, we highlight key drivers for financial technologies, and in particular a subset of fintech that is linked to big tech (i.e., big data), firms providing services to financial intermediaries or entering into financial services markets

2 Dirk A Zetzsche et al, "From FinTech to TechFin: The Regulatory Challenges of Data-Driven Finance" (2018) 14 NYUJ L & Bus 393 [Zetzsche et al, "From FinTech to TechFin"].

themselves. The next part argues that the advent of big tech in finance creates an unprecedented level of tech-based systemic risk, since both size and connectivity are present. The conclusion suggests a set of principles that may serve as the framework to address these sorts of risks going forward.

Size (TBTF) and Connectivity (TCTF) as Systemic Risk Measures

Systemic risk[3] has long been a major focus in the evolution of financial regulation, and banking regulation in particular. According to the Group of Twenty (G20), "Systemic financial risk is the risk that an event will trigger a loss of economic value or confidence in, and attendant increases in uncertainty about, a substantial portion of the financial system that is serious enough to quite probably have significant adverse effects on the real economy."[4]

Systemic financial risk includes contagion effects, in which a loss of confidence spreads to undermine markets; at times, such effects can arise from relatively small events that are disproportionate to their ultimate impact.[5] Prior to the 2008 GFC, financial stability regulation had emerged as a core regulatory function, focusing on the identification, prevention and management of systemic risk.[6] The focus generally was on banking — usually excluding non-bank financial institutions — and in particular on the size of individual institutions (the TBTF problem) and the payments system.

Despite decades of experience and analysis, systemic risk was a core feature of the 2008 GFC, highlighting distinct failures in financial stability regulation. Steven L. Schwartz rightfully pointed out at the peak of the GFC that — despite significant attention to systemic risk and financial stability prior to 2008 — "[t]here [was] widespread confusion, though, about the causes and even the definition of systemic risk, and uncertainty about how to control it."[7]

Since the GFC, large volumes of research have sharpened the understanding of systemic risk. As a baseline, there is a common understanding that size of intermediaries and interconnectivity are core sources of systemic risk. As defined by former US Federal Reserve Chair Ben Bernanke, a systemically important financial institution (SIFI) "is one whose size, complexity,

3 See the works by George G. Kaufmann, an economist at the US Federal Reserve, e.g. George G Kaufman, "Bank Failures, Systemic Risk, and Bank Regulation" (1996) 16 Cato J 16, n 5, quoting Alan Greenspan, former chair of the US Federal Reserve; George G Kaufmann & Kenneth E Scott, "What Is Systemic Risk, and Do Bank Regulators Retard or Contribute to It?" (2003) 7 Independent Rev 371 ("Systemic risk refers to the risk or probability of breakdowns in an entire system, as opposed to breakdowns in individual parts or components, and is evidenced by comovements (correlation) among most or all the parts" at 371; Kaufmann and Scott refer to Kaufmann's earlier work in the 1990s). See also Darryll Hendricks, "Defining Systemic Risk", Pew Financial Reform Project (8 July 2009), online: <www.pewtrusts.org/en/research-and-analysis/reports/2009/07/08/defining-systemic-risk> ("A systemic risk is the risk of a phase transition from one equilibrium to another, much less optimal equilibrium, characterized by multiple self-reinforcing feedback mechanisms making it difficult to reverse").

4 Group of Ten, *Report on Consolidation in the Financial Sector*, International Monetary Fund (2001), online: <www.imf.org/external/np/g10/2001/01/eng/pdf/file3.pdf>.

5 Federico Lupo-Pasini & Ross P Buckley, "Global Systemic Risk and International Regulatory Coordination: Squaring Sovereignty and Financial Stability" (2015) 30 Am U Intl L Rev 665 at 678.

6 See Douglas W Arner, *Financial Stability, Economic Growth and the Role of Law* (Cambridge, UK: Cambridge University Press, 2007).

7 See Steven L Schwarcz, "Systemic Risk" (2008) 97 Geo LJ 193. Schwarcz demands an integrated view on markets rather than institutions. His view indirectly supports the position presented herein that systemic risk is an established feature of the market governance objective of financial law.

interconnectedness, and critical functions are such that, should the firm go unexpectedly into liquidation, the rest of the financial system and the economy would face severe adverse consequences."[8] SIFIs — particularly global SIFIs (G-SIFIs) — have thus become a key focus for the G20 and its Financial Stability Board's (FSB's) post-crisis regulatory reform agenda, as well as a key focus of domestic and regional regulatory reforms over the past decade.

In the context of the TBTF paradigm, systemic significance follows from the size of a financial institution.[9] Under the TCTF paradigm, systemic importance follows from the fact that other financial intermediaries are engaged in business links with the intermediary that are crucial to the many intermediaries, while all of those intermediaries together are of critical importance for the financial system, and those links cannot be substituted for easily. The key post-crisis insight here is that interlinkages can take many forms, not just payment interlinkages, with a particular post-crisis focus on linkages from over-the-counter derivatives and the related counterparty risk. In addition, interlinkages are now seen as arising from common business models (for example, originate-to-distribute), contractual approaches (for example, standardized documentation such as that of the International Swaps and Derivatives Association) and commonalities across risk-management systems.

One consequence of systemic importance is that governments are pressed to provide support to SIFIs if they face financial problems. But, as Bernanke has framed it, this support is not due to "favoritism or particular concern for the management, owners, or creditors of the firm, but because they recognize that the consequences for the broader economy of allowing a disorderly failure greatly outweigh the costs of avoiding the failure in some way. Common means of avoiding failure include facilitating a merger, providing credit, or injecting government capital, all of which protect at least some creditors who otherwise would have suffered losses."[10]

Much of the FSB's post-crisis regulatory agenda thus focuses on prevention of systemic risk through a range of financial stability systems, including: microprudential supervision of SIFIs, and G-SIFIs in particular; macroprudential supervision to identify interconnections and risks prior to any crisis trigger; and strengthening core infrastructures, in particular in the context of systemically important infrastructures such as payment systems, securities settlement systems and central counterparties.[11] These have been undertaken through a wide range of efforts: domestic, regional and international, including regulatory changes and changes to the scope of regulatory mandates (in individual jurisdictions as well as through the FSB) and the creation of new systemic risk supervisory structures (such as the European Systemic Risk Board in the European Union and the Financial Stability Oversight Council in the United States).

8 Ben Bernanke, "Causes of the Recent Financial and Economic Crisis", testimony before the Financial Crisis Enquiry Commission, United States Congress (2 September 2010), online: <www.federalreserve.gov/newsevents/testimony/bernanke20100902a.htm>.

9 Luc Laeven, Lev Ratnovski & Hui Tong, "Bank Size and Systemic Risk" (2014) IMF Staff Discussion Note No SDN/14/04, online: <www.imf.org/external/pubs/ft/sdn/2014/sdn1404.pdf>.

10 Bernanke, *supra* note 8.

11 See Ross P Buckley, Emilios Avgouleas & Douglas A Arner, eds, *Reconceptualising Global Finance and Its Regulation* (Cambridge, UK: Cambridge University Press, 2016).

Fintech Factors — and the Advent of Big Tech

Fintech,[12] alongside related technologies such as big data[13] and artificial intelligence,[14] distributed ledgers and blockchain,[15] initial coin offerings (ICOs),[16] smart contracts,[17] regulatory technology (regtech)[18] and digital identity,[19] is transforming finance and challenging its regulation at an unprecedented rate. Over the past decade, a long-term process of digitization of finance has increasingly combined with datafication and new technologies — including cloud computing, blockchain, big data and artificial intelligence — to create a new era of fintech (financial technology). The result is novel services with disruptive effects on existing intermediaries, such as crowdfunding and crowdlending.[20]

However, most attention to date has focused on the general trajectory that technologized financial services will take[21] and how they will be regulated.[22] Special consideration has also been

12 *Cf* Douglas W Arner, Janos Barberis & Ross P Buckley, "The Evolution of FinTech: A New Post-Crisis Paradigm?" (2017) 47 Geo J Intl L 1271.

13 Julie E Cohen, "What Privacy Is For" (2013) 126 Harv L Rev 1904; Solon Barocas & Andrew D Selbst, "Big Data's Disparate Impact" (2016) 104 Cal L Rev 671; Daniel Martin Katz, "Quantitative Legal Prediction — or — How I Learned to Stop Worrying and Start Preparing for the Data Driven Future of the Legal Services Industry" (2013) 62 Emory LJ 909; Omer Tene & Jules Polonetsky, "Big Data for All: Privacy and User Control in the Age of Analytics" (2013) 11 Nw J Tech & IP 239; Zetzsche et al, "From FinTech to TechFin", *supra* note 2.

14 In computer science, artificial intelligence is defined as devices that perceive their environment and take actions that maximize their chance of successfully achieving their task. The baseline of artificial intelligence is a computer mimicking human cognitive functions such as learning and problem solving. Artificial intelligence today can be used to detect unexpected correlations in large data pools, test expected correlations for causation or determine an empirical probability of a predefined pattern. See David Lynton Poole, Alan K Mackworth & Randy Goebel, *Computational Intelligence: A Logical Approach* (Oxford, UK: Oxford University Press, 1998); Stuart J Russel & Peter Norvig, *Artificial Intelligence: A Modern Approach,* 3rd ed (Upper Saddle River, NJ: Prentice Hall, 2009). Russel and Norvig prefer the term "rational agent." From an ethical/policy perspective, see Dirk Helbing, "Societal, Economic, Ethical and Legal Challenges of the Digital Revolution: From Big Data to Deep Learning, Artificial Intelligence, and Manipulative Technologies" in Dirk Helbing, ed, *Towards Digital Enlightenment* (Berlin: Springer, 2018).

15 See Christian Catalini & Joshua S Gans, "Some Simple Economics of the Blockchain", NBER Working Paper No 22952, National Bureau of Economic Research, June 2018, online: <www.nber.org/papers/w22952>; Dirk A Zetzsche, Ross P Buckley & Douglas W Arner, "The distributed liability of distributed ledgers: legal risks of blockchain" (forthcoming) U Ill L Rev; Usha Rodrigues, "Law and the Blockchain" (forthcoming) Iowa L Rev.

16 Philipp Hacker & Chris Thomale, "Crypto-Securities Regulation: ICOs, Token Sales and Cryptocurrencies under EU Financial Law" (forthcoming) European Company & Finance L Rev; Dirk A Zetzsche et al, "The ICO Gold Rush: It's a Scam, It's a Bubble, It's a Super Challenge for Regulators" (2019) 63 Harv Intl LJ [Zetzsche et al, "The ICO Gold Rush"]; Saman Adhami, Giancarlo Giudici & Stefano Martinazzi, "Why Do Businesses Go Crypto? An Empirical Analysis of Initial Coin Offerings" (forthcoming) J Economics & Business.

17 Jeremy M Sklaroff, "Smart Contracts and the Cost of Inflexibility" (2017) 166 U Pa L Rev 263; Kevin Werbach & Nicolas Cornell, "Contracts Ex Machina" (2017) 67 Duke LJ 313; Max Raskin, "The Law and Legality of Smart Contracts" (2017) 1 Geo L & Tech Rev 304.

18 Douglas W Arner, Janos Barberis & Ross P Buckley, "FinTech, RegTech and the Reconceptualisation of Financial Regulation" (2017) 37 Nw J Intl L & Bus 371; Bart van Liebergen, "RegTech in Financial Services: Solutions for Compliance and Reporting" (2016) Institute of International Finance, online: <www.iif.com/system/files/regtech_in_financial_services_-_solutions_for_compliance_and_reporting.pdf>.

19 Douglas W Arner et al, "The Identity Challenge in Finance: From Analogue Identity to Digitized Identification to Digital KYC Utilities" (forthcoming) 19 European Business Organization L Rev.

20 John Armour & Luca Enrique, "The Promise and Perils of Crowdfunding: Between Corporate Finance and Consumer Contracts" (2018) 81 Mod L Rev 51; Dirk Zetzsche & Christina Preiner, "Cross-Border Crowdfunding: Towards a Single Crowdlending and Crowdinvesting Market for Europe" (2018) 19 European Business Organization L Rev 217.

21 Arner, Barberis & Buckley, *supra* note 12 at 1276–85.

22 See Dirk A Zetzsche et al, "Regulating a Revolution: From Regulatory Sandboxes to Smart Regulation" (2017) 23 Fordham J Corp & Fin L 31 [Zetzsche et al, "Regulating a Revolution"].

given to fintech's impact on banks and the payment services sector,[23] including the disruptive effects of crowdfunding and crowdlending[24] on existing intermediaries.

But most fintechs do not seek to disrupt the existing intermediaries; rather, they want to collaborate and seek intermediaries as clients.[25] It is here that true fintech innovation takes place — and at a rapid pace.[26]

This process of digitization and datafication combined with new technologies can be seen across developed global markets and also in emerging and developing markets, where the process of digital financial transformation is taking place even faster than in developed markets.

Two major trends stand out in the current period of fintech development. The first is the speed of change driven by the commoditization of technology, big data analytics, machine learning and artificial intelligence. The second is the increasing number and variety of new entrants into the financial sector, including pre-existing technology and e-commerce companies. This encompasses the transformation of techfins, which initially only provided data or information technology (IT) services to financial institutions, into entities that operate as data-based financial intermediaries.[27]

From a systemic risk perspective, we do not believe that the risk stems from fintechs as such. Fintechs tend to start small, as problem-driven firms, and then try to become big.[28] As such, balanced proportional approaches to regulation are most appropriate, as we have analyzed in detail elsewhere.[29]

Further, we do not believe that new technologies and innovations such as blockchain, cryptocurrencies and token sales create systemic risk of a magnitude to warrant intervention. While the growth of ICO volumes has been impressive indeed,[30] we lack evidence of significant involvement of regulated financial intermediaries in such products. Given the public statements by bank CEOs, quite the opposite seems to be true.[31] However, this may change and the first

23 See BCBS, "Sound Practices: Implications of Fintech Developments for Banks and Bank Supervisors", Bank for International Settlements, 19 February 2018, online: <www.bis.org/bcbs/publ/d431.pdf>; US Department of the Treasury, "A Financial System That Creates Economic Opportunities: Nonbank Financials, Fintech, and Innovation" (31 July 2018), online: <https://home.treasury.gov/sites/default/files/2018-08/A-Financial-System-that-Creates-Economic-Opportunities---Nonbank-Financials-Fintech-and-Innovation_0.pdf>; Lerong Lu, "Decoding Alipay: Mobile Payments, a Cashless Society and Regulatory Challenges" (forthcoming) Butterworths J Intl Banking & Fin L.

24 See John Armour & Luca Enriques, "The Promise and Perils of Crowdfunding: Between Corporate Finance and Consumer Contracts" (2018) 81 Modern L Rev 51; Zetzsche & Preiner, *supra* note 20.

25 Zetzsche et al, "From FinTech to TechFin", *supra* note 2 at 401–02; Arner, Barberis & Buckley, *supra* note 12 at 1309.

26 See e.g. Miklos Dietz, Jared Moon & Miklos Radnai, "Fintechs Can Help Incumbents, Not Just Disrupt Them" (2016) McKinsey & Company, online: <www.mckinsey.com/industries/financial-services/our-insights/fintechs-can-help-incumbents-not-just-disrupt-them>; European Banking Authority, "EBA Report on the Impact of FinTech on Incumbent Credit Institutions' Business Models" (3 July 2018), online: <www.eba.europa.eu/documents/10180/2270909/Report+on+the+impact+of+Fintech+on+incumbent+credit+institutions%27%20business+models.pdf>.

27 Zetzsche et al, "From FinTech to TechFin", *supra* note 2 at 409–11.

28 Daniel Drummer et al, "Fintech: Challenges and Opportunities" (2016) McKinsey & Company, online: <www.slideshare.net/DanielDrummerLLM/160512-fintechenglishdd>.

29 Zetzsche et al, "Regulating a Revolution", *supra* note 22.

30 See Zetzsche et al, "The ICO Gold Rush", *supra* note 16.

31 See e.g. Anthony Cuthbertson, "Bitcoin trading comes to Goldman Sachs after investment bank hires first cryptocurrency trader", *The Independent* (3 May 2018), online: <www.independent.co.uk/life-style/gadgets-and-tech/news/bitcoin-trading-latest-goldman-sachs-digital-asset-trader-investment-banks-a8334171.html>; Tae Kim, "Jamie Dimon says he regrets calling bitcoin a fraud and believes in the technology behind it", CNBC Markets (9 January 2018), online: <www.cnbc.com/2018/01/09/jamie-dimon-says-he-regrets-calling-bitcoin-a-fraud.html>.

indicators of such a change may be found in the apparently growing numbers of so-called crypto hedge funds and regulated investment funds getting involved in those markets.[32] Given the rapid growth of the ICO markets, regulators are well advised to enforce existing laws strictly, monitor developments closely and cooperate globally to ensure that systemic risk is kept under control.[33]

Rather, the clear risk of digitization — a process that, in many cases, covers entire businesses — is that of security, namely, cyber security and data protection.

Cyber security has become one of the leading areas of attention of financial regulators around the world as well as of governments and financial and tech firms. We would suggest that cyber security is now the most significant source of systemic risk, as well as one of the most significant issues of national security. From the standpoint of SIFIs, which have almost entirely digitized their operations, hacking, cyber theft, cyber terrorism, cyber activism and cyber attacks pose grave risks. While financial institutions have long focused on all forms of fraud and theft risk, digitization and globalization raise the potential for even simple fraud and theft to take on much greater scale: instead of robbing one account, office or firm, an attacker can potentially rob or attack all accounts and offices of multiple firms in multiple jurisdictions at the same time. The challenge here is clearly greater, given that much wider motivations for attackers are now common, beyond simple fraud and crime to a wide range of political and military activities.

While regulators — both in individual jurisdictions as well as internationally and regionally — are clearly focusing attention on related issues, the challenge is the wide range of actors and motivations: while it is clearly appropriate and necessary for all financial institutions and infrastructure providers to focus significant resources and efforts on cyber security, the widespread presence of state and state-supported actors highlights the difficulties of pushing the entire burden onto the financial sector.

As a result of increased state activity in cyber activities (including cyber warfare), there is a clear need for states to take a leading role in building systems to monitor and support key sectors of the economy — such as the financial sector — in addition to private and regulatory attention to issues of cyber security.

In addition to cyber security, the increasingly central role of data in the financial sector highlights the second major area of concern: data protection. This is in some ways related to cyber security but, at the same time, there is a range of underlying policies involved in data protection rules in jurisdictions around the world. These policies in particular relate to major questions about the role of data in digitized and datafied societies and economies: who owns and controls data? Different results are being arrived at in differing economies, with the United States, China and the European Union being the leading examples of differing legal approaches to the use and ownership of data resulting from different societal approaches. These, in turn, result in different market and business structures, with different legal requirements related to data protection and control. How societies address questions about the role of data and the related legal and

32 See Jemima Kelly & Maiya Keidan, "Bitcoin boom failing to attract big name investors", *The Independent* (23 October 2017), citing Autonomous NEXT, "Crypto Fund List" (5 April 2010), online: <https://next.autonomous.com/cryptofundlist/>.

33 Zetzsche et al, "Regulating a Revolution", *supra* note 22.

governance frameworks are likely to be among the most important questions of the twenty-first century.

Fintech, Techfin, Size and Connectivity

Beyond cyber security and data protection, the involvement of large data firms ("big tech") in financial matters is a reason for concern.[34] According to the Basel Committee on Banking Supervision, "BigTech refers to large globally active technology firms with a relative advantage in digital technology. Bigtech firms usually provide web services (search engines, social networks, e-commerce etc) to end users over the internet and/or IT platforms or they maintain infrastructure (data storage and processing capabilities) on which other companies can provide products or service."[35]

Those big techs are linked to financial markets in two ways. First, they can function as third-party providers to financial intermediaries. Cases include the cloud services provided by Amazon and others, or data feeds to banks and asset managers that are used to inform risk models and calculations. Second, big tech firms can move more directly into the provision of financial services, initially serving as conduits linking the financial service providers with the customers that the big tech typically already has, and over time potentially beginning to provide the financial service directly to customers: as techfins.[36]

Figure 1: Big Tech's Function in Finance

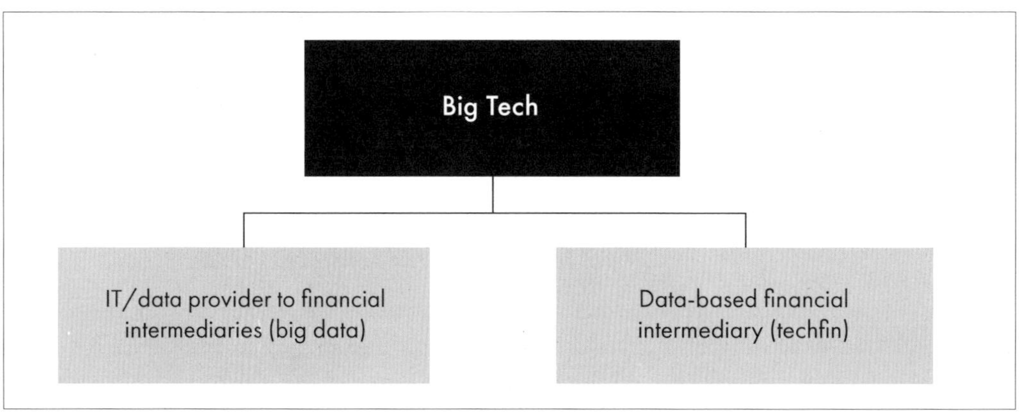

Source: Authors.

In the following sections we argue that big tech's involvement in finance pairs size with connectivity — a combination that creates sizable potential systemic risks. The lack of transparency and the potential to build up (further) size in financial services very rapidly complete the picture that regulatory action with regard to big tech should be on the regulators' agenda.

34 Current regulatory attention focuses on the systemic risk dimension of technology firms. The Bank for International Settlements/BCBS has entered into a global consultation, in particular, on the role of big tech. See BCBS, *supra* note 23 at 15.

35 BCBS, *supra* note 23 at 15.

36 Zetzsche et al, "From FinTech to TechFin", *supra* note 2.

Both big tech business models — be it third-party IT services (big data) or techfin-like provision of financial services — have the potential to create systemic risk, albeit in different ways.

Big Data

In the case of IT/data provision to financial intermediaries, the intermediaries are exposed to operational risks, and cyber risks in particular, from those third-party service providers. For instance, when Amazon's cloud computing data centre in Hong Kong failed, the website of the US Securities and Exchange Commission, as well as many consumer-oriented services, such as Netflix, went down.[37] We can also allocate here the development of large IT service platforms to which many financial intermediaries outsource core functions. For instance, Aladdin — the back office software platform developed by Blackrock, the world's largest asset manager[38] — is relied on by approximately 25,000 investment professionals[39] around the world and is used to manage approximately seven percent of the world's financial assets, including the assets of other top-10 asset managers.[40]

Financial supervision typically does not apply to the big data providers. IT/data providers usually fall outside the scope of financial regulation: financial regulators lack information regarding such firms and their potential roles in interconnectivity across the financial sector as well as tools of supervision or regulation.

Techfin

In contrast to fintechs, techfins — big tech firms entering into finance, often gradually over three stages[41] — are often very significant firms outside of financial services prior to stepping into the financial sector. Due to their scale, techfins are connected to many institutions from the moment they enter the financial services market, such as when the techfin functions as a conduit to licensed institutions. Moreover, due to their data power, techfins exercise influence over connected financial institutions from their moment of entry, and may often quickly control whole market segments when they finally provide regulated financial services.

The governance and disclosure frameworks for financial services are not designed to accommodate techfins: financial intermediaries should be experts in processing financial information so as to channel cash flows to their most efficient use, in terms of expected risk-to-return ratios. This paradigm is challenged by techfins. If techfins have better data than traditional financial institutions, techfins may provide the financial intermediary function more effectively. However, techfins, at least today, operate for the most part in an unregulated environment. Until rather late in their journey into financial services, at the point when they apply for a financial services licence, techfins will neither be subject to client/customer/investor protection rules nor subject

37 Elaine Ou, "Can't Stream Netflix? The Cloud May Be to Blame", *Bloomberg View* (3 March 2017), online: <www.bloomberg.com/view/articles/2017-03-02/can-t-stream-netflix-the-cloud-may-be-to-blame>.

38 See Aladdin by BlackRock, online: <www.blackrock.com/aladdin>.

39 See Aladdin Platform Overview, online: <www.blackrock.com/aladdin/offerings/aladdin-overview>.

40 "The monolith and the markets", *The Economist* (7 December 2013), online: <www.economist.com/briefing/2013/12/07/the-monolith-and-the-markets>.

41 Zetzsche et al, "From FinTech to TechFin", *supra* note 2.

to measures that ensure the functioning of financial markets and prevent the buildup of systemic risk.[42]

Moreover, from the perspective of incumbent licensed financial intermediaries, techfins provide unbalanced, and arguably unfair, competition. The fixed costs of an initial licence and the ongoing costs of supervision and related reviews by advisers (and so on) will mean licensed intermediaries bear higher costs than unlicensed ones. In the long run, licensed intermediaries are doomed to lose in such contests, given their higher cost base and limited flexibility to respond to competitive challenges. Such an uneven playing field clearly raises risks of regulatory arbitrage as well as unfair competition.

Risks arise from the potential for very rapid scaling in the techfin context, something we have previously highlighted in the context of the speed with which a firm or product can now move from "too small to care" to TBTF — a core feature of the fintech era that has emerged over the past decade.[43] For instance, Ant Financial runs a wealth management platform named Yu'e Bao. In its first 10 months of operation, Yu'e Bao[44] became the fourth-largest money market fund in the world, which led to a hasty response from Chinese regulators.[45] In April 2017, only four years after its creation, it assumed the top spot among all money market funds globally.[46] Alibaba's decision to separate Ant into a separate licensed financial services holding company — albeit under its continued control — by renaming its subsidiary Alipay in October 2014, was the direct result of regulators' fears over possible systemic risk arising from both Alipay and Yu'e Bao, resulting in China's decision to build a regulatory system to address fintech.[47] In a similar way, mobile money platforms such as M-Pesa have assumed systemic importance in some African countries,[48] as well as MercadoLibre (with payments and financial subsidiaries) and Russian financial platform provider Tinkoff in their respective home markets.

While arguably bringing important consumer benefits, the emergence of techfins highlights the emergence of large new firms that must be carefully considered from the standpoint of their potential risks, both from size as well as from interconnectivity and roles in providing systemically important infrastructure. But the result of trust and control over important market segments in financial services being in the hands of the few has led to major financial crises. One can highlight the examples of early-2000s accounting frauds[49] and of credit ratings agencies in

42 *Cf* Dirk Zetzsche, "Investment Law as Financial Law: From Fund Governance over Market Governance to Stakeholder Governance?" in Hanne S Birkmose, Mette Neville & Karsten Engsig Sørensen, eds, *The European Financial Market in Transition* (Alphen aan den Rijn, Netherlands: Kluwer Law International, 2012) 339.

43 Arner, Barberis & Buckley, *supra* note 12.

44 Jamil Anderlini, "Explosive Growth pushes Alibaba online fund up global rankings", *Financial Times* (10 March 2014), online: <www.ft.com/content/748a0cd8-a843-11e3-8ce1-00144feab7de>.

45 Zhou Weihuan, Douglas W Arner & Ross P Buckley, "Regulation of Digital Financial Services in China: Last Mover Advantage" (2015) 8 Tsinghua China L Rev 25.

46 See Yifan Xie & Chuin-Wei Yap, "Meet the Earth's Largest Money-Market Fund", *The Wall Street Journal* (13 September 2017), online: <www.wsj.com/articles/how-an-alibaba-spinoff-created-the-worlds-largest-money-market-fund-1505295000>.

47 *Ibid.*

48 See e.g. Kiarie Njoroge, "Report: This is What Would Happen to Kenya's Economy if M-Pesa was to Collapse", *Nairobi News* (30 November 2016), online: <http://nairobinews.nation.co.ke/news/treasury-report-reveals-fears-m-pesas-critical-role-economy/>; Frank Jacob, "The Role of M-Pesa in Kenya's Economic and Political Development" in *African Histories and Modernities* (London, UK: Palgrave MacMillan, 2016) 89.

49 See e.g. Sean Farrell, "The world's biggest accounting scandals", *The Guardian* (22 July 2015), online: <www.theguardian.com/business/2015/jul/21/the-worlds-biggest-accounting-scandals-toshiba-enron-olympus>; C William Thomas, "The Rise and Fall of Enron" (2002) 193:4 J Accountancy 41.

the 2008 crisis[50] in addition to the roles of SIFIs in many crises, not just the most recent.[51] Accounting firms and rating agencies are mere data providers linked to the system (similar to early stage techfins), while SIFIs are typically very large (like techfins that offer regulated services).[52] All three are strictly regulated today.[53]

Techfins are by no means risk free. Most importantly, without experience and monitoring, we simply do not know all the risks created by technology since information flow to financial regulators is not mandatory as long as techfins are beyond the scope of monitoring or supervision. We will only experience the outcome if the service is not performed properly, with often surprising results. This will be particularly so as artificial intelligence and machine learning (AI/ML) applications to large and/or novel data sets become more prevalent in financial services, but the underlying algorithms are very complex, almost opaque, and the behaviour of the self-learning algorithm becomes impossible to predict. Further, we lack experience with AI/ML-based pricing models over a full business cycle.

If financial law does not apply, potential systemic risk may build up unobserved, unmitigated and uncontrolled, and, looking longer-term, the next global financial crisis may well come from techfins rather than authorized financial institutions.

Addressing Big Tech and Techfin Systemic Risk

Big Data: Diversification as Second-best Solution

Financial law usually responds to risks created by non-supervised firms by imposing strict outsourcing requirements on financial firms. In particular, the financial firm needs to ensure systemic stability at all times, regardless of the outsourcing of IT. But how should a bank (even JP Morgan or Goldman Sachs) ensure that a major tech company (for example, Amazon, Apple, Google or Microsoft) provides appropriate service? Banks cannot police firms whose market value is a multiple of that of their own (if worse came to worst, Apple could buy Deutsche Bank with its pocket cash), nor can they apply controls that ensure that big tech's cloud centres work. In the end, financial intermediaries need to trust big tech.

The alternative to control over the service provider is diversification. For instance, financial law could require that any financial firm must have mirror cloud servers at three different providers, and that these providers be unrelated to each other. While mandatory diversification ensures some additional security and also has some positive effects on market structure in the provider market, it also comes with increased costs and other problems.

The first other problem is cyber security. The more providers hold the intermediaries' financial data, the greater is the risk of data corruption (stealing, manipulation or abuse) from the inside or a cyber attack from the outside. Second, mandatory diversification of data streams and server space takes away some of the benefits of datafication. It slows down IT processes and creates

50 Amanda J Bahena, "What Role Did Credit Rating Agencies Play in the Credit Crisis?" (March 2010).

51 Financial System Inquiry, "Too-big-to-fail and moral hazard" (7 December 2014), online: <http://fsi.gov.au/publications/interim-report/05-stability/too-big-to-fail/>.

52 Mustafa Yuksel, "Identifying Global Systemically Important Financial Institutions" (2014) Reserve Bank of Australia, online: <www.rba.gov.au/publications/bulletin/2014/dec/pdf/bu-1214-8.pdf>.

53 See e.g. Siegfried Utzig, "The Financial Crisis and the Regulation of Credit Rating Agencies: A European Banking Perspective" (2010) Asian Development Bank Institute Working Paper No 188.

risk of confusion: if data is stored on a blockchain comprising many different cloud providers, the storing of data on a blockchain itself costs time. If a brokerage system runs on three different data streams simultaneously, and one of the streams shows different data from the other two, which of the three data sets is correct, and on which should the broker base a multi-billion-dollar transaction? These risks are exacerbated by the fact that the market for cloud storage and related analytics as well as data provision for financial markets is highly concentrated.[54] Financial intermediaries have little choice and cyber attacks have easy targets.

Techfin: Regulate Data Analytics

While the cause of systemic risk in the case of big techs is connectivity (and that connectivity could be diversified away, at some cost), the systemic risk perspective of techfins rests on the assumption of size and connectivity, so diversification does not help.

At the core of our concern is the techfin's conduit function in their early stage: they stand between the financial intermediary and its clients. One could respond that the early stage techfin conduit function is merely one of data delivery, and data delivery is not a special activity warranting regulation.

Yet data provision in a highly concentrated market has prompted regulators to require financial institutions to diversify their data sources. The difference with techfins is that data delivery is a back-end function, while techfins also provide front-end, overlay services to the financial institutions, framed as financial ecosystem or platform technology. Techfins' conduit function cannot be addressed by diversification requirements since the financial institution cannot as readily change the "service provider" as it can a back-end relationship — terminating the cooperation with the techfin would cost the financial institution the link to its most precious asset: its clients.

For that reason we have proposed elsewhere to regulate data gathering and analytics by virtue of a moderate regulatory intervention, along the business evolution from "too small to care" to "too large to ignore," and then to TBTF.[55]

As techfins often do not seek access to client funds directly, many established financial regulatory thresholds based on balance sheet size, exposures or assets under management will fail to be triggered. In order to set appropriate thresholds, regulators must develop new criteria. These could include an overall number of data points, or holding data on a significant share of a population in the reference market, as both figures reflect a substantial data set.

If financial data gathering and analytics becomes a regulated activity, systemic risk measures will apply as soon as techfins become essential to financial stability, and this will be determined by the TBTF or TCTF tests. If the techfin is the main client channel for one important bank of systemic importance (or for many banks that together are of systemic importance), the importance of the techfin becomes like that of a new CEO or a new business model rather than infrastructure. To the same extent that a new bank CEO and other key staff would be subject to regulatory scrutiny, we would ask the techfin to meet the "fit and proper" requirement, and

54 See Zetzsche et al, "From FinTech to TechFin", *supra* note 2 at 31.

55 *Ibid.*

ask for adequate resources to maintain that function on the side of the techfin. This is where the systemic risk perspective indicates a case for regulation of techfins.

Once regulators come to the conclusion that a techfin is of systemic importance — for instance, once techfin data is essential for a SIFI, or the techfin provides the main client access for several financial institutions that together are of systemic significance — we recommend measures to control and limit systemic risk. In the first case, this could require the SIFI to diversify its data sources. In the second case, we recommend the following options. First, structural requirements could be imposed on techfins, including quarantine provisions as to the "fin" portion of the techfin's business; minimum capital for maintenance and clean-up; and country-by-country or market-by-market segregation of activities. Second, regulators could be empowered to shut down the activity, while preserving customer data. Finally, regulators could be empowered to appoint a commissioner to run the quarantined techfin part of the business in the public interest. As part of the resolution scheme, regulators will need to know how to ensure access to essential facilities in the event of a crisis. In the case of data-driven business models, such as those of techfins, the resolution plan must lay out how continued access to data is assured even if the financial business is bankrupt. Because continued data access is central to the viability of the firm, and the techfin arm of a big data firm will often not own the data it is using, we would prefer data-intensive financial firms to have licensing contracts with their data providers (be they other members of the corporate group or external entities) that ensure business continuity (i.e., further data feeds) even if the financial firm itself is insolvent for a period of time.

Systemic risk intervention could even go one step further. Since running a crucial data provider in the public interest is not a long-term solution, mandating an open data policy under certain circumstances (as a specific systemic risk measure for data-driven financial services) may reduce the need for additional regulatory intervention over the long term. Note that in contrast to open banking proponents, we do not argue for open data policies in all cases, but only as a specific crisis measure imposed on very large data-driven financial services firms.

The New Risk Paradigm: IT and Model Risk as Drivers of Systemic Risk

Even if policy makers and regulators follow our recommendations, one thing does not change and cannot be changed: the dependence on technology and the exposure to tech failures. At the same time, financial risks have not been reduced. Cyber risks, data risks, technological risks and financial risks add up. Digitization/datafication, cyber security and TBTF/TCTF considerations together create a world where the financial system is more vulnerable than before.

Within categories of operational risk, cyber security and technology risk have become more pressing than traditional financial risks. More so than market developments, technology risk functions as a new driver of instability, and regulators are well advised to focus on this new risk category.

How can regulators respond to this new reality? The deficiencies in the regulatory system with regard to global technology risks are similar to those that existed with regard to other new forms of systemic risk prior to the GFC. Those deficiencies include loopholes in regulation, lack of coordination among regulators, information asymmetry, lack of expertise on the side of financial intermediaries and regulators, and lack of awareness or investment on the side of intermediaries.

We encourage a new risk agenda that responds to global technology risks proactively. Such an agenda must include, from a regulatory perspective, five steps.

First, regulators must **prioritize technology risks**, and this prioritization must take place both internally and externally. The result of this prioritization is that technology risks play an equally important role as financial risks. This is particularly important in the context of monitoring these new sorts of risk and collecting non-traditional forms of information. This could be done by appointing a chief technology risk officer (CTRO) for the supervisory authority or creating a similar role at the board level in order to emphasize the significance of these sorts of risks. At the same time, financial intermediaries should be required to appoint CTROs (or equivalent senior management officers) as a main contact point responsible for cyber and technology risk, with board monitoring, perhaps in the context of the firm's risk committee. Further, the CTRO's report on cyber risk should be a core agenda item at all meetings of the authority's as well as the intermediary's senior management.

Second, regulators need to **strengthen in-house tech expertise** to understand the new vulnerabilities of the ecosystems they monitor and supervise, and to be able to discuss tech matters with intermediaries. We encourage, in particular, consultation with tech councils and tech expert groups at global policy bodies such as the FSB, the International Organization of Securities Commissions and others.

Third, regulators must continue to **enhance reporting requirements** with regard to details on the intermediaries' technology risk management strategies and the budget invested into and human resources devoted to system stability and cyber security. These reports should include technology details, and should be read by the supervisor's technology department.

Fourth, regulators must prioritize these sorts of risks in the context of both **on-site and off-site supervision** to understand whether intermediaries have understood the risks and how to address them. When they visit, regulators need to speak to tech people rather than upper management or the legal department. Of course, on the authorities' side, technology and regulatory experts should be present as well.

Fifth, regulators will have to **make use of new technologies themselves**, since only the user understands the issues with the application. This can be part of a major regtech strategy — which in many instances is overdue anyway — in order to respond to the enormous data streams regulators receive in response to GFC-related additional reporting requirements. We admit that regulators may at times suffer from the failures of technology, but if they do they will also learn to handle large tech projects — and know what they have to ask for from their intermediaries.

The world has become riskier, with technology risk being a prime driver as a result of fintech. The new technology risk will translate into financial risk sooner or later. A regulatory system that waits until financial risks have materialized as long-term impacts of technology risk has missed its task. Regulators need to face the unknown rather than fear it, and develop a degree of tech expertise matched only by the large — yet entirely unregulated — data-driven firms.

5

Regulating Systemic Risk in the EU Financial Sector

DANNY BUSCH AND MIRIK VAN RIJN

This chapter[1] seeks to contribute to the discussion on the development within the European Union of a regulatory regime that adequately addresses and mitigates the risk to financial stability posed by non-bank systemically important financial institutions (SIFIs). The first part of the chapter highlights the relevance of the problem by reiterating lessons learned from the global financial crisis (GFC), especially in respect of the systemic risk posed by non-bank financial institutions. The next three parts consider the existing body of EU financial regulation. We assess what has already been accomplished since the GFC and provide context to our proposed regime of non-bank SIFI supervision and resolution. The fifth part makes suggestions and explores legal possibilities for enhancing the existing body of EU financial regulation by including designation, supervision and resolution of non-bank SIFIs at the European level. The sixth part contains our concluding remarks.

1 This chapter was completed on August 24, 2018. No account could be taken of developments since that date. This chapter is based, in part, on the authors' article, "Towards Single Supervision and Resolution of Systemically Important Non-Bank Financial Institutions in the European Union" (2018) European Business Organization L Rev 301.

Systemic Risk

The GFC painfully demonstrated deficiencies in the regulation, supervision and resolution of financial institutions, not only in the traditional banking sector but also in other parts of the financial system. Indeed, systemic risk manifested itself to a large degree outside the traditional banking sector, especially in the lightly regulated shadow banking sector. The latter refers, quite ominously, to market-based credit intermediation outside the banking sector. Due to a lack of comprehensive regulation and supervision, banks increasingly shifted activities to the shadow banking sector in order to avoid tax, disclosure and capital requirements.[2] Such behaviour, which is designed to evade more stringent regulation and supervision or to evade regulation and supervision altogether, is known as regulatory arbitrage. The exploitation of regulatory gaps, however, creates risks to financial stability and undermines the notion of a level playing field.

To strengthen financial stability, we propose that non-bank financial institutions that are systemically relevant should be subjected to European prudential regulation and to a European supervisor and a European resolution authority.

Our proposals exclude banks that are already subject to stricter prudential regulation and, within the member states participating in the European Banking Union (EBU), are subject to the Single Supervisory Mechanism (SSM) and the Single Resolution Mechanism (SRM). Within the SSM, significant banks are directly supervised by the European Central Bank (ECB) and resolved by the Single Resolution Board (SRB).[3]

In accordance with the approach of the Financial Stability Board (FSB)[4] and the US Dodd-Frank reforms,[5] we advocate that the European Union's sectoral approach to financial regulation, supervision and resolution be complemented by a more risk-based identification, regulation, supervision and resolution of non-bank SIFIs. Any non-bank financial institution[6] that could pose a threat to financial stability — referred to as non-bank SIFIs — should therefore be subject to commensurate supervision, regulation and resolution, regardless of the legal categorization of the non-bank financial institution.[7] This would entail partial reform and extension of supervision, regulation and resolution of financial institutions in the European Union, which is presently organized largely along sectoral lines, and a move toward a more pan-sectoral regime for non-bank SIFIs. A cross-sectoral supervisory and resolution regime for non-bank SIFIs would correspond with the increasingly blurred distinction between markets,

2 See e.g. Tobias Adrian, Adam B Ashcraft & Nicola Cetorelli, "Shadow Bank Monitoring" in Allen N Berger, Philip Molyneux & John OS Wilson, eds, *The Oxford Handbook of Banking*, 2nd ed (Oxford, UK: Oxford University Press, 2015) 378 at 392.

3 As regards the EBU, see e.g. Danny Busch & Guido Ferrarini, eds, *European Banking Union* (Oxford, UK: Oxford University Press, 2015).

4 FSB, "Policy Measures to Address Systemically Important Financial Institutions" (4 November 2011) at para 3 [FSB, "Policy Measures"], online: <www.fsb.org/wp-content/uploads/Policy-Measures-to-Address-Systemically-Important-Financial-Institutions.pdf>.

5 12 USC § 5323.

6 "Financial institution" should be understood as a broad term encapsulating all financial sector entities.

7 The FSB defines SIFIs as "financial institutions whose distress or disorderly failure, because of their size, complexity and systemic interconnectedness, would cause significant disruption to the wider financial system and economic activity." See FSB, "Policy Measures", *supra* note 4 at para 3.

financial institutions and products.[8] It would also help to reduce regulatory arbitrage activities and gaps in coverage, as it would ensure that the risks posed by a non-bank SIFI are subject to commensurate regulation, regardless of the legal form of the entity. In order to properly identify non-bank SIFIs, robust monitoring of the entire European financial sector is necessary.

The proposed regime is in line with financial reform proposals issued by the FSB, which call for a level of supervision proportionate to the potential destabilization risk that a financial firm poses to the financial system.[9] Additionally, the FSB requires an effective resolution regime for all financial institutions that could be systemically significant or critical if they fail.[10]

For the development of such a regime, we draw on the aspirations and initial experience of the United States. Although the Trump administration intends to reverse the course of US financial regulation, non-bank financial companies have, in the past, been designated as systemically important.[11] Such designation puts them under federal supervision and, reflecting their importance to the financial system, makes them subject to specific prudential and living will requirements. Additionally, non-bank financial institutions posing a systemic risk may be subjected to a specialized resolution regime.

The GFC highlighted a number of structural weaknesses in the worldwide financial system and economies. One of the most important lessons was the generally unforeseen possibility of systemic risk originating from non-bank financial institutions.

Systemic risk is the risk that a regional, national or global financial system will break down.[12] Systemic risks manifest themselves where a localized shock — such as the failure of a financial institution — has repercussions that adversely affect the broader economy.[13] It thus poses a threat to financial stability.[14] Systemic risk can manifest itself in many different forms and within a range of financial institutions. As noted by Iman Anabtawi and Steven L. Schwarcz, systemic risks do not distinguish between financial market participants.[15] Systemic risk should therefore

8 Eilís Ferran, "Institutional Design: The Choices for National Systems" in Niamh Moloney, Eilís Ferran & Jennifer Payne, eds, *The Oxford Handbook of Financial Regulation* (Oxford, UK: Oxford University Press, 2015) 97; Robin Hui Huang & Dirk Schoenmaker, eds, *Institutional Structure of Financial Regulation: Theories and International Experiences* (Abingdon, UK: Routledge, 2014).

9 FSB, "Progress and Next Steps Towards Ending 'Too-Big-To-Fail' (TBTF)", Report of the Financial Stability Board to the G-20 (2013) at 18, online: <www.fsb.org/wp-content/uploads/r_130902.pdf>.

10 FSB, *Key Attributes of Effective Resolution Regimes for Financial Institutions* (October 2011), online: <www.fsb.org/wp-content/uploads/r_111104cc.pdf>.

11 The Financial Stability Oversight Council (FSOC) designated American International Group (AIG), General Electric Capital Corporation, Prudential Financial and MetLife to be non-bank financial companies whose material financial distress could pose a threat to US financial stability. Changes in the business of GE Capital Global Holdings (successor to General Electric Capital Corporation), AIG and Prudential Financial subsequently led FSOC to rescind their designations in, respectively, 2016, 2017 and 2018. MetLife successfully appealed its designation at the Federal District Court for the District of Columbia. The US Court of Appeal dismissed the appeal on January 23, 2018, on a motion to this effect filed jointly by MetLife and FSOC. See *MetLife, Inc v Financial Stability Oversight Council, CA No 15-0045 (DDC 2016)*.

12 Hal S Scott, "Reducing Systemic Risk Through the Reform of Capital Regulation" (2010) 13:3 J Intl Econ L 763 at 764.

13 Iman Anabtawi & Steven L Schwarcz, "Regulating Systemic Risk: Towards an Analytical Framework" (2011) 86:4 Notre Dame L Rev 1349 at 1351.

14 Rosa Lastra, "Systemic risk & Macro-prudential supervision" in Moloney, Ferran & Payne, *supra* note 8 at 312.

15 Anabtawi & Schwarcz, *supra* note 13, n 10.

be regarded as an elusive concept, not confined to certain institutions, markets or products.[16] Accordingly, financial regulation should have an equally flexible and open scope.

Despite the regulatory focus, it turned out that systemic risk was not confined to the (retail) banking sector. Non-bank financial institutions such as Long-Term Capital Management, American International Group (AIG) and Reserve Primary proved equally capable of creating systemic risk. This realization is reflected in the European Systemic Risk Board Regulation, which acknowledges that all types of financial intermediaries, markets and infrastructure may potentially be systemically important to some degree.[17] Asset management activities are another example of a potential source of non-bank systemic risk that has recently attracted attention.[18]

The European Commission's proposal for the establishment of a Capital Markets Union (CMU) is also of interest, as the envisaged growth of non-bank credit intermediation makes overarching checks on systemic risks even more pressing.[19] Designed to increase the supply of alternative sources of financing — thereby reducing dependence on funding through the banking sector — the CMU proposal looks to increase the role of non-bank financial intermediaries.[20] Such diversification of funding improves the allocation of capital and diversification of risk, and thereby strengthens the European financial system. At the same time, as recognized by the "Five Presidents' Report," closer integration of capital markets and gradual removal of remaining national barriers necessitates an expansion and strengthening of the available tools to manage financial players' systemic risks prudently (macroprudential tool kit) and to strengthen the supervisory framework to ensure the solidity of all financial actors.[21] This should, according to the report, ultimately lead to a single European capital markets supervisor.[22]

This shows that systemic risk can occur in different sectors, or indeed across different sectors, and have a variety of distinct characteristics; therefore, it might be difficult to identify such risks. It is therefore of great importance for jurisdictions to have a broad monitoring system in place, capable of identifying systemic risk throughout the entire financial sector.

16 Indeed, the creation of suitable regulation of markets and financial products — for example, by increasing market transparency and through product approval processes — is essential for the safeguarding of financial stability. However, this chapter focuses mainly on the regulation of entities, specifically non-bank SIFIs.

17 *Regulation (EU) No 1092/2010 of the European Parliament and of the Council of 24 November 2010 on European Union macro-prudential oversight of the financial system and establishing a European Systemic Risk Board*, [2010] OJ, L 331/1, art 2(c) [*ESRB Regulation*].

18 See FSB, *Policy Recommendations to Address Structural Vulnerabilities from Asset Management Activities* (12 January 2017), online: <www.fsb.org/wp-content/uploads/FSB-Policy-Recommendations-on-Asset-Management-Structural-Vulnerabilities.pdf>; Nicola Doyle et al, "Shadow banking in the euro area: risks and vulnerabilities in the investment fund sector" (2016) European Central Bank Occasional Paper Series No 174, online: <www.ecb.europa.eu/pub/pdf/scpops/ecbop174.en.pdf>.

19 See also Nicolas Véron & Guntram B Wolff, "Capital Markets Union: A Vision for the Long Term" (2016) 2:1 J Financial Regulation 130; Kern Alexander, "Capital Markets Union from the perspective of the banking industry and prudential supervision" (2015) 9:3 L & Financial Markets Rev 191.

20 EC, "Building a Capital Markets Union" (2015) Green Paper, COM(2015) 63 final.

21 Jean-Claude Juncker et al, *Completing Europe's Economic and Monetary Union* (2015) at 12, online: <www.ecb.europa.eu/pub/pdf/other/5presidentsreport.en.pdf>.

22 *Ibid*. For discussion on ESMA as a single European capital markets supervisor, see Emilios Avgouleas & Guido Ferrarini, "A single listing authority and securities regulator for the CMU and the future of ESMA" in Danny Busch, Emilios Avgouleas & Guido Ferrarini, eds, *Capital Markets Union in Europe* (Oxford, UK: Oxford University Press) 55. For discussion on the CMU in a general sense, see Busch, Avgouleas & Ferrarini (*ibid*); Danny Busch, "A Capital Markets Union for a Divided Europe" (2017) 3:2 J Financial Regulation 262.

Sectoral Reform in the European Union

In the European Union, the policy response to the GFC and the European sovereign debt crisis has remained organized largely along sectoral lines.

The EBU

The most notable reform has been the creation of the EBU, which entailed an extensive overhaul and transfer of bank supervision and resolution to the EU level, respectively to the ECB and the SRB.[23] However, since the focus of this contribution is on non-bank financial institutions, precisely because banks are already subject to stricter prudential regulation, we will not engage in a detailed discussion of the EBU.[24] It will suffice to conclude here that although the EBU is an ambitious and vigorous overhaul of banking supervision in the euro zone, it risks being inflexible and setting a non-future-proof regulatory perimeter due to the rigid scope of its application to banks.[25]

Besides the EBU, the European legislators have adopted numerous reform measures for the financial sector. These can largely be divided into regulation, either of markets or financial institutions, and supervisory infrastructure. Both are organized mainly along sectoral lines. Many of the regulatory reforms have, at least partially, a financial stability objective. This reduces the potential for regulatory arbitrage, at least with regard to the applicable entities.

Investment Funds

For instance, investment funds are subject to increased regulation under the Undertakings for Collective Investment in Transferable Securities (UCITS) Directive[26] or the Alternative Investment Fund Managers Directive (AIFMD).[27] Both directives have the effect of reducing liquidity risks in investment funds. The UCITS Directive requires investment funds to hold liquid assets only. Alternative investment funds (AIFs), other than unleveraged, closed-ended AIFs, must employ appropriate liquidity management and monitoring procedures for liquidity risks.[28] The liquidity profile of the investments must comply with the AIF's underlying obligations.

23 For a detailed discussion of the EBU, see e.g. Busch & Ferrarini, *supra* note 3.

24 *Ibid.*

25 A small reservation to this conclusion is in order, as the scope of the EBU does extend to certain non-bank entities and groups. The SSM also captures parent undertakings that are a financial holding or mixed financial holding company. The resolution mechanism also extends to 730,000 investment firms and financial institutions that are covered by the consolidated supervision of the parent undertaking by the ECB.

26 See *Directive 2009/65/EC of the European Parliament and of the Council of 13 July 2009 on the coordination of laws, regulations and administrative provisions relating to undertakings for collective investment in transferable securities*, [2009] OJ, L 302, arts 1, 3(b) [*UCITS Directive*].

27 See *Directive 2011/61/EU of the European Parliament and of the Council of 8 June 2011 on Alternative Investment Fund Managers and amending Directives 2003/41/EC and 2009/65/EC and Regulations (EC) No 1060/2009 and (EU) No 1095/2010*, [2011] OJ, L 174, art 4(a) [*AIFMD Directive*]. For a detailed discussion of the AIFMD, see Lodewijk Van Setten & Danny Busch, eds, *Alternative Investment Funds in Europe* (Oxford, UK: Oxford University Press, 2014); Dirk Zetzsche, ed, *The Alternative Investment Fund Managers Directive: European Regulation of Investment Funds*, 2nd ed (Alphen aan den Rijn, Netherlands: Kluwer Law International, 2015).

28 *AIFMD Directive*, *supra* note 27, art 16.

The UCITS Directive places direct restrictions on the use of leverage. A UCITS may only borrow up to 10 percent of its assets.[29] Additionally, synthetic leverage, which is acquired through derivatives and securities lending and measured in "global exposure," must not exceed the fund's total net asset value.[30] The AIFMD, in contrast, does not provide regulatory limits on the amount of leverage. Instead, the AIFM has to demonstrate that leverage limits set by it, for each AIF it manages, are reasonable and that it complies with them at all times. National authorities are competent to impose leverage limits on an AIF in its jurisdiction where they deem this necessary in order to ensure the stability and integrity of the financial system.[31] Furthermore, additional regulation is applicable to money-market funds to preserve the integrity and stability of the internal market.[32]

Insurance Sector

With regard to the insurance sector, the EU legislator adopted the Solvency II Directive, harmonizing EU insurance regulation.[33] The Solvency II Directive requires member states to ensure that their supervisory authorities can protect policyholders and, second, to contribute to the stability of the financial system as a whole.[34] Solvency II therefore requires insurers and regulators to take account of the asset-side risks, as capital needs to be held against market risks.

Over-the-counter Derivatives Clearing

A third example with an obvious financial stability objective is the European Market Infrastructure Regulation (EMIR).[35] EMIR is a centrepiece of the legislation introduced in the wake of the financial crisis to make financial markets safer and more transparent. A key pillar of EMIR is the requirement for standardized over-the-counter (OTC) derivatives contracts to be cleared through a central counterparty (CCP).[36] A CCP is a market infrastructure that reduces systemic risk and enhances financial stability by standing between the two counterparties to a derivatives contract (i.e., acting as buyer to the seller of risk, and seller to the buyer of risk) and thereby reducing the risk for both.[37] EMIR also introduced strict prudential, organizational and business conduct requirements for CCPs and established arrangements for their prudential supervision to minimize any risk to users of a CCP and to underpin systemic stability.[38]

29 *UCITS Directive, supra* note 26, art 83.

30 *Ibid*, art 51(3).

31 *AIFMD Directive, supra* note 27, art 25(3).

32 See *Regulation (EU) 2017/1131 of the European Parliament and of the Council of 14 June 2017 on money market funds*, [2017] OJ, L 169.

33 *Directive 2009/138/EC of the European Parliament and of the Council of 25 November 2009 on the taking-up and pursuit of the business of Insurance and Reinsurance*, [2009] OJ, L 335 [*Solvency II Directive*].

34 Michelle Everson, "Regulating the Insurance Sector" in Moloney, Ferran & Payne, *supra* note 8 at 433.

35 *Regulation (EU) 648/2012 of the European Parliament and of the Council of 4 July 2012 on OTC derivatives, central counterparties and trade repositories*, [2012] OJ, L 201 at 1–59 [*EMIR*].

36 *Ibid*, arts 4, 5 (for discussion on the clearing obligation).

37 Steven L Schwarcz, "Central Clearing of Financial Contracts: Theory and Regulatory Implications", 167:6 U Pa L Rev [forthcoming in 2019], online: <https://ssrn.com/abstract=3104079>. For the definition of CCP, see *EMIR, supra* note 35, art 2(1).

38 See *EMIR, supra* note 35, arts 16, 40–50 (prudential requirements), 26–39 (organizational and business conduct requirements).

Assessment

However, notwithstanding the increase in sector regulation, the potential for regulatory arbitrage remains. The ESRB, for instance, notes in its 2017 shadow banking report that hedge funds should be closely monitored, as they are not subject to leverage limits if regulated under the AIFMD.[39] More importantly, such an approach to financial regulation remains calibrated on "form over function"; in other words, the legal label of a financial institution is decisive for the applicable regulation and supervisor. In consequence, new financial market participants (for example, fintech entities) or formally different institutions performing similar activities may fall into regulatory gaps, thus creating systemic risk.[40]

The European Supervisory Agencies

Sectoral Approach

From a financial stability perspective, it is important to note that the institutional supervisory structure provided at the EU level mimics the sectoral approach in EU regulation. The European Supervisory Authorities (ESAs) were created in 2010 and consist of the European Banking Authority (EBA), the European Securities and Markets Authority (ESMA), and the European Insurance and Occupational Pensions Authority (EIOPA).[41] The ESAs are primarily responsible for drafting the binding technical standards and non-binding guidelines and recommendations that constitute, along with EU directives and regulations, the Single Rulebook that applies to their respective financial sectors.

Few Direct Supervisory Powers

Referring to the ESAs as supervisors is slightly misleading, as they mainly assist the European Commission in law making. Of the three ESAs, only ESMA currently has direct supervisory powers, namely over credit rating agencies (CRAs) and trade repositories (TRs), otherwise the national supervisors are still competent — except for significant banks in the euro zone where the ECB is in charge (see section above entitled "Systemic Risk"). Furthermore, the Commission recently proposed to grant ESMA additional direct supervisory powers with respect to data reporting services providers, approval of certain prospectuses, certain harmonized collective investment funds and benchmarks.

39 ESRB, *EU Shadow Banking Monitor* (May 2017) at 18, online: <www.esrb.europa.eu/pub/pdf/reports/20170529_shadow_banking_report.en.pdf>. For a discussion of the macroprudential elements and gaps in existing EU regulation, see ESRB, *Macroprudential policy beyond banking: an ESRB strategy paper* (July 2016), online: <www.esrb.europa.eu/pub/pdf/reports/20160718_strategy_paper_beyond_banking.en.pdf>.

40 See e.g. ESMA, "Opinion: Key principles for a European framework on loan origination by funds", ESMA/2016/596 (11 April 2016).

41 See *Regulation (EU) No 1095/2010 of the European Parliament and of the Council of 24 November 2010 establishing a European Supervisory Authority (European Securities and Markets Authority), amending Decision No 716/2009/EC and repealing Commission Decision 2009/77/EC*, [2010] OJ, L 331 [*ESMA Regulation*]; *Regulation (EU) No 1093/2010 of the European Parliament and of the Council of 24 November 2010 establishing a European Supervisory Authority (European Banking Authority), amending Decision No 716/2009/EC and repealing Commission Decision 2009/78/EC*, [2010] OJ, L 331 [*EBA Regulation*]; *Regulation (EU) No 1094/2010 of the European Parliament and of the Council of 24 November 2010 establishing a European Supervisory Authority (European Insurance and Occupational Pensions Authority), amending Decision No 716/2009/EC and repealing Commission Decision 2009/79/EC*, [2010] OJ, L 331 [*EIOPA Regulation*] at 48–83.

European Personal Pension Product Providers

In addition, in its proposal of June 29, 2017, the Commission proposed to introduce a pan-European Personal Pension Product (PEPP). PEPP providers will be supervised by the national competent supervisors, but a PEPP may only be manufactured and distributed in the European Union where it has been authorized by EIOPA.[42]

Crowdfunding Service Providers

Furthermore, there is the March 2018 Commission proposal for a Regulation on European Crowdfunding Service Providers for Business.[43] The proposal seeks to establish uniform rules on crowdfunding at the EU level. It does not replace national rules on crowdfunding where they exist. A crowdfunding service provider can choose to either provide or continue providing services on a domestic basis under applicable national law (including where a member state chooses to apply the Markets in Financial Instruments Directive II to crowdfunding activities), or seek authorization to provide crowdfunding services under the proposed regulation.

In the latter case, authorization allows crowdfunding service providers to provide crowdfunding services under a passport across all member states; a legal person that intends to provide crowdfunding services shall apply to ESMA for authorization as a crowdfunding service provider; and crowdfunding service providers shall provide their services under the supervision of ESMA. Note that the regulation does not apply to crowdfunding services that are provided by project owners that are consumers. But the persons at the other end (i.e., those who grant loans or acquire transferable securities through a crowdfunding platform [investors]) are also captured by the regulation if they are consumers.

OTC Derivatives Clearing

Last, but certainly not least, the Commission's proposal of June 13, 2017, is noteworthy. It proposes amendments to the EMIR and the ESMA Regulation, with a view to regulating and supervising the systemic risk posed by CCPs and strengthening the role of ESMA.[44] In order to avoid risks of regulatory and supervisory arbitrage, the "CCP executive session" — established within ESMA — will be responsible for a more coherent and consistent supervision of CCPs. To this effect, ESMA may determine a third-country CCP to be systemically important, thereby subjecting it to stricter requirements. Acting on a recommendation from ESMA, the Commission may also determine a third-country CCP to be substantially systemically important. Subsequent to such a determination, the Commission may declare that the CCP may provide services in the European Union only if it is authorized in the European Union.[45]

42 EC, *Proposal for a Regulation of the European Parliament and of the Council on a pan-European Personal Pension Product (PEPP),* COM(2017) 343 final (29 June 2017).

43 EC, *Proposal for a Regulation of the European Parliament and of the Council on European Crowdfunding Service Providers (ECSP) for Business,* COM(2018) 113 final (8 March 2018); EC, *Proposal for a Directive of the European Parliament and of the Council amending Directive 2014/65/EU on markets in financial instruments,* COM(2018) 99 final (8 March 2018).

44 EC, *Proposal for a Regulation of the European Parliament and of the Council amending Regulation (EU) No 1095/2010 establishing a European Supervisory Authority (European Securities and Markets Authority) and amending Regulation (EU) No 648/2012 as regards the procedures and authorities involved for the authorisation of CCPs and requirements for the recognition of third-country CCPs,* COM(2017) 331 final (13 June 2017).

45 See in more detail Danny Busch, "A Stronger Role for the European Supervisory Authorities in the EU27" in Busch, Avgouleas & Ferrarini, *supra* note 22.

The determination of systemic importance of CCPs by ESMA shows clear parallels with our proposed non-bank SIFI determination.

Assessment

Two elements in the makeup of the ESAs stand out. First, despite some coordination efforts, it is based on a sectoral approach to supervision.[46] As sectoral lines increasingly blur and new institutions outside the traditional institutional regulatory perimeter perform equivalent activities, an institutionally based layout of the supervisory organization may risk regulatory gaps. An institutional approach to financial regulation and supervision encourages regulatory arbitrage. It is therefore of critical importance that an institutional approach to financial regulation is supplemented by the existence of an authority with robust, financial sector-wide monitoring powers and, if deemed necessary, the power to pull non-bank SIFIs inside a suitable regulatory and supervisory perimeter. As discussed in the following section, the European Systemic Risk Board (ESRB) is responsible for monitoring the financial system within the European Union and identifying systemic risk. Its powers, however, are rather limited.

A second important element in the functioning of the ESAs is their limited powers of direct prudential supervision of financial institutions.[47] Instead, national authorities are responsible for day-to-day prudential supervision. Systemically important institutions expand, however, across many jurisdictions. Much the same arguments that underpin the creation of direct ECB supervision over significant banks therefore apply also to non-bank SIFIs. This line of reasoning is now familiar, for example, because a European authority is better placed to ensure a smooth and sound overview of the entire non-bank SIFI and its overall health, and would reduce the risk of different interpretations and contradictory decisions at the level of the individual entity, thereby enhancing market integration. In our proposal, designated non-bank SIFIs, like significant banks, should therefore be placed under direct prudential supervision by an EU authority. The intended reforms of the ESAs may therefore provide a connection with our proposal. They illustrate a developing inclination to endow the ESAs with more direct supervisory powers. Supervision of designated non-bank SIFIs by the most relevant ESA, as determined by the nature and activities of the non-bank SIFI, is in line with these developments.

The ESRB

Created in November 2010, the ESRB[48] is tasked with exercising "macroprudential oversight of the financial system within the Union, in order to contribute to the prevention or mitigation of systemic risks to financial stability in the Union."[49] Its oversight has a broad scope, as the ESRB Regulation recognizes that all types of financial intermediaries, markets and infrastructure may potentially be systemically important to some degree.[50] Macroprudential supervision

46 See also Dan Awrey, "Law, Financial Instability, and the Institutional Structure of Financial Regulation" in Anita Anand, ed, *Systemic Risk, Institutional Design, and the Regulation of Financial Markets* (Oxford, UK: Oxford University Press, 2016) 61 at 86.

47 As stated, only ESMA performs direct supervision, namely of CRAs and TRs.

48 *Regulation (EU) No 1092/2010 of the European Parliament and of the Council of 24 November 2010 on European Union macro-prudential oversight of the financial system and establishing a European Systemic Risk Board*, [2010] OJ, L 331 [*ESRB Regulation*].

49 *Ibid*, art 3(1).

50 *Ibid*, art 2(c).

focuses on systemic risks arising from the common exposure of many financial institutions to the same risk factors. In other words, whereas microprudential supervision focuses on the "tree," macroprudential supervision is all about the "forest."[51] In accordance with its macroprudential tasks, the ESRB monitors and assesses risks and, if necessary, adopts warnings and recommendations.

Pursuant to its monitoring tasks, the ESRB may request information from the European System of Central Banks, the ESAs, the national supervisory authorities or the national statistics authorities. If information remains unavailable, the ESRB may request it from the member states.[52]

When the ESRB identifies significant risks to financial stability, it must provide warnings and, where appropriate, issue recommendations for remedial action.[53] As the ESRB has no formal legal powers, its warnings and recommendations are non-binding, but they are subject to a "comply or explain" procedure.

All in all, and although highly reputed, the ESRB is a relatively weak institution with limited powers and a small budget.

More Is Needed in Europe to Address Systemic Risk

Addressing Systemic Risk: The Institutional Structure

Financial institutions falling outside the regulatory perimeter of traditional financial entities may engage in equivalent activities without being subjected to adequate regulation. In the same vein, sectoral supervisors can only monitor the buildup of systemic risk within their competence and thus, by definition, lack a comprehensive overview of the financial sector. The institutional financial supervisory structure in the European Union should, therefore, be supplemented by an institution charged with monitoring systemic risk buildup in any financial institution and, when necessary, bring them within an adequate regulatory and supervisory perimeter.

As demonstrated in the sections above, an institutional approach is still prevalent in the European Union's financial regulatory structure. Because such an approach is especially susceptible to regulatory gaps, it needs to be complemented by a robust monitoring mechanism that has an activity-based approach of detecting systemic risk across the entire financial sector. In the European Union, the ESRB provides for monitoring of systemic risks but lacks substantial formal legal power. The United States, in contrast, has equipped the Financial Stability Oversight Council (FSOC) with substantial systemic risk-monitoring powers and the competence to bring SIFIs within an adequate regulatory and supervisory perimeter.[54] An expansion of the ESRB's powers, providing it in imitation of the FSOC, with the competence

51 Jacques de Larosière, The High-Level Group on Financial Supervision in the EU, *Report* (2009) at 38, online: <http://ec.europa.eu/economy_finance/publications/pages/publication14527_en.pdf>.

52 *ESRB Regulation, supra* note 48, art 15(5).

53 *Ibid*, art 16(1).

54 12 USC § 5323.

to designate financial institutions as systemically important and, in consequence, to bring them within prudential supervision or enhanced supervision, would be in order.

Given the dual legal orders of the European Union and its member states, it is submitted that prudential supervision should be performed at the EU level by an EU institution. As SIFIs operate across national borders, regulation and supervision should not be confined within such borders. This brings to mind what Dirk Schoenmaker has called the "financial trilemma": increased financial integration due to globalization and, more specifically, to the creation of a European internal market is not compatible with both financial stability and national financial policies.[55] National supervision of non-bank SIFIs has proved inadequate.[56] This is, in part, due to inherent jurisdictional limitations and the corresponding fragmented view of the supervised institution.[57] Moreover, national authorities might be tempted to practise forbearance with regard to financial institutions perceived as national champions.[58]

Similarly, the resolution of non-bank SIFIs can best be achieved by an EU institution. Much the same arguments as for European supervision apply. Lacking a comprehensive view of a non-bank SIFI's business causes suboptimal resolution decisions. Moreover, national authorities have strong incentives to minimize the impact of failing non-bank SIFIs on their economy.[59] This can result in unilateral measures such as requiring higher capital and liquidity buffers or limiting intra-group transfers. Maintaining financial stability is not the prime aim of such measures. Consequently, they have the potential to cause unnecessary destruction of the non-bank SIFI's value and distort the functioning of the internal market.

Monitoring Systemic Risk

The GFC exposed the integrated nature, both cross-sectoral and cross-border, of financial markets and institutions. This warrants an integrated approach to the monitoring of financial risks. In the European Union, the ESRB is tasked with systemic risk monitoring. However, as discussed, the ESRB's powers are limited. It does not have formal powers and instead has to rely on systemic risk warnings and non-binding recommendations to EU members, which can be punctuated by a "comply or explain" mechanism.

With regard to the collection of information, it is of interest to note that the ESRB may request information of the ESAs, the ECB, the Commission and national supervisors, statistics

55 Dirk Schoenmaker, *Governance of International Banking: The Financial Trilemma* (Oxford, UK: Oxford University Press, 2013).

56 See de Larosière et al, *supra* note 51.

57 The Commission, for instance, notes in its consultation on the reform of the ESAs that stakeholders confirmed that the understanding and supervision of investment funds is very different among national competent authorities, which ultimately limits the uptake of these funds. See EC, *Public Consultation* (2017) at 17, online: <https://ec.europa.eu/info/sites/info/files/2017-esas-operations-consultation-document_en.pdf>. Similarly, recital 5 of the SSM Regulation grants that the creation of the SSM was prompted by the conviction that "[c]oordination between supervisors is vital, but the crisis has shown that mere coordination is not enough, in particular in the context of a single currency. In order to preserve financial stability in the Union and increase the positive effects of market integration on growth and welfare, integration of supervisory responsibilities should therefore be enhanced." This holds similarly true for the supervision of non-bank SIFIs.

58 Adam Posen & Nicolas Véron, "Europe's half a banking union" (19 September 2014), online: <http://bruegel.org/2014/09/europes-half-a-banking-union/>.

59 This is also cited as a basis for the creation of the SRM. See *Regulation (EU) No 806/2014 of the European Parliament and of the Council of 15 July 2014 establishing uniform rules and a uniform procedure for the resolution of credit institutions and certain investment firms in the framework of a Single Resolution Mechanism and a Single Resolution Fund and amending Regulation (EU) No 1093/2010*, [2014] OJ, L 225, rec 9.

authorities and member states. However, as the information provided is in aggregate form, it is impossible to distinguish individual firms. If, as we propose below, the ESRB is to be able to make non-bank SIFI designations comparable to the FSOC designations, this limitation should be removed.

In the United States, the FSOC is charged with identifying risks to the financial stability of the country, promoting market discipline and responding to emerging risks to the stability of the US financial system. Its powers include the designation of non-bank financial institutions and financial market utilities to be supervised by the Federal Reserve Board. It may issue recommendations on heightened prudential standards to supervisory authorities. Moreover, it makes recommendations on jurisdictional disputes and reports on regulatory gaps to Congress.

Non-bank SIFI Designation

It is submitted that the ESRB should be equipped with powers similar to those of the FSOC to designate non-bank financial companies as systemically important and, consequently, deserving of additional prudential regulation and supervision. This would go a long way toward alleviating systemic risks by creating a mechanism to ensure non-bank SIFIs are subjected to a regulatory requirement consistent with the risks they pose. Such a designation would be an important instrument in preventing regulatory arbitrage. Indeed, echoing the designation process of the FSOC, we would note that the level of regulatory scrutiny to which a non-bank SIFI is subjected is an important factor when deciding on a designation.

The ESRB could be given the power to designate non-bank SIFIs under article 114 of the Treaty on the Functioning of the European Union (TFEU), as it aims to improve the functioning of the internal market by helping to provide financial stability. Indeed, the very goal of such a designation is to make sure that such non-bank SIFIs are regulated to an extent consistent with the level of systemic risk they pose. Consequently, the power to make such a designation is conditional on whether it addresses a threat to financial stability and whether such a designation would alleviate the threat.

However, such a power of designation for the ESRB might be subject to legal constraints on the delegation of discretionary powers to agencies. The EU member states have delegated powers to the European Union through the treaties. In turn, the EU legislature may decide to delegate some of these powers to an agency in cases where the treaties provide for this possibility, either in a specific provision or in the form of a general competence such as article 114 of the TFEU.

The degree to which such delegation is allowed was addressed by the Court of Justice of the European Union (CJEU) in its *Meroni* ruling.[60] The CJEU distinguished between two types of delegation. Whereas purely executive powers may be delegated, as their exercise can be reviewed against objective criteria specified by the delegating authority, powers involving a wide margin of discretion in determining economic policy may not be delegated. Such delegation would replace the choices of the delegating authority by those of the delegatee and bring about an

60 *Meroni & Co, Industrie Metallurgiche, SpA v High Authority of the European Coal and Steel Community*, C-9/56, [1958] ECLI:EU:C:1958:7 [*Meroni*].

actual transfer of responsibility.[61] As a transfer of responsibility of this kind would alter the balance of power between the EU institutions, it would be incompatible with the treaties.[62]

In its *Short Selling* judgment,[63] the CJEU revisited and revised its *Meroni* doctrine. First, the CJEU emphasized that the contested delegation in *Meroni* concerned delegation to an entity governed by private law, whereas the contested delegation in the *Short Selling* case was to ESMA, which had been established pursuant to an EU regulation. The court went on to note that ESMA's power to prohibit or impose conditions on the entry by natural or legal persons into a short sale, or to require them to notify a competent authority or to disclose to the public details of net short positions,[64] does not confer any autonomous power that goes beyond the boundaries of the regulatory framework established by the ESMA Regulation.[65] Furthermore, and unlike the circumstances in *Meroni*, ESMA's discretionary powers with regard to short selling are circumscribed by various conditions and criteria.[66] The CJEU therefore held that the powers available to ESMA with regard to short selling are precisely delineated and amenable to judicial review in light of the objectives established by the delegating authority. Accordingly, it found that those powers comply with the requirements laid down in *Meroni*. Consequently, those powers do not imply that ESMA is vested with a "very large measure of discretion" that is incompatible with the treaties.[67]

In line with the *Short Selling* ruling, it could be argued that granting the ESRB the power to designate non-bank financial institutions as systemically important is not in breach of the *Meroni* constraints. Much the same conditions and restraints applicable to ESMA's short selling powers would be applicable to the designation procedure, as the ESRB too has to make an assessment of a possible threat to the stability of the whole or part of the financial system. The Commission could provide conditions detailing how such an assessment should be made in a delegated regulation. Judicial review of a designation would also be possible, as a designation is of direct and individual concern to the subject institution, opening up proceedings under article 263 of the TFEU, before the CJEU.

At the same time, we concede that in order to have in place a forward-looking system for the monitoring and designation of systemically important institutions, it is vital for the ESRB to have a degree of discretion. As the financial sector is ever evolving, the ESRB should not be subject to extremely detailed conditions limiting its ability to review and determine systemic relevance. As the FSOC also notes in its final rule and interpretive guidance on non-bank SIFI designation, a determination decision cannot be reduced to a formula.[68]

61 *Ibid* at 152.

62 *Ibid.*

63 *United Kingdom of Great Britain and Northern Ireland v European Parliament and Council of the European Union*, C-270/12, [2014] ECLI:EU:C:2014:18 [*Short Selling*].

64 As provided for under *Regulation (EU) No 236/2012 of the European Parliament and of the Council of 14 March 2012 on short selling and certain aspects of credit default swaps*, [2012] OJ, L 86/1, art 28.

65 *Short Selling*, *supra* note 63 at paras 43–44.

66 *Ibid* at paras 45, 53.

67 *Ibid* at paras 53, 54.

68 *Authority to Require Supervision and Regulation of Certain Nonbank Financial Companies*, 77:70 Fed Reg 21637 (2012) at 21642.

In order to loosen possible *Meroni* constraints, final determination could be subjected to validation by the Commission (or by non-objection within an appropriate timeframe). As the Commission has a direct basis in the treaties, it is not subjected to *Meroni* constraints. Such an arrangement has, for the same reasons, been used in the context of the SRM, where resolution decisions by the SRB are validated by the Commission. Additionally, in the recent legislative proposal on supervision of CCPs, ESMA may make a request to the Commission that a CCP may be of such systemic importance that it will be able to provide services in the European Union only if it establishes itself in the European Union. Again, the Commission officially makes the final determination.

Alternatively, the ESRB or a newly created institution could be endowed with designation powers in the treaty. This might be the preferable option, as it would provide a strong legal basis without complicating the governance structure by including the Commission. However, as it would require a treaty change, it seems politically unfeasible. On the other hand, political realities could turn out to fluctuate more than the financial markets.

Furthermore, designations must, of course, comply with fundamental principles of EU law, including the principle of proportionality and subsidiarity.[69] Accordingly, a designation must be necessary to achieve the goal of financial stability and must not exceed the limits of what is necessary to achieve this. It should be noted that in our proposal, a proportionality test is ingrained in the designation procedure. A non-bank SIFI designation should only take place after establishing deficiencies in the current regulation and/or supervision of the institution, and in order to alleviate these deficiencies. Allocating responsibility for designations to an EU authority is also in line with the subsidiarity principle. After all, establishing whether a designation is prudent requires an in-depth overview of its activities and current regulatory and supervisory regime, which likely extends across multiple national jurisdictions. This cannot be sufficiently achieved by national authorities whose powers stop at the border.

Non-bank SIFI Supervision

New prudential regulation in the United States rearranged and expanded financial regulation, supervision and resolution. FSOC-designated SIFIs are subject to the prudential regulations set out in Title I of the act and are supervised by the Federal Reserve Board (FRB). The latter has the discretion to impose additional tailor-made prudential standards and disclosure requirements.[70]

Following the example set by the FSOC, a designation by the ESRB should have the consequence of pulling a financial institution within an appropriate prudential regulatory perimeter and related supervision. This is not to say that a one-size-fits-all approach should be taken in determining prudential requirements. Instead, regulators should have the discretion to set specific requirements reflecting the specific business of a regulated entity. Following the example set by Dodd-Frank,[71] this should include requirements in relation to capital, leverage limits, liquidity, risk management, resolution planning and credit exposure reporting. Again, following the US model, the prudential standards should be tailored, on an individual basis

69 As provided in the *Treaty on European Union*, 7 February 1992, C 326/47, arts 5(3), (4) (entered into force 1 November 1993). Likewise, other fundamental principles, such as the right to good administration, must also be secured.

70 12 USC § 5365.

71 *Ibid.*

or by category, to the designated institution. Such standards should reflect the institutions' capital structure, riskiness, complexity, financial activities (including the financial activities of their subsidiaries), size and any other risk-related factors. In consequence, the resulting tailored prudential requirements address the systemic risks while providing a fair regulatory burden, taking into account the specific nature and activities of the institution.[72]

European supervision could be realized by having designated non-bank SIFIs fall within the scope of the EBU. In addition to supervising significant euro-zone banks, the ECB would then also be charged with supervising non-bank financial institutions designated by the ESRB as systemically important. In this scenario, it would be most sensible to have the ECB determine adequate prudential requirements for the designated institution.

Alternatively, another EU entity could be charged with supervision. A possible connection could be made with the intended or successive reforms of the ESAs. Pursuant to a non-bank SIFI designation by the ESRB, the ESA that has the most affinity with the designated institution would operate as direct prudential supervisor. Direct supervision by an ESA is not unprecedented, as ESMA already has direct supervisory tasks. Some would prefer this option, as it would remove the perception that designated institutions are regulated and supervised as banks by the ECB. At the same time, the ECB could profit from the resources and experiences gained in the context of the EBU and from a comprehensive overview of the financial sector. We will limit ourselves to the more fundamental contention that the prudential supervision of non-bank SIFIs, subject to a determination by the ESRB, should be performed by an EU authority as opposed to a national authority. It is, however, important to note that the scope of ECB supervision in the context of the EBU currently coincides with that of the euro zone, as no additional member states have acceded. This is more limited than the scope of the ESAs that operate throughout the European Union. We would prefer a broader scope.

This touches upon an important additional benefit of our proposed designation and supervision scheme for systemically important institutions. As Daniel Schwarcz and David Zaring point out, the benefits of a non-bank SIFI identification and supervisory scheme extend beyond the systemic risk mitigation of the supervised institution. First, the possibility to take over or provide additional supervision of designated firms deters the initial supervisors (if any, of course) of the non-bank institutions from applying lax supervisory standards or neglecting to take proper account of systemic risk.[73] This dimension is of extra importance in the context of the European Union, where non-bank financial regulation largely depends on national administration, as the looming threat of losing supervisory control to an EU authority would provide a strong incentive for national supervisors to redouble their efforts. Moreover, an instruction from EU authorities such as the ESRB itself or other agencies to national supervisors would have even greater impact if non-compliance could lead to a non-bank SIFI designation by the ESRB.

72 The proposed rules of the FRB regarding capital requirements for supervised institutions significantly engaged in insurance activities in the United States follow a similar approach. See *Capital Requirements for Supervised Institutions Significantly Engaged in Insurance Activities*, 81 Fed Reg 38631 (2016), online: <www.govinfo.gov/content/pkg/FR-2016-06-14/pdf/2016-14004.pdf>.

73 Schwarcz and Zaring indicate that the threat of designation incentivizes primary regulators of non-banks to implement reform aimed at limiting systemic risk and to take proper account of changes in financial markets that warrant a change in their regulatory approach. See Daniel Schwarcz & David Zaring, "Regulation by Threat: Understanding Dodd-Frank's Regulation of Systemically Significant Non-bank Financial Companies" in *Regulation by Threat* (preliminary version) at 41, online: <www.law.ox.ac.uk/sites/files/oxlaw/regulation_by_threat_nov_6_-_zaring.pdf>.

Another benefit of the designation regime is that it compels financial institutions to exercise self-restraint when confronted with the threat of being designated as a non-bank SIFI. Financial institutions that add value through regulatory arbitrage activities might be deterred from engaging in these activities if they knew that this might bring them within the scope of a non-bank SIFI designation. In other words, the possibility of being designated as systemically important curbs the risk appetite of institutions. These effects are already apparent in the United States, where General Electric has greatly reduced its risk profile in a successful effort to have its non-bank SIFI status rescinded.

The scope of the SSM will have to be expanded in order to bring supervision of designated non-bank SIFIs within the scope of the EBU. However, the scope of the SSM is subject to treaty limitations.

Article 127(6) of the TFEU grants the council the power to confer specific tasks upon the ECB concerning policies relating to the prudential supervision of credit institutions and other financial institutions with the exception of insurance undertakings. It follows that although the basic treaty provision allows for a broader scope than merely credit institutions, the SSM does not reflect this.

The scope of the SSM could therefore be expanded to include other financial institutions, provided they do not qualify as insurance undertakings. It could, perhaps, be argued that the term "insurance undertaking" should be narrowly defined to exclude institutions that deal in bank-like products, as AIG did when it took large positions in credit default swaps.

However, a more legally satisfying approach, albeit perhaps a politically less feasible one, would be to amend the TFEU. The primary function of such an amendment would be to confer on a European body the power to supervise all non-bank SIFI-designated entities. Logically, this would be the same body as is in charge of supervision under the SSM.

Alternatively, an ESA could be tasked with the direct prudential supervision of designated non-bank SIFIs. To this end, EU legislators could adopt a regulation based on article 114 of the TFEU in which they delegate these tasks to a European agency. Article 114 of the TFEU provides a suitable legal basis, as EU supervision harmonizes the supervisory practices and thereby improves the conditions for the establishment and functioning of the internal market. This is also in compliance with the principle of subsidiarity and proportionality, since the execution of supervision at the EU level is motivated precisely because fragmented supervision at the national level has proven inadequate. Additionally, proportionality is an important element in the determination whether to designate a financial institution as a non-bank SIFI and place it under direct supervision.

In view of the *Short Selling* judgment, direct prudential supervision by an EU agency seems legally possible when the execution of supervision is circumscribed by various conditions and criteria that limit the discretionary powers of the agency and the acts of the agency are amenable to judicial review. However, as discussed above, the associated legal uncertainty is troublesome. Furthermore, the fact that no regulatory powers may be conferred on the agency renders it impossible for the agency to adopt tailored prudential requirements for non-bank SIFIs without approval by an EU institution with a treaty basis.

Non-bank SIFI Resolution

A credible resolution regime for non-bank SIFIs is of paramount importance in order to create a credible alternative to publicly funded bailouts and help safeguard financial stability by providing for orderly liquidation and allowing for the continued operation of systemically important business processes. Such a regime subjects non-bank SIFIs to market discipline, as it cancels out their too-big-to-fail (TBTF) status and associated implicit guarantees.

The EBU provides a resolution regime for banks and, subject to certain conditions, their parent companies if they are a financial holding company or mixed financial holding company. Additionally, 730,000 investment firms and financial institutions' subsidiaries may also fall within the resolution scope of the EBU. This creates a complicated and opaque resolution regime, with some entities within a group falling within the resolution scope and others not. The scope of resolution is governed not by the systemic risk posed by an institution and whether this may be mitigated by placing it under resolution, but instead by inflexible and arbitrary legal norms.

This leads to regulatory gaps, regulatory arbitrage, an uneven playing field and an incomplete tool box for addressing systemic risk, which may manifest itself in different and, to some extent, unknown forms. A resolution regime needs to reflect this. Therefore, non-bank SIFIs should also qualify for liquidation under a European resolution mechanism. This creates a more flexible, open-ended and forward-looking approach aimed at preventing the next crisis, not the last one.

Inspiration can, again, be drawn from the resolution regime created by the Dodd-Frank Act in the United States. This regime, known as the Orderly Liquidation Authority, captures any non-bank financial institution whose failure would seriously impact financial stability in the United States.[74]

A possible way of strengthening the European resolution regime and mitigating the systemic risks stemming from non-bank entities would be to widen the scope of the SRM to include all financial institutions that pose systemic risk. Alternatively, a separate resolution regime and authority may be established on the basis of article 114 of the TFEU, with the understanding that, as is now also required in the SRM, compliance with the *Meroni* doctrine might necessitate an endorsement of the resolution decision by the Commission.

Conclusion

The GFC revealed that the migration of financial activities outside the traditional banking sector was accompanied by a huge and unchecked buildup of systemic risk. National and/or sectorally organized regulation and supervision proved insufficient, owing to the continued integration and interconnectedness of financial markets, institutions, products and services. Gaps in the coverage of regulation and supervision led to an inconsistent regulatory treatment of equivalent products and/or services. This, in turn, caused an uneven playing field and encouraged regulatory arbitrage behaviour, which caused a migration of activities and a buildup of systemic risk in the less regulated or unregulated parts of the financial system.

74 12 USC § 5381ff.

We propose that equivalent financial products and/or services should be subject to an integrated European regulatory and supervisory approach. Above all, institutions that pose systemic risk should be brought within a regulatory environment consistent with the risk they pose to financial stability.

A European body should therefore be in charge of monitoring financial institutions active in the European Union and should identify institutions that pose systemic risk. It should, subsequently, have the discretion to designate a non-bank financial firm as a non-bank SIFI. Such designation would ensure a level of regulatory supervision consistent with the risks to financial stability posed by a financial institution. Given its current tasks, the ESRB seems best suited for this task.

After an institution has been designated as a non-bank SIFI, it comes under (stricter) European supervision. As such, a regime has been created for banks in the form of the EBU, and designated non-bank SIFIs could be brought within the perimeter of the EBU. While the treaties exclude insurance companies, other financial institutions can be brought under supervision of the ECB without the need for treaty change. The ECB would then be able to supervise and impose enhanced prudential standards on designated non-bank SIFIs. Alternatively, another EU entity could be charged with supervision, for example, the relevant ESA.

In keeping with the second pillar of the EBU, a regime should also be in place to ensure that non-bank SIFIs can be resolved without causing systemic risk. This would resolve the TBTF dilemma and subject the institutions concerned to market discipline. A connection could be made with the EBU's second pillar by expanding the scope of the SRM to include designated non-bank SIFIs. Such an inclusion could be based on article 114 of the TFEU, as the alleviation of systemic risk greatly improves the functioning of the internal market.

The development of such a regime could be based on the example of the United States, where the Dodd-Frank Act provides for the designation of non-bank SIFIs and their regulation, supervision and possible resolution.

Ensuring that non-bank SIFIs are properly regulated, supervised and, if necessary, resolved would help to eliminate supervisory and regulatory gaps, reduce regulatory arbitrage activities, enhance the level playing field and contribute to the stability of the financial system as a whole.

6

Clearing Houses and Systemic Risk

PAOLO SAGUATO AND GUIDO FERRARINI

Ten years ago, the engine of the global financial markets halted and the financial system experienced one of the most severe crises of the last two centuries. Many segments of and players in the financial system were investigated, market and structural failures were identified, and radical reforms were implemented. The over-the-counter (OTC) derivatives markets were among the market segments most heavily scrutinized.[1] Commentators and policy makers questioned the systemic resilience and efficiency of the pre-crisis OTC derivatives markets. Having grown exponentially since the early 2000s and accounting for trillions of dollars' worth of transactions,[2] the derivatives markets raised four main concerns in the aftermath of the 2008 crises: the concentration of the market in a few dealers acting as market makers exacerbated the interconnectedness of market participants and the risk of domino defaults; the absence of any system-wide, shock-absorbing mechanisms aggravated the risk of contagion in situations of distress; the opacity of the markets hindered the oversight capacity of public authorities and the ability of market participants to effectively understand and price the risks therein; and, finally,

1 Lynn A Stout, "Derivatives and the Legal Origin of the 2008 Credit Crisis" (2011) 1 Harv Bus L Rev 1 at 21 .

2 Bank for International Settlements, "OTC derivatives outstanding", online: <www.bis.org/statistics/derstats.htm>.

the lack of any formal public regulatory and supervisory apparatus caught regulators unprepared to deal with a crisis.

Policy makers responded to these structural fragilities and built a new regulatory framework whose cardinal priorities are the reduction of financial institutions' moral hazard and the containment of systemic risk. At the international level, the Group of Twenty (G20) and the Financial Stability Board (FSB) recommended moving OTC derivatives into centralized and organized markets.[3] The intervention of financial market infrastructures (FMIs)[4] in the OTC derivatives ecosystem was designed to increase transparency, enhance transactional efficiency and mitigate systemic risk.[5] Central clearing counterparties (CCPs) — or clearing houses — are the cornerstone of this new architecture.[6] Clearing houses act as middlemen in their markets, interpose themselves between contractual parties and become the central nodes of a multitude of trades.[7] By centralizing contractual positions, clearing houses operate as risk managers: they compress exposures and provide a pre-funded mechanism to absorb losses. In addition, clearing houses have the tools to manage the default of their counterparties, internalize the costs and risks thereof, and avoid the risk of systemic spillovers.

Implementing the international recommendations, national lawmakers mandated the use of clearing houses for all standardized derivatives; regulated their internal governance and risk management mechanisms; and established procedures for cross-border regulatory and supervisory cooperation. Title VII and Title VIII of the Dodd-Frank Act in the United States[8] and the European Market Infrastructure Regulation (EMIR) in the European Union[9] set the new comprehensive regulatory regime for derivatives markets and clearing houses, address some of the pre-crisis market fragilities, and contribute to the overall containment and reduction of systemic risk in the financial system.[10] Nevertheless, this new regulatory architecture is not flawless. Policy makers overlooked and underestimated some features of the internal organization of clearing houses that, if not addressed, might increase the moral hazard of these firms and threaten their systemic resilience.

3 The international guidelines set by the G20 and the FSB envisioned three pillars to support more efficient and stable derivatives markets: mandatory trading of standardized derivatives in trading venues; mandatory reporting of all derivatives to trade repositories; and mandatory central clearing of eligible derivatives through central counterparties. See "Leaders' Statement: The Pittsburgh Summit" (2009), online: <www.treasury.gov/resource-center/international/g7-g20/Documents/pittsburgh_summit_leaders_statement_250909.pdf>; FSB, *Implementing OTC Derivatives Market Reforms* (2010), online: <www.fsb.org/2010/10/fsb-report-on-implementing-otc-derivatives-market-reforms/>.

4 See Ruben Lee, *Running the World's Markets: The Governance of Financial Infrastructure* (Princeton, NJ: Princeton University Press, 2011).

5 See Guido Ferrarini & Paolo Saguato, "Regulating Financial Market Infrastructures" in Niamh Moloney, Eilís Ferran & Jennifer Payne, eds, *The Oxford Handbook of Financial Regulation* (Oxford, UK: Oxford University Press, 2015) 568.

6 See Craig Pirrong, "The Economics of Central Clearing: Theory and Practice" (2011) International Swaps and Derivatives Association Discussion Papers Series No 1, online: <www2.isda.org/attachment/MzE0Ng==/ISDAdiscussion_CCP_Pirrong.pdf>; see the section below entitled "Clearing Houses: Functions and Organization" (discussing the differences between clearing houses and central clearing counterparties).

7 See Paolo Saguato, "The Ownership of Clearinghouses: When 'Skin in the Game' Is Not Enough: The Remutualization of Clearinghouses" (2017) 34 Yale J Reg 601 at 605, n 13 (reviewing the academic literature on central clearing houses), 614–23.

8 *Dodd-Frank Wall Street Reform and Consumer Protection Act,* Pub L No 111-203, 124 Stat 1376-2223 (2010) (codified as amended in scattered sections of 7 USC, 12 USC, 15 USC) [*Dodd-Frank Act*].

9 *Regulation (EU) No 648/2012 of the European Parliament and of the Council of 4 July 2012 on OTC derivatives, central counterparties and trade repositories,* [2012] OJ, L 201 at 1 [*EMIR*].

10 See Kevin McPartland, *Systemic Risk and the Impacts of Central Clearing* (Stamford, CT: Greenwich Associates, 2015), online: <www.greenwich.com/sites/default/files/reports_pdf/IS-Systemic_Risk-2015-GR.pdf> (reporting the results of an industry survey, according to which 80 percent of global fixed-income investors believe that systemic risk was reduced by the increased use of central clearing for derivatives).

Historically, clearing houses developed as mutual firms owned by their members. They operated as private ordering mechanisms compressing trades, achieving netting efficiencies[11] and mutualizing losses. In addition, members of clearing houses *ex ante* agreed to internalize and share any costs associated with the eventual default of other members. Nowadays, however, clearing houses are different firms — they are demutualized entities. They are often subsidiaries or business units of large public corporations. Members do not own clearing houses (instead, members pay to access their services), but clearing houses fully rely on members to absorb the costs of the clearing business. The open issues for post-crisis derivatives clearing houses are primarily a matter of incentives that manifest in their internal organization.

This chapter looks at how the current regime for clearing houses interacts with systemic risk, discusses two critical shortcomings in the current regulatory apparatus and offers some policy considerations on how to increase clearing houses' systemic resilience.[12] First, clearing houses are systemically important players in the post-crisis markets: they act as systemic risk managers; they centralize and manage risk; and they provide a counter-cyclical mechanism to internalize losses. However, because of their systemic role, any risk connected to their business becomes systemic. Is the current organizational structure of clearing houses adequate to internalize the risks spilling from their systemic importance? Have risk-taking and risk-allocation incentives been properly tuned and aligned to control rights at a firm level? Second, derivatives markets are global in nature and players in these markets operate cross-border. The current tensions in international economic relations — Brexit and the current "trade wars" — are threatening the already fragile equilibrium in the cross-border prudential and supervisory agreements for clearing houses. How can the risk of cross-border spillovers be contained? And how does the current regulatory architecture cope with cross-border risk?

This chapter intends to raise awareness of a few overlooked issues in the internal organization of post-crisis derivatives clearing houses and how they affect their systemic resilience in order to contribute to a better-informed policy dialogue on the regulation of clearing houses. Post-crisis reforms were driven by the need to promptly stabilize the markets and understandably reflected a contingent situation. Ten years after the crisis, with the new regime for financial markets having been rolled out and market developments having occurred, a reassessment of the crisis-driven regulation might be appropriate.

After this introduction, the next section, "Clearing Houses: Functions and Organization," briefly analyzes the economic functions and the organizational features of post-crisis derivatives clearing houses. The two sections entitled "The Systemic Resilience of Clearing Houses in the Current Regulatory Landscape" and "The Cross-border Resilience of Clearing Houses in the Current Regulatory Regime" look at how systemic risk interacts with clearing houses in post-crisis markets. Post-crisis reforms centralized the risks of dealing in derivatives in clearing houses, making them systemically important, and making the risk of their failure systemic. Each section raises some unresolved critical issues and vulnerabilities in the existing regulatory regime and offers some policy considerations. The chapter ends with some brief conclusions.

11 Netting is the process of compressing reciprocal and opposite positions; see Paolo Saguato, "Unbundling Complexity: The Law and Economics on Netting", online: <https://ssrn.com/abstract=3269062>.

12 See Steven L Schwarcz, "Systemic Risk" (2008) 97 Geo LJ 193 (defining systemic risk as "the risk that (i) an economic shock such as market or institutional failure triggers…either (X) the failure of a chain of markets or institutions or (Y) a chain of significant losses to financial institutions, (ii) resulting in increases in the cost of capital or decreases in its availability, often evidenced by substantial financial-market price volatility" at 204).

Clearing Houses: Functions and Organization

Clearing houses are the product of the synergies of market participants to create a mechanism to centralize, pool, manage and, ultimately and eventually, share the risks and losses of transacting in financial contracts.[13] Widely used in both securities and derivatives markets, clearing houses operate in the post-trading phase of a transaction, confirming and reconciling the contractual terms, administrating and managing the provision of contractual guarantees (i.e., collateral), and ensuring the performance of the contract. To effectively manage risks and compress exposures, clearing houses act as central counterparties.[14] By a process of novation,[15] a clearing house breaks the original contract between two parties into two offsetting contracts, interposes itself between the original parties, and becomes the buyer to the original seller and the seller to the original buyer.

Operating as a central counterparty, a clearing house provides several main functions: multilateral netting, centralized risk management and loss-absorbing capacity.[16] The first two features operate as microprudential and transactional tools to mitigate systemic risk. Multilateral netting is the process of compressing offsetting positions. When executed on a rolling basis, it mitigates counterparty credit exposures and optimizes the use of collateral. When, on the other hand, it is triggered by the default of a contractual party, it expedites the liquidation of the defaulted party's positions.[17] Becoming the central node for the market and accessing the information about all cleared transactions, the clearing house can effectively and more accurately assess, price and monitor the risks in the market. In addition, clearing houses build robust risk-management practices to contain counterparty credit risk. At a microprudential level, clearing houses collect collateral as margin from their clearing members. Margins are transactional guarantees and serve an important risk mitigation function, acting as the first line of defence to absorb the risk and losses of the default of one of the clearing members.[18]

In addition to transactional defences, clearing houses have developed a unique risk mitigation resource, the so-called default guaranty fund. Each clearing member must contribute to the guaranty fund in proportion to the volume and riskiness of the cleared transactions.[19] The guaranty fund acts as a loss-sharing defence and provides a counter-cyclical pre-funded resources "cushion" to mutualize losses among the clearing members and contain, within the clearing

13 See Pirrong, *supra* note 6.

14 A clearing house provides its services to its customer-members either as a central counterparty on a principal-principal basis or by acting as an agent for its contractual parties. The former business model is commonly used in the derivatives markets while the latter applies in the securities markets and repurchase agreements markets.

15 Novation is a legal process of substitution of an original obligation or party with a new one; see Robert Bliss & Chryssa Papathanassiou, "Derivatives clearing, central counterparties and novation: The economic implications" (2006), online: <www.ecb.europa.eu/events/pdf/conferences/ccp/BlissPapathanassiou_final.pdf>.

16 Two additional functions performed indirectly by clearing houses are transparency enhancement (by reporting data of cleared transactions) and contract standardization (as a basic prerequisite to perform their business and operate with a "matched book.")

17 See Richard Squire, "Clearinghouses and Liquidity Partitioning" (2014) 99 Cornell L Rev 857 at 891–906.

18 Clearing houses collect "initial margin" at the time the transaction is cleared and "variation margin" throughout the lifespan of the contract.

19 In order to access the clearing house's services, a market participant must be admitted as a clearing member. Being admitted as a member imposes duties. In addition to contributing to the guaranty fund, each member is subject to disclosure and an oversight regime by the clearing houses, and members commit to inject fresh resources to keep the clearing house afloat even when the guaranty fund is depleted.

house, the losses caused by the default of one or more of them.[20] The fund intervenes only after all the transactional guarantees pledged by the defaulted member are completely depleted. Furthermore, if the default guaranty fund is depleted, then members are under the obligation to replenish it through so-called assessment rights. Because of these specific features, clearing houses also perform a macroprudential function in mitigating systemic risk: the counter-cyclical nature of the fund reduces the likelihood of contagion, absorbs shocks and strengthens contractual links among derivatives counterparties.

Being born out of the private initiative of market participants to reduce transaction costs and manage counterparty default risk in an orderly fashion, clearing houses were originally organized as member-owned mutual enterprises, either directly owned by the clearing members or organized as subsidiaries or business units of a mutual exchange.[21] A clearing member was required to be an owner (either shareholder or partner) of the clearing firm, and the two qualities could not be decoupled. However, starting in the early 2000s, derivatives exchanges and their clearing houses decided to demutualize their ownership structure, opening up their capital to external equity investors.[22] Looking at the largest derivatives clearing houses operating worldwide, they are all now part of large corporate groups,[23] whose parent company is listed on a public market, and where trading and post-trading are provided in a vertical structure.[24] Being wholly owned subsidiaries of a listed firm, or being one of its internal divisions, means that the clearing house's directors are appointed by the parent firm, and its management has a duty to maximize the firm's value.[25] Members do not have any formal control or governance right in the clearing house, however, they fully contribute to the guaranty fund and have full skin in the game in the clearing business. Simply put, clearing houses demutualized their ownership structure to external shareholders, but they kept the risk and losses mutualized among its clearing members.[26]

20 In jargon, the ensemble of all financial resources used by a clearing house to deal with the default of a clearing member is called "default waterfall," where transaction-specific resources (margin) are used before tapping into the default guaranty fund (mutualization defence).

21 For a more comprehensive account of the historical evolution of the clearing industry, see Saguato, *supra* note 11 at 123–30; Peter Norman, *The Risk Controllers: Central Counterparty Clearing in Globalised Financial Markets* (Chippenham, UK: Wiley, 2011).

22 Norman, *supra* note 21 at 183–84, 274–76.

23 The London Clearing House (part of the London Stock Exchange group), Eurex Clearing (part of the Deutsche Börse Group), the Chicago Mercantile Exchange and its clearing division, and ICE Clear Credit (part of the Intercontinental Exchange group) are the most important derivatives clearing houses.

24 See Guido Ferrarini & Paolo Saguato, "Governance and Organization of Trading Venues: The Role of Financial Market Infrastructures Groups" in Danny Busch & Guido Ferrarini, eds, *Regulation of the EU Financial Markets* (Oxford, UK: Oxford University Press, 2015) (defining these corporate groups as "financial market infrastructural groups" at 285).

25 It is outside the scope of this chapter to discuss the complex issue of the corporate purpose; for completeness, the other corporate purpose theory of "shareholders primary" claims that the duty of management is to maximize shareholders' value.

26 See Robert T Cox & Robert S Steigerwald, "'Incomplete demutualization' and financial market infrastructure: central counterparty ownership and governance after the crisis of 2008–9" (2016) 4:3 J Financial Market Infrastructures 25 (describing as "incomplete demutualization" the separation of ownership from clearing participation).

The Systemic Resilience of Clearing Houses in the Current Regulatory Landscape

Title VII and Title VIII of the Dodd-Frank Act and EMIR mandated the use of clearing houses to manage systemic risk in the derivatives markets. Trillions of dollars' worth of financial transactions were rechannelled to clearing houses. The systemic risk that characterized the pre-crisis derivatives markets was not fully eliminated — and it would be naive to think so — but it did shift from the markets to clearing houses. Clearing houses have become systemically important: they process trillions of dollars' worth of transactions, are significantly exposed to clearing members' counterparty risk and, because of their public role as systemic risk managers, their mismanagement or failure might result in a systemic disruption of crucial infrastructural services.[27]

There is no doubt that the post-crisis system has in place more resilient mechanisms to deal with risk and more counter-cyclical resources allotted to absorb systemic shocks. What is critical, however, is the regulatory approach to the internal governance and risk management of clearing houses. The vulnerabilities of the current regulatory framework and organizational design of clearing houses reflect the political environment during which post-crisis reforms were adopted. In the United States, Title VII and Title VIII were adopted after the catastrophic failure of American International Group (AIG) due to its derivatives exposures and the "uncontrolled" derivatives liabilities built by many broker-dealers in the run-up to the crisis.[28] Derivatives dealers and their moral hazard were pointed out as a primary cause of the OTC derivatives markets' instability. Lawmakers were pushed to drastically reduce derivatives dealers' influence in the post-crisis derivatives markets. Thus, they mandated the use of clearing houses and trading facilities to shrink derivatives dealers' influence and expand public and open markets for derivatives.

Aware of the systemic importance of clearing houses in the post-crisis landscape, both EU and US lawmakers set enhanced prudential requirements and risk-management standards for these firms. Detailed rules cover the operations of the default waterfall and both the transactional and mutualization defences a clearing house deploys to handle the failure of its members. A clear stand was taken about CCPs' internal governance.[29] Clearing houses are required to have a risk committee responsible for setting the firm's risk appetite, overseeing the firm's activities and

27 The systemic severity of the default of a clearing house would be caused by the lack of viable substitute firms that could replace a defaulted clearing house (i.e., existing clearing houses have built expertise in clearing only specific derivatives); the sudden halt of provision of essential infrastructural services in the financial markets; or the acceleration of fire sales in the asset classes accepted by CCPs as collateral.

28 Colleen M Baker, "Regulating the Invisible: The Case of Over-the-Counter Derivatives" (2010) 85 Notre Dame L Rev 1287.

29 See *Requirements for Derivatives Clearing Organizations, Designated Contract Markets, and Swap Execution Facilities Regarding the Mitigation of Conflicts of Interest,* 75 Fed Reg 63732 (proposed 18 October 2010), online: <www.cftc.gov/idc/groups/public/@lrfederalregister/documents/file/2010-26220a.pdf>; *Governance Requirements for Derivatives Clearing Organizations, Designated Contract Markets, and Swap Execution Facilities; Additional Requirements Regarding the Mitigation of Conflicts of Interest,* 76 Fed Reg 722 (proposed 11 January 2011) [*Requirements for Derivatives Clearing Organizations*], online: <www.cftc.gov/idc/groups/public/@lrfederalregister/documents/file/2010-31898a.pdf> (nine years after these rules were published, they are still proposed rules).

advising the board on any risk-related matters.[30] The risk committee, while critical for the sound and prudent operation of a clearing business, has a mere consultative role, with no binding power over the board of directors; the board retains the ultimate authority to decide any matter relating to the clearing business. By law, no members' representatives are required to sit on it; however, clearing houses generally offer members the majority of the seats on the risk committee.[31]

In the United States, strict rules discipline the internal governance of clearing houses. Clearing members, the "too-big-to-fail" derivatives dealers whose moral hazard was identified as one of the primary causes of the crisis, saw their role in running and managing the clearing house's risk drastically curtailed. They are required, on one side, to provide all the financial resources necessary to fill the guaranty fund and to pre-emptively agree to further financially support the clearing house in a situation of severe distress; on the other, they are restricted to owning shares or beneficial interests in the clearing house. In addition, they are not given any formal rights in the governance of the firm's risk management.

A different approach was taken in the European Union. EMIR requires a multi-stakeholder representation on the risk committee:[32] members' representatives must sit on the risk committee; their prescriptions are not, however, binding on the board. At the same time, members are not subject to ownership restrictions and their representatives can meet the independence requirements — something that is, at the moment, excluded in the proposed rules on the governance of clearing houses in the United States.[33] Finally, both jurisdictions — the United States and the European Union — reserve an enhanced supervisory role for their central banks, and clearing houses are granted special privileges to access public financial support.

Despite significant differences in approaching clearing houses' regulations, both regimes are vulnerable to the same critiques: the restrictions on members' rights in the governance of risk, in the United States, and the direct and intrusive public intervention in risk management, especially in the European Union,[34] might increase clearing houses' moral hazard, reshuffle and distort the risk-taking incentives of the risk managers, and ultimately create a new form of systemic risk. The current allocation of control rights and final risk-bearing costs create a potential misbalance in the governance structure of clearing houses that might threaten the systemic resilience of the firms. In particular in the United States, the stakeholders who set the risk profile and appetite of the firm and who have a formal say in its risk management are not the ones bearing the final costs if the clearing house were to be in distress.

30 See *Requirements for Derivatives Clearing Organizations, supra* note 29 at 63750, proposed rule § 39.13. In more detail, the risk committee assists the board of directors in the identification of risks in the firms' business; the assessment, review and oversight of the firm's risk management practices; the evaluation of the effectiveness, integrity and adequacy of the risk management programs and mechanisms; and the organization and performance of the firm's risk management functions.

31 See e.g. ICE Clear Credit LLC, *Disclosure Framework* (2019) at 11–12, online: <www.theice.com/publicdocs/clear_credit/ICEClearCredit_DisclosureFramework.pdf>; CME Group, *CME Clearing: Principles for Financial Market Infrastructures Disclosure* (2017) at 22–23, online: <www.cmegroup.com/clearing/risk-management/files/cme-clearing-principles-for-financial-market-infrastructures-disclosure.pdf>.

32 See *EMIR, supra* note 9, art 28.

33 See *Requirements for Derivatives Clearing Organizations, supra* note 29 at 63742; see *Dodd-Frank Act, supra* note 8 at § 825 (requiring that clearing houses include market participants — customers of the clearing members — in the composition of their governing board or committees), but excluding from the definition of "public directors" (i.e., independent directors) employees of the clearing members.

34 See Paolo Saguato, "Financial Market Infrastructures: The Essential Role of Risk Management" in Danny Busch, Guido Ferrarini & Gerard van Solinge, *Governance of Financial Institutions* (Oxford, UK: Oxford University Press, 2019) at 228.

Clearing houses are public corporations and they operate with a unique dual-layered capital structure:[35] shareholders provide the equity capital and clearing members fully finance the guaranty fund. If the resources provided by a defaulted member are insufficient to cover the costs of its default, then the guaranty fund, to which all members fully contributed, absorbs the remaining losses. In addition, the clearing house itself participates in the default waterfall with some of its own resources — its so-called skin in the game — and absorbs part of the default losses before they are fully mutualized among the non-defaulted members. While aiming to align the clearing house's risk-taking incentives with those of its members, the amount of the clearing house's skin in the game is relatively small with respect to the amount of the guaranty fund.[36] In the current economic structure of the default waterfall, clearing members, and not the firm's shareholders, are the final underwriters of the clearing risk. This decoupling of final risk-bearing costs from control rights reverses the traditional view of a corporation, where shareholders are considered the residual claimants and the final risk bearers of any business risk. Here, shareholders shift the costs of running the business onto the firm's members (users): this creates delicate and risky agency costs between the shareholders (agents) and the members (principals).[37] These agency costs are exacerbated rather than reduced by the current regulatory framework. The presence of these agency costs might result in the clearing house taking excessive risk in its clearing business in order to maximize profits for its shareholders and externalizing any potential cost onto its members.[38]

A second and mostly overlooked aspect of clearing houses is the fact that they are not stand-alone entities but subsidiaries of large infrastructural groups. Clearing houses and their activities are not ring-fenced from the risks that might spill over from the group's other business lines. Large infrastructural groups have engaged in acquisition campaigns and have expanded their activities to new sectors; yet, as of today, no legal restrictions would prevent them from engaging in highly leveraged activities. Finally, the culture of infrastructural groups, in particular in the European Union, is changing. After their demutualization, these groups maintained strong ties with their former members and maintained an internal management that represented the old guard of the member-owned firm. Today, the London Stock Exchange, Deutsche Börse and ICE are all managed by former investment bankers. And while culture is a soft element that might affect the governance of a business, we do not think it is a pure coincidence that the majority of clearing houses are now run by former risk takers rather than risk managers.

35 For the purpose of this chapter, we use the concept of "capital" in its broadest meaning to refer to any operating financial resources received by the clearing house from its stakeholders — i.e., shareholders and members in particular.

36 As of January 2019, CME Clearing House had a total of US$250 million of "designated corporate contributions" (i.e., skin in the game) in the default waterfall and US$7.326 billion in guaranty fund contributions from its clearing members (with the power to assess US$11.184 billion in additional capital contributions from its members). See CME Group, "CME Clearing's Financial Safeguards System", online: <www.cmegroup.com/clearing/cme-clearing-overview/safeguards.html>. CME Group, the parent company of CME Clearing, has an equity capital of US$23 billion and a market capitalization of US$64.8 billion. See Bloomberg, "CME:US", online: <www.bloomberg.com/quote/CME:US>. Similarly, ICE Clear Credit has US$50 million worth of skin in the game and US$667.6 million in guaranty fund contributions; see ICE, "Regulation", online: <www.theice.com/clear-us/regulation>. ICE has equity capital of US$17 billion and a market capitalization of US$42.91 billion; see Bloomberg (*ibid*).

37 See Saguato, *supra* note 7 at 659.

38 Examples of degradations in risk management could take the form of lowering membership requirements, acceptance for clearing highly volatile and risky products, broadening types of classes of acceptable collaterals as margin, reuse of the pledged collateral in leveraged transactions and so forth.

A third critical aspect of the current regime of clearing houses is the approach to their recovery and resolution.[39] First, clearing houses are not banks. Each clearing house operates on a matched book, runs a single line of business (i.e., clearing) and is not a leveraged institution (a clearing house, generally speaking, does not issue debt to finance its activities). Second, despite not being banks, the general discourse around clearing houses' recovery and resolution tends to gravitate around concepts and institutions that belong to the banking world. Bail-in mechanisms,[40] the break-up of the institution in a bad clearing house (with the defaulted and defaulting portfolios) and in a good clearing house (with the profitable positions), or the creation of a bridge institution, are options that will not effectively work in the clearing houses context. In their current structure, clearing houses do not have liabilities or convertible debt instruments that can be easily written off or converted into equity to refinance the firm.[41] The only creditors available are the clearing members that have open positions with the clearing house. In addition, the idea of a bridge clearing house that would intervene to separate the good clearing business from the troubled one is not easily applicable. In general, and historically, clearing houses faced financial distress when they wrongly programmed their risk models, and creating a bridge clearing house that would use proven flawed risk models would just replicate the same risks in the new firm. Furthermore, writing new risk models requires time and resources, both of which are lacking in a situation of distress. Finally, a third solution discussed in many policy fora is the so-called variation margin gains haircut (VMGH). Put simply, the clearing house would take some collateral posted as margin by the non-defaulted members and use them to cover the remaining outstanding losses. This mechanism not only reveals the complete failure of the clearing house's existing risk models, but further exacerbates the moral hazard of the firm. Risks and losses caused by the firm's failure in setting effective risk models would be externalized again onto the clearing members and not onto the clearing house's shareholders (who set the risk profile). Furthermore, VMGH would be eventually triggered during an already existing crisis and after all mutualization resources have already been wiped out. Rather than containing the crisis, VMGH (and the assessment rights of the clearing house) would act as procyclical tools, exacerbating the risk of fire sales and weakening the already fragile members.[42]

Undoubtedly, clearing houses have concentrated risk and have become systemically important infrastructures in the post-crisis markets. Clearing houses must be systemically resilient because of the public policy function assigned to them by lawmakers. Their unique capital profile, however, creates a potentially extremely fragile structure: the complete misalignment of final

39 The recovery and resolution tool box would come into play at the end of the default waterfall, after all margins posted by the defaulted member are liquidated, the resources pledged in the guaranty fund are depleted and the additional contributions collected by exercising the assessment rights are exhausted. See e.g. Darrell Duffie, "Resolution of Failing Central Counterparties" in Kenneth E Scott, Thomas H Jackson & John B Taylor, eds, *Making Failure Feasible: How Bankruptcy Reform Can End "Too Big to Fail"* (Stanford, CA: Hoover Institution Press, 2015) 87; Manmohan Singh & Dermot Turing, "Central Counterparties Resolution — An Unresolved Problem" (2018) IMF Working Paper 65, online: <www.imf.org/en/Publications/WP/Issues/2018/03/20/Central-Counterparties-Resolution-An-Unresolved-Problem-45727>.

40 A bail-in mechanism supports the recovery of a troubled financial institution by allocating losses on the firm's creditors, either by writing off liabilities or, when convertible instruments are issued, by converting debt into equity instruments (i.e., at the same time recapitalizing the firm and reducing its liabilities).

41 See Paolo Saguato, "The Unfinished Business of Regulating Systemic Risk Managers" (2018) SSRN, online: <https://ssrn.com/abstract=3269063>.

42 VMGH would be triggered after a billion dollars' worth of collateral had already been sold on the market, likely at a discounted price. VMGH would be triggered in a market with pre-existing fire-sale activities. Requiring margin to be additionally haircut would leave the existing open positions with the clearing house undercollateralized, thus exposing the clearing house even more to fragility.

risk-bearing costs and control rights among clearing houses' stakeholders increases the moral hazard of the firm. The limited equity contributions and skin in the game of shareholders, together with the mechanics of the default waterfall, externalize the costs of the clearing business onto members that do not have, per se, any control rights over the firm's risk management. Finally, this unbalanced economic and organizational structure, compounded with the systemic role of clearing houses, creates a new manifestation of systemic risk overlooked by the crisis-driven regulation.

The obvious next step in this discussion is to determine how we can make clearing houses more systemically resilient and reduce the moral hazard and misaligned risk-taking incentives in clearing houses, when ownership is demutualized to external shareholders and risk is mutualized among members. Policy makers should have better analyzed the economic implications of the incomplete demutualization and the decoupling of final risk-bearing costs and control rights in demutualized derivatives clearing houses when drafting the post-crisis reform.[43] Demutualized clearing houses face the delicate balancing of their public policy function as systemic risk managers with their for-profit nature as public corporations.[44] This balance is further exacerbated by the externalization on members of the costs of (poor) risk management. So how can these two roles be better aligned? In this chapter, we focus on four market solutions to create more systemically resilient clearing houses.

The two policy solutions on the extremes of the spectrum are remutualization of clearing houses and nationalization of these firms. Both solutions address, in different ways, the risk concentration issue and would assign control and ownership rights to the stakeholders that are likely going to be the clearing business's final risk bearers. The remutualization of clearing houses would combine the role of member and shareholder. In doing so, the agency costs between members and shareholders would be completely reconciled. Full internalization of the clearing business's risk would be achieved, and clearing houses would vest again the "clothes" of private ordering mechanisms.[45] The other extreme policy solution would be the nationalization of clearing houses.[46] Because of the direct regulation of multiple aspects of the clearing business and its risk management, a failure of a clearing house would be a regulator's failure. The political and administrative capital at stake would be substantial. Furthermore, a public financial intervention — with taxpayers being the final risk bearers — would be the implied final solution in a default scenario.[47] Both radical solutions find their potential implementation environment during or after a clearing-house crisis.

The two other intermediate options would operate on the internal resilience of clearing houses and affect shareholders' skin in the game and members' control rights, respectively. To have their risk-taking incentives aligned with those of the members, the clearing house's shareholders should

43 See Saguato, *supra* note 7.

44 See Steven L Schwarcz, "Misalignment: Corporate Risk-Taking and Public Duty" (2016) 92 Notre Dame L Rev 1 (elaborating a public governance duty as a mechanism to reduce systemic externalities).

45 See Saguato, *supra* note 7 at 659–61.

46 The Federal Reserve would not be a newbie in running a clearing house. Its historical foundations lie in payments clearing business, the Chicago federal regional offices have been historically engaged with the derivatives markets, and the Dodd-Frank Act empowered the Fed to draft critical regulation on the governance and risk management of systemically important financial market utilities — Title VIII — and assigned the Fed a backstop and support function for clearing houses in distress. See Saguato, *supra* note 7 at 665–66; see also Stephen J Lubben, "Failure of a Clearinghouse: Dodd-Frank's Fatal Flaw?" (2015) 10 Va L & Bus Rev at 149.

47 See *Dodd-Frank Act*, *supra* note 8, § 806.

be subject to a contingent liability regime. Instead of having clearing members replenishing the guaranty fund upon exhaustion, the clearing house's shareholders should be responsible for it. By doing so, shareholders would have actual (*ex post*) skin in the game in the business and they would be incentivized to effectively monitor the clearing house's management and to implement robust risk models.[48] Finally, and more easily achievable by private action, clearing houses could create a hybrid governance mechanism that would reflect the double-layered capital structure of the firm. Members should be assigned special voting rights that are proportional to the amount they contribute to the guaranty fund. These special hybrid financial instruments issued to members would assign voting rights to appoint the majority of the clearing house board of directors and members of the risk committee. By empowering members to govern and police the firm's risk profile and management, members would have fewer conflicts or problems with the operation of the loss mutualization mechanism.[49]

A corollary aspect that policy makers should consider is to require clearing houses that are part of an FMI group to be ring-fenced from the corporate group's other activities and risks.[50] Ring-fencing would not only prevent the FMI group from leveraging the clearing business from investing in risky activities, but would also reduce the risk of intra-group spillovers (from the clearing business to the rest of the FMI group activities and vice versa) and simplify public oversight of the clearing business.[51]

Here, we share a final comment on the systemic resilience of clearing houses and the debate on firms' recovery and resolution. As previously mentioned, although a clearing house failure is (generally) caused by a failure of its risk models, it is also (generally) triggered by the default of one of the clearing members (i.e., counterparty credit risk).[52] The current VMGH approach dealing with recovery and resolution raises perplexity because of its procyclical nature. It might stabilize the clearing house, but it would do so to the detriment of its members and the markets in general. Reassessing the unstable organizational structure of clearing houses should be, in our opinion, a priority for policy makers. Reducing risk-taking incentives and containing the agency costs between members and shareholders would reduce the likelihood of engaging in recovery and resolution actions. However, in our view, policy makers should focus their attention not just on the node of the system (the clearing house) but also on its links. In other words, if the clearing house faces distress and one or more of its members defaults, it is very likely the whole system would be facing distress, including (and especially) clearing members. Regulators should strengthen the legal obligations of members to fulfill their assessment rights, including in the scenario of a clearing member under a recovery and resolution regime. And a better alignment of risk-bearing costs and control rights, achieved through one of the four policy solutions described above, would increase the incentives of the firm to build more robust buffers of loss-absorbing resources and invest in an alternative risk-sharing and hedging mechanism (i.e., insurance).

48 See Saguato, *supra* note 7 at 662–64.

49 *Ibid* at 664–65.

50 See Ferrarini & Saguato, *supra* note 24 at 294 (suggesting the ring-fencing of the clearing business within large FMI groups); Steven L Schwarcz, "Central Clearing of Financial Contracts: Theory and Regulatory Implications", 167 U Pa L Rev [forthcoming in 2019], online: <https://ssrn.com/abstract=3104079> (raising the same argument in favour of ring-fencing).

51 See Steven L Schwarcz, "Ring-Fencing" (2013) 87 S Cal L Rev 69.

52 It is also possible that a clearing house would fail because of operational risk.

Cross-border Resilience of Clearing Houses in the Current Regulatory Regime

Derivatives markets are cross-border in nature. The four main global clearing houses provide their services in multiple jurisdictions and their membership pool represents about 30 global financial institutions. The risk that might spill from the frictions or discrepancies between conflicting regulatory approaches and regimes is the second aspect of systemic risk that potentially affects the global clearing markets.

In the immediate aftermath of the crisis, national lawmakers were fully aware of the risk of cross-border contagion and spillovers and responded by bringing the post-crisis reform debate to an international level. The FSB has been the main driver of international dialogue and coordination for the regulation of financial markets. However, international financial regulation has weak foundations: it operates like a pendulum. In the aftermath of a crisis revealing that some risks and failures were triggered by foreign institutions or were exacerbated by foreign supervisory or regulatory failures, the "pendulum of concern" swings into action and national lawmakers deem international coordination necessary. Thus, in the immediate aftermath of a crisis, the demand for international coordination is generally high; national lawmakers push to create a level playing field to seal arbitrage loopholes and to create more resilient markets.

However, as soon as the memory of a crisis begins to fade and the compliance costs of the new regulatory regime imposed by what are generally referred to as unaccountable and non-legitimate international organizations begin to hit the financial system, national lawmakers begin to question the merit of being subject to rules set by non-national and non-elected officials. At that point, tensions rise and the pendulum swings to the other extreme. National lawmakers disengage from international fora, they cease to recognize the merit of coordinated action and question the merit of implementing international guidelines at a national level. When the pendulum moves to this extreme (where the benefits of international financial regulation are questioned), danger mounts. The atmosphere is made more tense when political decisions are made that undermine the legitimacy of international coordination, most recently Brexit and the trade wars between the United States and its trading partners.[53] These political decisions, whose merit is outside the scope of this chapter to evaluate, create significant fragilities in the regulation and supervision of the global financial markets, opening up the risk of cross-border spillovers, contagion and critical arbitrage opportunities.

This political skepticism about international coordination is not always shared by national regulators and by the financial industry. Financial market participants that operate in multiple jurisdictions have economic interests in calling for further cross-border financial harmonization to reduce compliance costs and bring more certainty to the markets. In addition, some regulators,

53 With the Brexit referendum, British citizens expressed their intent to exit the European Union. The British government acted on the electors' decision and triggered article 50 of the Treaty on European Union to activate the negotiation to withdraw from the European Union. See Guido Ferrarini & Davide Trasciatti, "OTC Derivatives Clearing, Brexit and the CMU" in Danny Busch, Guido Ferrarini & Emilios Avgouleas, eds, *Capital Markets Union in Europe* (Oxford, UK: Oxford University Press, 2018) 140 (discussing the effect of Brexit on the future of the EU internal markets); Guido Ferrarini & Davide Trasciatti, "Brexit and OTC Derivatives Clearing: The Role of Politics" (2018) European Banking Institute Working Paper Series 2018 No 21, online: <https://ssrn.com/abstract=3142197> (offering policy solutions on the delicate issue of the effect of Brexit on the European clearing markets).

echoing the industry, stress the importance of preserving clear and stable mechanisms to regulate and supervise cross-border entities and activities as an effective mechanism to tackle cross-border risk and strengthen market oversight.[54]

The critical issue linking Brexit to the general discourse of international financial regulation is the policy and supervisory approach to clearing houses that provide cross-border services[55] (i.e., either offering their services to foreign customers or providing clearing of instruments denominated in a foreign currency).[56] The two main alternatives to cross-border clearing issues are relocation of the clearing business in each foreign jurisdiction or regulatory recognition and supervisory cooperation.[57] The former approach would require a clearing house to set up a subsidiary in each jurisdiction in which it operates, set up jurisdiction-specific financial resources and break down its members' portfolios of cleared transactions across multiple local clearing houses. Some policy makers support location policies on the main rationale of keeping national control over a critical market infrastructure.[58] Location policy as a regulatory approach to cross-border clearing houses, however, raises a serious concern. Clearing houses can more efficiently and effectively perform their function as systemic risk managers if they can achieve scale and scope economies in their multilateral netting activities. By breaking up the derivatives business into smaller national clearing pools, clearing houses and their members would reduce their ability to achieve multilateral netting benefits and face higher clearing costs. In addition, as previously mentioned, the clearing market is highly concentrated in a few global players: four main clearing houses offer their services to a small group of members that are generally members in every single clearing house. For members, the location policy would drastically increase the cost of their derivatives-dealing activities: each member would have to contribute to the default guaranty fund of every clearing house in each jurisdiction. From a systemic perspective, the location policy would substantially increase market transaction costs, but in some way, it would reduce the concentration of risk in a handful of global clearing houses.

The alternative solution to the location policy is a regime where regulators from different jurisdictions compare the substance of their individual regulations, eventually determine their equivalence and allow their market participants to access their respective markets by complying with their home regime. Determining the substantial equivalence of two regulatory regimes is

54 Recently, both the Commodity Futures Trading Commission and the Fed re-emphasized the importance of cross-border dialogue in financial regulation; see Ryan Tracy, "Fed's Quarles Defends Global Regulatory Bodies", *The Wall Street Journal* (27 June 2018); J Christopher Giancarlo, "Cross-Border Swaps Regulation Version 2.0: A Risk-Based Approach with Deference to Comparable Non-U.S. Regulation" (2018) White Paper (retracting the overreach of the extraterritorial application of US law embraced in the aftermath of the 2008 crisis and calling for a more effective approach to substitute compliance and equivalence [i.e., comparability] for the regulation and supervision of cross-border entities and activities).

55 The term "foreign" is used to refer to a jurisdiction or market other than the home jurisdiction where the clearing house is incorporated and originally authorized to offer its services.

56 See Yves Mersch, member of the Executive Board of the European Central Bank, "Euro Clearing — the open race" (Keynote speech delivered at the Frankfurt Finance Summit, Frankfurt, 29 May 2018), online: <www.ecb.europa.eu/press/key/date/2018/html/ecb.sp180529.en.html>.

57 See generally Danny Busch, "A Stronger Role for the European Supervisory Authorities in the EU27" in Busch, Ferrarini & Avgouleas, *supra* note 53 at 28 (on the current EU approach to cross-border clearing houses).

58 Location policy, for instance, is used in the United States for foreign bank holding companies; see 12 CFR § 225.124 – foreign bank holding companies. The European Central Bank (ECB) attempted in 2011 to require the FMIs used for the euro area to be located in the euro zone; see ECB, *Eurosystem Oversight Policy Framework* (2011), online: <www.ecb.europa.eu/pub/pdf/other/eurosystemoversightpolicyframework2011en.pdf>; see also the European Court of Justice decision that annuls the ECB location policy decision; *United Kingdom of Great Britain and Northern Ireland v European Central Bank* (ECB) (2015), No T-496/11, online: <https://eur-lex.europa.eu/legal-content/EN/TXT/PDF/?uri=CELEX:62011TJ0496&from=EN>.

a coordination tool delegated to administrative agencies but strongly embedded in the political arena. Here is a simplified version of the equivalence process: the host jurisdiction negotiates with the home country of a clearing house the substantial and functional equivalence of their regulatory and supervisory regimes for their clearing market (a highly political process). Then, if the countries agree on the equivalence of their respective regimes, and they agree to mutually recognize the equivalence of their regimes, the home country clearing house can access the market of the host jurisdiction by substantially complying with its own country regime.

Theoretical evidence shows that a small number of clearing houses — if properly managed and with an effective economic and organizational structure — more effectively manage and mitigate systemic risk.[59] Fragmenting the global derivatives markets into national entities and fragmenting their loss-absorbing capacity risk would threaten the efficiency and resilience of the markets. The FSB should rechannel its attentions on its core and original mission, i.e., investigating and proposing cross-border policy solutions to mitigate and tackle systemic risk, and providing frameworks and tools to facilitate international dialogues and coordination, with the ultimate goal of smoothing the equivalence procedure and international supervision of global players.

Conclusion

Clearing houses are the central nodes in the post-crisis derivatives markets. While in the pre-crisis markets, financial risk was spread across the system, now the risk of dealing in derivatives is concentrated in clearing houses. This new architecture makes it more efficient for regulators and supervisors to monitor the risk and eventually intervene. However, it makes the firms entrusted to keep the market functioning and managing the risk therein systemically important.

Ten years after the crisis, systemic risk has been reduced, but it has not disappeared: it has been transformed and centralized in systemic risk managers. The crisis-driven reforms, focusing on reducing the impact and role of systemic financial institutions, miscalibrated the regulation of the internal governance of clearing houses. The agency costs between shareholders and members (the former participating in the profits of the business, and the latter bearing the final costs of the business) increase the moral hazard of these institutions and threaten clearing houses' systemic resilience. The situation is further exacerbated by the cross-border nature of the derivatives markets: clearing houses operate cross-border, therefore, the lack of coordination between domestic regulators might exacerbate the costs of providing clearing business and might result in weak risk management practices.

We recommend that domestic and international policy makers should more effectively reassess the internal organization of clearing houses to better align the incentives of the shareholders with those of the clearing members, and strengthen the international framework of regulatory and supervisory equivalence to contain the risk of arbitrage opportunities and spillovers.

Authors' Note

This chapter is substantially based on Paolo Saguato, "The Unfinished Business of Regulating Systemic Risk Managers", online: <https://ssrn.com/abstract=3269063>.

59 See Darrell Duffie & Haoxiang Zhu, "Does a Central Clearing Counterparty Reduce Counterparty Risk?" (2011) 1:1 Rev Asset Pricing Studies 74.

7

Tackling Systemic Risk for Banks and Countries:

Perspectives from the United States and Europe

RON FELDMAN AND PAUL HIEBERT

As the understanding of systemic risk remains nascent, post-crisis policies still need fleshing out to better account for incentives and measurement. Fragilities can hold both at the level of financial institutions and of country financial systems (see Figure 1). In the United States, the debate continues on policies to tackle the too-big-to-fail (TBTF) issue, following lessons from the failure of Lehman Brothers in 2008. In Europe, the debate continues on enhancing the basis for effective counter-cyclical policies at the national level, following a bout of highly contagious country stress over the period 2010–2012.

The second section of the chapter, "The Minneapolis Plan to Fix TBTF," argues that the new system in the United States to limit taxpayer support for failed bank creditors will fail in its ultimate goal. In short, the so-called TBTF problem still exists. The section goes on to propose an alternative set of reforms, focused on dramatically increasing the equity funding of the largest

Figure 1: Systemic Risk — Financial Institutions and Country Dimension

Financial Institutions (global financial crisis)	Country Dimension (euro-area debt crisis)
(Micro)prudential regulation underestimated externalities 1. System → financial institution 2. Financial institution → system	*Time series and cross-sectional aspects* • Buildup of country vulnerabilities, e.g., indebtedness (public and private) • Country spillovers and contagion

Policy Domain	**Objective**		**Systemic Risk Treated as**
Microprudential supervision and regulation	Ensure soundness of individual financial institutions		exogenous
Macroprudential oversight	Limit systemic risk	Increase resilience	endogenous
		Lean against the financial cycle	endogenous

Source: European Central Bank (ECB).

banks. The Federal Reserve Bank of Minneapolis has made this proposal, which is called the "Minneapolis Plan."[1]

The third section of the chapter, "Measuring — and Attenuating — the Buildup of Systemic Risk in Euro-area Countries," argues that a better monitoring of country risk buildup is needed to inform enhanced crisis prevention policies. The section outlines key aspects of a counter-cyclical framework designed to inform policies to counteract the buildup of country vulnerabilities, such as those that resulted in euro area strains of 2010–2012. Empirical methods are presented for capturing and measuring the buildup of systemic risk at the national level. While still in their infancy, effective counter-cyclical macroprudential policies can eventually serve as a useful complement to more mature policies aimed at macroeconomic stabilization.

The Minneapolis Plan to Fix TBTF

The TBTF problem arises when the largest and most systemically important banks fail and impose their losses onto other banks. The spread of these losses fuels contagion as turmoil spreads throughout financial markets and into the rest of the economy. As the US economy experienced in the most recent crisis, these spillover losses have the ability to cause massive and widespread economic devastation. When faced with economic catastrophe, government leaders

1 Federal Reserve Bank of Minneapolis, "The Minneapolis Plan to End Too Big to Fail" (December 2017), online: <www.minneapolisfed.org/~/media/files/publications/studies/endingtbtf/the-minneapolis-plan/the-minneapolis-plan-to-end-too-big-to-fail-final.pdf?la=en>.

are inevitably compelled to stop the hemorrhaging by bailing out large banks, bank managers and those who lent money to the banks.

In 2008, the risk of contagion presented by TBTF banks was central to the financial crisis. As a result, trillions of dollars in American wealth was destroyed. Even now, nine years later, the effects of the crisis continue to be felt throughout the economy.

Soon after the crisis, federal policy makers moved swiftly to approve reforms to the financial system to help move the country in the right direction. These reforms, such as those contained in the Dodd-Frank Act, have indeed strengthened the financial system, and we support many of these efforts. However, some experts agree that TBTF still exists today because current plans to address it have not been fully implemented. More importantly, we believe that the government's current plan, even when fully implemented, will not sufficiently minimize the threat of TBTF.

The current plan fundamentally rests on the belief that the government will, through a complicated scheme, force debt holders of TBTF banks to absorb losses — even when the economy and financial markets appear weak. Yet our experience in the 2008 crisis teaches us that when markets show weakness, even debt holders of TBTF financial firms who were informed that they would bear losses in such times of distress do not actually incur any hit. This recent lesson of history and human behaviour in times of market stress makes clear that it is not credible that any scheme, especially a complicated one, would work to impose losses on debt holders of TBTF banks when the next crisis occurs. We have no reason to believe that the government will follow through on its current plan in the next crisis because imposing losses on debt holders of TBTF banks in a weak environment will be viewed as too risky and complex, with a high likelihood of intensifying a crisis. In fact, the most recent experience with European debt holders of banks who were supposed to take losses to avoid bailouts confirms our view that debt holders, in general, continue to be protected.[2]

Ending TBTF through Four Steps

In Step 1, the Minneapolis Plan will significantly increase the minimum capital requirements for covered banks.[3] The equity capital requirement would be 23.5 percent of risk-weighted assets (which is equivalent to a 13 percent leverage ratio, using a methodology explained in the Minneapolis Plan). New covered banks that come into existence due to mergers, acquisitions or the formation of a new holding company will be subject to the requirements upon completion of the corporate action. The Minneapolis Plan will index the $250 billion[4] in assets threshold that defines covered banks to nominal GDP so that it continues to target relatively large banks in the future. Covered banks will have five years following plan implementation before they must comply with this requirement.

2 Neel Kashkari, "New Bailouts Prove 'Too Big to Fail' Is Alive and Well", *The Wall Street Journal* (9 July 2017), online: <www.minneapolisfed.org/news-and-events/messages/wsj-op-ed-new-bailouts-prove-too-big-tofail-is-alive-and-well>.

3 "Covered banks" are bank holding companies in the United States with assets equal to or greater than $250 billion. We chose the $250 billion level as our initial threshold, as this size is consistent with an important definition of systemically important banks. For example, the Federal Reserve requires banks of this size to comply with the Liquidity Coverage Ratio. Covered banks, as of the November 2016 draft plan, were Bank of America Corporation, Bank of New York Mellon Corporation, Citigroup, Capital One Financial Corporation, Goldman Sachs Group, HSBC North America Holdings, JPMorgan Chase & Company, Morgan Stanley, PNC Financial Services Group, State Street Corporation, TD Group US Holdings, US Bancorp and Wells Fargo & Company. We do not address the treatment of financial market utilities in our Plan. As of June 30, 2017, State Street Corporation had dropped below $250 billion.

4 Unless otherwise stated, all dollar figures are in US dollars.

In Step 2, the Minneapolis Plan will force these banks to either cease being systemically important — as judged by the Treasury Secretary — or face the Systemic Risk Charge (SRC), bringing their total equity capital up to a maximum of 38 percent over time. This process will also start five years after enactment of the proposal.

In Step 3, the Minneapolis Plan will impose a tax on the borrowings of shadow banks[5] with assets of more than $50 billion. Shadow banks that are not systemically important will face a tax rate of 1.2 percent of borrowings outstanding. The shadow banks that remain systemically important will face a tax rate of 2.2 percent. The plan will also index the $50 billion threshold to nominal GDP. This aspect of the Plan will go into effect five years after enactment.

Finally, in Step 4, we propose creating a much simpler and less burdensome supervisory and regulatory regime for community banks. This recommendation reflects the ultimate goal of the Minneapolis Plan: to create a safe and sound banking system serving firms and households with effective and appropriately sized regulation and supervision.

Before providing more details on the Minneapolis Plan, we note that any analytical effort to determine an appropriate level of capital or tax for systemically important banks and shadow banks with the goal of eliminating TBTF will face significant uncertainty and sensitivity in its calculations. The full plan provides sensitivity analysis.

The Minneapolis Plan to End TBTF

In this section, we summarize the key features of each aspect of the Minneapolis Plan. We first offer two ways to understand the plan in its totality.

The first way focuses on the treatment of banks and is captured visually in Figure 2. The treatment that banks face under the Minneapolis Plan varies by two factors: asset size and systemic risk. The larger a bank is, the more onerous the capital and regulatory regime it will face. Banks that are systemically risky face a more onerous capital regime than banks that are not. Naturally, firms that are both large and systemically important face the highest capital requirements, while small community banks face the least costly regime, consistent with the risks they pose.

There are three key asset size groupings in the plan: banks with assets greater than $250 billion; banks with assets between $10 billion and $250 billion; and banks with assets less than $10 billion. We define banks with asset sizes less than $10 billion as community banks. Under our plan, these banks will face a simpler and more risk-focused capital regime and regulatory and supervisory regime in general than they face today. Banks with assets greater than $10 billion, but less than $250 billion, will face the same capital and regulatory regime that they face today. Finally, covered banks with assets greater than $250 billion will have a minimum equity capital requirement of 23.5 percent of risk-weighted assets.

Size intersects with systemic risk to make the final determination of capital and other requirements that the banks face. Under our proposal, the Treasury Secretary will have to certify when banks are not systemically important. The Treasury Secretary will not be bound by any other international or

5 Shadow banks are defined more specifically in the third section of this chapter, "Measuring — and Attenuating — the Buildup of Systemic Risk in Euro-area Countries."

Figure 2: Summary of Steps 1, 2 and 4 of the Minneapolis Plan

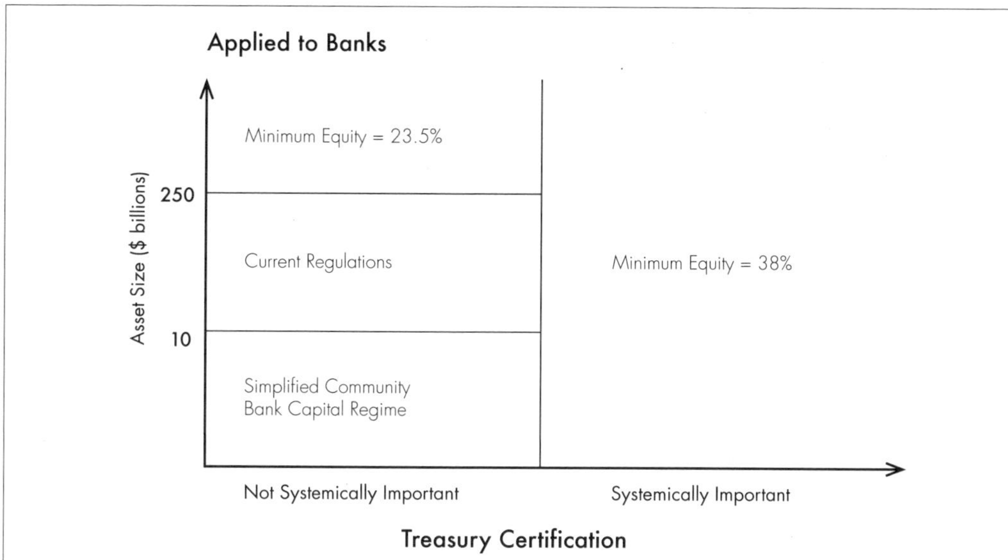

Source: Federal Reserve Bank of Minneapolis.

domestic designation of banks as systematically important when making that determination. The Treasury Secretary will have to review the systemic risk of covered banks but can, at the secretary's discretion, identify banks with fewer assets as remaining systemically important. Our plan's default position is that community banks will face an appropriate risk-focused level of capital and other regulations, while banks between $10 billion and $250 billion in assets will continue to face the current regime. But it is possible that the Treasury Secretary will deem a relatively larger but not covered bank, with assets greater than $10 billion but less than $250 billion, as remaining systemically important.

It is less clear, a priori, if banks with assets greater than $250 billion will be designated by the Treasury Secretary as not systemically important. Banks with assets greater than $250 billion that are designated as not systemically important will face a minimum equity capital requirement of 23.5 percent. Banks that do not receive that designation will face an increasing SRC until they reach a maximum equity capital requirement of 38 percent.

Figure 3 illustrates how the shadow banking tax applies to non-banks, depending on their Treasury certification (systemically important or not systemically important) and their asset size (more or less than $50 billion). This tax, by definition, applies to financial firms that are not banks.

A second way to understand the Minneapolis Plan focuses on the relationship between the two capital levels the plan imposes on banks. Our plan has a minimum capital requirement (Step 1) and a higher SRC level of capital (Step 2). The minimum capital requirement applies to banks that the Treasury Secretary certifies do not pose systemic risk. The higher capital level applies to banks that continue to pose systemic risk. Banks that are subject only to Step 1 will no longer be systemically important because many will have responded to the threat of the higher capital

Figure 3: Summary of Step 3 of the Minneapolis Plan

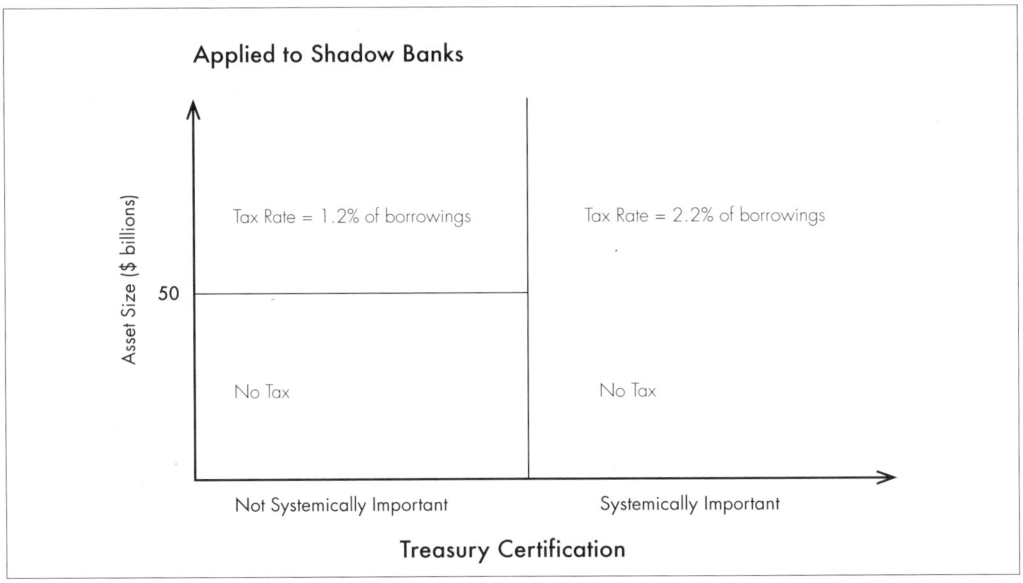

Source: Federal Reserve Bank of Minneapolis.

standards of Step 2 by lowering their own risk so that they can earn the Treasury Secretary's certification. They will do this by shedding assets and restructuring their business lines so that their failure cannot inflict systemic harm on the banking sector. Of course, not all business lines or activities will have equal systemic risk implications; we are confident that this designation process will focus on those activities that pose the greatest systemic risk.

But the potential for an individual bank to trigger systemic damage is not merely a function of that individual bank's assets and liabilities. It is also a function of the strength and capital position of the rest of the banking sector. For example, if an individual $250-billion-plus bank failed when all other $250 billion-plus banks had at least 23.5 percent capital, we believe that failure would likely not pose a systemic risk. However, if that individual $250-billion bank failed when all other large banks were lightly capitalized, that failure could pose a systemic risk. Hence, the minimum 23.5 percent capital requirement for all large banks is essential to enabling individual firms to make themselves no longer TBTF. The higher level of capital is needed for the banks that continue to pose systemic risk to get their chance of failure down to minimal levels. At this level of equity funding, the expected benefits of the total increase in equity funding exceeds its costs. We would not support higher equity levels as that would lead to higher costs than benefits.

We now discuss more details of the Minneapolis Plan.

Step 1: Minimum Capital Requirement Proposal — Key Features

- Only common equity or closely related items count toward the requirement. Common equity is the most robust form of capital for absorbing losses.
- Under current Federal Reserve-issued rules, long-term debt counts toward measures of total loss-absorbing capacity (TLAC). We do not believe long-term debt will actually

absorb losses in a time of market stress. Historical evidence shows that only bank equity holders absorb losses. In contrast, there is little US evidence to support the notion that bank debt holders will absorb losses. There would be tremendous downside to taxpayers if the government counted on debt holders to absorb bank losses and they did not.

- The 23.5 percent figure will apply to covered banks.

- The proposal also does not vary the minimum level of equity capital by bank or over time. This approach does have a potential downside of imposing similar capital requirements on banks with different levels of systemic risk. Despite this downside, we prefer a less complex capital regime. Our benefit and cost analysis leads us to conclude that 23.5 percent is the right minimum level of capital that all covered banks should maintain.

- The 23.5 percent capital level is measured as a share of risk-weighted assets. The equivalent leverage ratio is 15 percent of total assets.

- We chose this level of minimum capital based on a benefit and cost analysis and by referencing current proposals.

In summary, we consider the benefit of higher capital to be its ability to reduce the likelihood of a banking crisis. We look at historical data on banking crises to calculate how a change in the capital level of banks would reduce the chance of a country having a crisis and requiring government interventions such as liquidity support, restructuring, asset purchases, deposit freezes or other guarantees. We consider such actions to constitute bailouts. In the historical data we review, there is a one-to-one relationship between calling an event a banking crisis and having a bank bailout.

The cost of higher capital is measured as the reduction in GDP that occurs because the cost of lending goes up and, thus, less lending occurs. Here, we follow the general methodology of the regulatory community and apply it using one of the Federal Reserve Board of Governors' models of the US economy.

This benefit and cost approach finds that a minimum capital requirement of about 22 percent maximizes net benefits. That is, it is the point at which the marginal benefits of increased capital equal the marginal costs. The exact level of 23.5 percent came from the TLAC proposal issued by the board of governors, which has become a final rule.[6] The proposal applied to banks in the United States considered to be global systemically important banks (G-SIBs). The proposal set the amount of financial resources that the board thought G-SIBs should have such that they could come out of an extraordinarily stressful period without relying on public resources. A level of 23.5 percent of risk-weighted assets is the level of TLAC that the board proposed requiring of JPMorgan Chase at the time the proposed TLAC rule was released, which is the highest

6 Board of Governors of the Federal Reserve System, "Depiction of Proposed LTD Requirement + Fully Phased-in Tier 1 Risk-Based Capital Requirements", online: <www.federalreserve.gov/aboutthefed/boardmeetings/ltd-chart-20151030.pdf>. For the TLAC proposal, see Board of Governors of the Federal Reserve System, Press Release, "Federal Reserve Board proposes new rule to strengthen the ability of largest domestic and foreign banks operating in the United States to be resolved without extraordinary government support or taxpayer assistance" (30 October 2015), online: <www.federalreserve.gov/newsevents/press/bcreg/20151030a.htm>. For the final rule, see Board of Governors of the Federal Reserve System, Press Release, "Federal Reserve Board adopts final rule to strengthen the ability of government authorities to resolve in orderly way largest domestic and foreign banks operating in the United States" (15 December 2016), online: <www.federalreserve.gov/newsevents/pressreleases/bcreg20161215a.htm>.

requirement for any bank. We believe the board's sizing of financial resources that covered banks should have is reasonable.

Step 1 goes into effect five years after enactment of our proposal.

Step 2: SRC — Key Features

- Five years after the enactment of our proposal, and every year thereafter, the Treasury Secretary must certify that covered banks are not systemically important. The Treasury Secretary will also have the discretion to review the systemic risk posed by any bank.
- Firms that receive that certification continue to face the minimum capital requirement spelled out in Step 1 of our plan.
- Firms that do not receive this certification face an SRC, which will increase by five percentage points each year until either the Treasury Secretary makes the certification or the equity capital level reaches 38 percent.
- Thirty-eight percent equity capital represents the level that is needed to drive the chance of a bailout to nine percent. At this level of equity funding, the net benefits of the increase in equity funding are on the order of 15 percent of US GDP (relative to pre-crisis equity funding).

We encourage the Treasury Secretary to start the analysis of a bank's systemic risk with the same metrics regulators use today for measuring that risk. We believe that many firms currently considered systemically important will restructure themselves to greatly reduce their systemic risk rather than issue equity up to the maximum SRC. Firms that do issue equity equal to the maximum SRC will have a much lower chance of failure (and consequent bailout) as well, given their exceptionally high ability to absorb losses.

Step 3: Shadow Banking Tax — Key Features

- The Treasury Secretary will, within five years, certify whether shadow banks are systemically important and will have the discretion to review all non-bank financial firms when certifying that a given firm is not systemically important.
- A two-tier shadow banking tax rate system mirrors our two-tier capital proposal.
- The tax applies to borrowings of shadow banks.
- A lower tax rate equal to 1.2 percent of borrowings applies to shadow banks with assets that exceed $50 billion that are not systemically important.
- A higher tax rate equal to 2.2 percent of borrowings applies to shadow banks with assets that exceed $50 billion that are systemically important.
- We describe the methodology by which we set the tax in the third and final sections of this chapter. The general idea is that the government should want the overall cost of funds within the shadow banking system to be the same as in the traditional banking system. We calculate the shadow leverage tax rate so that the 1.2 percent tax rate equalizes the

funding costs of banks and shadow banks at the 23.5 percent capital requirement. The 2.2 percent tax rate makes funding costs equal at the SRC of 38 percent. This outcome will discourage the movement of leveraged activity from the standard banking sector to the shadow banking sector. Moreover, this tax effectively removes the tax preference for debt issuance for shadow banks.

- The tax will apply to firms specified in our proposal as non-banks or shadow banks. We rely on the work of the Financial Stability Board (FSB) to identify types of firms that are considered shadow banks. We include hedge funds, mutual funds and finance companies as shadow banks under this approach. The Treasury Secretary will have the discretion, however, to look beyond this list of shadow banks in certifying that a given financial institution is not systemically important.
- The tax will go into effect five years after enactment of the Minneapolis Plan.
- We make very conservative assumptions in making this calculation. At the same time, we recognize that the analytical framework to support the shadow banking tax is in early stages of development.

Step 4: Right-sized Community Bank Supervision and Regulation – Key Features

- Make the capital risk-weighting regime for community banks much less complicated, so that it largely mirrors Basel I.[7]
- Create a default mode for supervision of community banks where supervisors would only review, subject to an exception process: how banks comply with specific laws passed by Congress (and the rules and guidance issued to implement those laws); or operations, policies or procedures of a bank for which the banking agencies have empirical evidence supporting a correlation with materially weaker bank conditions.
- Impose a wide range of specific risk-focused reforms, including but not limited to a longer exam cycle, appraisal reform, reductions in call report collections, and a review of the Current Expected Credit Loss accounting standard.
- Repeal solvency and other non-compliance-related provisions of the Dodd-Frank Act[8] that apply to community banks and that do not have a strong link to their chance of failure.

These proposed reforms are similar to ones passed into law in May 2018 in the Economic Growth, Regulatory Relief, and Consumer Protection Act.[9] Our proposals would make more robust changes to risk focus supervision of community banks. In other areas, the act would go further than our proposal.

7 The Basel I Capital Accord, a set of international banking regulations developed by the Basel Committee on Bank Supervision, was created in 1988. With the goal of strengthening the stability of the international banking system and minimizing credit risk, the regulations set out the minimum capital requirements of financial institutions.

8 *The Dodd-Frank Wall Street Reform and Consumer Protection Act,* Pub L No 111-203, 1376 Stat 124 (2010).

9 *Economic Growth, Regulatory Relief, and Consumer Protection Act,* Pub L No 115-174 (2018).

Measuring — and Attenuating — the Buildup of Systemic Risk in Euro-area Countries

The scars of the GFC in Europe relate importantly to an unchecked buildup of country risk. From a European perspective, the GFC can be viewed not as a continuous event, but rather as a collection of phases — two distinct phases when tracing out impacts on each side of the Atlantic Ocean, illustrating the multifaceted nature of systemic risk. In an initial phase, during 2008-2009, the collapse of a single institution in the United States — Lehman Brothers — triggered the spread of stress throughout not only the US financial system but also the global financial system. This illustrated that system stability was not an additive function of its constituent parts, but rather a function of their interaction. A second distinct phase, from 2010 to 2012, illustrated the contagious potential of strains in single countries could ripple through to several other European countries — as strains in Greece eventually culminated in European/international assistance aid packages for Cyprus, Ireland, Portugal and Spain. The spread of systemic risk in this phase of the crisis was mainly to countries that had seen a credit-fuelled buildup of asset prices.

The European experience with crisis has elevated the importance of attenuating the financial cycle, with the aim of mitigating systemic risk buildup. Empirically, financial cycles are intimately related to the concept of leverage cycles,[10] whereby credit and asset prices reinforce one another to create both virtuous cycles in a systemic risk buildup phase and vicious cycles in a systemic risk materialization phase. This strong procyclical dynamic inherent to the financial system augurs for counter-cyclical macroprudential policies both to prevent excessive risk buildup and also to ensure adequate resilience through the cycle.

Financial cycles are often treated synonymously (but erroneously) with credit cycles. While a necessary input to a financial cycle, a broader consideration of the value of collateral in the system is central to the buildup of systemic risk, whereby leverage ebbs and flows as collateral valuations embed accelerator-like properties. The propensity of such properties to create large swings in financial activity may differ significantly across countries, depending on structural features of the economy, such as home ownership or standard contractual features of debt contracts, down to deep parameters governing societal preferences, thereby requiring methods aimed at country-specific empirical measurement..

The Financial Cycle: From Concepts to Measurement

Stylized representations of the financial cycle often treat countries similarly, failing to take into account the prospect of strong country-specific features. In particular, approaches can gloss over important elements of such cycles — notably their length, their amplitude and any prospect of asymmetry of upturns and downturns. These three features of cycles may differ significantly across countries, thereby requiring methods aimed at country-specific empirical measurement.

The main building block of any financial cycle is the evolution of credit. Credit growth is clearly a *necessary* element of any financial cycle, given the widespread findings on its role in the run-up

10 See e.g. John Geanakopolos & Ana Fostel, "Leverage Cycles and the Anxious Economy" (2008) 98:4 American Economic Rev 1211.

to crises. The work of Yves Schüler, Paul Hiebert and Tuomas Peltonen, and others, underscores this notion.[11] Frédéric Boissay, Fabrice Collard and Frank Smets in particular demonstrate mechanisms through which financial recessions follow credit booms,[12] also supported by empirical applications such as those demonstrated by Òscar Jordà, Moritz Schularick and A. M. Taylor.[13] These notions are also supported by the seminal work of Hyman Minsky, who argued that credit can be a source of financial instability and not only an amplifier.[14]

Credit is not *sufficient* as an element of a financial cycle (or as a predictor for buildup of systemic stress). A focus on credit growth alone or in relation to the economy might be misleading as a gauge of risk buildup, given the prospect of credit deepening; it is important to note that not all credit booms end in financial recessions.[15] Asset prices are an essential complement to credit in determining system leverage — in particular, the common evolution of credit and asset prices as a fundamental driver of leverage cycles.

Empirical measures of financial cycles can be extracted as common movements of national credit and asset price developments, closely linked to this concept of leverage cycles. Schüler, Hiebert and Peltonen introduced a two-part methodology to capture these common movements as country financial cycles.[16] First, a novel multivariate spectral methodology identifies country-specific cycle frequencies, using more than 45 years of quarterly data for country credit growth and asset price inflation across all market segments. Second, these identified frequencies inform a time-varying aggregation emphasizing systemic developments. This can be either a *narrow* measure of the cycle (extracting common movement inherent to credit and house prices) or a *broad* measure with a more complete portfolio choice aspect (extracting common movements of weighted average of national credit and asset price developments across all main asset market segments: real estate, bond, equity).

A judicious combination of spectral analysis and informed averaging can extract common movements in credit and asset price variables, and can improve crisis prediction. Initially, country-specific estimates of cycle length can be obtained from historical relationships, using a novel spectral approach of *power cohesion*. The latter methodology extracts common cyclical frequencies within the frequency domain from a set of indicators characterizing the financial cycle. This consists of three steps. First, a set of normalized cross-spectra for all combinations of cycle components are needed — similar in spirit to cross correlations, but in the frequency domain. Second, we average across the absolute value of these cross-spectra to understand commonalities of movement. Third, we identify the peak co-movement of indicators, spanning a window around it to discover dominant financial cycle frequencies. This resulting power cohesion method has the advantage of discarding phase shifts between variables and parsing

11 Yves Schüler, Paul Hiebert & Tuomas Peltonen, "Characterising the Financial Cycle: A Multivariate and Time-Varying Approach" (2015) ECB Working Paper No 1846 ["Characterising the Financial Cycle"]; Yves Schüler, Paul Hiebert & Tuomas Peltonen, "Coherent Financial Cycles for G-7 Countries: Why Extending Credit Can Be an Asset" (2017) ESRB Working Paper No 43 [Schüler, Hiebert & Peltonen, "Coherent Financial Cycles"].

12 Frédéric Boissay, Fabrice Collard & Frank Smets, "Booms and Banking Crises" (2016) 142 J Political Economy 489.

13 Òscar Jordà, Moritz Schularick & AM Taylor, "Leveraged Bubbles" (2015) 76 J Monetary Economics S1.

14 Hyman P Minsky, "The Financial Instability Hypothesis: An Interpretation of Keynes and an Alternative to 'Standard' Theory" (1977) 20:1 Challenge 20, online: <www.tandfonline.com/doi/abs/10.1080/05775132.1977.11470296>.

15 See e.g. Gary Gorton & Guillermo Ordoñez, "Good Booms, Bad Booms" (2016) NBER Working Paper No 22008.

16 Schüler, Hiebert & Peltonen, "Characterising the Financial Cycle", *supra* note 11; Schüler, Hiebert & Peltonen, "Coherent Financial Cycles", *supra* note 11.

out the contribution of different cycle lengths to the overall co-variance of indicators. This joint consideration also yields a more robust view on financial cycle characteristics, reconciling a long-standing empirical puzzle concerning cycle properties when using two popular alternative methodologies: frequency decompositions and standard turning point analysis. Combining information in an informed country-specific way also helps to improve crisis prediction. A key value of the derived financial cycles lies in their ability to predict systemic banking crises. Specifically, the common movement is assessed as one that can be used both as a coincident and an early warning indicator of systemic banking crises. Schüler, Hiebert and Peltonen report that results from a signalling exercise extracting the pseudo real-time forecasting performance of financial cycles vis-à-vis individual variables reinforce the case for aggregation, and suggest that combining information helps to improve the capacity of financial variables to predict the start and vulnerability periods prior to systemic banking crises.

These country-specific estimates of dominant frequencies help to inform choices when applying a filter. Such a filter, parsing out low-frequency movements common to credit and asset prices, is achieved by standardizing variables in different measurement units, then aggregating these standardized indicators into composite financial and business cycle series by means of time-varying aggregation weights that exploit changing correlation structures between variables.

The results for G7 countries suggest considerable heterogeneity of financial cycles. Schüler, Hiebert and Peltonen show that for almost all G7 countries financial cycles are long — often more than 15 years in length.[17] Germany remains a notable exception, where financial cycles have tended be shorter and closely associated with business cycles. For Germany, and to a lesser extent the United Kingdom and Canada, shorter financial cycles relate to a stronger importance for equity and bond prices, reducing cycle length for these open economies.

Taking these dominant frequencies common to credit and asset prices away from the frequency domain and back to the more familiar time domain, resulting financial cycles tend to yield a slow and predictable buildup in systemic risk. The use of a statistical filter merely emphasizes a low-frequency variation already present in the common movement of credit and asset prices (see Figure 4, which depicts the composite financial cycle indices for the United States and euro area). That is, the mere aggregation confirms a strong cyclical impetus, further emphasized by means of filtering. This, in turn, suggests that high-frequency noise surrounding certain financial asset prices, such as equity prices, are effectively dampened as part of the aggregation process. The right panel complements this information, showing both the narrow and broad composite financial cycle as well as the business cycle. It is important to keep in mind that we construct cycles of credit and asset prices in growth rates. A peak is reached when the composite indices pass from above the normalized historical median of 0.5 to below; a trough when indices pass from below 0.5 to above.

Relative to business cycles drawn from a comparable methodology, financial cycles differ in their amplitude and persistence — albeit with heterogeneity across countries. A standard set of indicators is selected to encapsulate a reference business cycle, based on the same approach used to identify financial cycles. These indicators are output, consumption, investment and hours

17 Schüler, Hiebert & Peltonen, "Coherent Financial Cycles", *supra* note 11.

worked.[18] Comparing these comparably computed cycles, three main facts stand out. First, average financial cycle length is considerably longer — at around 15 years — compared with business cycles of around nine years (or 6.7 years if Japan is excluded). Second, country financial cycles tend to be more distinct across countries than business cycle counterparts. Financial cycle synchronization is strong for most countries, but not for all. In contrast, business cycles relate homogeneously. That said, business cycles tend to embed multiple peaks — with business cycles embedding a strong medium-term component in Canada, Germany and Japan. For Canada and Germany, this may relate to a relative lack of systemic banking crises over the last half century, while Japan has a distinctive history, including a substantial cycle buildup, followed by a lengthy correction phase beginning in the early 1990s — the so-called lost decade. Third, economic downturns tend to be amplified when coincident with financial cycle contractions. Financial cycles tend to match to periods of recession quite closely. This applies regardless of the application of the filter (simply extracting low-frequency cyclical movement common to these credit and asset price series); troughs match National Bureau of Economic Research recession periods well (see Figure 4).

Focusing instead on EU countries, a close correspondence may be expected given common institutional aspects. Paul Hiebert, Ivan Jaccard and Yves Schüler drill down further for these countries on empirical features of financial and business cycles, and possible economic rationale for their divergence.[19] Results are similar to those for the G7, notably that financial cycles have a high amplitude, are longer, and are more symmetric than their business cycle counterparts. Financial cycles tend to be long, in particular in upswing phases and with important dispersion across country cases. Concordance of financial and business cycles is observed only two-thirds of the time. While a similar degree of concordance for financial cycles is apparent across countries, heterogeneity is high; that is, where a cluster of countries tends to exhibit a high synchronization in their financial cycle phases to their business cycle counterparts, it is found that financial cycles have a higher amplitude, a longer duration and exhibit far greater symmetry. Already at indicator level, real GDP growth is left-tailed (negative skewness), while credit and house price growth are rather symmetric. For financial cycles, expansions (seven-and-a-half years) tend to last longer than contractions (four years). For business cycles, by contrast, contractions are short (a little over one year), while expansions long (around six years). Mostly owing to this difference in symmetry, the authors find that financial and business cycles synchronize on average only two-thirds of the time, exhibiting weaker concordance in countries having experienced very persistent financial downturns.

Hiebert, Jaccard and Schüler also document several candidate theoretical mechanisms that could explain these differences. Five strands stand out. First, *debt overhang* may be present, whereby measures of the financial cycle, such as credit and house prices, recover more slowly following recessions than output. Debt overhang deters new investment because the benefit of new investment will go to the existing creditors, not to the investors, if the firm goes bankrupt. Second, *financial shocks* play a more important role than what is typically predicted by models developed during the Great Moderation period. Third, *learning and deviations from rational expectations* may occur in lengthy booms, when expectations can become myopic (assigning

18 See e.g. Craig Burnside, "Detrending and business cycle facts: A comment" (1998) 41:3 J Monetary Economics 513.

19 Paul Hiebert, Ivan Jaccard & Yves Schüler, "Contrasting financial and business cycles: Stylized facts and candidate explanations" (2018) 38 J Financial Stability 72.

an important role to past observations). Fourth, *strategic complementarities* can be present in financial booms, whereby the payoff from individual excess optimism can increase with the number of others holding this view. Fifth and last, *financial structures* might amplify credit booms, whereby structural characteristics, notably in housing markets (such as the dominant national preference for owning or renting homes) can allow for divergence between financial and business cycles.

Figure 4: Financial Cycle Estimates

United States

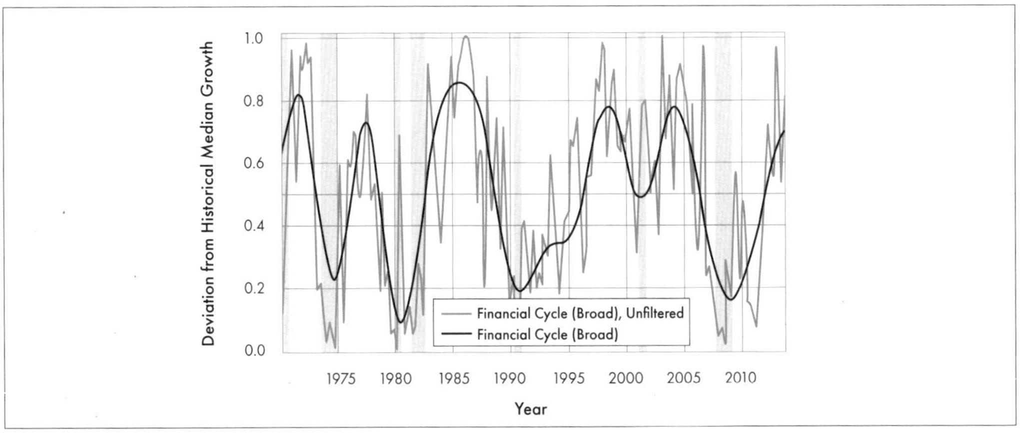

Euro Area

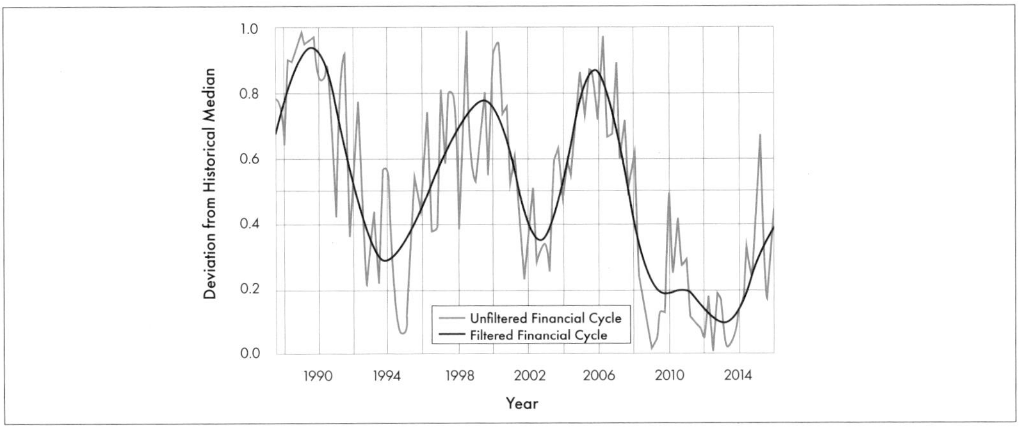

Source: ECB.

The Financial Cycle and Fragility in the Cross Section: Bringing Together the Two Dimensions of Systemic Risk

Financial cycles are broader than just risk buildup. While the financial cycle is often treated synonymously with the *time series* dimension of systemic risk, this applies only in a risk buildup phase. In a downturn phase of the financial cycle, the time series dimension and also the other dimension of systemic risk — the *cross-sectional* dimension — coalesce.[20] Figure 5 depicts the phases of a financial cycle, along with measurement considerations.

Unfortunately, it is rarely the case that theoretical and empirical approaches are considered holistically. This is important for policy — where both strands should mutually reinforce one another. As noted by Sylvain Benoit et al., while several theoretical mechanisms exist for the purpose of evaluating the rationale for buildup of systemic risk, other branches of the systemic risk literature have tended to evolve largely independently — leading to a situation in which several strands of the academic literature are not speaking to one another.[21] Methods that track the buildup of systemic risk are brought together with amplification mechanisms (for example, liquidity spirals, classical bank runs) or interconnectedness-contagion issues (for example, those deriving from network analytics).

Figure 5: Critical Phases of a Financial Cycle

Phase	Type of Systemic Risks	Measurement Focus	Dimension	Examples of Vulnerabilities/ Externalities	Modelling Approach
Risk buildup	Cyclical risks	Probability of default	Time	Asset price misalignment, excessive leverage, maturity mismatch	Time series models, early-warning models, market-based indicators
Amplification of shocks	Contagion and spillovers	Loss given default	Cross-sectional, cross-border	Interconnectedness, commonalities in exposures	Networks, spillover models, conditional loss probabilities, structural

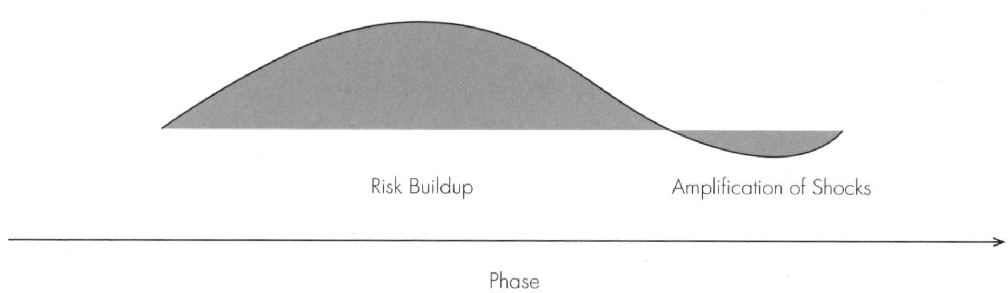

Source: Constâncio, *supra* note 20.

20 See Vítor Constâncio, "Macroprudential policy at the ECB", ECB Occasional Paper (forthcoming in 2019).

21 See Sylvain Benoit et al, "Where the Risks Lie: A Survey on Systemic Risk" (2017) 21:1 Rev Finance 109.

Figure 6: An Index for Each Phase of the Financial Cycle

a. A euro-area wide FSRI and coincident systemic stress (CISS)

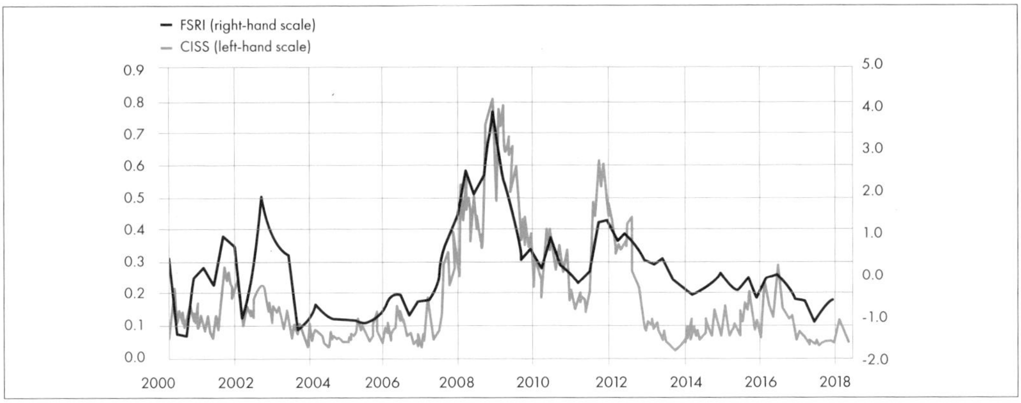

b. A CSRI for euro-area countries

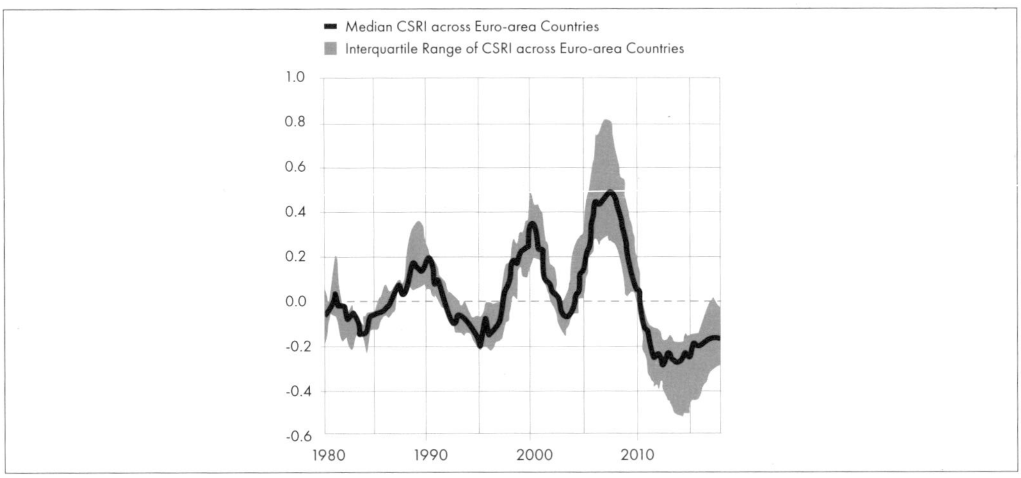

Source: ECB, *supra* note 24.

A holistic view of the interaction between the time series and cross-sectional dimensions systemic risk is essential to accurately gauge the real economy repercussions of financial crises (which are the ultimate focus of financial stability monitoring and policy makers). In marrying the time series and cross-sectional aspects of systemic risks, it is critical to measure the interplay of institutional fragility with national financial cycles.[22] An encompassing policy approach should also take into account that financial stability consists of intertemporal tradeoffs — thereby embedding a term structure of systemic risk, both near- and medium-term.[23]

At the ECB, a metric has been estimated to gauge latent losses for near-term and medium-term settings of the financial cycle, depicted in Figure 5. A financial stability risk index (FSRI) predicts the near-term recessionary effects of financial stress, while a cyclical systemic risk indicator

22 See Miguel Segoviano et al, "Latent Fragility: Conditioning Bank Distress on the Financial Cycle" (Mimeo).

23 See Tobias Adrian et al, "The Term Structure of Growth-at-Risk" (2018) IMF Working Paper No 18/180.

(CSRI) anticipates the medium-term consequences of financial instability.[24] The FSRI, on the one hand, is an encompassing index predicting near-term risks (i.e., less than one year) of deep recessions in the euro area. By extending a standard set of financial stability indicators with indicators capturing spillover and contagion risks, the index has predictive power for the near-term risk of deep recessions. The empirical performance of the index benefits from combining a large set of macro-financial indicators with spillover and contagion risk indicators. The CSRI, on the other hand, is an early warning indicator of systemic stress (more than one year), for early detection of systemic risk buildup in euro-area countries. Risks at this horizon stem from domestic credit, real estate markets, asset prices, external imbalances and cross-country spillovers. The CSRI increases, on average, several years before the onset of systemic financial crises and its level is highly correlated with measures of crisis severity. Model estimates suggest that high values of the CSRI contain information about large declines in real GDP growth three to four years down the road, as it precedes shifts in the entire distribution of future real GDP growth and especially of its left tail — thereby providing a timely signal of the buildup of systemic risk.

Where Do We Stand on Counter-cyclical Policies?

Despite the prominence of the counter-cyclical mandate, the active use of macroprudential instruments predominantly earmarked for combatting the financial cycle has thus far been limited in Europe and elsewhere. Most notably, the use of the counter-cyclical capital buffer — the policy instrument specifically earmarked for the buildup of systemic risk at the country level — has been used sparingly to date. Within the 30-country European Economic Area, only eight member states had enacted positive settings for the counter-cyclical capital buffer by June 2019, although several have announced an intention to tighten (see Figure 7, panel A). This limited use could reflect a combination of the only nascent legislation, as well as cyclical temperance, as several countries continue on the path of recovery since the GFC.

More globally, the broader palette of macroprudential policies has gained considerable traction both in Europe and around the world more generally. An IMF survey reports that macroprudential tools were applied widely in the last years.[25] Indeed, by February 2018, 141 of their 192 reporting countries indicated a total of 1,313 macroprudential measures (equating to an average of 9.3 measures per country). The application of these policies appears to be mainly drawing from the granular and targeted features of these tools. Looking across countries, only one-third of policies applied to all (aggregate) exposures of the banking system ("broad-based tools"). Of these instruments, the majority were capital conservation buffers, with far less use to date of the counter-cyclical capital buffer (as in Europe). An interesting contrast is also apparent for advanced versus emerging market economies. Around one-quarter of countries — mainly advanced economies — have favoured tools that address risks from banks' exposure to households or to address risks from banks' exposure to non-financial firms. In contrast, around one-third of countries — mainly emerging market economies — have favoured tools to address liquidity risks and foreign exchange mismatches in the banking sector.

24 See ECB, *Financial Stability Review* (May 2018).

25 See IMF, *The IMF's Annual Macroprudential Policy Survey: Objectives, Design, and Country Responses* (April 2018).

Figure 7: Macroprudential Policies

a. Counter-cyclical Capital Buffer rates, European Economic Area (shading represents level of buffer, from 0.5 to 2 percent)

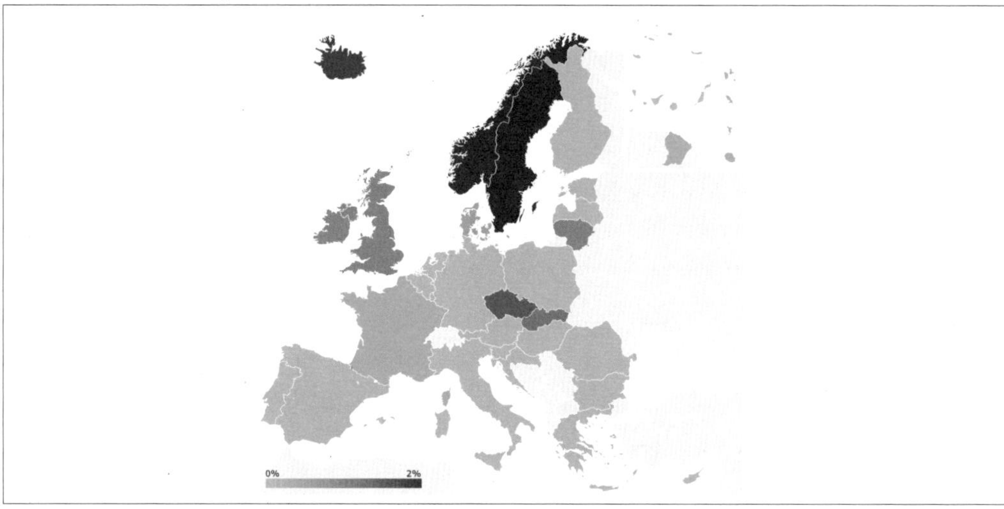

b. Macroprudential Policies at the Global Level (number of measures and percentage of total in parentheses)

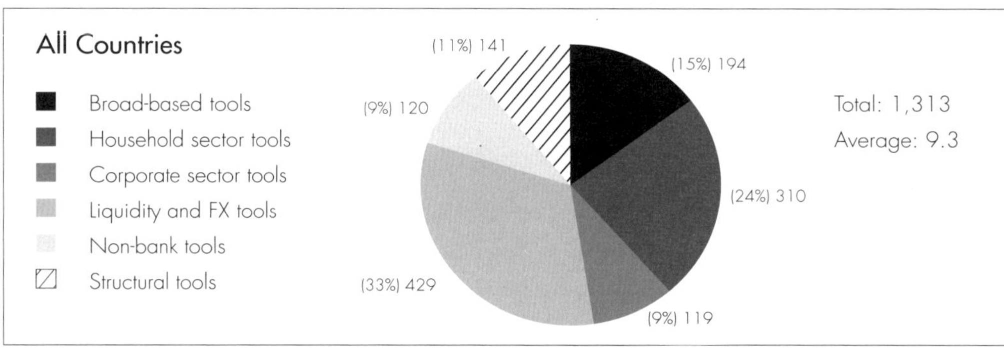

Source: European Systemic Risk Board, IMF.

As macroprudential policy making matures, so too will its relationship with other policy levers. One key interaction is that with monetary policy — itself having exhibited a marked shift toward unconventional tools when facing the zero lower bound post-crisis. On this point, debate continues on the appropriate interplay of macroprudential and monetary tools in tackling the buildup phase of systemic risk. Ultimately, discussion continues on the dichotomy presented by Frank Smets, contrasting several views of policy interplay.[26] On one end of the spectrum are arguments for policy separation between blunt and wider-ranging monetary policies versus granular and targeted macroprudential policies (see Table 1). On the other end of the spectrum are arguments for a strong role for financial stability considerations in monetary policy, given concerns about effectiveness and reach of macroprudential policies. Resolution of this debate would require accounting for open issues associated with any given alternative. Coordination issues are paramount, given complementarities between monetary and macroprudential policies.

26 Frank Smets, "Financial Stability and Monetary Policy: How Closely Interlinked?" (2014) Intl J Central Banking.

A clear attribution of responsibilities between such policies requires a better understanding of country financial cycles and their interaction with business cycle counterparts. While the debate continues, within the European Monetary Union a consensus has emerged that the country-specific nature of financial cycles translates into a need for effective country-specific policies as a natural financial stability complement to a common monetary policy focused on its primary — and necessary — objective of price stability.

Table 1: Evaluating Policy Tradeoffs

	Modified Jackson Hole Consensus	Leaning against the Wind Vindicated	Financial Stability Is Price Stability
Monetary Policy	• Framework largely unchanged • Limited effects on credit and risk taking • Blunt instrument to deal with imbalances	• Financial stability as secondary objective; lengthening of horizon • Affects risk taking • "Gets in all the cracks"	• Twin objectives on equal footing • Unblocks balance sheet impairments; avoids financial imbalances in upturns
Macroprudential Policy	Granular and effective	Cannot fully address financial cycle; arbitrage	Indistinguishable from monetary policy
Interaction of Above Policies	Limited interaction and easy separation of objectives, instruments	Financial fragility affects monetary transmission and price stability	Financial stability and price stability are intimately interlinked
Open Issues	Coordination? Lender of last resort?	Coordination? Overburden monetary policy?	Time inconsistency problems?

Source: Authors; adapted from Smets, *supra* note 26.

Conclusion

This chapter has reviewed challenges central to financial sector regulation and supervision on both sides of the Atlantic. For the United States, the post-crisis focus has centred on the effective tackling of the TBTF issue at the level of systemic financial institutions. The Minneapolis Federal Reserve Bank has taken the position that the TBTF problem in the United States remains present. The Minneapolis Plan would address this issue by forcing the most systemically important banks and non-banks to greatly reduce their leverage. For Europe, the post-crisis focus has centred on a more effective means of monitoring and tackling the buildup of systemic risk at the level of country financial systems. In this way, the chapter has reviewed the case for a more effective measurement of the buildup of systemic risk. This more effective framework for understanding country financial cycles and why they differ can play a key role in governing policies to attenuate the buildup of systemic risk — thereby complementing macroeconomic and other policies aimed at financial stabilization.

8

The Data Standardization Challenge

Richard Berner and Kathryn Judge

> *"Quality information is the lifeblood of strong, vibrant markets. Without it, investor confidence erodes. Liquidity dries up. Fair and efficient markets simply cease to exist. As the quantity of information increases exponentially through the Internet and other technologies, the quality of that information must be our signal priority."*[1]
>
> **— US Securities and Exchange Commission (SEC) Chairman Arthur Levitt**

> *"Data standards are the rules by which data are described and recorded."*[2]
>
> **— United States Geological Survey**

1 Arthur Levitt, "Quality Information: The Lifeblood of Our Markets" (Speech to the Economic Club of New York, 18 October 1999), online: <www.sec.gov/news/speech/speecharchive/1999/spch304.htm>.

2 United States Geological Survey, Data Standards, online: USGS Data Management <www2.usgs.gov/datamanagement/plan/datastandards.php>. That this definition comes from an entirely different discipline than finance illustrates the universality of the need for standardized data.

Information is the lifeblood of finance. The role the financial system plays in moving capital from savers to borrowers and projects is inherently informational. Banks, investment banks, asset managers, insurance companies and other financial firms add value in part by producing, verifying and disseminating the information needed to determine who should get financing, on what terms and the risks involved. Financial markets, and institutional structures such as exchanges, play essential roles in aggregating and translating information into price signals. Institutional investors aggregate capital and further contribute to the information-generating role of the financial system. Many significant financial innovations, like securitization, exist not just to redistribute or manage risks, but to do so in a manner that alters the information sensitivity of the financial instruments available in the market to meet participants' needs.[3] Likewise, other financial-system functions, such as pooling and reallocating risks and providing liquidity, depend on the sector's information-related roles.[4]

The integral role of information in finance also helps to explain much financial regulation. Securities regulation, for example, reduces the costs investors incur gathering, analyzing and verifying information.[5] Similarly, cornerstones of bank regulation, such as capped deposit insurance, coupled with supervision, can be framed as efforts to reallocate monitoring and other information-production to the parties best suited to undertake it. Regulators also require information to fulfill many of their mandates, in particular with respect to promoting systemic stability and resilience.

Designing and implementing appropriate data standards is an important mechanism through which the government can fulfill these dual roles of enhancing the efficiency of private activity and obtaining the high-quality information necessary to better serve the public at large. Standardization is essential to compare and aggregate data and can enable firms and regulators to produce more accurate and timely information about a host of issues at lower expense. Firms benefit by better understanding their clients' needs, and in pricing and managing risk. Regulators benefit by being better able to identify trends across firms and markets, and potentially being better able to assess the local and systemic risks associated with those changes. Standardization also facilitates sharing data so that firms and regulators can use and understand the same data within and across jurisdictions, reducing redundancy and misunderstanding. At its best, data standardization can serve as a crucial ingredient in building and sustaining the trust, accountability, adaptability and efficiency that are essential to finance.

Well designed and broadly used data standards also have the potential to promote systemic resilience. The financial crisis of 2007–2009, commonly known as the global financial crisis (GFC), vividly illustrates the potential for how information gaps that grow in the absence of quality data contribute to systemic fragility. When subprime mortgage-backed securities proved to be more risky than their ratings suggested, the extent of the market dysfunction that followed far exceeded that which could be readily explained by the potential actual losses on those instruments. The averted failure of Bear Stearns and actual failure of Lehman Brothers entailed

3 Gary Gorton & George Pennacchi, "Security Baskets and Index-Linked Securities" (1991) National Bureau of Economic Research Working Paper No 3711.

4 See e.g. Douglas Diamond & Raghuram Rajan, "A Theory of Bank Capital" (2000) 55:6 J Finance 2431; Charles W Calomiris & Charles M Kahn, "The role of demandable debt in structuring optimal banking arrangements" (1991) 81:3 American Economic Rev 497.

5 Zohar Goshen & Gideon Parchomovsky, "The Essential Role of Securities Regulation" (2006) 55 Duke LJ 711 at 715.

similar dynamics, as knowable unknowns (that is, information gaps) exacerbated fragility and impeded the ability of government actors to intervene in a timely and proportionate way. Had firms and regulators been able to use standardized, reliable information to assess more accurately the origins and impact of these developments, the overall course of the crisis might have been far less severe.

Hence, as explained by the Financial Stability Board (FSB) and the International Monetary Fund (IMF), "the recent crisis has reaffirmed an old lesson — good data and good analysis are the lifeblood of effective surveillance and policy responses at both the national and international levels."[6] Data standardization alone obviously cannot produce a stable financial system, but in improving data quality, it represents a critical tool to build and sustain a resilient system — that is, one that can take a few knocks and still get back on its feet without significant spillover on the real economy.

This chapter's first contribution is to show why data standardization deserves a higher place on the post-crisis regulatory priority list. Although there has been some progress toward the development of and mandates to employ data standards in the decade since the GFC, improvements in data standardization have been slow, hard won, and, in many areas, elusive. The examination here reveals numerous, often unexciting, but consequential, impediments to data standardization. Collective action problems, positive externalities, and governance and incentives challenges are among the many factors impeding progress.

It might seem like an odd time to be making data standardization such a priority. With the massive technological changes of the last few years, some might believe that these issues will solve themselves. We think otherwise. A core assumption underlying our analysis is that it is not enough to increase the scope and quantity of information; if anything, today we are overwhelmed by the quantity. This makes efforts to address the qualitative characteristics of the input data — whether it is sufficiently reliable, adequately defined and well understood — all the more important. These aims are at the core of data standardization. Improving data standards and promoting more widespread standardization have the potential to unleash real gains for public and private stakeholders and society more generally. By illuminating those gains and myriad impediments, this chapter helps explain the mixed progress over the past decade and how to do better in the decades ahead.

The chapter's second contribution is to use data standardization as a lens for understanding the challenges that impede effective financial regulation more generally. Data standardization has the potential to benefit banks, other financial firms and the public generally. Why, then, haven't we seen more progress? The answer suggested here is that mundane details can matter as much as abstract incentives. The benefits of standardization accrue slowly, are spread widely and are only partially captured by financial firms, while the costs are borne upfront and mainly by those firms.

Also significant, and telling, is that data standardization doesn't fit neatly into either a "tough on finance" or a deregulatory agenda. Oftentimes, financial regulation is depicted as a battleground. In this frame, the public is assumed to benefit from more regulation and is situated on one side,

6 FSB & IMF, "The Financial Crisis and Information Gaps," Report to the G-20 Finance Ministers and Central Bank Governors, IMF Staff & FSB Secretariat (29 October 2009), online: <www.imf.org/external/np/g20/pdf/102909.pdf>.

with banks and other financial firms, who are assumed to oppose regulation, on the other. Close discussions between regulators and financial firms, of the kind that are critical to producing high-quality standards, are seen by some as troubling evidence of regulatory capture. At the same time, because of coordination and other challenges, the efficacy of data standards often depends on broadly applicable government mandates. As a result, standardization is not deregulatory, as that term is commonly understood.

The good news is that standardization is now under way in a number of domains. Standards that emerged in response to weaknesses revealed by the GFC are slowly becoming more widely required, and there is new leadership in efforts to develop more thoughtful data standards in other areas. Given the clear value of thoughtful standardization and the many impediments slowing adoption, examining data standardization illuminates systemic challenges that impede both the efficiency of financial firms and the quality of financial regulation.

Background: What Was Learned from the Crisis

This section explores what the GFC revealed about the importance of data standardization and why post-crisis developments accentuate the public and private value of well-designed data standards.

This volume commemorates (if such a word can be used for such an event) the 2007–2009 GFC, so that is our starting point. The decade that has passed since the crisis reached its nadir in the wake of the failure of Lehman Brothers in 2008. Most analysts agree that adverse information dynamics played a central role, contributing to the scope of the market dysfunction and the adverse spillover effects on the real economy that made the crisis so tragic. The authors have each addressed elsewhere the important role of information gaps in contributing to the crisis.[7] Instead of reiterating that work here, this chapter will illustrate how information gaps contribute to fragility with a focus on the failure of Lehman Brothers, and on how the government's information production and dissemination helped restore stability through the market's positive response to the first round of stress tests.

With the benefit of hindsight, it is clear that the actual losses incurred as a direct result of Lehman Brothers' failure were not sufficient to compromise directly the vitality of any major financial institution or key market structure. Nonetheless, Lehman's failure triggered widespread market dysfunction. One reason was the inability of market participants to quickly assess their total exposures to Lehman, including its numerous subsidiaries and affiliates, or to know the exposures of their other counterparties. Financial regulators were also in the dark. A market reaction that is outsized relative to the content of new information is the very definition of systemic fragility.[8] Had standardized, reliable information been available to assess the origins and impact of these developments, the overall course of the crisis might have been far less severe.

The massive runs on money market mutual funds (MMMFs) that followed offer examples of information-gap spillovers. One fund, the Primary Reserve Fund, which held US$785 million

7 Kathryn Judge, "The first year: the role of a modern lender of last resort" (2016) 843 Colum L Rev 116; Kathryn Judge, "Information Gaps and Shadow Banking" (2017) 103:3 Va L Rev 101; US, Senate, Senate Banking Subcommittee on Economic Policy, *Testimony of Richard Berner, Director of the Office of Financial Research, U.S. Department of the Treasury* (29 January 2014), online: <www.banking.senate.gov/imo/media/doc/BernerTestimony12914EP.pdf>.

8 Franklin Allen & Douglas Gale, "Financial Fragility, Liquidity, and Asset Prices" (2004) 2:6 J European Economic Assoc 1015.

in commercial paper issued by Lehman Brothers, was forced to "break the buck" — to redeem shares below the $1.00 net asset value typically assigned to MMMF shares. At the lowest, shares in the fund were redeemed at 97 cents, and most holders eventually received 99 cents on the dollar. No other MMMF ended up breaking the buck. Not one.

Nonetheless, these events triggered a massive run (US$400 billion, or 20 percent, in a few days) on MMMFs holding privately issued debt. MMMF investors had only limited information about the actual assets and their creditworthiness backing their claims, so it was easier, cheaper and safer to run than to learn more about the actual risks of sticking around. As Ricardo Caballero and Alp Simsek demonstrate formally, most financial firms may have been able to assess their rough exposure to Lehman Brothers, but they could not readily ascertain the exposure and soundness of other financial firms. So they withdrew from activities that might expose them to credit risk, which impaired liquidity and market functioning.[9] The resulting significant ripple effects on short-term money markets were halted only through government intervention.

The positive impact of the first round of stress tests illustrates the flipside — the important role of more information in facilitating market functioning. By early 2009, the government had engaged in massive efforts to stabilize the financial system. Among those efforts: implementing a range of non-bank liquidity facilities and guarantees of deposits and new senior debt; providing massive support to American International Group (AIG); converting key non-banks to bank holding companies; creating the Troubled Asset Relief Program; offering capital to many banks through a voluntary Capital Purchase Program; and announcing that stress tests would be used to assess banking system capital needs. These steps brought about significant improvements in market functioning, but normalcy remained out of reach.

Then, on May 7, 2009, the Federal Reserve and other bank regulators announced the results of the Supervisory Capital Assessment Program (SCAP — the stress tests). The tests provided market participants much-needed information that they could verify and trust. The Fed deliberately disclosed the results of the SCAP. In providing an unprecedented level of detail regarding the methodology and inputs used in reaching those results, the Fed turned on its head the assumption that bank supervision should always be secret. Both gambles paid off. As then Federal Reserve Chair Ben Bernanke later observed: "The SCAP stands out…as one of the critical turning points in the financial crisis. It provided anxious investors with something they craved: credible information about prospective losses at banks."[10]

These contrasting episodes reveal that lack of information contributed to the fragility that became manifest during the crisis, and the provision of information played an important role in helping to restore stability. Although there is a gap between data and information, high-quality data standards are one of the most effective ways of narrowing that gap and enabling timely information production.

The remainder of this chapter will explore why data standardization might seem to be easy, and why it nonetheless has proven difficult and slow.

9 Ricardo Caballero & Alp Simsek, "Fire Sales in a Model of Complexity" (2013) 68:6 J Finance 2549.

10 Board of Governors of the Federal Reserve System, "Lessons from the Failure of Lehman Brothers", Testimony to the Committee on Financial Services, US House of Representatives, 20 April 2010, online: <www.federalreserve.gov/newsevents/testimony/bernanke20100420a.htm>.

Why It Should Be Easy

Obstacles to data standardization would be understandable if the only gain were enhanced systemic stability at some point in the future. This section shows why well designed and comprehensively implemented data standardization also confers benefits outside of crisis periods. In so doing, it shows why data standardization seems like it should be easier to implement than post-crisis reforms that impose only costs outside of crisis periods or that benefit the public at the expense of regulated institutions.

Firms Benefit

Firms benefit from quality data standards by better understanding their clients' needs, and being better able to price and manage risk. Effective risk management requires coordination. The capacity of senior management to oversee and coordinate actions among various divisions within their organizations depends on standardized information.

While key players are accountable for important functions, everyone working in a financial institution should be attuned to business risks. Such a structure requires that all members of the team communicate effectively. To do so requires that they have appropriate access to the same high-quality, accurate facts as the basis for risk detection, understanding, monitoring, remediation and recovery, and that the firm assures policies for standardization that are followed and create accountability for data quality throughout the firm. If a firm has an operational incident that impairs, corrupts or loses data, it will be easier to recover and recreate client and transaction data if they are standardized. Standardized, high-quality data are also critical for effective use of third-party vendors for risk management or compliance functions.

Standards can also help reduce regulatory compliance costs. As standards become more widely understood and used, regulatory demands for duplicate information in slightly different forms should decline. Standardization could make it easier for firms to communicate with regulators, ensuring that they precisely define what they are measuring and why.

Supervisors and Other Regulators Benefit

Regulators benefit from quality data standards by being better able to spot risks in firms, markets and across the system, and to design effective, efficient and appropriately tailored remedies to mitigate those risks. The interests of prudential regulators and regulated firms should be well aligned: each wants firms to be profitable, well managed and well capitalized, taking risk knowingly and managing that risk appropriately.

But a core challenge for bank and other supervisors is that a regulated firm inevitably knows far more about its operations and risk exposures than its supervisors. Data standardization will not eliminate this asymmetry, but it can help to mitigate it. For example, when bank supervisors regularly rotate among firms, as they now do, standardized data can enable regulators to compare risk management practices across firms and quickly assess a new firm's practices. Standardized data could, in time, help regulators to develop or improve the robustness of their techniques to assess firms' risk and risk-management capabilities.

The Fed's stress tests are an example of a domain where greater standardization enhances the accuracy of supervisory efforts. Clearly, both regulators and firms have made progress in this area since the GFC. The challenge is to do so more effectively than in current practice. Were the Fed to embrace data standards in stress testing and other supervisory activities, they and the firms they supervise would benefit.

Using standards facilitates sharing data appropriately and securely so that firms and regulators can use and understand the same data within and across jurisdictions, and so that duplication of data reporting can be reduced, if not eliminated. Both benefit by building and sustaining the trust, accountability, adaptability and efficiency in finance essential to its functioning. These efficiency gains could help boost economic productivity by allocating funds to their highest uses and could also prove crucial in the ever-more-competitive and ever-more-global financial markets.

Society Benefits

The microprudential benefits of standardization are significant. However, the most important public value served by greater standardization is the potential for enhanced system-wide resilience. Financial crises are informational events. Many of the classic forms of market dysfunction, from runs by short-term creditors (such as depositors) to liquidity providers refusing to continue playing that role, are, at least in part, the by-product of incomplete or asymmetric information about events or changes in circumstances.

As a consequence, when it comes to thinking about the system as a whole, the alignment mentioned above between the interests of prudential regulators and regulated firms is asymmetric. System-wide, financial stability or macroprudential policies are needed because neither firm risk management nor microprudential policies are sufficient to deal with the system-wide externalities and market failures that can arise from asymmetric information and mispriced guarantees. And, as a practical matter, market participants and regulators are constantly operating with only a subset of the information that could be pertinent to the decisions they are making. Given the costs and other frictions inhibiting data compilation, distribution and analysis, this is inevitable. The critical point is that these information gaps are an increasingly important source of systemic fragility.

The flip side of the challenge posed by information gaps is the opportunities that they create. When market participants are reluctant to transact because of a lack of information that recent events have made pertinent, filling in those gaps can be an important mechanism through which regulators help restore functionality. High-quality information about the location of capital deficiencies, interconnections among firms, and other vulnerabilities can also help regulators identify and address fragilities in a timely fashion. Data standardization is one component of a broader information infrastructure that can and must be built in "peacetime" if we expect regulators to have any chance of producing timely and relevant information once panic sets in.

Of course, the benefits of risk management and financial stability activities are often not obscured during periods of calm. More generally, systemic resilience is a good that benefits far more than the firms engaged in standardization, creating the typical challenges that arise with positive externalities.

Nonetheless, one lesson of the financial crisis is that vigilance — and the investments needed to achieve it — in peacetime is essential. Because the next crisis is unlikely to replicate those of the past, we do not know in advance what information will be needed, which means an expansion of the range of possible infrastructures that must be built in advance. Data standardization is critical to that undertaking. This is one of the core lessons of 2008 that has been only partially realized thus far.

Why It Is Often Quite Hard

Having argued that market participants and regulators both stand to gain from improved data standardization, the natural question to ask is why we haven't seen more of it? That's even more perplexing, given that industry has long recognized and supported the need for standardization. To quote from John Bottega and Linda Powell's seminal "Linchpin" paper on entity identification: "The financial services industry has been exploring the issue of unique entity identification for decades. More recently, several [industry] efforts have been made to advance the idea of a standard LEI [Legal Entity Identifier], but competing priorities, funding issues, and an evident lack of industry focus have kept such a standard, and the benefits it could have yielded, from being implemented."[11]

To be sure, in the decade since the crisis, there has been meaningful progress toward the development of and mandates to employ data standards. In derivatives markets, for example, regulators globally have started to require the LEI to identify parties to financial transactions ("who is who")[12] and the relationships among those parties ("who owns who").[13] LEIs have the potential to make precise entity and counterparty identification frictionless, thus improving the quality of the information that firms use to manage risk and report to supervisors.[14] There has also been some progress made in efforts to standardize transactions and products ("who owns what"), which is equally important in interconnected, global markets.[15] At the same time,

11 John A Bottega and Linda F Powell, "Creating a Linchpin for Financial Data: Toward a Universal Legal Entity Identifier" (2011) Finance and Economics Discussion Series Working Paper 2011-07, Divisions of Research & Statistics and Monetary Affairs Federal Reserve Board, Washington, DC, online: <www.federalreserve.gov/pubs/feds/2011/201107/201107pap.pdf>.

12 The LEI is a 20-digit, alpha-numeric code that clearly and uniquely identifies parties to financial transactions; specifically, the legal entities within companies participating in global financial markets. Thanks to public and private collaboration, use of the LEI system is now widespread — to date, more than 1.4 million LEIs are in use — but it is far from ubiquitous. Global Legal Entity Identifier Foundation (GLEIF), "LEI Statistics" (2018), online: <www.gleif.org/en/lei-data/global-lei-index/lei-statistics>.

13 These are established with so-called Level 2 LEI data; see <www.gleif.org/en/lei-data/access-and-use-lei-data/level-2-data-who-owns-whom#>.

14 GLEIF, "LEI in KYC: A New Future for Legal Entity Identification" (2018), online: <www.gleif.org/en/lei-solutions/lei-in-kyc-a-new-future-for-legal-entity-identification>; McKinsey & Company and GLEIF, "The Legal Entity Identifier: The Value of the Unique Counterparty ID" (2018), online: <www.gleif.org/en/lei-solutions/mckinsey-company-and-gleif-creating-business-value-with-the-lei>.

15 Benoît Cœuré remarked on this progress in 2017 at the third workshop of the Office of Financial Research/European Central Bank/Bank of England, "Setting Global Standards for Granular Data: Sharing the Challenge" (28 March 2017), online: <www.ecb.europa.eu/press/key/date/2017/html/sp170328.en.html> ("The interconnectedness of financial markets establishes an obvious need to improve our global ability to collect, aggregate, disseminate and share data"). And in April 2019, the GLEIF and the Association of National Numbering Agencies published the first pilot project linking newly issued International Securities Identification Numbers and LEIs. It was created to improve the transparency of exposure by linking the issuer and issuance of securities. This enables firms to aggregate data that clearly shows their securities exposure in relation to an individual issuer and its related entities. Stephan Wolf, "A Progress Report on the ANNA and GLEIF Mapping Initiative: First Pilot ISIN-to-LEI Relationship File Published", GLEIF blog, online: <www.gleif.org/en/newsroom/blog/a-progress-report-on-the-anna-and-gleif-mapping-initiative-first-pilot-isin-to-lei-relationship-file-published>.

improvements in data standardization remain sluggish and are a long way from addressing even those problems revealed to be pressing in the GFC. LEI adoption remains incomplete and progress on other fronts has been even slower.[16] The use of LEIs in derivatives and, increasingly, in other markets is a good example of a post-crisis reform that has been slow but meaningful.[17] Work is also progressing to create coherent reference data — the data that help define financial instruments and the taxonomy or ontology to establish how instruments relate to one another.[18] Work is likewise progressing to move from a sometimes duplicative documents-plus-data financial reporting regime to data-centric reporting.[19]

That slow progress is not from lack of industry support. Since the Linchpin paper was published in 2011, industry has strongly supported standards initiatives and provided leadership in this area. The Data Coalition, a non-profit supported by industry, has supported the need for data standards, both in financial services and in the federal government.[20] Market participants on the Financial Research Advisory Committee of the Office of Financial Research have urged broader adoption.[21]

Moreover, industry and regulators have worked together on these initiatives. The industry supported the creation of the GLEIF. On behalf of JP Morgan, Robin Doyle, managing director of the Office of Regulatory Affairs, noted that recent efforts at data standardization have entailed "a unique collaboration among industry, regulators, and other standard-setting bodies to develop data and reporting standards and to create global systems to manage and maintain the standards."[22]

Despite this meaningful progress and support, however, the improvements have lagged far behind the need. It has been more than a decade since the GFC hit its nadir and not one of the initiatives just described has been fully implemented; some have been poorly implemented, requiring rework; and far more work remains to be done in other domains. Part of what makes data standardization a useful lens is that progress is heterogeneous. It's not that it's not happening, but it is happening inconsistently across substantive domains and across jurisdictions. Understanding where it is proceeding more quickly and the challenges that have impeded effective standardization shows that significant improvements are possible, but they are not assured.

16 See e.g. Bank for International Settlements and International Organization of Securities Commissions, *Harmonisation of critical OTC derivatives data elements (other than UTI and UPI)*, Committee on Payments and Market Infrastructures (April 2018), online: <www.bis.org/cpmi/publ/d175.pdf>.

17 See the introductory section of this chapter. See also EC, *Commission Directive 2014/65/EU on markets in financial instruments* [2014] OJ, L 173 at 349; Bertrand Couillault, Jun Mizuguchi & Matthew Reed, "Collective Action: Toward Solving a Vexing Problem to Build a Global Infrastructure for Financial Information" (2017), Office of Financial Research, online: <www.financialresearch.gov/briefs/2017/02/02/collective-action-toward-solving-a-vexing-problem-to-build-global-infrastructure/>.

18 One example is the Financial Industry Business Ontology (FIBO). EDM Council, *FIBO Primer* (2018), online: <https://cdn.ymaws.com/edmcouncil.org/resource/collection/16D6DC67-430E-4F75-9E07-08B1EC228091/FIBO_Primer_v0.2.pdf>.

19 Data Coalition, Press Release, "After Five Years the SEC Votes to Adopt Inline XBRL for Corporate Financial Filings" (2018), online: <www.datacoalition.org/press-releases/after-five-years-the-sec-votes-to-adopt-inline-xbrl-for-corporate-financial-filings/>.

20 Data Coalition, "Policy Agenda", online: <www.datacoalition.org/issues/policy-agenda/>.

21 Office of Financial Research, Financial Research Advisory Committee, online: <www.financialresearch.gov/frac/2017/02/23/committee-meeting/>.

22 Robin Doyle, "Data Standardization: A Call To Action", JP Morgan (2 May 2018), online: <www.jpmorganchase.com/corporate/news/insights/data-standardization-call-to-action.htm>.

The following section attempts to answer the question of why data standardization has been so slow and difficult, given its recognized importance and the apparent alignment of public and private interests.

Short-term Costs, Long-term Gains

Standardizing data is not a free good. The costs of developing standards, testing them, retooling firm and regulatory systems to use them, and working out the kinks in implementation are considerable, and the costs of these investments are incurred early on. The benefits follow with a lag, and the benefits aren't restricted to those who incur the bulk of the costs.

In addition, the connection between bad data and financial instability is far harder to understand than the moral hazard and unfairness of bailouts, and far less tangible than corrupt bankers who can be blamed when something goes wrong. So, while some regulators are engaging in a time-consuming process of helping to design and implement well-crafted data standardization requirements, universal regulatory support for data standards, at least in the United States, is lacking. Few voters will demand that their elected representatives legislate data standardization (although a bipartisan trio of visionary members of Congress did exactly that[23]).

Collective action problems, positive externalities and other classic but still meaningful challenges associated with governance and incentives compound the challenge.[24] This externality creates a free rider issue — gains aren't equally shared, so there's a first mover disadvantage. As in other public finance projects that entail upfront costs and an uncertain stream of long-term benefits to all, mandates and incentives are required to promote action.

Coordination Challenges

Another core challenge is that data standardization requires coordination from diverse parties, not only government and market actors, but various groups within those broad categories. Thus, the problem is not only a coordination problem of the kind recognized by Mancur Olson decades ago, but also a cultural one.[25] Effectively implementing data standardization requires groups who think about issues in slightly different ways — business leaders, risk managers, legal officers, data scientists and financial economists — to understand how others see the world. They must find vocabulary and figure out collectively how to devise standards that can serve related, but not identical, aims.

An additional challenge: private and public actors will only fully benefit from switching their current proprietary systems to new models that use standardized inputs when there is widespread adoption. So maintaining legacy systems while putting new ones in place adds to the costs. These network externalities underscore the need for government coordination and mandates.

Inadequate IT and Data Infrastructure at Firms

In theory, private firms stand to enjoy an array of gains from well-designed data standards. To fully enjoy these gains, however, firms need the technology and enterprise-wide data

23 Data Coalition, "The Financial Transparency Act," online: <www.datacoalition.org/issues/financial-transparency-act/>.

24 Couillault, Mizuguchi & Reed, *supra* note 17.

25 Mancur Olson Jr, *The Logic of Collective Action* (Cambridge, MA: Harvard University Press, 1971).

management and governance practices that will allow them to use the data to better identify and manage their risks.

The evidence available suggests that many firms are not yet in a position to harness these gains. According to a 2013 report by the Basel Committee on Banking Supervision (BCBS): "One of the most significant lessons learned from the global financial crisis that began in 2007 was that banks' information technology (IT) and data architectures were inadequate to support the broad management of financial risks. Many banks lacked the ability to aggregate risk exposures and identify concentrations quickly and accurately at the bank group level, across business lines and between legal entities."[26]

Although there has been significant progress, these IT-related challenges remain. A 2018 Progress Report by the BCBS brings this point home. According to the report, "banks have increasingly recognised the value of implementing the Principles and have stepped up their efforts to do so," yet progress toward those goals has been insufficient.[27] Only three global systemically important banks are fully compliant with the principles, and most have not taken a sufficiently comprehensive approach to assuring the principles' goals. Further progress will be essential to produce comprehensive, high-quality, interoperable data.

Fragmented Regulatory Structure and Path Dependence

In the United States, the balkanized regulatory structure is an obstacle to adoption of data standards. Regulators are free to use whatever mode of collection they choose. The Commodity Futures Trading Commission (CFTC) and the SEC did choose to require the LEI to report swap and securities-based swap data.[28] But in most cases the agencies request, rather than require, its use.[29] This may reflect a lack of regulatory understanding regarding the benefits or a failure to adequately value gains that accrue outside a particular regulator's mandate.

Adding to the challenge, no higher authority can compel agencies to use a particular standard. The Financial Stability Oversight Council, which was created to solve collective action problems among regulators, can make recommendations, but it has no authority to require member agencies to adopt data standards. The other post-crisis change, the newly formed Office of Financial Research (OFR), does have authority to require standards in data it collects or that member agencies collect on behalf of the council, but it has no authority to require their use for other data those agencies collect.[30]

In Europe, the situation is the opposite. Despite the fragmentation resulting from 28 sovereigns in the European Union, the European Securities and Markets Authority and other pan-European

26 BCBS, *Principles for effective risk data aggregation and risk reporting,* January 2013, online: <www.bis.org/publ/bcbs239.pdf>.

27 BCBS, *Progress in adopting the "Principles for effective risk data aggregation and risk reporting"*, June 2018, online: <www.bis.org/bcbs/publ/d443.pdf>.

28 See Levitt, *supra* note 1; US SEC, *Public Statement: Statement on Proposal of FAST Act Modernization and Simplification of Regulation S-K, Commissioner Kara M Stein,* online: <www.sec.gov/news/public-statement/stein-statement-101117>.

29 GLEIF, "Regulatory Use of the LEI" (2018), online: <www.gleif.org/en/lei-solutions/regulatory-use-of-the-lei>.

30 *Dodd-Frank Wall Street Reform and Consumer Protection Act,* 12 USC (2018), § 5343(c)(2). Helpfully, the OFR has helpfully proposed a rule for collecting bilateral repo data that requires the use of standards.

regulators have required the use of the LEI in all but a handful of reporting requirements.[31] And even post-Brexit, it seems likely that the United Kingdom will retain those requirements. That Europe has moved more quickly than the United States to impose a broadly applicable requirement that parties use the LEI highlights the challenge of entrenched interests and the way newcomers can leapfrog over incumbents. More specifically, Europe is in the position of trying to create a Capital Market Union. In contrast to the United States, where capital markets have long provided roughly two-thirds of all intermediation, Europe remains more reliant on banks and thus capital flows across countries remain lower than would seem optimal. This creates the motivation needed to adopt new rules, at least some of which — like the broad LEI requirement — are closer to the current state of the art than the United States.

A Look Ahead

We believe that data standards have benefits that greatly exceed the costs, but that, as a classic public good, government must solve the collective action problem by mandating their use. That said, data standards work well only when well designed, and that also requires meaningful participation from industry and public-private cooperation and partnerships to align actions and interests.

We close with two examples that illustrate both the potential of such participation and the need for further progress.

Derivatives

New, post-crisis rules sometimes require and otherwise strongly incentivize central clearing of derivatives.[32] These changes have brought a host of new challenges and opportunities, only some of which are informational. One of those aims was to promote post-trade transparency in derivatives for both market participants and regulators through the establishment of swap data repositories (SDRs, known as trade repositories in Europe) and trade reporting requirements. As mentioned earlier, in the United States, the CFTC required the LEI in swap reporting, which improved the quality and the value of those data. The industry has also supported the use of standards. But implementation fell short. Initial efforts to collect swap data left it up to the CCPs or their SDRs to decide what data elements should be collected, and how they should be reported. So each SDR reported data in its own idiosyncratic way, with different data elements in different formats. The result, in the words of a senior official, was a "meteor storm."[33]

There has been meaningful progress. According to a recent CFTC report, "in 2014, roughly half of all reports for the highly standardized credit default swaps (CDS) lacked complete price information, and approximately 15% of all CDS trades lacked a legal entity identifier, making

31 See Steven Maijoor, "MiFID II Implementation: Achievements and Current Priorities" (Address to the Federation of European Securities Exchanges convention, Vienna, 21 June 2018), online: <www.esma.europa.eu/document/mifid-ii-implementation-%E2%80%93-achievements-and-current-priorities-steven-maijoor-fese>. For a thorough overview of the current requirements and how they changed in the Markets in Financial Instruments Directive II (MiFID II), see Danny Busch, "MiFID II and MiFIR: stricter rules for the EU financial markets" (2017) 11:2-3 L & Financial Markets Rev 126.

32 See generally *Dodd-Frank Wall Street Reform and Consumer Protection Act,* 12 USC (2018), Title VII, 21 July 2010.

33 CFTC leadership acknowledged these issues back in 2013, but it took until 2017 to specify solutions. CFTC, "Speeches & Testimony: Making the CFTC's Surveillance Work: Efficient Data Management and Clear Rule Implementation" (2013), online: <www.cftc.gov/PressRoom/SpeechesTestimony/opaomalia-24>.

it difficult to identify the counterparty. By early 2018, roughly 95% of all CDS trades had complete counterparty and price information."[34]

Nonetheless, significant challenges remain. SDR requirements are not yet harmonized between the SEC and CFTC, nor are they harmonized between the United States and the European Union — another area in which public-private cooperation could help solve this coordination problem. The sheer volume of granular data and their lack of comparability has limited the ability to manage and process the data collected and to extract useful information. As a result, regulators cannot fully compare the data currently being produced with other data sets to effectively oversee or stress test CCPs.

In response, the CFTC announced in July 2017 that it was launching a new review of the swap data reporting regulations, and it subsequently announced a wholesale review of swaps regulations and reporting.[35] Leadership is key, and the CFTC is now trying to provide that.

The role of a leader here is to identify and draw attention to key issues, keep other parties motivated, learn from mistakes, work with key stakeholders and counterparts at home and abroad, and use the force of law needed to produce uniformity of adoption once a usable set of standards and data elements have been identified. In that regard, as noted earlier, the FSB has provided leadership through its Data Gaps Initiative to coordinate efforts to improve the scope and quality of global financial data.[36]

Another key element is willingness by all to listen, learn and compromise. As the experience in this domain reflects, going it on one's own doesn't work. Uniformity is key, and can only be achieved when there is broad buy-in and a well-designed standard. Similarly, the more regulators are willing to work together to produce standards that can serve multiple aims, the greater the potential efficiency gains in terms of reduced reporting requirements. These small compromises can be hard won, but over time can enable a far more productive dialogue by getting disparate regulators and market participants on the same page.

Industry can also play an important leadership role in helping to develop usable standards and to work with regulators to help them understand how that data can help them achieve specified aims. As the flurry of post-crisis reforms recedes, but the volume of financial activity increases, and fragilities remain, now is a ripe moment for progress.

Fintech

The current excitement surrounding financial technology (fintech) may seem to make standardization all the more banal. Why is there a need for standardization and all of the associated upfront costs when innovations such as distributed ledger technology (which reliably

34 JC Giancarlo & Bruce Tuckman, "Swaps Regulation Version 2.0: An Assessment of the Current Implementation of Reform and Proposals for Next Steps" (2018), CFTC White Paper, online: <www.cftc.gov/sites/default/files/2018-04/oce_chairman_swapregversion2whitepaper_042618.pdf>.

35 *Ibid*; CFTC, "Roadmap to Achieve High Quality Swaps Data" (2017), online: <www.cftc.gov/sites/default/files/idc/groups/public/@newsroom/documents/file/dmo_swapdataplan071017.pdf>; CFTC, "Amendments to the Swap Data Access Provisions of Part 49 and Certain Other Matters" (2018), RIN Number 3038-AE44, online: <www.cftc.gov/sites/default/files/2018-06/Federalregister06052018a.pdf>.

36 FSB, "Addressing Data Gaps," online: <www.fsb.org/what-we-do/policy-development/additional-policy-areas/addressing-data-gaps/>.

stores information about transactions) and artificial intelligence might obviate the need for such infrastructure?

We believe that just the opposite is closer to the truth. Technology demands precision and interoperability, and standards help provide both.[37] Distributed ledger technology and machine learning, for example, demand quality data inputs.[38] Industry-wide technology standards are also critical to avoid repeating past mistakes, with siloed solutions that can't be reconciled.

History also shows that financial-system vulnerabilities often grow just outside the regulated perimeter. With the financial system evolving at an ever more rapid rate, and the potential for new entrants to gain market share quickly, the threat of unexpected systemic disruptions cannot be ignored. New modes of gathering and analyzing disparate bits of data may yield real gains, but without quality data inputs, they could also create new information-related vulnerabilities. When the limits of these developments come to the fore, as they did with securitization a decade ago, high-quality, credible information will be critical to minimizing the disruption that results.

Data Standardization as Microcosm

The core claim here is that data standardization is important and should be prioritized. But there is also an important second lesson. The firms and countries that have long been the financial leaders are facing increasing threats for that dominance. Fintech and globalization are among the forces that make it possible for power dynamics to change quickly, even if the top players seem inevitable right up until their downfall. That well-designed standardization has the potential to enhance the operations of firms in addition to promoting resilience suggests that delays in implementation may well signal bigger problems. Firms and regulators can get trapped by inertia. Legacy assets within firms may go underutilized or pose risks that are not justified at the entity-level because of a failure to accept the short-term costs necessary to realize long-term gains. Turf wars and more subtle forms of provincialism among regulators can also impede widespread adoption of standards. To remain dominant in today's dynamic financial system requires that countries and firms be ahead — or at least not too far behind — in implementing value-creating reforms. When that is not happening — and the slow pace and mixed quality of data standardization suggests it is not — more monumental change may well be lurking in the shadows.

The core takeaway is this: details matter. Stylized accounts of finance suggest regulation is only needed to address market failures, and those failures are most apparent when interests conflict. Although there are positive externalities from standardization, there is also a lot of overlap between the types of reforms that will benefit industry and those that will promote public aims. The slow progress on data standardization suggests that frictions too banal to merit serious academic inquiry can have first-order effects on progress, or lack thereof. A willingness to grapple with these details, institutional and substantive, is key to producing financial regulatory schemes that work as well in practice as they do in theory.

37 It is worth noting here that both standards and a governance structure to standardize data across a firm are needed.

38 See e.g. Luke Clancy, "RiskTech Start-ups: Survival of the Fittest?" *Risk.net* (13 August 2018), online: <www.risk.net/our-take/5858356/risk-tech-start-ups-survival-of-the-fittest>.

Conclusion

Information is the lifeblood of finance. New technologies are only accentuating its importance and making urgent the need to govern and manage it. As finance continues to evolve, the capacity of the financial system to achieve the promise of enhanced efficiencies will depend, in part, on its capacity to gather, analyze and make productive use of available information. Information is also critical to promoting the resilience and health of the financial system. Data standards that are well designed, broadly understood, and widely used are a critical component to these undertakings. The process of designing standards forces communication and lays the groundwork for those standards to evolve when and as needed.

As the pace of finance continues to reach ever more dizzying speeds, the value of high-quality information and the threats posed by information gaps continue to grow. Given the myriad frictions that stand in the way of optimal policy, what is needed for success is leadership, creativity and a willingness to look to the future and to work across firm, industry and national bounds. Some progress has been made already. More is needed, and we think possible. Only vision and leadership are the missing ingredients.

9

Central Banks as Macroprudential Authorities:

Economics and Politics

DONATO MASCIANDARO

The 2007-2008 global financial crisis (GFC) highlighted the need for financial stability. Reforms of financial regulation in numerous countries were motivated by the fact that paying attention only to monetary stability and micro supervision (the stability of individual institutions and markets) was not enough to guarantee the safety and soundness of the financial industry. A broader approach, known as macroprudential policy (the use of prudential tools to mitigate systemic risk),[1] was deemed necessary for ensuring the resilience of the financial system as a whole.

Reforms of financial supervision and the establishment of macroprudential regimes have gone hand in hand with various degrees of involvement on the part of central banks. It's a matter of fact[2] that today, among the 111 countries where macroprudential institutional architectures are present, the central bank play a relevant role in 80 jurisdictions, and in 39 of them the central

1 In line with the International Monetary Fund's (IMF's) definition, the focus is on the concept of systemic risk, i.e., the risk of disruptions to the provision of financial services caused by an impairment of all or parts of the financial system, which can have serious negative consequences for the real economy.

2 IMF, *Annual Macroprudential Policy Survey: Objectives, Design and Country Responses* (Washington, DC: IMF, 2018).

bank is the sole authority. Central banks are almost always involved in macroprudential settings, but their role is far from homogeneous across countries. A central bank can be lightly involved if the responsibility of ensuring financial stability is shared by multiple agencies. The opposite is true when the central bank is the sole holder of the macroprudential mandate. Intermediate settings, in which a central bank acts as a coordinator or as the leading authority among multiple agencies, can also occur.[3]

How can the key role played by central banks in new macroprudential architectures be explained? From a theoretical point of view, the extension of central bank influence into macroprudential policies has pros and cons. Therefore, policy makers must address a series of possible trade-offs between the expected benefits and costs of allowing the monetary authority to have more or less influence on macroprudential strategies. The question that naturally arises is then genuinely empirical: is it possible to identify common drivers that explain political choices concerning central bank involvement in macroprudential governance?

This chapter proceeds as follows. The first section presents the state of the art. The second section offers a discussion of the relationships among political incentives, central bank design and macroprudential policies, highlighting the empirical drivers that may explain central bank involvement in the macroprudential perimeter. The third section provides conclusions.

Macroprudential Governance and Central Bank Involvement: The State of the Art

Macroprudential policy and its relationship with central banking[4] are topics that have long been

3 *Ibid.*

4 Charles Goodhart & Dirk Schoenmaker, "Should the functions of monetary policy and banking supervision be separated?" (1995) 47:4 Oxford Economic Paper No 539; Donato Masciandaro, "Designing a Central Bank: Social Player, Monetary Agent or Banking Agent?" (1995) 6:4 Open Economies Rev 399 [Masciandaro, "Designing a Central Bank"]; Donato Masciandaro, "Divide et Impera: Financial Supervision Unification and the Central Bank Fragmentation Effect" (2007) 23:2 European J Political Economy 285 [Masciandaro, "Divide et Impera"]; Ben Bernanke, "Central Banking and Bank Supervision in the United States" (Speech delivered at the Allied Social Sciences Association Annual Meeting, Chicago, 5 January 2007); Ben Bernanke, "The Effects of the Great Recession on Central Bank Doctrine and Practice" (2011) (Speech delivered at the Board of Governors of the Federal Reserve System 56th Economic Conference, Boston, 18 October 2011) [Bernanke, "Effects of the Great Recession"]; Richard J Herring & Jacopo Carmassi, "The Structure of Cross-Sector Financial Supervision" (2008) 17:1 Financial Markets, Institutions & Instruments 51; Olivier Blanchard, Giovanni Dell'Ariccia & Paolo Mauro, "Rethinking Macroeconomic Policy" (2010) 42:1 J Money, Credit & Banking; Erlend Walter Nier, "Financial Stability Frameworks and the Role of Central Banks: Lessons from the Crisis" (2009) IMF Working Paper No 70; Alan S Blinder, "How Central Should the Central Bank Be?" (2010) 48:1 J Economic Literature 123; Charles Goodhart, "The Changing Role of Central Banks" (2010) Bank for International Settlements (BIS) Working Paper No 326; Markus Brunnermeier et al, "The Fundamental Principles of Financial Regulation" (2010) Geneva Reports on the World Economy No 11; Claudio Borio, "Monetary and Prudential Policies at a Crossroads? New Challenges in the New Century" (2010) BIS Working Paper No 216; Claudio Borio, "Central Banking Post-Crisis: What Compass for Uncharted Waters?" (2011) BIS Working Paper No 353 [Borio, "What Compass?"]; Erlend Nier et al, "Towards Effective Macroprudential Policy Frameworks: An Assessment of Stylized Institutional Models" (2011) IMF Working Paper No 11/250; Stephen G Cecchetti et al, "The Future of Central Banking under Post-Crisis Mandates" (2011) BIS Paper No 55; Charles Bean, "Central Banking Then and Now" (Sir Leslie Melville Lecture, Australian National University, Canberra, 2011); Itai Agur & Maria Demertzis, "Will Macroprudential Policy Counteract Monetary Policy's Effects on Financial Stability?" (2015) IMF Working Paper No 15/283; Eugenio Cerutti et al, "Changes in Prudential Policy Instruments: A New Cross-country Database" (2017) Intl J Central Banking; Eugenio Cerutti, Stijn Claessens & Luc Laeven, "The Use and Effectiveness of Macroprudential Policies: New Evidence" (2017) 28 J Financial Stability 203; Javier Bianchi, Enrique G Mendoza, "Optimal Time-Consistent Macroprudential Policy" (2018) 126:2 J Political Economy; Codruta Boar et al, "What Are the Effects of Macroprudential Policies on Macroeconomic Performance?" (2017) BIS Q Rev.

studied in advanced, emerging[5] and developing economies. The same is true for macroprudential policy and its connection to other government agencies responsible for financial stability.[6] In such debates, a crucial point is the link between macroprudential policy and monetary policy.

The evolution of the economics and the political economy of monetary policy in the three decades prior to the GFC of 2007-2008 is a story of two intertwined tales. The first is a tale of ways to govern money and interest rates in the short run. The second is a tale about ways to design monetary architectures for the long run.

Thirty years ago, economic theory did not attribute any importance to the concept of central bank governance. Institutional arrangements increased in importance only when economic theory began to stress their role in determining macroeconomic performance.[7]

Essentially, optimal central bank governance has two key aspects. First, the central banker has to be independent. Second, the central banker must be conservative, where conservativeness refers to the importance assigned to price stability in relation to other macroeconomic objectives. The trade-off between conservativeness and independence[8] can be addressed by using independence as a tool to implement conservative monetary policies. However, private agents will trust the central banker only if effective rules on accountability and transparency hold.

The relationship between independence and accountability represents the core of central bank governance. In turn, central bank governance becomes the institutional setting for day-to-day monetary policy: given the long-run goal of avoiding the risk of inflation, the modern central banker can also smooth real business cycles[9] using monetary policy rules.[10] Monetary policy becomes the final outcome of the complex interactions among three main components: monetary institutions, central banker preferences and policy rules.[11]

In this respect, the literature on central bank governance has been developed in a two-stage process. Initially, scholars in the field focused on verifying the theoretical conjectures through

5 Masahiro Kawai & Peter J Morgan, "Central Banking for Financial Stability in Asia" (2012) ADBI Working Paper Series No 377; BIS, "Macroprudential Frameworks, Implementation and Relationship with Other Policies" (2017) BIS Paper No 94.

6 Stefan Gerlach, Alberto Giovannini & Cédric Tille, "Are the Golden Years of Central Banking Over? Monetary Policy after the Crisis" (2009) Geneva Reports on the World Economy 10; Paolo Angelini, Stefano Neri & Fabio Panetta, "Monetary and Macroprudential Policies" (2012) European Central Bank Working Paper No 1449.

7 Robert J Barro & David B Gordon (1983), "Rules, Discretion and Reputation in a Model of Monetary Policy" (1983) 12 J Monetary Economics 101; David Backus & Edward Driffill, "Inflation and Reputation" (1985) 75 American Economic Rev 530; Kenneth Rogoff, "The Optimal Degree of Commitment to an Intermediate Monetary Target" (1985) 100 QJ Economics 1169; Susanne Lohmann, "Optimal Commitment in Monetary Policy: Credibility versus Flexibility" (1992) 82:1 American Economic Rev 273.

8 Sylvester CW Eijffinger & Marco Hoeberichts, "The Trade off between Central Bank Independence and Conservativeness" (1998) Oxford Economic Paper No 50.

9 Ben S Bernanke & Mark L Gertler, "Inside the Black Box: The Credit Channel of Monetary Policy Transmission" (1995) 9:4 J Economic Perspectives 27; Richard Clarida, Jordi Galí & Mark Gertler, "The Science of Monetary Policy: A New Keynesian Perspective" (1999) 37 J Economic Literature 1661; Michael Woodford, "Optimal Interest Rate Smoothing" (2003) 70:4 Rev Economic Studies 861.

10 John B Taylor, "Discretion versus Policy Rules in Practice" (1993) 39 Carnegie-Rochester Conference Series on Public Policy 195; Dale W Henderson & Warwick J McKibbin, "A Comparison of Some Basis Monetary Policy Regimes for Open Economies: Implications of Different Degrees of Instrument Adjustment and Wage Persistence" (1993) 39 Carnegie-Rochester Conference Series on Public Policy 221; Carl E Walsh, "Optimal Contracts for Central Bankers" (1995) 85:1 American Economic Rev 150.

11 Torsten Persson & Guido Tabellini, "Designing Institutions for Monetary Stability" (1993) 39 Carnegie-Rochester Conference Series on Public Policy 53; Lars EO Svensson, "Optimal Inflation Targets, 'Conservative' Central Banks, and Linear Inflation Contracts" (1997) 87:1 American Economic Rev 98.

comparative, institutional and empirical analyses.[12] The first wave of studies on monetary regimes — including those adopting critical views[13] — took an important step in terms of considering central bank governance as an endogenous (dependent) variable that needed to be explained.[14]

These studies acquire greater importance in certain periods, such as the period after the 2007-2008 GFC. The recent debate reawakened political and academic interest in macroprudential policy[15] and the corresponding institutional settings.[16] The crucial point is that the scientific literature offers two main and contradictory results, which can be summarized as opposite answers to the following question: given two policies — monetary policy and macro supervision policy — with two different macro goals, what is the optimal degree of involvement for the monetary agent (i.e., the central bank) in supervisory responsibilities?[17] So far, two answers have been offered: the integration view and the separation view (Table 1).

Table 1: Integration and Separation Views on Central Bank Involvement in Macroprudential Policies

Integration View	Separation View
Information gains	Tool misallocation risk
Skill gains	Goal overriding risk
Independence gains	Super bureaucracy risk

Source: Author.

The integration view is based on three different categories of argument: information gains, skill gains and independence gains. The integration view suggests that the more the central bank gains information, the more its leading role in the definition and implementation of macro supervision is supported. Such gains can also increase the probability of coordination between monetary and macroprudential policies. Notwithstanding, it is worth noting that the coordination between the two policies can present macroeconomic risks.[18] In other words, having the central bank

12 Vittorio Grilli et al, "Political and Monetary Institutions and Public Financial Policies in the Industrial Countries" (1991) 6:13 Economic Pol'y 341; Alex Cukierman, Geoffrey P Miller & Bilin Neyapti, "Central Bank Reform, Liberalization and Inflation in Transition Economies: An International Perspective" (2002) 29:2 J Monetary Economics 237; Alberto Alesina & Lawrence H Summers, "Central Bank Independence and Macroeconomic Performances: Some Comparative Evidence" (1993) 25:2 J Money, Credit & Banking 151.

13 Bennett T McCallum, "Two Fallacies Concerning Central Bank Independence" (1995) 85:2 American Economic Rev 207.

14 Adam S Posen, "Declarations Are Not Enough: Financial Sector Sources of Central Bank Independence" in Ben S Bernanke & Julio J Rotemberg, eds, *NBER Macroeconomics Annual 1995* (Cambridge, MA: MIT Press, 1996).

15 Papa MBP N'Diaye, "Countercyclical Macro Prudential Policies in a Supporting Role to Monetary Policy" (2009) IMF Working Paper No 09/257; Alasdair Scott, Pau Rabanal & Prakash Kannan, "Monetary and Macroprudential Policy Rules in a Model with House Price Booms" (2009) IMF Working Paper No 09/251; Luisa Lambertini, Caterina Mendicino & Maria Teresa Punzi, "Leaning against boom-bust cycles in credit and housing prices" (2013) 37:8 J Economic Dynamics & Control 1500; Denis Beau et al, "Macro-Prudential Policy and the Conduct of Monetary Policy" in Sofía Bauducco, Lawrence Christiano & Claudio Raddatz, eds, *Macroeconomic and Financial Stability: Challenges for Monetary Policy*, ed 1, vol 19, (Santiago: Central Bank of Chile, 2014) 273; Angelini, Neri & Panetta, *supra* note 6.

16 Donald Kohn, "Implementing Macroprudential and Monetary Policies: The Case for Two Committees" (Speech delivered at the Federal Reserve Board, Boston, 2 October 2015); Ricardo Correa, Rochelle M Edge & Nellie Liang; *A New Dataset of Macroprudential Policy Governance Structures* (2017) Board of Governors of the Federal Reserve System; Turalay Kenç, "Macroprudential Regulation: History, Theory and Policy" (2016) BIS Working Paper No 86. For a systematic survey, see Diana Lima, "Institutional Setups of Monetary Policy and Banking Regulation and Supervision: A Survey" (2018) School of Economics Discussion Paper 0718, University of Surrey.

17 Masciandaro, "Designing a Central Bank", *supra* note 4.

18 Alejandro Van der Ghote, "Coordinating Monetary and Financial Regulatory Policies" (2018) European Central Bank Working Paper No 2155, as well as the related literature he cites.

as the leading actor in both policies increases the likelihood that Tinbergen's principle (i.e., consistency between different goals and different tools) is respected.[19]

The integration view is also based on the fact that the central banker is the country's liquidity manager, and that he or she obtains information on the health of the banking and financial system by carrying out that role.[20] As sources of liquidity, central banks naturally serve as leaders in preventing and managing systemic banking crises in advanced, emerging[21] and developing countries. Moreover, other government agencies entrusted with responsibility for financial stability[22] serve as the central bank's de jure or de facto subordinates.

At the same time, the risks of having both policies in the same hands can be increased by the fact that the central bank is also the liquidity manager, as has been evident since the beginning of the 2007-2008 GFC. Supervisory and regulatory responsibilities have been piled onto the central banks, thereby intensifying the relationships among banking, fiscal and monetary policies.[23] The mix between banking and monetary policies can produce the so-called "three D" effects.[24] The distributional effect results from changes in interest rates. The directional effect captures the impact of public policy on a certain sector and/or constituency of the economy, such as the banking industry.[25] The duration effect measures the monetary policy's effect on overall public sector liabilities, including the central bank's balance sheet within the public sector.[26]

The boundaries between the central bank's role as liquidity manager and the government's solvency support for banking and financial institutions have been blurred, inevitably triggering a debate on the shape of central bank settings,[27] especially with regard to the features of central

19 In the debate on the relationships between monetary and supervisory tasks, the importance of consistency with respect to Tinbergen's principle is highlighted in Frank Smets, "Financial Stability and Monetary Policy" (2014) 10:2 Intl J Central Banking 264. On the economics of macroprudential policy, see Salim Dehmej & Leonardo Gambacorta, "Macroprudential Policy in a Monetary Union" (2017) Document du travail 2017-4, Bank Al-Maghrib, Département de la Recherche; Bálint Horváth & Wolf Wagner, "Macroprudential Policies and the Lucas Critique" (2016) BIS Working Paper No 86; Enrique G Mendoza, "Macroprudential Policy: Promise and Challenges" (2016) National Bureau of Economic Research (NBER) Working Paper No 22868; Thierry Tressel & Yuanyan S Zhang, "Effectiveness and Channels of Macroprudential Instruments: Lessons from the Euro Area" (2016) IMF Working Paper No 16/4; Lars EO Svensson, "Cost-Benefit Analysis of Leaning Against the Wind" (2017) 90 J Monetary Economics 193 [Svensson, "Cost-Benefit Analysis"]; Lars EO Svensson, "Leaning Against the Wind: The Role of Different Assumptions about the Costs" (2017) NBER Working Paper No 23745 [Svensson, "Leaning Against the Wind"].

20 José Tuya & Lorena Zamalloa, "Issues on Placing Banking Supervision in the Central Bank" in Tomás JT Baliño & Carlo Cottarelli, eds, *Frameworks for Monetary Stability* (Washington, DC: IMF, 1994) 663; Goodhart & Schoenmaker, *supra* note 4; Rafael Repullo, "Who Should Act as Lender of Last Resort? An Incomplete Contracts Model" (2000) 32:3 J Money, Credit & Banking 580; Paul De Grauwe, "There is More to Central Banking than Inflation Targeting" in Andrew Felton & Carmen Reinhart, eds, *The First Global Financial Crisis of the 21st Century* (London, UK: VoxEU/Centre for Economic Policy Research (CEPR) Press, 2008); Brunnermeier et al, *supra* note 4; Borio, "What Compass?", *supra* note 4; Erlend Nier et al, "Institutional Models for Macroprudential Policy" (2011) IMF Staff Discussion Notes No 11/18.

21 Kawai & Morgan, *supra* note 5.

22 De Grauwe, *supra* note 20; Gerlach, Giovannini & Tille, *supra* note 6; Angelini, Neri & Panetta, *supra* note 6. For a survey, see Sander Oosterloo & Jakob de Haan, "Central banks and financial stability: a survey" (2004) 1:2 J Financial Stability 257.

23 Tamim Bayoumi et al, "Monetary Policy in the New Normal" (2014) IMF Staff Discussion Notes No 14/3; Jakob de Haan & Sylvester CW Ejiffinger, "Central Bank Independence under Threat?" (2017) CEPR Policy Insights No 87.

24 Charles Goodhart & Rosa Lastra, "Populism and Central Bank Independence" (2018) 29:1 Open Economies Rev.

25 Markus K Brunnermeier & Yuliy Sannikov, "Redistributive Monetary Policy" (Paper delivered at Jackson Hole Symposium, Federal Reserve Bank of Kansas City, 1 September 2012).

26 Michele Cavallo et al, "Fiscal Implications of the Federal Reserve's Balance Sheet Normalization" (2018) Federal Reserve Bank of New York Staff Reports No 833.

27 Nier, *supra* note 4; Bean, *supra* note 4; Cecchetti et al, *supra* note 4; Stefan Ingves & Sveriges Riksbank, "Central Bank Governance and Financial Stability" (2011) BIS/Central Bank Governance Group; Ricardo Reis, "Central Bank Design" (2013) 27:4 J Economic Perspectives 17.

bank independence.[28] These aspects have also been in focus from a historical perspective.[29] In this vein, an important question is whether the policy-blurring effect has made the pendulum swing, hampering the independence of the central banks as monetary authority. Thus far, however, comparative analyses have not delivered homogeneous results.[30]

The central bank's leading role in macro supervision is also supported by arguments related to the skill gains and economies of scale gains that derive from bringing all functions together under the same umbrella.[31] Finally, it has been claimed that the macroprudential policy function should be assigned to independent agencies with technical expertise (i.e., those with an institutional profile that — at least in advanced economies — matches the central bank's characteristics).[32]

The separation view is essentially based on three different categories of argument that have been alluded to in illustrating the integration view: tool misallocation risks, goal overriding risks and super-bureaucracy risks.

First, the separation view claims that if the central bank is the leading macro supervisor, there is a risk that the instruments of one policy can be assigned to the wrong objectives[33] and/or

28 Alex Cukierman, "Central Bank Independence and Monetary Policymaking Institutions: Past, Present and Future" (2008) 24:4 European J Political Economy 722; Alex Cukierman, "Monetary Policy and Institutions before, during and after the Global Financial Crisis" (2013) 9:3 J Financial Stability 373; Stephen G Cecchetti, "Central Bank Independence: A Path Less Clear" (Speech delivered at an international conference of the Bank for International Settlements, Mexico City, 14 October 2013); John B Taylor, "The Effectiveness of Central Bank Independence vs. Policy Rules" (2013) 48:3 Business Economics 155; Willem H Buiter, "Central Banks: Powerful, Political and Unaccountable" (2014) CEPR Discussion Paper No DP10223; Christopher A Sims, "Fiscal Policy, Monetary Policy and Central Bank Independence" (Paper delivered at Jackson Hole Symposium, Federal Reserve Bank of Kansas City, 26 August 2016); Alan S Blinder et al, "Necessity as the Mother of Invention: Monetary Policy after the Crisis" (2016) NBER Working Paper No 22735.

29 Michael D Bordo & Pierre L Siklos, "Central Banks: Evolution and Innovation in Historical Perspective" (2017) NBER Working Paper No 23847.

30 Cristina Bodea & Masaaki Higashijima, "Central Bank Independence and Fiscal Policy: Can the Central Bank Restrain Deficit Spending?" (2017) 47:1 British J Political Science 47; Jakob de Haan et al, "Central Bank Independence Before and After the Crisis" (2018) Comparative Economic Studies 1; Donato Masciandaro & Davide Romelli, "Peaks and Troughs: Economics and Political Economy of Central Bank Independence Cycles" in David G Mayes, Pierre L Siklos & Jan-Egbert Sturm, eds, *Oxford Handbook of the Economics of Central Banking* (New York: Oxford University Press, 2019).

31 Peter Docherty, "Basel II and the Political Economy of Banking Regulation and Monetary Policy Interaction" (2008) 37:2 Intl J Political Economy 82; Richard K Abrams & Michael Taylor, "Issues in the Unification of Financial Sector Supervision" (2000) IMF Working Paper No 00/213; Herring & Carmassi, *supra* note 4; Jeroen Klomp & Jakob de Haan, "Central Bank Independence and Financial Stability" (2009) 5:4 J Financial Stability 321; Luis Garicano & Rosa Lastra, "Towards a New Architecture for Financial Stability: Seven Principles" (2010) 13:3 J Intl Economics L 597; Blanchard, Dell'Ariccia & Mauro, *supra* note 4; Blinder, *supra* note 4; Cecchetti et al, *supra* note 4; Bernanke, "Effects of the Great Recession", *supra* note 4; Erlend W Nier et al, "Institutional Models for Macroprudential Policy" (2011) IMF Staff Discussion Notes 11/18.

32 Tuya & Zamalloa, *supra* note 20; Abrams & Taylor, *supra* note 31; Nier et al, *supra* note 31; IMF, *Staff Guidance Note on Macroprudential Policy: Considerations for Low Income Countries* (Washington, DC: IMF, 2014); Samuel McPhilemy, "Integrating Macroprudential Policy: Central Banks as the 'Third Force' in EU Financial Reform" (2016) 39:3 West European Politics 526; Deepal Basak & Yunhui Zhao, "Does Financial Tranquility Call for Stringent Regulation?" (2018) IMF Working Paper No 18/123.

33 The literature confirms the following well-known rule: given different objectives, different policy instruments are needed (e.g., price stability and interest rates [monetary policy] versus loan-to-output ratio stability and capital buffers [macroprudential policy]). A deep analysis of the tools and goals of macroprudential policy is beyond the scope of this chapter. For a comprehensive survey, see Jan Brockmeijer et al, "Macroprudential Policy: An Organizing Framework" (2011) IMF Policy Paper 14. See also Piergiorgio Alessandri & Fabio Panetta, "Prudential Policy at Times of Stagnation: A View from the Trenches" (2015) Banca d'Italia Occasional Paper No 300; Erlend Nier & Heedon Kang, "Monetary and Macroprudential Policies—Exploring Interactions" (2016) BIS Working Paper No 86; Timothy Lane, "Monetary Policy and Financial Stability—Looking for the Right Tools" (Speech delivered by the Deputy Governor of the Bank of Canada, Montreal, 8 February 2016); Aino Silvo, "The Interaction of Monetary and Macroprudential Policies in Economic Stabilisation" (2016) Bank of Finland Research Discussion Paper No 1/2016; Andreas Beyer et al, "The Transmission Channel of Monetary, Macro- and Microprudential Policies and Their Interactions" (2017) European Central Bank Occasional Paper No 191; Lima, *supra* note 16.

organizational dysfunctions can arise[34] (tool misallocation risk). The misallocation risk can arise when the central bank, having macroprudential responsibilities, uses the monetary policy tools to pursue the financial stability goal, as in the case of the Leaning Against the Wind (LAW) policies. The costs of LAW seem to be higher than the benefits, by a substantial margin.[35]

At the same time, when the central bank is the main actor responsible for maintaining financial stability, the risk of goal overriding risk — the likelihood that financial stability concerns will undermine both the central bank's credibility and effectiveness as the monetary authority[36] — can increase.

Finally, the literature has focused on the potential role of political drivers that can shape policy makers' decisions. Recently, this assumption has been tested in different studies that endogenized the shape of financial supervision setting, taking the political cost and benefit analysis into account.[37] These studies followed the central bank governance literature on the drivers of the monetary setting, which showed that political incentives can be a crucial factor in explaining different degrees of central bank independence.[38] The political economics perspective is based on the hypothesis that the gains and losses of a given macroprudential regime are variables computed by the incumbent policy maker, who maintains or reforms any institutional setting in line with his or her own preferences.[39] In this case, an additional driver of the actual

34 Garicano & Lastra, *supra* note 31; John Vickers, "Central Banks and Competition Authorities: Institutional Comparisons and New Concerns" (2010) BIS Working Paper No 331.

35 Tuya & Zamalloa, *supra* note 20; Goodhart & Schoenmaker, *supra* note 4; Charles AE Goodhart, Pojanart Sunirand & Dimitrios P Tsomocos, "A Model to Analyse Financial Fragility" (2006) 27:1 Economic Theory 107; Joseph G Haubrich, "Combining Bank Supervision and Monetary Policy" (1996) Federal Reserve Bank of Cleveland Economic Commentary; Carmine Di Noia & Giorgio Di Giorgio, "Should Banking Supervision and Monetary Policy Tasks Be Given to Different Agencies?" (1999) 2:3 Intl Finance 361; Vasso P Ioannidou, "Does Monetary Policy Affect the Central Bank's Role in Bank Supervision?" (2005) 14:1 J Financial Intermediation 58; Mark S Copelovitch & David Andrew Singer, "Financial Regulation, Monetary Policy and Inflation" (2008) 70:3 J Politics 663; Blinder, *supra* note 4; Svensson, "Cost-Benefit Analysis", *supra* note 19; Svensson, "Leaning Against the Wind", *supra* note 19; Lars EO Svensson, "Monetary Policy and Macroprudential Policy: Different and Separate?" (2018) CEPR Discussion Paper No 13043; John C Williams, "Macroprudential Policy in a Microprudential World" (2015) Federal Reserve Bank of San Francisco Economic Research. For a different view, see Jeremy C Stein, "Overheating in Credit Markets: Origins, Measurement, and Policy Responses" (Speech delivered at the "Restoring Household Financial Stability after the Great Recession: Why Household Balance Sheets Matter" research symposium, Federal Reserve Bank of St Louis, St Louis, Missouri, 7 February 2013). For a more cautious take, see Diana Lima, Ioannis Lazopoulos & Vasco J Gabriel, "The Effect of Financial Regulation Mandate on Inflation Bias: A Dynamic Panel Approach" (2016) Discussion Papers in Economics No 6, University of Surrey.

36 Blanchard, Dell'Ariccia & Mauro, *supra* note 4; Smets, *supra* note 19; Kenichi Ueda & Fabian Valencia, "Central Bank Independence and Macro-Prudential Regulation" (2012) 125:2 Economic Letters 327. Financial dominance can also have redistributive effects (see Buiter, *supra* note 28). On central banking, financial stability and redistributive effects, see Donato Masciandaro & Francesco Passarelli, "Bank Bailouts and Redistributive Monetary Policy: Voting on Central Bank Independence" (2013) Baffi Center Research Paper No 2013-146. On the redistributive effects of financial regulation, see Anton Korinek & Jonathan Kreamer, "The Redistributive Effects of Financial Deregulation" (2014) 68 J Monetary Economics S55.

37 Donato Masciandaro, "E Pluribus Unum? Authorities Design in Financial Supervision: Trends and Determinants" (2006) 17 Open Economies Rev 73; Masciandaro, "Divide et Impera", *supra* note 4; Donato Masciandaro, "Politicians and Financial Supervision outside the Central Bank: Why Do They Do It?" (2009) 5 J Financial Stability 12; Donato Masciandaro & Marc Quintyn, "Helping Hand or Grabbing Hand? Politicians, Supervision Regime, Financial Structure and Market View" (2008) 19 NA J Economy & Finance 153; Donato Masciandaro & Alessio Volpicella, "Central Banking, Macroprudential Supervision and Insurance" in Jan Monkiewicz & Marian Malecki, eds, *Macroprudential Supervision in Insurance* (London, UK: Palgrave Macmillan 2014) 167.

38 Alex Cukierman & Steven B Webb, "Political Influence on the Central Bank: International Evidence" (1995) 9:3 World Bank Economic Rev 397; Peter Moser, "Checks and Balances, and the Supply of Central Bank Independence" (1999) 43:8 European Economic Rev 1569; Philip Keefer & David Stasavage, "The Limits of Delegation: Veto Players, Central Bank Independence, and the Credibility of Monetary Policy" (2003) 97:3 American Political Science Rev 407 [Keefer & Stasavage, "The Limits of Delegation"].

39 Alberto Alesina & Guido Tabellini, "Bureaucrats or Politicians" (2004) NBER Working Paper No 10141.

role of the central bank in macro supervisory governance is its political role as an independent authority: politicians may fear creation of an overly powerful bureaucracy, i.e., the existence of a super-bureaucracy risk, especially given that implementation of effective macro supervisory action is often believed to require constrained discretion.[40]

Historically it has been noted that the choice between the integration view and the separation view has been influenced by two distinct traditions: the English tradition (integration) and the German tradition (separation).[41]

Finally, a separate discussion is needed when considering the role of central banks as micro supervisors. In fact, if the central bank is also a micro supervisor, there is a risk of capture by banks.[42] Therefore, the overall effect of the role of the central bank as a micro supervisor is theoretically ambiguous and must be analyzed empirically.

In summary, the literature suggests that when selecting the optimal level of central bank involvement in macro supervision, policy makers face a trade-off. On the one hand, there are potential net gains, which can be influenced by the fact that the central bank is also deeply involved in micro supervision. On the other hand, risks of capture, policy tool misallocation and an overly powerful bureaucracy arise. Notably, economic and econometric analyses of the relative merits of assigning the central bank a leading role in macroprudential governance are, so far, rare.[43]

40 Goodhart, Sunirand & Tsomocos, *supra* note 35; Haubrich, *supra* note 35; Roger W Ferguson, "Alternative Approaches to Financial Supervision and Regulation" (2000) 17:1 J Financial Services 297; Masciandaro, "Divide et Impera", *supra* note 4; Donato Masciandaro, Marc Quintyn & Michael W Taylor, "Inside and Outside the Central Bank: Independence and Accountability in Financial Supervision: Trends and Determinants" (2008) 24:4 European J Political Economy 833; Paul Tucker, "The political economy of macroprudential regimes" in Dirk Schoenmaker, ed, *Macroprudentialism* (London, UK: VoxEU/CEPR Press) 61.

41 Haubrich, *supra* note 35; Docherty, *supra* note 31; Lima, *supra* note 16.

42 Pierre C Boyer & Jorge Ponce, "Regulatory Capture and Banking Supervision Reform" (2012) 8:3 J Financial Stability 206. On the relationships between financial stability and the central bank's role in micro supervision, see Michael Koetter, Kasper Roszbach & Giancarlo Spagnolo, "Financial Stability and Central Bank Governance" (2014) 10:4 Intl J Central Banking 31.

43 Claudio Borio & Ilhyock Shim, "What can (macro)prudential policy do to support monetary policy?" (2007) BIS Working Paper No 242; Cheng Hoon Lim et al, "The Macroprudential Framework: Policy Responsiveness and Institutional Arrangements" (2013) IMF Working Paper No 166.

Politicians, Central Banks and Macroprudential Policies

Given the above list of pros and cons that can shape the decision regarding central bank involvement in macroprudential governance, we arrive at the crucial question: is it possible to identify common drivers to explain political decisions concerning such involvement? A recent econometric cross-sectional analysis of the determinants of central bank involvement in macroprudential governance[44] shed light on this issue by testing different assumptions made in the theoretical and institutional literature. In general, the empirical results indicate the following: central banks acting as micro supervisors of the banking industry are more likely to be given more macroprudential powers; higher central bank political independence is associated with lower involvement in macro supervision; and central banks pursuing specific price-stability objectives are more likely to be endowed with macro supervisory responsibilities. These results can be interpreted using a political economy perspective.

The political economy perspective differs from the extant literature in two main respects. First, while the interaction between macroprudential policies and monetary policies has been studied,[45] no research has examined the drivers of governance arrangements. At the same time, such perspective enriches research focusing on the effects of statutory central bank independence (CBI). As we have already mentioned in the previous section, since its onset in the 1990s,[46] CBI has been considered a major determinant of macroeconomic performance.[47] The economic literature has re-examined the relationship between CBI and monetary policy;[48] the effect of CBI on financial stability,[49] inflation[50] and government deficits;[51] central banks' micro involvement;[52] and the political, institutional and cultural factors influencing the effectiveness of

44 Donato Masciandaro & Alessio Volpicella, "Macro Prudential Governance and Central Banks: Facts and Drivers" (2016) 61 J Intl Money & Finance 101.

45 Schoenmaker, *supra* note 40; Smets, *supra* note 19.

46 Michael Parkin & Robin Bade, "Central Bank Laws and Monetary Policy: A Preliminary Investigation" (1978) Department of Economics Research Reports No 7804, University of Western Ontario; Grilli et al, *supra* note 12; Cukierman, Miller & Neyapti, *supra* note 12.

47 Cukierman, *supra* note 28; Jakob de Haan, Donato Masciandaro & Marc Quintyn, "Does Central Bank Independence Still Matter?" (2008) 24:4 European J Political Economy 717; Charles T Carlstrom & Timothy S Fuerst, "Central Bank Independence and Inflation: A Note" (2009) 47:1 Economic Inquiry 182; Sami Alpanda & Adam Honig, "Political Monetary Cycles and a De Facto Ranking of Central Bank Independence" (2010) 29:6 J Intl Money & Finance 1003; Alberto Alesina & Andrea Stella, "The Politics of Monetary Policy" in Benjamin M Friedman & Michael Woodford, eds, *Handbook of Monetary Economics* (Amsterdam: Elsevier, 2010) vol 3, 1001; Jeroen Klomp & Jakob de Haan, "Central Bank Independence and Inflation Revisited" (2010) 144:3 Public Choice 445.

48 Ian Down, "Central Bank Independence, Disinflations and Monetary Policy" (2004) 37:4 Compartive Political Studies 399; Aleksandra Maslowska, "Using Taylor Rule to Explain Effects of Institutional Changes in Central Banks" (2009) Aboa Centre for Economics Discussion Paper No 46; Sami Alpanda & Adam Honig, "The Impact of Central Bank Independence on Political Monetary Cycles in Advanced and Developing Countries" (2009) 41:7 J Money, Credit & Banking 1365.

49 Martin Čihák, "Central Bank Independence and Financial Stability: A Survey of Financial Stability Reports" (Paper presented at the Seminar on Current Developments in Monetary and Financial Law, Washington, DC, 23–27 October 2006); Klomp & de Haan, *supra* note 31.

50 Marco Arnone & Davide Romelli, "Dynamic Central Bank Independence Indices and Inflation Rate: A New Empirical Exploration" (2013) 9:3 J Financial Stability 385.

51 Cristina Bodea, "Independent Central Banks, Regime Type, and Fiscal Performance: The Case of Post-Communist Countries" (2013) 155:1–2 Public Choice 88.

52 Lucia Dalla Pellegrina, Donato Masciandaro & Rosario Vega Pansini, "The Central Banker as Prudential Supervisor: Does Independence Matter?" (2013) 9:3 J Financial Stability 415.

CBI.[53] This broader picture can be enriched by exploring the relationship between CBI and an important institutional feature: macro supervision. The results suggest that CBI is relevant not only owing to its beneficial effects on macroeconomic variables, but also because it influences policy makers' decisions. In the last two decades, policy makers have increasingly realized the importance of central bank design and the role of central bankers. In fact, at times they have used central bankers as scapegoats.[54]

The empirical analysis is based on data collected for 31 countries that are heterogeneous in terms of institutional framework and stage of economic development. In order to shed light on the drivers that have influenced the buildup of macroprudential settings, qualitative information must first be transformed into quantitative variables. Two main indicators can be used to measure the key features of the central bank's role in financial supervision. The central bank's involvement in macro supervision is the dependent variable in the econometric tests, while the central bank's role as a micro supervisor serves as a proxy for the role of the central bank as the leading authority in micro supervision, as discussed above.

The macroprudential index[55] (MAPP) (Figure 1) is used to measure the central bank's involvement in macro supervision. The Central Bank as Banking Authority (CBBA) index (Figure 2) is applied to measure the central bank's involvement in the micro supervision of the banking industry. This index is a dummy variable that takes a value of one if the central bank is the main banking supervisory authority, and zero otherwise.

In addition, we can use an index of involvement for the central bank's micro supervision of the financial system as a whole (i.e., banking, securities and insurance). To do so, we adopt a two-step procedure. The first stage uses the Financial Supervision Herfindahl Hirschman (FSHH) Index,[56] which measures the extent to which supervisory powers are consolidated.

In the second stage, the Central Bank Supervisor Share (CBSS) index[57] is used to build up the index of central bank involvement in micro supervision. Figure 2 presents the distribution of central banks' involvement as micro supervisors.

53 Philip Keefer & David Stasavage, "Checks and Balances, Private Information, and the Credibility of Monetary Commitments" (2002) 56:4 Intl Organization 751; Keefer & Stasavage, "The Limits of Delegation", *supra* note 38; Sylvester CW Eijffinger & Patrick Stadhouders, "Monetary Policy and the Rule of Law" (2003) CEPR Discussion Paper No 3698; Daron Acemoglu et al, "When Does Policy Reform Work? The Case of Central Bank Independence" (2008) Brookings Papers on Economic Activity No 1; Marc G Quintyn & Sophia Gollwitzer, "The Effectiveness of Macroeconomic Commitment in Weak(er) Institutional Environments" (2010) IMF Working Paper No 10/193; Kai Hielscher & Gunther Markwardt, "The Role of Political Institutions for the Effectiveness of Central Bank Independence" (2012) 28:3 European J Political Economy 286; Niclas Berggren, Sven-Olov Daunfeldt & Jörgen Hellström, "Social Trust and Central-Bank Independence" (2014) 34 European J Political Economy 425.

54 Alesina & Stella, *supra* note 47.

55 Lim et al, *supra* note 43. We normalize the index to facilitate its use. For an EU-specific comparative analysis of the institutional arrangements for macroprudential policy, see Jedrych A Matysek, "Institutional Arrangements for Macroprudential Policies: On Differences Across the EU Countries" (2018) 21:2 Comparative Economic Research37.

56 Albert O Hirschman, "The Paternity of an Index" (1964) 54:5 American Economic Rev 761. See also Donato Masciandaro & Marc Quintyn, "The Architecture of Insurance Supervision: Global Trends Before and After the Financial Crisis" in Patrick M Liedtke & Jan Monkiewicz, eds, *The Future of Insurance Regulation and Supervision: A Global Perspective* (London, UK: Palgrave Macmillan, 2011) 109 [Masciandaro & Quintyn, "Architecture of Insurance Supervision"].

57 The index in Masciandaro & Quintyn ("Architecture of Insurance Supervision", *supra* note 56) is similar to the one suggested in Lim et al, *supra* note 43.

Figure 1: Central Banks as Macro Supervisors

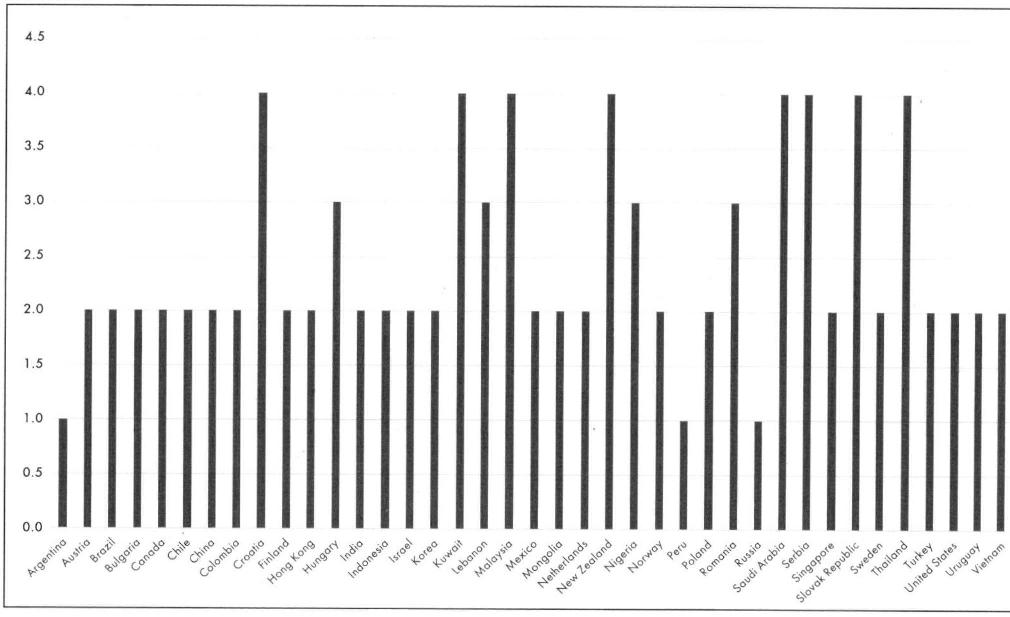

Source: Masciandaro & Volpicella, *supra* note 44.

Figure 2: Central Banks as Micro Supervisors

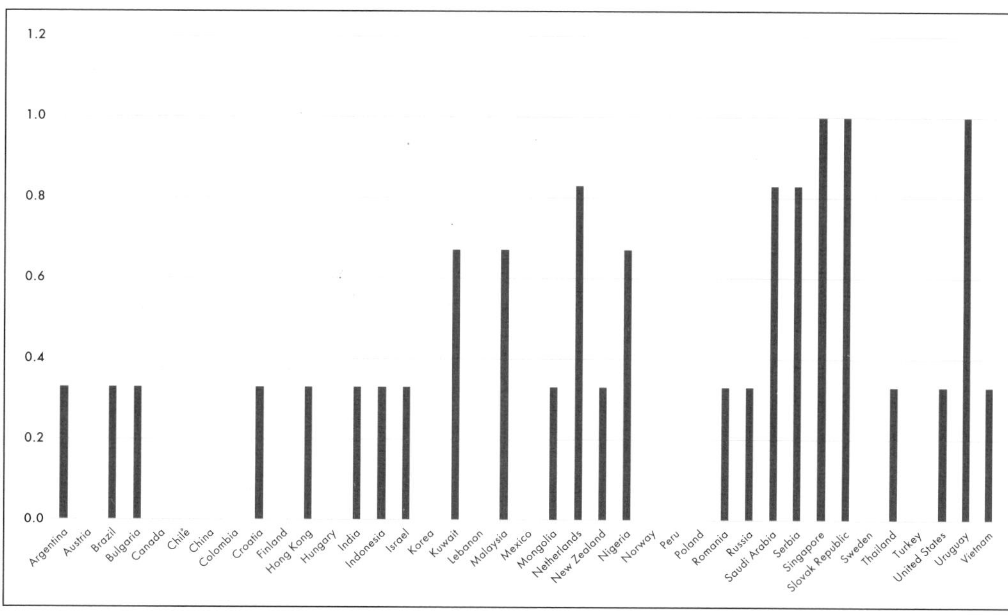

Source: Author. *Data source:* Robert Pringle, "How Countries Supervise their Banks, Insurers and Securities Markets" (New York: Central Banking Publications, 2009).

As a result, we have two alternative indices that measure the impact of the central bank's role as micro supervisor. The expected sign of both variables is undetermined: higher levels of either the CBBA or the CBSS index are likely to be associated with higher levels of the MAPP variable if the information-gain effect prevails. The opposite is true if the capture-risk effect dominates.

Given the discussion in the previous section, it is necessary to measure two potential shortcomings associated with deep central bank involvement in macro supervision: too much bureaucratic independence in the institutional setting and excessive discretion in defining monetary policy.

A proxy for central bank independence can be found in the extant literature. Acknowledging that de facto independence can sometimes lead to a different framework than de jure independence — in emerging and developing countries in particular[58] — this analysis focuses on the legal features of independence. This choice is justified by the fact that central bank independence cannot be ensured without proper legal provisions.[59]

In terms of determining the most relevant index among those proposed in the literature[60] for capturing either the political or operational dimensions of CBI, this study uses the index developed by Vittorio Grilli, Donato Masciandaro and Guido Tabellini (GMT Index),[61] mainly owing to its robustness. In fact, the literature on CBI generally uses two different strategies to capture the degree of independence of a central bank: indices based on central bank legislation (de jure); or the turnover rate of the central bank governor (de facto). De jure indices are more likely to capture the degree of CBI, for several reasons. First, turnover rates relate the independence of central banks to the autonomy of their governors. While extensively used, this approach has been shown to be less robust in empirical estimations as compared to the GMT Index of legal independence.[62] Second, the legal measures of CBI are more likely to reflect the true relationships between the central bank, policy makers and bankers, especially in countries where the rule of law is more strongly embedded in the political culture, as in many developed economies.[63] Third, to capture the change, if any, in the level of CBI post-2008, given that many post-crisis reforms have been related to the involvement of the central bank in supervision, it is more efficient to restrict our attention to de jure indices that can capture such changes.[64] Figure 3 shows the distribution of central bank independence.

58 Cukierman, *supra* note 28.

59 Lorenzo Bini Smaghi, "Central Bank Independence in the EU: From Theory to Practice" (2008) 14:4 Eur LJ 446.

60 For a survey, see Amirul Ahsan, Michael Skully & J Wickramanayake, "Central Bank Independence and Governance: Definitions and Modelling" (2008) 1 J Administration & Governance 46.

61 Grilli et al (*supra* note 12) set up the index, which was updated in Bernard J Laurens et al, "Central Bank Autonomy: Lessons from Global Trends" (2007) 56:2 IMF Staff Paper No 07/88.

62 Aleksandra Maslowska, "Quest for the Best: How to Measure Central Bank Independence and Show its Relation with Inflation?" (2008) Aboa Centre for Economics Discussion Paper No 37.

63 De Haan, Masciandaro & Quintyn, *supra* note 47.

64 Donato Masciandaro & Davide Romelli, "Central bankers as supervisors: Do crises matter?" (2017) 52 European J Political Economy 120; Masciandaro & Romelli, *supra* note 30.

Figure 3: Central Bank Independence

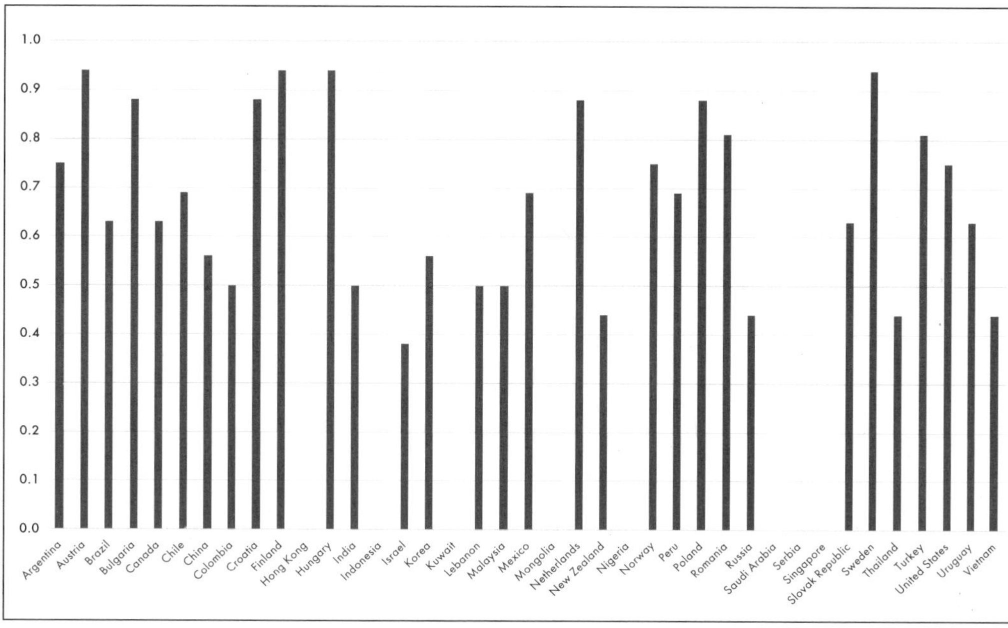

Source: Masciandaro & Volpicella, *supra* note 44.

Given this overall setting, we can frame the specific results regarding the drivers of central bank involvement in macro supervision. The empirical results show that central banks acting as micro supervisors of the banking industry are more likely to be given more extensive macroprudential powers; higher central bank political independence is associated with lower involvement in macro supervision; and central banks pursuing specific price-stability objectives are more likely to be endowed with macro supervisory responsibilities.

Conclusion

This chapter discussed the economic and political drivers of policy makers' decisions to assign macro supervisory powers to central banks. The empirical analysis that has been discussed shows that the central bank's role as a micro supervisor of the banking industry can be a significant driver of its macroprudential involvement. The bottom line is that micro supervisory powers serve as a proxy for the information advantages available to the central bank. Furthermore, greater central bank political independence, which increases the risk of an overly powerful monetary authority, seems to imply fewer macro supervisory powers. Finally, rule-based monetary policy focused on inflation targeting, which reduces monetary policy discretion, weakly increases the odds of a central bank being involved in macro supervision. Politicians seem wary of placing too much power in the hands of independent and/or discretionary central banks, although it is worth noting that the first feature — independence — seems to be more relevant.

The stability and general applicability of these results regarding the incentives of politicians in this context should be checked in future research. At the same time, other assumptions regarding what drives politicians to modify supervisory architectures over time need to be tested in the field of macro supervision. For example, in a 2017 publication I co-authored with Davide Romelli, we suggested the existence of two main drivers of reforms. We found, first, that systemic banking crises significantly increase the probability that a country will change its supervisory structure; and second, an equally important "bandwagon" effect seems to matter: countries are more likely to change their supervisory architectures when the share of countries undertaking reforms around the world or on the same continent is high.

10

Activities Are Not Enough! Why Non-bank SIFI Designations Are Essential to Prevent Systemic Risk

JEREMY C. KRESS, PATRICIA A. MCCOY AND DANIEL SCHWARCZ

The 2008 financial crisis demonstrated indisputably that non-bank financial firms such as investment banks and insurance companies can threaten the global economy.[1] Since the crisis, policy makers have conceived of two different approaches to combatting emerging forms of non-bank systemic risk. The first, dubbed an entity-based approach, empowers a public entity such as the Financial Stability Oversight Council (FSOC) to designate individual non-bank systemically important financial institutions (SIFIs) for enhanced regulation and supervision. The second, known as an activities-based approach, seeks to regulate financial activities that can produce systemic risk.

1 See e.g. Daniel Schwarcz & Steven L Schwarcz, "Regulating Systemic Risk in Insurance" (2014) 81:4 U Chi L Rev 1569 at 1601; Kathleen C Engel & Patricia A McCoy, *The Subprime Virus: Reckless Credit, Regulatory Failure, and Next Steps* (New York: Oxford University Press, 2011) at 25–27, 69–75; Hilary J Allen, "The SEC as Financial Stability Regulator" (2018) 43:4 J Corp L 714; John Armour et al, *Principles of Financial Regulation* (Oxford, UK: Oxford University Press, 2016) 445–48; Michael S Barr, Howell E Jackson & Margaret E Tahyar, *Financial Regulation: Law and Policy* (St. Paul, MN: Foundation Press, 2016) at 60.

During the first several years after the crisis, governments and multinational standard setters embraced both entity- and activities-based approaches to the problem of non-bank systemic risk. More recently, however, an emerging view has begun to dominate the financial regulatory community: that regulators should focus principally on an activities-based, rather than an entity-based, approach. This view emerged out of US regulatory circles, gained momentum after President Donald Trump's election in 2016, and is now exerting significant influence globally. Indeed, just a week after this view became the official policy of the US Treasury Department,[2] the Financial Stability Board (FSB) announced it would not update its list of international insurance SIFIs and instead would focus on developing an activities-based approach.[3]

This chapter challenges the emerging consensus that FSOC and its international counterparts should rely predominantly or exclusively on an activities-based, rather than an entity-based, approach to non-bank systemic risk. Proposals to eliminate an entity-based approach in favour of an activities-based approach assume that appropriately regulating systemically risky activities will prevent systemically important non-banks from failing. Although intuitively attractive, this assumption is wrong.

Even a reasonably well-implemented, activities-based approach is insufficient to prevent non-bank systemic risk unless it is supplemented with a robust entity-based approach. At root, this is because an individual firm's systemic riskiness is a product of the interrelations among its various activities and risk-management practices. Individual activities may pose limited systemic risk in isolation, but much greater systemic risk when combined with one another at a single firm. American International Group (AIG), for instance, nearly failed because of the toxic interactions between its derivatives and securities lending operations.[4] An activities-based approach is blind to this cumulative nature of a firm's systemic risk profile. Even more importantly, identifying ahead of time which new financial activities may create systemic risk is a nearly impossible assignment for regulators, given the varied forms such risk can take and the constant evolution of activities to evade regulatory restrictions.

In contrast to an activities-based approach, an entity-based approach is reasonably well designed to limit the risk that a systemically important non-bank will fail. Perhaps most obviously, the content of entity-based regulation — such as capital, liquidity and risk-management requirements — is inherently focused on the cumulative impact of a firm's activities. Moreover, an entity-based approach is a more effective deterrent against firms taking on systemic risk than an activities-based approach, as firms can quickly adjust to new activities-based rules through regulatory arbitrage.[5] An entity-based approach is also inherently more reliable than the alternative, as identifying systemically significant firms is substantially easier than identifying systemically significant activities *ex ante.*

2 US Department of the Treasury, *Financial Stability Oversight Council Designations: Report to the President of the United States Pursuant to the Presidential Memorandum Issued April 21, 2017* [Treasury, *FSOC Report*].

3 FSB, Press Release, 44/2017, "FSB statement on identification of global systemically important insurers" (21 November 2017), online: <www.fsb.org/2017/11/fsb-statement-on-identification-of-global-systemically-important-insurers/>.

4 See Daniel Schwarcz, "A Critical Take on Group Regulation of Insurers in the United States" (2015) 5 UC Irvine L Rev 537 at 553–54.

5 Daniel Schwarcz & David Zaring, "Regulation by Threat: Dodd-Frank and the Nonbank Problem" (2017) 84 U Chi L Rev 1813 at 1835–38.

None of this is to say that a well-designed, activities-based approach cannot help preserve financial stability. To the contrary, as we have written elsewhere, activities-based regulation has the potential to combat some (but not all) sources of non-bank systemic risk, if it is configured appropriately.[6] Our focus here, however, is on the conclusion that, in the absence of a robust and complementary entity-based approach, activities-based strategies alone are insufficient to reliably mitigate non-bank systemic risk.

The Emergence of Entity- and Activities-based Approaches to Non-bank Systemic Risk

The financial crisis demonstrated that non-bank financial companies can destabilize the financial system when not regulated appropriately. There is little doubt, for instance, that non-bank financial firms were central in creating and propagating the mortgage-linked securities that sowed the seeds of the crisis. Nor is there any doubt that the failure or near failure of certain non-bank financial firms — including Bear Stearns, Lehman Brothers and AIG — destabilized the broader financial system. This section describes how, after the crisis, policy makers in both the United States and the international arena quickly moved to address financial stability risks arising from non-banks.

United States

In the United States, lawmakers passed the Dodd-Frank Wall Street Reform and Consumer Protection Act (Dodd-Frank) in the wake of the crisis. The act created FSOC and empowered it to designate non-bank financial entities as systemically significant. This authority has come to be known as the "entity-based approach." Under Dodd-Frank, FSOC may designate a non-bank financial company for heightened oversight if the firm "could pose a threat to the financial stability of the United States." Any firm that FSOC designates as a non-bank SIFI becomes subject to consolidated supervision and regulation by the Federal Reserve.[7] Critically, the Federal Reserve's oversight of non-bank SIFIs targets financial stability risks through tools such as leverage and risk-based capital requirements, stress tests, liquidity rules and risk-management standards. This macroprudential orientation is important because traditional non-bank regulation, including state-based insurance regulation and oversight of broker-dealers by the US Securities and Exchange Commission (SEC), is not designed to address risks to financial stability.[8] Instead, non-bank financial oversight generally focuses on other goals, such as solvency and market conduct.

This entity-based approach, of course, mirrors traditional financial regulation insofar as it attaches different regulatory regimes to different types of financial firms. Oftentimes in the United States, a legal entity's charter type dictates its applicable regulatory regime, with investment

6 See Jeremy C Kress, Patricia A McCoy & Daniel Schwarcz, "Regulating Entities and Activities: Complementary Approaches to Nonbank Systemic Risk" 92 S Cal L Rev [forthcoming in 2019] (arguing that properly configured activities-based regulation can limit systemic correlations among firms, safeguard conduct that is inadequately addressed by entity-based regulation and prevent some forms of regulatory arbitrage).

7 See 12 USC § 5365(b)(1)(A).

8 See e.g. Schwarcz & Schwarcz, *supra* note 1 at 1627–34; Allen, *supra* note 1. Broadly speaking, macroprudential regulation addresses the stability of the financial system as a whole, while microprudential regulation focuses on the stability of individual financial institutions.

banks subject to one set of regulatory restrictions, insurers a second set and commercial banks a third. FSOC's entity-based approach departs from this tradition because its enhanced regulation applies to all non-bank SIFIs, regardless of their charter types. But aside from this design feature, FSOC's entity-based approach fits comfortably within traditional entity-based schemes of financial regulation while addressing systemic risk.

In the years immediately following the crisis, FSOC wielded its entity-based designation power aggressively. In one of its first major actions, the council established a process for evaluating whether a company could pose a threat to US financial stability.[9] After finalizing its designation procedures, FSOC quickly began evaluating non-bank financial companies. In 2013, it designated insurance-focused companies AIG and Prudential, as well as General Electric's captive finance subsidiary, GE Capital.[10] The following year, FSOC added MetLife, Inc., another insurance-focused firm, as a designee.[11] The council closely analyzed five additional firms, but ultimately opted not to designate them.[12]

In addition to its entity-based approach, Dodd-Frank empowered FSOC to pursue an activities-based approach by making non-binding recommendations to primary financial regulators regarding the oversight of potentially risky non-bank financial activities. For example, FSOC might recommend that the SEC or the Commodity Futures Trading Commission adopt new rules governing particular financial activities, but the agencies are not obligated to implement FSOC's activities-based recommendations.

As with its entity-based approach, FSOC's activities-based authority is hardly unique from the standpoint of regulatory architecture. In fact, many types of US financial regulations are organized around activities, rather than firms. For instance, Dodd-Frank's derivatives reforms generally target the activity of derivatives trading, not the entities that conduct this trading. Thus, while the procedures associated with FSOC's activities-based authority — in particular its non-binding status — are unusual, the idea of organizing financial regulation around activities, rather than firms, is not.

In contrast to its multiple entity-based designations, FSOC used its authority to recommend activities-based reforms only once during the Obama administration. In 2012, Treasury Secretary Timothy Geithner asked FSOC to recommend regulations to curb runs on money market mutual funds (MMMFs) after the SEC declined to adopt long-anticipated rules for these funds.[13] Exercising its activities-based power, FSOC requested public comment on

9 See *Financial Stability Oversight Council Guidance for Nonbank Financial Company Determinations*, 12 CFR part 1310, Appendix A (2018) [*FSOC Guidance*].

10 See FSOC, *Basis for the Financial Stability Oversight Council's Final Determination Regarding American International Group, Inc.* (2013); FSOC, *Basis for the Financial Stability Oversight Council's Final Determination Regarding General Electric Capital Corporation, Inc.* (2013); FSOC, *Basis for the Financial Stability Oversight Council's Final Determination Regarding Prudential Financial, Inc.* (2013).

11 See FSOC, *Basis for the Financial Stability Oversight Council's Final Determination Regarding MetLife, Inc.* (2014).

12 See FSOC, *2017 Annual Report* at 120, online: <www.treasury.gov/initiatives/fsoc/studies-reports/Documents/FSOC_2017_Annual_Report.pdf>.

13 See Kirsten Grind, "Funds Face New Battle on Rules", *The Wall Street Journal* (5 October 2012), online: <www.wsj.com/articles/SB10000872396390443493304578038410540850592>. MMMFs are specialized pooled investment vehicles that typically invest in low-risk assets such as commercial paper and government securities. See Hester Peirce & Robert Greene, "Opening the Gate to Money Market Fund Reform" (2014) 34:3 Pace L Rev 1093 at 1093.

regulatory approaches to mitigate systemic risk posed by MMMFs.[14] The SEC responded to FSOC's recommendations by adopting its own MMMF reforms the following year.[15] FSOC considered — but declined to pursue — other activities-based recommendations during the Obama administration. In late 2014, for example, FSOC sought public comment on whether the products and activities of asset managers, including hedge funds, could pose a risk to financial stability.[16] In response to public input, FSOC created an interagency working group to monitor the use of leverage by hedge funds and analyze the sufficiency of hedge funds' data reporting.[17] FSOC, however, stopped short of recommending enhanced regulation of any asset managers' activities.[18]

In sum, FSOC initially developed a robust system of entity-based regulation of non-bank SIFIs, while de-emphasizing its weaker, activities-based authority.

International

International financial regulators adopted a similar approach to non-bank systemic risk in the years after the crisis. In 2009, the Group of Twenty (G20) formed the FSB to coordinate the development of a comprehensive program to bolster the resilience of the global financial system.[19] Much of the FSB's focus was on strengthening systemically important banks.[20] The FSB had another top priority, however: addressing weaknesses in the regulation of *non-bank* systemic risk.

To accomplish this, the FSB and fellow international financial regulators first developed the infrastructure to implement an entity-based approach. At the urging of the FSB,[21] the International Association of Insurance Supervisors (IAIS) developed a methodology for identifying global systemically important insurers (G-SIIs).[22] Beginning in 2013, the IAIS published annual lists of such firms, identifying nine G-SIIs, including AIG, MetLife and Prudential.[23] The FSB and the International Organization of Securities Commissions (IOSCO) likewise began developing assessment methodologies for identifying non-bank, non-insurer global systemically important financial institutions (NBNI G-SIFIs).[24]

14 See FSOC, *Proposed Recommendations Regarding Money Market Mutual Fund Reform*, 77 Fed Reg 69455 (19 November 2012).

15 See SEC, *Money Market Fund Reform; Amendments to Form PF*, 79 Fed Reg 47736 (14 August 2014). The SEC's MMMF rules, however, were less stringent than the approaches FSOC had proposed. See Hilary J Allen, "Putting the 'Financial Stability' in Financial Stability Oversight Council" (2015) 76 Ohio St LJ 1087 at 1119.

16 See FSOC, *Notice Seeking Comment on Asset Management Products and Activities*, 79 Fed Reg 77488 (24 December 2014).

17 FSOC, *Update on Review of Asset Management Products and Activities* (2016) at 20–21, online: <www.treasury.gov/initiatives/fsoc/news/Documents/FSOC%20Update%20on%20Review%20of%20Asset%20Management%20Products%20and%20Activities.pdf>.

18 *Ibid.*

19 FSB, *Implementation and Effects of the G20 Financial Regulatory Reforms: 3 July 2017 3rd Annual Report* (2017) at 6 [FSB, *3rd Annual Report*], online: <www.fsb.org/wp-content/uploads/P030717-2.pdf>.

20 *Ibid* at 7–9.

21 See e.g. FSB, *Reducing the moral hazard posed by systemically important financial institutions* (20 October 2010) at 1, online: <www.fsb.org/wp-content/uploads/r_101111a.pdf>.

22 See IAIS, *Global Systemically Important Insurers: Initial Assessment Methodology* (2013) [IAIS, *Initial Assessment Methodology*]; FSB, *3rd Annual Report*, *supra* note 19 at 10. The IAIS and FSB defined G-SIIs as insurers whose "distress or failure would cause significant dislocation in the global financial system" (*ibid* at 3).

23 See FSB, "Global Systemically Important Financial Institutions", online: <www.fsb.org/what-we-do/policy-development/systematically-important-financial-institutions-sifis/global-systemically-important-financial-institutions-g-sifis/>.

24 FSB & IOSCO, *Assessment Methodologies for Identifying Non-Bank Non-Insurer Global Systemically Important Financial Institutions* (2014), online: <www.fsb.org/wp-content/uploads/r_140108.pdf>.

Next, international financial regulators created a companion policy framework for the regulation and oversight of firms identified as global non-bank SIFIs.[25] In general, the standard-setting bodies instructed global non-bank SIFIs' home country regulators to subject these firms to enhanced macroprudential oversight. Specifically, the policy framework's recommendations for systemically important non-banks included capital adequacy requirements, liquidity buffers, leverage limits and asset concentration caps, where appropriate for the line of business.[26] Subsequently, the IAIS began developing a pilot global risk-based insurance capital standard for internationally active insurance groups, with a final version slated for 2019.[27]

Adoption of the policy framework's entity-based standards remains a work in progress.[28] In 2017, the FSB reported that its member jurisdictions still had substantial gaps in tracking and regulating systemic risks from non-banks. These gaps included insufficient processes for monitoring and gauging non-bank risks, incomplete data, failures to bring systemically significant non-banks inside the regulatory perimeter and obstacles to cross-border cooperation.[29] These challenges can be seen, for example, in the European Union, where there is no system of non-bank SIFI designation and no single consolidated EU-level supervisor to oversee non-bank SIFIs for systemic risk, using enhanced prudential standards.[30] Through peer reviews of countries and thematic initiatives, the FSB continues to shed light — and nudge countries to act — on these and similar areas needing reform.[31]

Meanwhile, international regulators also worked to develop an activities-based approach to some non-bank systemic risks. However, these efforts have been piecemeal and generally focused on discrete markets and issues. The FSB has achieved its greatest progress to date in the adoption of over-the-counter derivatives reforms, although more work is necessary.[32] The FSB also published recommendations on repo (repurchase) financing transactions, including minimum haircut requirements, but countries have only begun implementing those recommendations.[33] Separately, IOSCO published recommendations to lower the risk of runs on MMMFs. Those recommendations have been implemented in some nations, but not all.[34]

Like the United States, international financial regulators initially focused the bulk of their attention on developing an entity-based approach to non-bank SIFI regulation. Global

25 See e.g. FSB, *Strengthening Oversight and Regulation of Shadow Banking: Policy Framework for Strengthening Oversight and Regulation of Shadow Banking Entities* (2013) at 13–14, online: <www.fsb.org/wp-content/uploads/r_130829c.pdf>; see also FSB, *Thematic Review on the Implementation of the FSB Policy Framework for Shadow Banking Entities: Peer Review Report* (2016) at 26–33 [FSB, *Shadow Banking Thematic Review*], online: <www.fsb.org/wp-content/uploads/Shadow-banking-peer-review.pdf>.

26 See FSB, *Shadow Banking Thematic Review, supra* note 25 at 31–33, table 2.

27 FSB, *3rd Annual Report, supra* note 19 at 9–10.

28 See FSB, *Shadow Banking Thematic Review, supra* note 25 ("implementation of the FSB Policy Framework remains at a relatively early stage" at 33), Annex H at 70–75.

29 FSB, *3rd Annual Report, supra* note 19 at 16, 26; see also FSB, *Shadow Banking Thematic Review, supra* note 25 at 34.

30 See Danny Busch & Mirik BJ van Rijn, "Towards Single Supervision and Resolution of Systemically Important Non-Bank Financial Institutions in the European Union" (2018) 19 European Business Organization L Rev 301 at 345–50, 352–55.

31 See e.g. FSB, *3rd Annual Report, supra* note 19 at 12; FSB, *Shadow Banking Thematic Review, supra* note 25; FSB, *Second Thematic Review on Resolution Regimes* (2016), online: <www.fsb.org/wp-content/uploads/Second-peer-review-report-on-resolution-regimes.pdf>; FSB, *Thematic Review of OTC Derivatives Trade Reporting* (November 2015), online: <www.fsb.org/2015/11/thematic-review-of-otc-derivatives-trade-reporting/>.

32 See FSB, *3rd Annual Report, supra* note 19 at 12–13, 15, 19–23.

33 *Ibid* at 17.

34 *Ibid* at 15–16.

implementation of that approach remains uneven, but the FSB's framework for entity-based regulation of systemically significant non-banks is well fleshed out. Meanwhile, global progress in developing activities-based regulation for non-banks mirrored that in the United States and generally lagged entity-based regulation immediately following the crisis.

The Gradual Demise of the Entity-based Approach to Non-bank Systemic Risk

Over the past several years, policy makers have coalesced around a consensus that non-bank systemic risk regulation should focus primarily or exclusively on an activities-based, rather than an entity-based, approach. This section details how the entity-based approach has recently fallen out of favour with both US and international policy makers, who have shifted their focus to activities-based systemic risk regulation.

United States

In response to FSOC's initial emphasis on its entity-based authority, opponents of non-bank SIFI designations urged the council to abandon its efforts to designate individual firms as systemically significant and concentrate on activities-based regulation. An activities-based approach, these critics insisted, would more effectively mitigate non-bank risks by providing clear guidance about how a broad range of financial firms could mitigate their systemic significance.[35] Moreover, critics insisted, activities-based regulation would avoid problems inherent in the United States' entity-based approach, such as the creation of an uneven playing field for designated firms and the application of bank-centric rules to non-bank SIFIs by the Federal Reserve.[36] Thus, for example, MetLife's CEO Steven A. Kandarian implored FSOC to "adopt an activities-based approach to systemic risk, rather than an institutions-based approach."[37] Critics, in sum, portrayed an activities-based approach as an alternative, rather than a complement, to the entity-based approach.

Over time, these criticisms have evolved into a consensus among Trump administration policy makers that FSOC should focus on an activities-based approach in lieu of entity-based designations. With many of President Trump's top financial regulators serving as voting members of FSOC, a majority of the council now holds this view. In fact, FSOC has shifted its focus to activities-based regulation in two different ways.

First, FSOC reversed each of its entity-based designations, freeing the four non-bank SIFIs from Federal Reserve oversight. Even before President Trump's election, FSOC voted unanimously to rescind GE Capital's designation after the company shrunk by more than half and substantially simplified its activities in an effort to reduce its systemic footprint.[38] More controversially, after many of President Trump's nominees took office and assumed seats on FSOC, the council

35 See e.g. *The Arbitrary and Inconsistent Non-Bank SIFI Designation Process: Hearing Before the H. Comm. on Fin. Servs.*, 115th Cong (2017) at 5 (statement of Douglas Holtz-Eakin, president, American Action Forum).

36 See e.g. Steven A Kandarian, chairman, president and CEO of MetLife, Inc., "Life Insurers as SIFIs: A Case of Mistaken Identity?" (Keynote address delivered at the US Chamber of Commerce Capital Markets Summit, 10 April 2013).

37 *Ibid.*

38 See FSOC, *Basis for the Financial Stability Oversight Council's Rescission of its Determination Regarding GE Capital Global Holdings, LLC* (2016) at 2.

voted six to three to rescind AIG's designation.[39] Later, FSOC freed MetLife from enhanced regulation by dropping its appeal of a district court order overturning the company's designation on procedural grounds.[40] Finally, FSOC rescinded Prudential's systemically important label in October 2018, leaving no remaining non-bank SIFIs.[41]

Second, FSOC is in the process of adopting formal policies prioritizing its activities-based authority over its entity-based designation power. In November 2017, the Treasury Department issued a report urging FSOC to focus on an activities-based approach and to resort to entity-based designations in exceedingly rare circumstances.[42] Thereafter, FSOC proposed amendments to its internal processes that would codify many of the Treasury Department's recommendations.[43] In a March 2019 release, the council stated that it would "prioritize its efforts to identify, assess, and address potential risks...through an activities-based approach" and resort to non-bank SIFI designations "only in rare instances."[44] Moreover, FSOC proposed a series of procedural hurdles that would make new non-bank SIFI designations exceedingly difficult. For example, the council suggested that it would conduct detailed statistical assessments for each non-bank SIFI designation, including a quantitative cost-benefit analysis and an assessment of the firm's vulnerability to distress. In light of the complexity and unpredictability inherent in macroeconomic forecasting, however, such empirical analyses would be nearly impossible for FSOC to perform with anything approximating precision.[45] These onerous requirements, therefore, could deter the council from even attempting to use its entity-based designation authority in the future, as they would open any new designations to the prospect of judicial challenge. Nonetheless, FSOC unanimously approved these proposed revisions and released them for public comment. The council, however, has neither issued any new activities-based recommendations, nor suggested specific activities it would seek to regulate under this new approach.

International

Mirroring these domestic developments, international policy makers have likewise changed their orientation to non-bank systemic risk. Despite their initial entity-based focus, international standard-setting bodies have ceased efforts to label individual non-banks as systemically

39 See FSOC, *Notice and Explanation of the Basis for the Financial Stability Oversight Council's Rescission of its Determination Regarding American International Group, Inc. (AIG)* (2017) at 12; *cf* Gregg Gelzinis, "Deregulating AIG Was a Mistake", Center for American Progress (11 October 2017), online: <www.americanprogress.org/issues/economy/reports/2017/10/11/440570/deregulating-aig-mistake/> (arguing that AIG did not sufficiently simplify itself to warrant de-designation).

40 See Alistair Gray, "Trump Administration Drops Appeal in MetLife 'Too Big to Fail' Case", *Financial Times* (19 January 2018), online: <www.ft.com/content/cfc31764-ff65-351d-95f2-78e7b413af4f>.

41 See FSOC, *Notice and Explanation of the Basis for the Financial Stability Oversight Council's Rescission of its Determination Regarding Prudential Financial, Inc.* (2018). For an argument that Prudential's de-designation was both misguided and against the law, see Jeremy C Kress, "The Last SIFI: The Unwise and Illegal Deregulation of Prudential Financial" (2018) 71 Stan L Rev Online 171.

42 See Treasury, *FSOC Report*, *supra* note 2. The Treasury Department issued its report in response to a directive by President Trump ordering FSOC to discontinue new non-bank SIFI designations while the Treasury Department conducted a thorough review of FSOC's designation process. See White House, "Presidential Memorandum for the Secretary of the Treasury" (21 April 2017), online: <www.whitehouse.gov/presidential-actions/presidential-memorandum-secretary-treasury/>.

43 See FSOC, *Authority to Require Supervision and Regulation of Certain Nonbank Financial Companies*, 84 Fed Reg 9028 (13 March 2019).

44 *Ibid* at 9039, 9045.

45 See Kress, McCoy & Schwarcz, *supra* note 6 at 24–30.

important and instead have shifted to an activities-based approach to asset management and insurance regulation.

The demise of the international entity-based approach originated in the asset management sector. In June 2015 — just three months after the FSB and IOSCO proposed assessment methodologies for NBNI G-SIFIs — IOSCO backtracked and asserted that "a full review of asset management activities and products...should be the immediate focus of international efforts to identify potential systemic risks."[46] Shortly thereafter, the FSB announced that it would stop working to identify NBNI G-SIFIs in order to focus on stability risks posed by asset management activities.[47] The FSB stated that, in conjunction with IOSCO, it would later revisit NBNI G-SIFI designations if any residual sources of systemic risk could not be addressed through an activities-based approach.[48]

The FSB's asset management review culminated with policy recommendations to address stability risks from asset management activities in January 2017.[49] The FSB identified two primary structural vulnerabilities in the asset management sector: liquidity mismatch and leverage. The FSB recommended a series of reforms to address these risks, including liquidity risk management tools and enhanced oversight of funds' leverage.[50] IOSCO issued final recommendations seeking to improve liquidity risk management in open-end funds in early 2018, and IOSCO is expected to report on additional leverage reforms in the near future.[51] As with all FSB and IOSCO recommendations, however, these reforms are strictly precatory, and jurisdictions have no legal obligation to implement them.[52] Neither the FSB nor IOSCO has indicated that they plan to revisit entity-based designations for asset managers, and as of the end of 2018, the NBNI G-SIFI assessment methodologies for asset managers remain unfinished.

The collapse of the international entity-based approach continued in the insurance sector. In early 2017, the IAIS announced that it would begin developing an activities-based approach to systemic risk in insurance.[53] Later that year — in fact, one week after the US Treasury Department recommended that FSOC de-emphasize entity-based designations — the FSB announced that it would not update its list of G-SIIs for the first time since it began identifying such firms.[54] The FSB stated that it "welcomes and encourages the work being undertaken by the IAIS to develop an Activities-Based Approach to systemic risk in the insurance sector." Such an approach, the FSB cryptically suggested, "may have significant implications for the

46 IOSCO, Media Release, IOSCO/MR/23/2005, "Meeting the Challenges of a New Financial World" (17 June 2015), online: <www.iosco.org/news/pdf/IOSCONEWS384.pdf>.

47 FSB, Press Release, 47/2015, "Next Steps on the NBNI G-SIFI Assessment Methodologies" (30 July 2015) [FSB, "Next Steps"], online: <www.fsb.org/2015/07/next-steps-on-the-nbni-g-sifi-assessment-methodologies/>.

48 *Ibid.*

49 FSB, *Policy Recommendations to Address Structural Vulnerabilities from Asset Management Activities* (2017), online: <www.fsb.org/wp-content/uploads/FSB-Policy-Recommendations-on-Asset-Management-Structural-Vulnerabilities.pdf>.

50 *Ibid* at 11–29.

51 IOSCO, *Recommendations for Liquidity Risk Management for Collective Investment Schemes: Final Report* (2018), online: <www.iosco.org/library/pubdocs/pdf/IOSCOPD590.pdf>; FSB, "Next Steps", *supra* note 47.

52 *Cf* Stavros Gadinis, "The Financial Stability Board: The New Politics of International Financial Regulation" (2013) 48 Tex Intl LJ 157.

53 IAIS, Press Release, "IAIS Announces Systemic Risk Assessment and Policy Workplan" (28 February 2017), online: <www.iaisweb.org/page/news/press-releases/file/65229/iais-press-release-systemic-risk-assessment-workplan>.

54 FSB, Press Release, 44/2017, "FSB statement on identification of global systemically important insurers" (21 November 2017), online: <www.fsb.org/2017/11/fsb-statement-on-identification-of-global-systemically-important-insurers/>.

assessment of systemic risk in the insurance sector and hence for the identification of G-SIIs and for G-SII policy measures."[55]

Just a few weeks after the FSB's announcement, the IAIS issued an interim public consultation laying out broad principles for implementing an activities-based approach in the insurance sector.[56] The IAIS insisted that its existing entity-based approach "may not completely address any potential (systemic) impacts that may stem from the collective actions or distress of insurers that are jointly exposed to certain risks."[57] Thus, the IAIS proposed to focus its activities-based approach on insurers' liquidity and macroeconomic risk exposures, which the IAIS asserted "could be strongly correlated across institutions and have the potential to cause a number of correlated cases of distress."[58] The IAIS suggested several activities-based reforms to address these risks, focusing on gaps in existing international standards.[59] It simultaneously cautioned that the development of an activities-based approach to insurance may affect the continued role of entity-based G-SII designations in international systemic risk regulation.[60]

Almost a year after its interim public consultation, the IAIS proposed a "holistic framework" for addressing systemic risk in the insurance sector.[61] The framework, to be adopted in 2020, largely embraced the activities-based approach outlined in the interim public consultation. Specifically, the IAIS proposed a package of supervisory tools — including liquidity risk management standards and stronger solvency assessments — and suggested that national authorities apply these tools with graduated intensity in relation to an insurer's size and risk profile.[62] The IAIS further recommended a global monitoring exercise to detect the buildup of systemic risk throughout the global insurance sector.[63] This "holistic" approach, according to the IAIS, would "address activities and exposures…targeted to a broader portion of the insurance sector."[64] The IAIS therefore proposed to formally eliminate the annual identification of systemically important insurers on the grounds that the holistic framework would eliminate the need for an entity-based approach.[65]

Thus, both domestically and internationally, policy makers have turned their attention to developing an activities-based approach to non-bank systemic risk. In the meantime, entity-based designations have ground to a halt, and new non-bank SIFI designations appear exceedingly unlikely any time in the near future.

55 *Ibid.*

56 See IAIS, "Public Consultation: Activities-based Approach to Systemic Risk" (8 December 2017), online: <www.iaisweb.org/page/consultations/closed-consultations/2018/activities-based-approach-to-systemic-risk> [IAIS, "Public Consultation"].

57 *Ibid* at 7.

58 *Ibid* at 12. More typically, rules aimed at ensuring adequate liquidity at the enterprise level are part of an entity-based approach.

59 *Ibid* at 28–29.

60 *Ibid* at 31.

61 See IAIS, *Holistic Framework for Systemic Risk in the Insurance Sector: Public Consultation Document* (Basel, Switzerland: IAIS 2018).

62 *Ibid* at 27–34.

63 *Ibid* at 42–54.

64 *Ibid* at 5. The IAIS asserted that "[t]o stress the importance of this holistic perspective, the IAIS proposes to move away from using the [activities-based] and [entity-based] terminology" (*ibid* at 9).

65 The IAIS recommended that the FSB review the need to re-establish G-SII designations in 2022. See *ibid* at 6.

Why an Activities-based Approach Must Be Supplemented with an Entity-based Approach

These evolving barriers to entity-based approaches in the United States and internationally are deeply misguided. This section explains why even a well-executed, activities-based approach, standing alone, cannot reliably prevent individual firms from becoming systemically important. It asserts that, by contrast, entity-based designation schemes are reasonably well tailored to promote this objective.

An Activities-based Approach Is Poorly Suited to Prevent Systemic Insolvencies

Proposals to de-emphasize an entity-based approach presume that regulators can prevent systemic non-bank failures such as AIG and Lehman Brothers by appropriately overseeing financial activities. This presumption, however, is false. While activities-based regulation may mitigate some sources of systemic risk, even well-designed, activities-based rules cannot prevent non-banks from experiencing systemic insolvencies. At bottom, this is because the risk that a firm will experience a systemic failure is a product of the interrelations among its various activities. Individual activities may pose limited systemic risk in isolation, but much greater systemic risk when combined at an individual firm. An activities-based approach is inherently blind to these realities.

This point is well understood with respect to individual firms. Indeed, modern risk management emphasizes the importance of understanding and managing a firm's risks holistically, across the entire enterprise.[66] Failure to take such an "enterprise-wide" approach to managing risk can result in problems that cross-cut a firm's operations remaining undiagnosed or ignored. But the centrality of the relationships among a firm's individual activities is equally applicable to the effective management of systemic risk.

Consider, for instance, a firm's susceptibility to a run, which is perhaps the single most important characteristic of systemically important financial firms. To be vulnerable to a run, a firm normally must fund itself with some form of short-term liabilities payable in cash. Examples include repo transactions, securities lending, warehouse lines of credit and commercial paper. Firms that pair such short-term liabilities with long-term illiquid assets are vulnerable to run-like dynamics because they may be required to dump their illiquid assets at fire-sale prices in order to raise enough cash to meet creditor demands. Knowing this, creditors may rush to claim repayment before the firm's cash reserves run out, in a classic case of the prisoner's dilemma. Creditors' uncertainty about the firm's true financial health often exacerbates this stampede.

A non-bank financial firm's susceptibility to a run cannot be effectively managed through an activities-based approach because it is inherently a by-product of the interrelations among a firm's activities. This is for three interconnected reasons.

First, numerous types of activities are known to create run risk, and many other activities may create run risk in ways that are not yet fully understood. As suggested above, any type of short-

66 See e.g. American Law Institute, *Principles of Risk Management*, § 4.02 (Preliminary Draft No 4, September 2018).

term borrowing can cause a run at a non-bank financial firm. Yet there are nearly infinite ways to structure short-term borrowing arrangements. Securities lending and repo transactions exploited this fact in different ways, but they are merely specific examples of the broader principle. It is therefore nearly impossible to define in advance all of the different forms that short-term borrowing might take, at least with the specificity that activities-based regulation requires.[67]

Not only are there innumerable potential types of short-term borrowing, but short-term borrowing is not the only type of liability that can generate a run. For instance, the crisis illustrated that run risk can also arise from any transaction that potentially requires a firm to post increasing amounts of cash collateral. AIG's credit default swaps (CDSs) are the poster child for this type of cash collateral-driven run.[68] These derivatives allowed counterparties to insist on increasing amounts of cash collateral to back the firm's insurance-like promises as either the firm's credit rating declined or the mortgage-backed securities they referenced decreased in value. The redeemable equity issued by MMMFs is yet another type of liability that generated runs in the crisis, but that was not short-term borrowing. Instead, it constituted equity that investors could redeem on demand, at the fund's net asset value, causing investors to run from these funds by seeking to withdraw their investments en masse once one large MMMF "broke the buck," disclosing that the value of its assets had fallen below the one-dollar threshold.[69]

So far, this litany of activities that creates run risk consists of examples that precipitated runs during the crisis. But innumerable other activities could also create run risk. For instance, many life insurers sell products that provide policyholders with an immediate right to withdraw their investment or borrow against their policy value.[70] Other examples include guaranteed investment contracts, funding agreements and certain variable annuity contracts.[71] As insurers' product designs change in the future, still other innovations could trigger a run.[72]

The prospect of new and unanticipated sources of run risk is particularly troubling because financial regulators are almost certain to fail to identify them ahead of time. Financial activities constantly evolve to evade regulatory restrictions when doing so can produce significant financial returns or lower costs, as in the case of cheap short-term funding.[73] The predictable result is that regulators will consistently be one step behind the financial sector in identifying new and emerging sources of run risk.[74]

67 Morgan Ricks offers one definition of short-term borrowing. See Morgan Ricks, *The Money Problem: Rethinking Financial Regulation* (Chicago: University of Chicago Press, 2016). But Ricks' proposal — to treat all short-term borrowing as a type of money creation — does not require him to differentiate among the numerous different subclasses of short-term debt. Any activities-based regulatory strategy would have to do this under the current regulatory framework, and could not therefore rely on a broad standard that lumped together all different types of short-term borrowing.

68 See Schwarcz, *supra* note 4 at 553–54. A CDS insures against the risk that securities referenced in the agreement will fare poorly. See *ibid.*

69 See Steven M Davidoff & David Zaring, "Regulation by Deal: The Government's Response to the Financial Crisis" (2009) 61 Admin L Rev 463 at 505.

70 See Schwarcz & Schwarcz, *supra* note 1 at 1619–23.

71 See Robert McMenamin et al, "How Liquid Are U.S. Life Insurance Liabilities?" (2012) 302 Chicago Fed Letter, online: <www.chicagofed.org/publications/Chicago-fed-letter/2012/September-302>.

72 See Schwarcz & Schwarcz, *supra* note 1 at 1619–23.

73 See Schwarcz & Zaring, *supra* note 5 at 1830–34.

74 See e.g. *Examining How the Dodd-Frank Act Could Result in More Taxpayer-Funded Bailouts: Hearing Before the H. Comm. on Fin. Servs.*, 113th Cong (2013) at 80 (statement of Richard W Fisher, president and CEO, Federal Reserve Bank of Dallas).

The second reason that run risk is inherently a by-product of the interrelations among firms' activities is that an individual firm's exposure to a run ultimately depends on its aggregate reliance on all activities that create run risk. The inherently cumulative nature of run risk follows from the fact that all of a firm's potential sources of run risk are likely to be triggered when it faces acute financial distress. This point is nicely illustrated by the collapse of AIG. As AIG's precarious financial position became clear throughout 2008, its CDS counterparties insisted that it post cash collateral on its derivatives at the same time that its securities lending counterparties terminated their transactions.[75] It was hardly fortuitous that this run on AIG implicated two different activities operated out of different subsidiaries; as AIG's counterparties realized the extent of the firm's troubles, they ran however they could to avoid experiencing losses if AIG defaulted.

An activities-based approach fails to address the risk that a combination of activities — none of which necessarily creates excessive short-term liabilities individually — might generate excessive run risk in the aggregate. Activities-based regulation generally seeks to limit the risks of an activity that necessarily creates short-term liabilities by, for instance, requiring that firms engaging in the activity maintain specified levels of liquid assets or creating mechanisms by which counterparties' capacity to run is suspended.[76] In doing so, activities-based regulation sets these safeguards only by reference to the prospect that the underlying activity, considered in isolation, might generate a run. In the absence of a complementary entity-based regime, however, activities-based regulation cannot calibrate customized safeguards for an individual firm's cumulative activities, in the aggregate.

The third, and final, reason that run risk is inherently a by-product of firms' cumulative risk profiles is that it depends on the interactions between firms' liabilities and assets. For instance, a seemingly reasonable amount of short-term debt might create dangerous run risk for a firm that overinvests in highly illiquid assets. As such, even a single activity that creates potential short-term liabilities may have a very different valance when it is combined with other activities that are not ordinarily considered systemic in isolation. An activities-based approach is limited in its capacity to respond to such interactions between the asset and liability sides of firms' balance sheets.

We focus on the inherently cumulative nature of run risk here both because runs are one of the central ways that an entity can become systemically risky and because an activities-based approach does indeed have some potential strengths in addressing this risk. But various additional criteria are, of course, relevant to the prospect that an individual firm will prove systemically significant in a crisis. These include a firm's size, connections to other major financial institutions and pre-existing regulatory scrutiny.

Like run risk, all of these additional indicia of systemic significance cannot be meaningfully policed by an activities-based approach. A firm's interconnectedness, for instance, necessarily depends on the cumulative impact of its activities. Innumerable financial activities — ranging from ordinary borrowing, to securities management, to derivatives, to the issuance of insurance policies — expose a non-bank firm's counterparties to the risk that the firm might fail. It

75 See Schwarcz, *supra* note 4 at 554.

76 The SEC's reforms of MMMFs provide examples of these strategies.

is presumably for these reasons that the IAIS's first report on designing an activities-based approach for systemic risk in insurance provides that "with regards to counterparty exposure… the IAIS tentatively concluded that [it is] mainly [an] entity-specific concept."[77]

An Entity-based Approach Is Well Structured to Limit the Costs of Systemic Insolvencies

In contrast to an activities-based approach, entity-based regimes that target systemic non-bank firms for heightened regulatory scrutiny can be reasonably well designed to limit the risk that firms will experience systemic insolvencies. This is because such schemes inherently focus on the cumulative impact of a firm's activities across the entire financial conglomerate, as well as interactions between its assets and liabilities. For instance, consolidated risk-based capital requirements and leverage limits ensure that SIFIs maintain a sufficient capital cushion to absorb potential losses.[78] Liquidity rules require a SIFI to hold a minimum amount of liquid assets to protect against runs and reduce the likelihood that it will have to sell illiquid assets in a fire sale.[79] Stress tests simulate adverse economic conditions to ensure that SIFIs could withstand a severe downturn.[80] And corporate governance reforms focus on improving enterprise risk management across SIFIs' operations.[81]

Entity-based non-bank SIFI regulation can also prevent systemic insolvencies indirectly by causing designated firms to shed risk in an effort to jettison their SIFI designations. The various extra regulatory restrictions and costs that designated firms experience are significant.[82] For this reason, non-banks that are designated as SIFIs have strong incentives to cease activities that may create the prospect of a systemic failure.[83] This reality has been vividly demonstrated with respect to firms that had been designated as SIFIs by FSOC: GE Capital and AIG both restructured their businesses in successful bids to shed their status as non-bank SIFIs.[84] Even MetLife, which embraced a successful legal and political strategy to escape its status as a non-bank SIFI, simultaneously reduced its participation in certain potentially systemic activities.[85]

Additionally, identifying systemically significant non-bank firms is much more manageable than correctly identifying all systemically significant activities *ex ante*. As discussed above, it is extremely difficult for regulators to anticipate new and emerging systemic activities. Relative

77 IAIS, "Public Consultation", *supra* note 56 at 12.

78 See 12 USC § 5365(b)(1)(A)(i) (2012); see also Barr et al, *supra* note 1 at 259–60. The Federal Reserve has not yet finalized rules implementing several non-bank SIFI standards mandated in Dodd-Frank, including capital and leverage requirements.

79 See 12 USC § 5365(b)(1)(A)(ii).

80 See 12 USC § 5365(i); see also Robert Weber, "A Theory for Deliberation-Oriented Stress Testing Regulation" (2014) 98 Minn L Rev 2236 at 2237–40.

81 See *Proposed Guidance on Supervisory Expectations for Boards of Directors*, 82 Fed Reg 37219 (9 August 2017). Oversight of an institution's board of directors and independent risk management function is a key element of an entity-based approach. These governance mechanisms are uniquely positioned to prevent excessive risk taking or misconduct that could transmit financial instability. See Jeremy C Kress, "Board to Death: How Busy Directors Could Cause the Next Financial Crisis" (2018) 59 Boston College L Rev 877 at 888–91. An entity-based approach allows regulators to monitor the effectiveness of a non-bank SIFI's corporate governance through regular on-site supervision.

82 See Schwarcz & Zaring, *supra* note 5 at 1851–55.

83 *Ibid.*

84 *Ibid.*

85 *Ibid.*

to these difficulties, entities such as FSOC and the FSB are much more likely to be able to consistently and accurately identify non-bank SIFIs. Although the distinction between firms that are systemically significant and those that are not is notoriously blurry, it is generally straightforward to identify which firms are plausibly close to the line and which are clearly on one side or the other.[86] Moreover, both US and international actors have developed detailed frameworks for identifying systemically significant firms, which have produced results similar to those of alternative methodologies.[87]

Perhaps even more importantly, an entity-based approach need not perfectly distinguish between non-banks that are systemically significant and those that are not to deter non-banks from seeking out systemic risk.[88] To the contrary, so long as the designation process is even roughly accurate, non-bank firms will have strong incentives to avoid pursuing strategies that could result in their failure propagating systemic risk. This is because the mere prospect of being designated as a SIFI — and thus facing increased regulatory restrictions and compliance burdens — creates real risks and uncertainties for firms, which they will seek to avoid.

By contrast, an activities-based approach in isolation affirmatively incentivizes non-banks to engage in regulatory arbitrage by seeking out activities that have not been identified or appropriately regulated. Doing so offers all the ordinary potential benefits to firms of systemic risk — the ability to reap the upside reward of risk, while externalizing some of the downside — but only limited costs. This is because the firm does not bear the full costs of engaging in such an activity until it is regulated appropriately. Financial firms are accustomed to adjusting as the regulatory landscape changes, and they can choose either to substitute a less highly regulated activity for a newly identified systemic activity or conform to the new regulatory standards. And unlike in an entity-based regime, either choice could be implemented immediately because changes in activities do not usually require affirmative approval by regulators.

An entity-based approach to financial stability can also complement activities-based regulation by helping regulators to identify potentially systemic activities *ex ante*, and by allowing them to assess how well activities-based reforms are curbing risk. An entity-based approach produces these benefits through regular on- and off-site supervision of non-bank SIFIs. Continuous monitoring — a hallmark of entity-based systemic risk oversight — allows officials to observe the impact of different activities across time.[89] This unique vantage point allows them to more quickly identify troubling activities. For instance, if supervisors observe that several non-bank SIFIs are suddenly engaging in a new activity at accelerating rates, this is likely to trigger enhanced scrutiny of the activity itself, in a way that might otherwise be overlooked.[90] Likewise,

86 See *FSOC Guidance, supra* note 9, part 1310, Appendix A, § II.

87 See Acharya et al, "Measuring Systemic Risk" (2017) 30:1 Rev Financial Studies 2 at 39 (identifying Bear Stearns, Lehman Brothers, Morgan Stanley, Goldman Sachs and Merrill Lynch among the top 10 systemically risky financial firms in 2006-2007 in back-testing of authors' marginal expected shortfall approach to systemic risk); Christian Brownlees & Robert F Engle, "SRISK: A Conditional Capital Shortfall Measure of Systemic Risk" (2017) 30:1 Rev Financial Studies 48 at 62–63 (finding that back-testing of authors' SRISK metric identified Morgan Stanley, Bear Stearns, Lehman Brothers, Fannie Mae and Freddie Mac as top systemic risk contributors as early as the beginning of 2005).

88 See Schwarcz & Zaring, *supra* note 5 at 1858.

89 See Board of Governors of the Federal Reserve System, *Consolidated Supervision Framework for Large Financial Institutions* (2012), SR 12-17 at 9–10 (discussing Federal Reserve supervision of non-bank SIFIs).

90 See Matthew C Turk, "The Convergence of Insurance with Banking and Securities Industries, and the Limits of Regulatory Arbitrage in Finance" (2015) 2015:3 Colum Bus L Rev 967 at 1040, 1053.

firm-wide examinations and continuous off-site monitoring can help supervisors detect when non-bank SIFIs respond to activities-based rules by changing their business models to continue taking systemic risks. In this way, regular entity-based non-bank SIFI supervision can help overcome some of the limitations inherent in an activities-based approach.

In sum, entity-based systemic risk regulation is uniquely capable of preventing catastrophic non-bank failures. Non-bank SIFI oversight takes into account the cumulative effect of all of a firm's activities and is relatively easy to target. An activities-based approach, by contrast, is severely limited along these dimensions, as it focuses on a firm's activities in isolation and is difficult to target effectively due to constant efforts by firms to avoid regulatory restrictions. Entity-based non-bank SIFI designations are therefore critical to prevent a recurrence of the systemic non-bank insolvencies from 2008.

Authors' Note

This chapter is substantially based on a more detailed law review article: Jeremy C Kress, Patricia A McCoy & Daniel Schwarcz, "Regulating Entities and Activities: Complementary Approaches to Nonbank Systemic Risk" 92 S Cal L Rev [forthcoming in 2019].

11

Toward a Better Bail-in Tool: Observations from a European Perspective

TOBIAS H. TRÖGER

After the financial crises of 2007 and 2008, governments around the world vowed to end "too big to fail" (TBTF) and avert the moral hazard problems arising from anticipated bailouts.[1] A main pillar of the regulatory strategy to achieve this goal was to enhance resolution frameworks

1 The first notice of intent occurred at the Group of Twenty (G20) summit in Pittsburgh in 2009; see *Leaders' Statement: The Pittsburgh Summit* (2009) at 9, online: <www.oecd.org/g20/summits/pittsburgh/G20-Pittsburgh-Leaders-Declaration.pdf>. For key policy documents, see Financial Stability Board (FSB), *Reducing the moral hazard posed by systemically important financial institutions* (2010) at 3–6, online: <www.fsb.org/wp-content/uploads/r_101111a.pdf>; High-level Expert Group on reforming the structure of the EU banking sector, *Final Report* (2012) at 81–83, 92–93 [*Liikanen Report*], online: <https://ec.europa.eu/info/system/files/liikanen-report-02102012_en.pdf>; Paul Tucker, "Resolution and future of finance" (Speech delivered at the International World Congress of the International Association of Restructuring, Insolvency and Bankruptcy Progessionals, The Hague, 20 May 2013), online: <www.bis.org/review/r130606a.pdf>.

and thus make failure an option even for the largest financial institutions.[2] If indeed a failing bank could be wound down or reorganized without implications for financial stability, a bailout with taxpayers' money would no longer be warranted as a matter of sound banking and economic policy. Instead, the private sector would have to bear the losses the ailing institution incurred. This would not only preserve public finances *ex post*, but also instill market discipline *ex ante*. Investors would price bank capital with a view only to the default probability as determined in the asset valuation process and not in light of distorting implicit government guarantees.

The introduction of the bail-in tool,[3] which compels investors in bank capital to absorb the losses of a failing institution according to a predetermined waterfall[4] and thereby to assume the primary burden in the bank's recapitalization, is a cornerstone of the reform agenda.[5] Only if a credible device existed for achieving such a significant private sector involvement (PSI) in bank resolution existed — without conjuring up threats for financial stability — would markets discard the possibility of a government intervention to support bank capital.

However, translating conclusive policy recommendations into operable regulation (law) has its own intricacies. Desirable market discipline can only be induced if investors can predict the risk of their capital instruments being written off or converted with reasonable certainty. To be sure, a significant amount of uncertainty is inherent in the pertinent determinations as a result of their forecasting nature, which is particularly true if conversion creates a potential upside in the future. Yet, these inevitable difficulties that stem from projecting a financial institution's destiny (failure and resurrection) should not be aggravated by a complex and highly discretionary regulatory framework for PSI. Predicting the timing and outcome of resolution should not require a wild guess. Otherwise, investors would find it even harder to determine expected losses in a bail-in. The prices of the relevant financial instruments would be a noisy indicator for the

2 For a discussion of the essential features of an adequate policy framework to counter the TBTF problem, see Inci Ötker-Robe et al, "The Too-Important-to-Fail Conundrum: Impossible to Ignore and Difficult to Resolve" (2011) International Monetary Fund (IMF) Staff Discussion Note SDN/11/12 at 10–21, online: <www.imf.org/external/pubs/ft/sdn/2011/sdn1112.pdf>; for a review of the academic literature, see Philip E Strahan, "Too Big to Fail: Causes, Consequences, and Policy Responses" (2013) 5 Annual Rev Financial Economics 43; for an insightful survey of the shortcomings of the institutional framework for bank failures prior to the financial crises and the lessons learned with a specific view to the European developments, see Jens-Hinrich Binder, "Resolution: Concepts, Requirements and Tools" in Jens-Hinrich Binder & Dalvinder Singh, eds, *Bank Resolution: The European Regime* (Oxford, UK: Oxford University Press, 2016) at paras 2.05–2.19.

3 The basic concept of private sector burden sharing predates the recent financial crisis; see e.g. Barry Eichengreen & Christof Rühl, "The bail-in problem: systematic goals, ad hoc means" (2001) 25:1 Economic Systems 3. The development of the contemporary, bank-specific implementations is frequently credited to a financial press contribution; see Paul Calello & Wilson Ervin, "From bail-out to bail-in", *The Economist* (28 January 2010) 95.

4 The most explicit codification occurs in the European Union; see *Directive 2014/59/EU of the European Parliament and of the Council of 15 May 2014 establishing a framework for the recovery and resolution of credit institutions and investment firms and amending Council Directive 82/891/EEC, and Directives 2001/24/EC, 2002/47/EC, 2004/25/EC, 2005/56/EC, 2007/36/EC, 2011/35/EU, 2012/30/EU and 2013/36/EU, and Regulations (EU) No 1093/2010 and (EU) No 648/2012, of the European Parliament and of the Council,* [2014] OJ, L 173/190, art 44 [*BRRD*]. The special resolution regime for systemically important financial institutions (SIFIs) in the United States implements private sector loss absorption rather indirectly; for a description, see Simon Gleeson & Randall Guynn, *Bank Resolution and Crisis Management* (Oxford, UK: Oxford University Press, 2015) at paras 6.52–6.54; Jeffrey N Gordon & Wolf Georg Ringe, "Bank Resolution in the European Banking Union: A Transatlantic Perspective on What it Would Take" (2015) 115 Colum L Rev 1297 at 1325–30; see also Federal Deposit Insurance Corporation, *The Resolution of Systemically Important Financial Institutions: The Single Point of Entry Strategy*, 78 Fed Reg 76614 (2013).

5 See Ötker-Robe et al, *supra* note 2 at 20–21. The DNA of the European regime stems from the FSB, "Key Attributes of Effective Resolution Regimes for Financial Institutions" (2011), ss 3.5, 3.6, online: <www.fsb.org/wp-content/uploads/r_111104cc.pdf>, which remained unchanged in the most recent version, FSB, "Key Attributes of Effective Resolution Regimes for Financial Institutions" (2014), ss 3.5, 3.6, online: <www.fsb.org/wp-content/uploads/r_141015.pdf>.

default risks associated with the investment and hence the effect of "market discipline" would be ambiguous as well.

Unfortunately, the bail-in tool under the Bank Recovery and Resolution Directive (BRRD) and the Single Resolution Mechanism Regulation (SRM Regulation)[6] provides for a highly complicated and detailed regulatory framework that gives a multitude of authorities ample discretion in compelling PSI, and requires significant inter-agency cooperation and information sharing. The publicly administered ad hoc bail-in tool under the BRRD complicates the prediction of outcomes and thus impairs an optimal implementation of the main policy objectives legislators pursued in the regulatory overhaul that reacted to the financial and sovereign debt crises.[7] Alongside the fundamental policy lesson that militates in favour of disentangling PSI from the broader resolution process[8] — and may also be achieved by private sector solutions such as early-triggering contingent convertible bonds (CoCos)[9] — this chapter draws attention to two further regulatory features that need to be added to the current regime to make it viable. In particular, this chapter makes the case for extensive buy-side monitoring and argues in favour of a bail-in maximum, because both aspects are pivotal for making PSI credible and generating the desirable market discipline.

To make this argument, this chapter first highlights the policy rationale that calls for mandatory PSI and its interplay with political economy and financial stability considerations. From this analysis, it revisits the key features for an effective bail-in tool that intends to foster market discipline and thus needs to thwart politicians' and regulators' appetite for bailouts. The chapter continues with brief case studies that look at the European resolution episodes of the summer of 2017. These episodes can be understood as anecdotal evidence for the European resolution framework's likely ineffectiveness in establishing adequate market discipline through risk-reflecting prices for bank capital. Finally, the contribution shows how both insufficient monitoring of investors who hold bank capital instruments subject to bail-in and potentially unlimited PSI create a proclivity among politicians and regulators to avoid the European

6 *Regulation (EU) No 806/2014 of the European Parliament and of the Council of 15 July 2014 establishing uniform rules and a uniform procedure for the resolution of credit institutions and certain investment firms in the framework of a Single Resolution Mechanism and a Single Resolution Fund and amending Regulation (EU) No 1093/2010,* [2014] OJ, L 225/1 [*SRM Regulation*].

7 For an in-depth analysis, see Tobias H Tröger, "Too Complex to Work: A Critical Assessment of the Bail-in Tool under the European Bank Recovery and Resolution Regime" (2018) 4:1 J Financial Regulation 35 at 47–69 [Tröger, "Too Complex to Work"] (showing the many choices resolution authorities have to make under the EU regime and their impact on investors' risk assessment and pricing); see also Tobias H Tröger, "Why MREL Won't Help Much", 20 J Banking Regulation [forthcoming in 2019] (showing that even the prescription of a cushion of debt instruments subject to bail-in will not cure the deficits of the EU regime).

8 See Tröger, "Too Complex to Work", *supra* note 7 at 69–73.

9 For a discussion of the policy rationale that underpins contingent capital and is identical to that of a statutory bail-in tool, see Darrell Duffie, "A Contractual Approach to Restructuring Financial Institutions" in George P Shultz, Kenneth E Scott & John B Taylor, eds, *Ending Government Bailouts as We Know Them* (Stanford, CA: Hoover Institution Press, 2010) 109 at 109–10; Ceyla Pazarbasioglu et al, "Contingent Capital: Economic Rationale and Design Features" (2011) IMF Staff Discussion Note SDN/11/01 at 7–8, online: <www.imf.org/external/pubs/ft/sdn/2011/sdn1101.pdf>. For the original vision, largely dwelling on the market-disciplining effect of contingent capital, see Mark J Flannery, "No Pain, No Gain? Effecting Market Discipline via 'Reverse Convertible Debentures'" in Hal S Scott, ed, *Capital Adequacy Beyond Basel: Banking, Securities, and Insurance* (Oxford, UK: Oxford University Press, 2005) 171 at 173, 175–82. For a contribution pointing especially to the desirability of CoCos' resolution remoteness, see Enrico Perotti & Mark Flannery, "CoCo design as a risk preventive tool", *VOX* (9 February 2011), online: <http://voxeu.org/article/coco-bonds-way-preventing-risk>.

resolution regime, with its rather rigid and far-reaching bail-in requirement.[10] The chapter also shows how these undesirable effects could be addressed by regulation, followed by concluding remarks.

Policy Objectives of Bail-in

This section briefly revisits the policy rationale that underpins mandatory PSI in bank resolution and delineates the relation between effective recapitalization of the failing bank and the re-establishment of market discipline. It also pays particular attention to the limits that follow from the paramount objective to resolve failing banks without creating financial instability.

Reinvigorate Market Discipline for Bank Funding

Bailout Rationality and Defunct Debt Governance

The failure of a SIFI can[11] affect other financial institutions because it is a counterparty for many other market participants; it is forced to fire-sell assets, which leads to depressed prices for assets that other institutions use as collateral (demand for higher margins), and its default sparks a panic that spreads to other institutions.[12] These consequences, in turn, carry over to the real economy.[13] If the proper functioning of the financial sector is impaired, for instance, because interbank lending dries up when confidence in borrowers' viability dwindles, financial institutions start to stash cash and the real economy receives less liquidity to finance productive activities. The lack of credit drives down total output, and the ensuing growth and welfare losses ultimately imperil political stability and democracy. In this scenario, government interventions that take the form of bank bailouts at an early stage are a fully rational reaction to imminent threats.

10 In resolution, BRRD articles 56(1) and 37(10)(a) prescribe that at least eight percent of an institution's total liabilities are bailed-in before any government support in the form of a capital contribution or even the nationalization of the bank can be extended under BRRD articles 57 and 58; similarly, BRRD article 45(5) requires a minimum bail-in of the same proportion before resolution financing arrangements can take any losses. See generally Tobias H Tröger, "Regulatory Influence on Market Conditions in the Banking Union: the Cases of Macro-Prudential Instruments and the Bail-in Tool" (2015) 16:3 European Business Organization L Rev 575 at 590 [Tröger, "Regulatory Influence"].

11 To be sure, even the failure of large banks must not necessarily trigger systemic implications; see Joseph H Sommer, "Why Bail-In? And How!" (2014) 20 Federal Reserve Bank of New York (FRBNY) Economic Policy Rev 207 at 214 (stressing that even "megabanks" often collapse in isolation and go down smoothly).

12 For illustrations of all types of systemic impact during the financial crisis of 2007 and 2008, see Markus K Brunnermeier, "Deciphering the Liquidity and Credit Crunch 2007–08" (2009) 23:1 J Economic Perspectives 77; Darrell Duffie, *How Big Banks Fail and What to Do About it* (Princeton, NJ: Princeton University Press, 2010) at 23–36; Viral V Acharya, Hyun Song Shin & Tanju Yorulmazer, "Crisis Resolution and Bank Liquidity" (2011) 24:6 Rev Financial Studies 2166; Gary Gorton & Andrew Metrick, "Securitized banking and the run on repo" (2012) 104:3 J Financial Economics 425.

13 For a detailed description of the macroeconomic links between the financial system and the real economy that precipitate policy makers' incentives to bail out SIFIs, see Jonathan R Macey & James P Holdcroft, Jr, "Failure Is an Option: An Ersatz-Antitrust Approach to Financial Regulation" (2011) 120:6 Yale LJ 1368 at 1375–83; Tobias H Tröger, "Organizational Choices of Banks and the Effective Supervision of Transnational Financial Institutions" (2013) 48:2 Tex Intl LJ 178 at 187–90. But see also Mathias Dewatripont, "European banking: Bailout, bail-in and state aid control" (2014) 34 Intl J Industrial Organization 37 at 39–40 (showing that the social costs of bailout restrictions potentially comprise losses in total output caused by lasting instability).

Beyond the perils of a bank-sovereign feedback loop,[14] the economic logic that motivates bailouts also allows markets to anticipate government behaviour and thus factor in an implicit government guarantee in the price of bank capital. This tacit guarantee provides a lower bound to the value of assets on a bank's balance sheet and thus shifts the default probability downward compared to a model with endogenously determined (asset valuation process) bank failure. Banks that benefit from implicit guarantees — because they are deemed TBTF — enjoy lower risk premiums and can thus raise capital from rational investors at lower prices.[15] Distorted market pricing bears on the liability side of banks' balance sheets because they can raise capital at costs that are insensitive to their risk-taking behaviour and thus serve the appetite of equity holders and managers to build leverage.[16] Hence, the government subsidy allows bank equity holders and executives to fund excessive risk-taking (moral hazard) and thus leads to inefficient investment decisions on the asset side of the institutions' balance sheets.[17] In essence, debt governance does not work because financial institutions' risk-bearing capacity does not drive the pricing of their capital (no market discipline).

Regulatory Intervention to Induce Risk Sensitivity of Banks' Cost of Capital

The observable market failure warrants regulatory intervention. The bail-in tool seeks to address the root cause of the problem: its objective is to credibly ensure PSI in a bank's failure (i.e., to

14 Bank rescues can lead to unsustainable public finances that put banks with significant exposures to sovereign debt into further solvency stress; see Jianping Zhou et al, "From Bail-out to Bail-in: Mandatory Debt Restructuring of Systemic Financial Institutions" (2012) IMF Staff Discussion Note SDN/12/03 at 4, online: <www.imf.org/~/media/Websites/IMF/imported-full-text-pdf/external/pubs/ft/sdn/2012/_sdn1203.ashx>; Emilios Avgouleas & Charles Goodhart, "A Critical Evaluation of Bail-Ins as Bank Recapitalisation Mechanisms" (2014) Centre for Economic Policy Research Discussion Paper 10065 at 1, online: <http://ssrn.com/abstract=2478647>.

15 For empirical evidence of the effect, see Donald P Morgan and Kevin J Stiroh, "Too Big to Fail after All These Years" (2005) FRBNY Staff Report No 220, online: <www.newyorkfed.org/medialibrary/media/research/staff_reports/sr220.pdf> (showing that the relationship between bond spreads and ratings was lower for TBTF banks than for other financial institutions during the 1990s); Kenichi Ueda & Beatrice Weder di Mauro, "Quantifying Structural Subsidy Values for Systemically Important Financial Institutions" (2012) IMF Working Paper No WP/12/128, online: <www.imf.org/~/media/Websites/IMF/imported-full-text-pdf/external/pubs/ft/wp/2012/_wp12128.ashx> (estimating an increase from 60 to 80 basis points between 2007 and 2009 in the structural subsidy as measured in big banks' credit ratings); Zoe Tsesmelidakis & Robert C Merton, "The Value of Implicit Guarantees" (2012) Working Paper, online: <http://ssrn.com/abstract=2231317> (estimating the funding advantage of 74 US financial institutions benefiting from implicit government guarantees totalling $365 billion); Frederick A Schweikhard & Zoe Tsesmelidakis, "The Impact of Government Interventions on CDS and Equity Markets" (2012) American Finance Association 2012 Chicago Meetings Working Paper, online; <http://ssrn.com/abstract=1573377> (showing how model-estimated risk premiums for bank debt deviated significantly from actual market premiums charged for major US banks in credit default swaps markets through the financial crisis); João AC Santos, "Evidence from the Bond Market on Banks' 'Too-Big-To-Fail' Subsidy" (2014) 20:2 FRBNY Economic Policy Rev 29 (showing that between 1985 and 2009, investors accepted significantly lower spreads on bonds issued by the largest US banks than on bonds issued by small banks). For an estimation of the potential impact that credible PSI through bail-in would have, according to standard rating methodology, see Frank Packer & Nikola Tarashev, "Rating methodologies for banks" (2011) BIS Q Rev 39 at 50.

16 On the basic incentive structure that is rooted in the ability to shift risk to existing creditors, see e.g. Anat R Admati et al, "Fallacies, Irrelevant Facts, and Myths in the Discussion of Capital Regulation: Why Bank Equity is Not Socially Expensive" (2013) Max Planck Institute for Research on Collective Goods 2013/23, online: <https://ssrn.com/abstract=2349739>. On the motivation of managers, see Lucian A Bebchuk & Holger Spamann, "Regulating Bankers' Pay" (2010) 98:2 Geo LJ 247 at 255–57.

17 For evidence, see Blaise Gadanecz, Kostas Tsatsaronis & Yener Altunbaş, "Spoilt and Lazy: The Impact of State Support on Bank Behavior in the International Loan Market" (2012) 8 Intl J Central Banking 121; Luis Brandao Marques, Ricardo Correa & Horacio Sapriza, "International Evidence on Government Support and Risk Taking in the Banking Sector" (2013) IMF Working Paper No WP/13/94, online: <www.imf.org/external/pubs/cat/longres.aspx?sk=40501>; Gara Afonso, João AC Santos & James Traina, "Do 'Too-Big-To-Fail' Banks Take on More Risk?" (2014) 20:2 FRBNY Economic Policy Rev 41. On the anticompetitive effect of the subsidy that allows big banks to push smaller competitors out of the market by aggressively cutting margins, see Reint Gropp, Hendrik Hakenes & Isabel Schnabel, "Competition, Risk-shifting, and Public Bail-out Policies" (2010) 24:6 Rev Financial Studies 2084.

compel risk-bearing of agents who provide banks' capital).[18] If effective, it undoes government guarantees (no bailout). Banks' funding thus becomes sensitive to the risks the institutions are running and puts an end to excessive risk-taking, over-investment and other behaviours induced by moral hazard.[19]

The indispensable precondition for such a regime to work is that the bail-in tool allows losses to be passed on to investors in bank capital in a way that does not shatter the confidence of bank clients in the continuous provision of critical financial services (liquidity provision, insurance-type risk-shifting) throughout and beyond resolution. In other words, PSI must not impair the (short- to medium-term) viability of the essential functions of the resolved institution. Only under this precondition can it prevent overly disruptive effects of bank failure.[20] After all, bankruptcy law also allocates losses to the insolvent entity's creditors, yet it does so without paying attention to the peculiarities of financial institutions.[21] Instead, a bank-dedicated regime for PSI would carefully avoid destroying the additional value that certain liabilities of banks convey to the claimholder beyond the rights to future cash flows.[22]

The (Implied) Systemic Exception

Bank resolution without injection of public funds poses a problem if it occurs in the middle of a systemic crisis. In fact, financial history teaches that a tough stance by governments that refuse to

18 See John C Coffee, Jr, "Bail-Ins Versus Bail-Outs: Using Contingent Capital to Mitigate Systemic Risk" (2010) Columbia Law and Economics Working Paper No 380 at 35, online: <http://ssrn.com/abstract=1675015>; Zhou et al, *supra* note 14 at 5, 20; Thomas F Huertas, "The Case for Bail-ins" in Andreas Dombret & Patrick S Kenadjian, eds, *The Bank Recovery and Resolution Directive: Europe's Solution for "Too Big To Fail"?* (Berlin: De Gruyter, 2013) 167 at 168; Avgouleas & Goodhart, *supra* note 14 at 2; Karl-Philipp Wojcik, "Bail-in in the Banking Union" (2016) 53:1 CML Rev 91 at 107; see also Zhou et al, *supra* note 14 at 7 (describing bail-in as a concept of insurance provided by subordinated term debtors); Gordon & Ringe, *supra* note 4 at 1355–56. The description of PSI as a "penalty for failure" imposed on investors in bank capital (see e.g. Avgouleas & Goodhart, *supra* note 14 at 2) can be misleading because bail-in does primarily aim at an efficient allocation of risk and does not express any normative judgment as to who is to blame for the bank's failure.

19 See also Tröger, "Regulatory Influence", *supra* note 10 at 588, figure 3. For tentative empirical evidence that actual bail-ins indeed shape market expectations, see Alexander Schäfer, Isabel Schnabel & Beatrice Weder di Mauro, "Bail-in Expectations for European Banks: Actions Speak Louder than Words" (2016) Centre for Economic Policy Research Discussion Paper 11061, online: <www.cepr.org/active/publications/discussion_papers/dp.php?dpno=11061> (gauging price reactions to pre-BRRD bail-ins in equity and credit default swap markets).

20 Bail-in can be understood as an instrument to facilitate a large bank's (financial conglomerate's) swift recapitalization. Therefore, it prevents liquidity stress, averts fire sales and, ultimately, the disorderly liquidation of financial contracts ("runs"); see Zhou, *supra* note 14 at 5, 7; Sommer, *supra* note 11 at 217–23; Wojcik, *supra* note 18 at 92, 107; see also Binder, *supra* note 2 at para 2.57 (emphasizing that bail-in preserves the incentives attributed to insolvency proceedings but avoids disruptive effects).

21 For a theoretical discussion that complex and time-consuming bankruptcy proceedings under regular insolvency laws are apt to undermine confidence and destabilize markets, see Andrei Schleifer & Robert Vishny, "Fire Sales in Finance and Macroeconomics" (2011) 25:1 J Economic Perspectives 29; for specific assessments of the ineptness of the US Chapter 11 proceedings, see Sommer, *supra* note 11 at 225–28; for a pre-crisis statement to the contrary, see David A Skeel, "The Law and Finance of Bank and Insurance Insolvency Regulation" (1998) 76:4 Tex L Rev 723; for post-crisis proponents of Chapter 11 proceedings for banks, see Kenneth Ayotte & David A Skeel, "Bankruptcy or Bailouts?" (2009) 35 J Corp L 469; Stephen J Lubben, "Systemic Risk and Chapter 11" (2009) Temp L Rev 433; Douglas G Baird & Edward R Morrison, "Dodd-Frank for Bankruptcy Lawyers" (2011) 19 Am Bankr Inst L Rev 287; for a comprehensive project seeking to propel bank-specific amendments to the US bankruptcy code, see Thomas H Jackson, "Bankruptcy Code Chapter 14" in Kenneth E Scott & John B Taylor, eds, *Bankruptcy Not Bailout: A Special Chapter 14* (Stanford, CA: Hoover Institution Press, 2012) 25.

22 Critical client relations appear on the liability side of the failed bank's balance sheet. Therefore, their treatment in ordinary insolvency law would destroy value beyond the nominal value of the claim. For instance, the automatic stay impairs the liquidity-providing function of deposits and the loss participation of risk-shifting derivatives destroys hedges; see Sommer, *supra* note 11 at 209–13 (highlighting the specific characteristics of "financial liabilities" whose social value exceeds their nominal one and may have a firm-specific element). Hence, the cost-minimizing social optimum can only be achieved if these liabilities receive a special (preferred) treatment in insolvency; Avgouleas & Goodhart, *supra* note 14 at 12 (same, with diverging terminology).

backstop the financial system aggravates the impact of the event.[23] Hence, any regime that seeks to compel PSI applies only under the condition — either expressly stipulated in the statutory foundations or included as an implied term — that no systemic crisis looms absent government intervention. The key question is thus how to balance the inevitable systemic exception with the goal of instilling market discipline. In other words, how can regulators provide a safety valve without sacrificing the credibility of the regime altogether?[24] The answer certainly is not an easy one, but has to carefully consider how even a well-designed PSI might indeed contribute to system-wide adverse effects. In this regard, it is worth noting that PSI (bail-in) may be a pro-cyclical crisis accelerator, for instance, because haircuts chill investors and thus make it harder for struggling banks to refinance themselves.[25]

Minimized Incentives for Bailouts as a Precondition for an Efficient Bail-in Regime

The objective of the bail-in tool to induce adequate pricing of the risk of bank failure by all investors who provide capital determines the preconditions under which a regulatory intervention can lead to efficient outcomes. The key desideratum is that — at least — sophisticated investors must be able to price the risk adequately, which requires a reasonably certain *ex ante* designation of the likelihood and extent of their loss-bearing.[26] The latter aspect hinges, *inter alia*, on minimizing politicians' and resolution authorities' incentives to bail out failing banks. If government-funded bank rescues continue to exist as a realistic alternative to PSI, the undesirable price distortions in bank capital markets and the related inefficiencies survive (see section above entitled "Bailout Rationality and Defunct Debt Governance"). Therefore, an adequately designed regime for PSI must pay close attention that the application of the bail-in tool does not destabilize financial markets, either because it adversely affects other market participants that provide critical functions or because it triggers panic-driven runs. Moreover, beyond financial stability concerns, it has to ensure that political economy considerations do not fuel bailout desires.

23 The conventional wisdom is informed by the Federal Reserve's policy mistakes (allowing monetary contraction also by letting banks fail across the board) in the run-up to and during the Great Depression; see e.g. Lester V Chandler, *American Monetary Policy 1928 to 1941* (New York: Harper & Row, 1971); Barry Eichengreen, "The Origins and Nature of the Great Slump Revisited" (1992) 45:2 Economic History Rev 213; Christina D Romer, "The Nation in Depression" (1993) 7:2 J Economic Perspectives 19; Ben S Bernanke, "The Macroeconomics of the Great Depression: A Comparative Approach" in Ben S Bernanke, ed, *Essays on the Great Depression* (Princeton, NJ: Princeton University Press, 2000) 5.

24 For a discussion of the trade-off between *ex ante* incentive effects and *ex post* stabilization objectives, see Christos Hadjiemmuil, "Bank Stakeholders' Mandatory Contribution to Resolution Financing: Principle and Ambiguities of Bail-in" in European Central Bank (ECB), *ECB Legal Conference 2015* (Frankfurt am Main: ECB, 2015) 225 at 245–48; Daniel Gros, "The SRM and the dream to resolve banks without public money" (2013) Centre for European Policy Studies (CEPS) Papers No 8774, online: <https://ideas.repec.org/p/eps/cepswp/8774.html>. For a more optimistic view that considers bail-in constructive, even in a systemic crisis, see Zhou et al, *supra* note 14 at 22.

25 Avgouleas & Goodhart, *supra* note 14 at 16. See also section below entitled "Run Risks."

26 For more detailed accounts of the optimal regulatory design of bail-in regimes, see Tröger, "Too Complex to Work", *supra* note 7 at 45–46; Jan Pieter Krahnen & Laura Morretti, "Bail-In Clauses" in Esther Faia et al, eds, *Financial Regulation: A Transatlantic Perspective* (Cambridge, UK: Cambridge University Press, 2015) 136; John Armour, "Making Bank Resolution Credible" (2014) European Corporate Governance Institute (ECGI) Law Working Paper No 244/2014 at 20–21, online: <http://ssrn.com/abstract=2393998>; Huertas, *supra* note 18 at 173. The Liikanen Report contains a condensed view of the issue; *cf Liikanen Report*, *supra* note 1 at 103–4.

Looming Knock-on Effects

Threats for financial stability may arise if the holder of capital instruments subject to bail-in provide critical functions for financial markets themselves. If these essential market participants cannot bear the losses imposed on them without being drawn into solvency problems themselves, a bail-in of their respective investments is not a viable option and instead the incentives to bail out the failing institution dominate. In order to prevent such knock-on effects, the bail-in-able instruments should be held outside the banking sector by investors with sufficient loss-bearing and risk-management capacity (for example, insurance companies, pension funds, high-net-worth individuals and hedge funds).[27]

Run Risks

The policy objectives of PSI are also undermined if a bail-in triggers a bank run. If investors are fully rational, however, bail-in as such does not trigger a systemic crisis because its mechanics confine loss bearing.[28] This is certainly true if bail-in is limited to one institution, however large. Yet, even where a higher number of banks fail, for instance because information revelation at one bank causes sector-wide markdowns of certain assets, recapitalization through PSI remains a plausible element of the strategy to extinguish the fire. The only precondition for establishing sufficient trust in the regained viability of the resolved organizations is that the sector has issued adequate capital subject to reduction, write-down or conversion, or bail-in[29] and central bank liquidity (emergency lending) is available in sufficient proportions.[30]

Yet, if rationality assumptions are relaxed, runs may occur even if investors have no verifiable reason to believe that their institution is in trouble.[31] Limiting negative effects of haircuts imposed on creditors of failing banks thus also requires attenuating (irrational) fears that PSI will occur at other, similarly situated institutions as well.[32] Only this induces investors in runnable debt to wait out the crisis. The first line of defence against investor panic obviously

27 See Zhou et al, *supra* note 14 at 22; Krahnen & Morretti, *supra* note 26 at 140; Tröger, "Regulatory Influence", *supra* note 10 at 589; Martin R Götz & Tobias H Tröger, *Should the marketing of subordinated debt be restricted/different in one way or the other? What to do in the case of mis-selling?* (European Parliament, 2016) at 6, online: <www.europarl.europa.eu/RegData/etudes/IDAN/2016/497723/IPOL_IDA(2016)497723_EN.pdf>. See also section below entitled "Minimum Requirements for Investors in Bail-in-able Debt."

28 See Sommer, *supra* note 11 at 214, 222.

29 The European resolution framework executes PSI through the reduction of Common Equity Tier 1 (CET1) (*BRRD*, *supra* note 4, art 60[1][a]), the write-down or conversion of Additional Tier 1 (AT1) and Tier 2 (T2) ("relevant capital instruments") (*ibid*, art 59[2]) and the bail-in of liabilities (*ibid*, arts 43[1], 63[1]). This chapter uses the term "capital" in a non-technical manner to describe all capital instruments and liabilities subject to PSI.

30 For discussion on the critical importance of central bank liquidity assistance, see Thomas Philippon & Aude Salord, *Bail-ins and Bank Resolution in Europe: A Progress Report* (Geneva: International Center for Monetary and Banking Studies, 2017) at 48; for a discussion on restrictions that might result from a lack of central-bank-eligible collateral, see Avgouleas & Goodhart, *supra* note 14 at 17. As a consequence, the ECB has pushed for special liquidity facilities in resolution (Eurosystem Resolution Liquidity) not subject to the restrictions of regular emergency lending operations; see Alexander Weber & Alessandro Speciale, "ECB Weighs Emergency Cash Injections to Smooth Bank Rescues", *Bloomberg* (9 April 2018), online: <www.bloomberg.com/news/articles/2018-04-09/ecb-considers-proposal-for-new-cash-line-to-aid-bank-rescues>.

31 For the seminal model, see Douglas W Diamond & Philip H Dybvig, "Bank Runs, Deposit Insurance, and Liquidity" (1983) 91:3 J Political Economy 401. For an extension that shows that modern bank runs occur not only at deposit-taking credit institutions but also at similarly financed commercial and investment banks, see Gary Gorton, "The Panic of 2007" in Federal Reserve Bank of Kansas City (FRBKC), *Maintaining Stability in a Changing Financial System* (FRBKC, 2009) 131 at 199–231; Gary Gorton, "Information, Liquidity, and the (Ongoing) Panic of 2007" (2009) 99 AER Papers & Proceedings 567.

32 See Avgouleas & Goodhart, *supra* note 14 at 11, pointing to the experience reported in Timothy F Geithner, *Stress Test: Reflections on Financial Crises* (New York: Broadway Books, 2014) at 306.

is the prescription of a sufficiently large layer of long-term (non-runnable), high-quality and easy-to-bail-in capital that assures other creditors that PSI will not reach their claims.[33] Ultimately, however, with bounded rationality and the scope of the crisis unclear, the existence of a second bulwark is even more important. Only if a credible government backstop is in place for situations in which the predestined cushion for bail-in is insufficient, will other claimholders refrain from withdrawing their funds. Counter to the immediate intuition, PSI thus requires a strong backstop for all runnable positions on the liability side of banks' balance sheet, absent which it accelerates ensuing crises. This observation does not impair the policy objective of instilling market discipline because the sufficiently thick layer of easy-to-bail-in, high-quality bank capital elicits adequate debt governance, precisely because potential systemic implications of PSI are attenuated and the bail-in threat therefore becomes credible.

Political Economy Considerations

Investors in bank capital other than SIFIs also need to have sufficient loss-bearing capacity to endure damages when their debt is written-down or converted into equity. As conversion occurs during periods of distress, new equity holdings will initially be of substantially lower value than the nominal value of prior debt holdings. If, for instance, households invest a large fraction of their wealth in banks' bail-in capital, losses incurred in PSI potentially lead to adverse social and/ or psychological consequences that, in turn, may induce politicians to spare their constituents and bail out banks instead. Where markets anticipate these motives, the credibility of a regime of mandatory PSI is significantly weakened, no matter which pledges legislators make at the time of promulgation. Similarly, politicians' resentments vis-à-vis hedge funds[34] may lead to similar time inconsistencies if, after a bail-in, the banking system was owned by these funds. Hence, an adequately designed regime for PSI has to monitor holders of bail-in debt closely.[35]

The European Experience of 2017

Recent resolution episodes in the European Union corroborate the identified shortcomings of the framework for PSI under the BRRD and SRM Regulation. A closer look at the main facts of the cases illustrates that decision makers in and beyond the agencies involved have an inclination to interpret the exceptions from mandatory PSI under the resolution regime extensively to afford themselves sufficient leeway to spare certain investors and to stabilize ailing banks with government money instead of executing a full-blown bail-in. The resolution cases are not only highly idiosyncratic on the facts, but also with regard to the legal solutions found, and therefore do not add up to a clear European standard of PSI in bank resolution that could shape market expectations.

33 In principle, a sufficiently upholstered, comforting capital cushion could prevent more senior claimants of all sorts from running and thus prevent contagion that would otherwise loom; see Stefano Micossi, Ginevra Bruzzone & Miriam Cassella, "Bail-in Provisions in State Aid and Resolution Procedures: Are they consistent with systemic stability?" (2014) CEPS Policy Brief No 318 at 9, online: <www.ceps.eu/ceps-publications/bail-provisions-state-aid-and-resolution-procedures-are-they-consistent-systemic/>; Avgouleas & Goodhart, *supra* note 14 at 17–18.

34 For evidence that this view may have no sound factual basis, see Jan Bena et al, "Are Foreign Investors Locusts? The Long-Term Effects of Foreign Institutional Ownership" (2016) ECGI Finance Working Paper No 468/2016, online: <https://ssrn.com/abstract=2640045> (showing that foreign institutional investor ownership increases long-term investment).

35 Philippon & Salord, *supra* note 30 at 43; for the various reasons why redress in securities litigation is inapt to internalize the social costs of mis-selling and rectify incentives *ex ante*, see Götz & Tröger, *supra* note 27 at 13–15.

In the resolution of Spain's Banco Popular, all CET1 and AT1 instruments were reduced or (converted and) written down entirely and T2 capital was converted into equity; the new shares were transferred to Santander for the symbolic price of one euro.[36] The Single Resolution Board (SRB) thus only used the write-down and conversion tool[37] in conjunction with the reduction power and did not touch (subordinated) debt instruments that rank below a bank's own funds in the waterfall in a bail-in. The SRB could resolve the failed banking group with limited PSI *inter alia* because a credible private sector backstop was available. As a consequence, investors learned little to nothing for resolution cases in which market confidence would have to be restored through bail-in alone.

Although Banco Popolare di Vicenza and Veneto Banca failed, they were not put in resolution under the BRRD because the SRB in both cases denied a public interest in applying the special regime[38] and remitted the institutions to wind-downs in orderly insolvency proceedings under national bankruptcy laws.[39] PSI thus occurred under Italian insolvency laws and was cushioned by injections of government money, approved by the European Commission's state aid division, to facilitate a partial sale to Intesa, a large bank.[40]

Long-ailing Monte dei Paschi di Siena was rescued by a publicly funded "precautionary recapitalization" that avoids triggering resolution with the significant eight percent minimum bail-in under the BRRD.[41] Hence, at this stage, investors in bank (subordinated) debt remained untouched by the rescue efforts and the European Commission once again did not object to the government aid.[42]

With regard to this chapter's objective, the main takeaway from these three cases is that the European resolution framework indeed opens many routes for stabilizing wobbly banks. They involve vastly diverging degrees of PSI. Therefore, the BRRD may work as a tool to achieve efficient outcomes *ex post*, yet it does not provide the required predictability for PSI to induce risk-adequate pricing of bank capital *ex ante*. Quite importantly, decision makers at resolution authorities responding to political pressure have ample opportunity to avoid PSI under the

36 SRB, *Decision of the Single Resolution Board in its executive session of 7 June 2017 concerning the adoption of a resolution scheme in respect of Banco Popular Español, S.A.*, SRB/EES/2017/08 at 17–19.

37 *BRRD, supra* note 4, art 59(2) allows to write down and convert AT1 and T2 instruments immediately once the bank reaches the point of non-viability (i.e., provides an instrument for PSI distinct from bail-in); see Anna Gardella, "Bail-in and the Financing of Resolution within the SRM Framework" in Danny Busch & Guido Ferrarini, eds, *European Banking Union* (Oxford, UK: Oxford University Press, 2015) at para 11.49.

38 *BRRD, supra* note 4, art 32(1)(c), (5) requires a determination that the resolution objectives can be better achieved under the special resolution regime than under regular insolvency laws; for an extensive discussion, see Tröger, "Too Complex to Work", *supra* note 7 at 52–53.

39 SRB, *Decision concerning the assessment of the conditions for resolution in respect of Veneto Banca SpA*, SRB/EES/2017/11 at 11–21; SRB, *Decision concerning the assessment of the conditions for resolution in respect of Banca Popolare di Vicenza SpA*, SRB/EES/2017/12 at 11–21.

40 European Commission, *State Aid SA.45664 (2017/N) – Italy – Orderly liquidation of Banca Popolare di Vicenza and Veneto Banca – Liquidation aid,* COM C (2017) 4501 final at 20–24.

41 See *BRRD, supra* note 4, art 32(4)(1)(d). For an extensive discussion of this highly discretionary, politically charged exception, see Tröger, "Too Complex to Work", *supra* note 7 at 49–50.

42 European Commission, *State Aid SA.47677 (2017/N) – Italy – New aid and amended restructuring plan of Banca Monte dei Paschi di Siena,* COM C (2017) 4690 final at 17–23.

BRRD. In particular, the recent experience in Italy indicates[43] that bailout-avid regulators and politicians can exploit the exception to avoid inflicting losses on investors and stabilize failing banks with government money instead; EU state-aid rules provide only a lax restriction in this regard.[44]

Bail-in 2.0

One possible reaction to the deficiencies of the existing framework could seek to amend the BRRD and the SRM Regulation in order to close the loopholes that allow avoiding PSI. However, such a strategy would arguably reorganize the army to win a past war, but leave the forces unprepared for the next one.[45] Instead, it seems more appealing to remodel the regulatory environment in a way that largely eliminates the incentives to avoid PSI in the first place.

To achieve this goal, a rather radical departure from key premises of the current resolution regime is required. It seems to be common ground that PSI should be without limits and, in principle, should affect the whole liability side of a bank's balance sheet.[46] Yet, such an unconditional bail-in largely misses the threat of a systemic crisis that can emanate from the inherent fragility of any banking system in case of bail-in (see sections above entitled "Looming Knock-on Effects" and "Run Risks"). Moreover, such an undiscriminating approach tends to be agnostic vis-à-vis the characteristics of the buy side of bail-in bonds that influence politicians' and bureaucrats' incentives to oppose efficient PSI for political economy reasons (see section above entitled "Political Economy Considerations").[47] To counter these blind spots effectively, this chapter proposes not only a close monitoring of the investors in bail-in-able debt, but also a more nuanced view of bank liabilities potentially subject to PSI that balances a bank's moral hazard incentive and the run-risk inherent in bank investments.[48]

43 In June 2017, the Italian government injected €17 billion into Veneto Banca and Banca Popolare di Vicenza and thus protected senior bond holders in full, the junior claims being held by a government-orchestrated rescue fund already; see Deborah Ball, "Italy to Spend Up to $19 Billion to Bail Out Two Banks", *The Wall Street Journal* (25 June 2017), online: <www.wsj.com/articles/italy-is-prepared-to-spend-billions-in-shutdown-of-two-banks-1498418669>; "Bank Bail-Outs Italian Style", Editorial, *The Wall Street Journal* (26 June 2017), online: <www.wsj.com/articles/bank-bailouts-italian-style-1498517158>; Rachel Sanderson et al, "Italy sets aside €17bn to wind down failing lenders", *Financial Times* (26 June 2017), online: <www.ft.com/content/83ad52a8-59a5-11e7-9bc8-8055f264aa8b>.

44 For the view in the daily press that regular insolvency proceedings were favoured in order to avoid full PSI in resolution, see Simon Nixon, "Deal on Italian Banks Raises Questions About Euro-zone Rules", *The Wall Street Journal* (25 June 2017), online: <www.wsj.com/articles/deal-on-italian-banks-raises-questions-about-eurozone-rules-1498407926>; Paul J Davies, "Why Italy's Bank Rescue Looks a Backward Step for Europe", *The Wall Street Journal* (25 June 2017), online: <www.wsj.com/articles/why-italys-bank-rescue-looks-a-backward-step-for-europe-1498479633>; Editorial, "Italy shows EU banking union still has far to go", *Financial Times* (26 June 2017), online: <www.ft.com/content/f01db25e-5a70-11e7-9bc8-8055f264aa8b>; Lucrezia Reichlin, "The European banking union falls short in Italy", *Financial Times* (26 June 2017), online: <www.ft.com/content/3b8bc570-5a7e-11e7-b553-e2df1b0c3220>.

45 Luca Enriques, "Regulators' Response to the Current Crisis and the Upcoming Reregulation of Financial Markets: One Reluctant Regulator's View" (2009) 30 U Pa J Intl L 1147 at 1153 (arguing that crisis-driven regulation is prone to miss future challenges); for a similar assessment, see Steven L Schwarcz, "The Functional Regulation of Finance" (2014) Working Paper at 3–4, online: <http://ssrn.com/abstract=2437544>.

46 See *BRRD*, *supra* note 4, art 44(1): "Member States shall ensure that the bail-in instrument can be applied to all the liabilities of an institution"; for a more nuanced delineation, including the limited exceptions under BRRD, articles 44(2) and (3), see Tröger, "Too Complex to Work", *supra* note 7 at 57–60.

47 For the seminal analysis that highlights how decision makers in public administration are driven by personal motives such as personal power and prestige, see William A Niskanen, Jr, *Bureaucracy & Representative Government* (London, UK: Routledge, 1971) at 36–42.

48 For an earlier version of the following, see Martin R Götz, Jan P Krahnen & Tobias H Tröger, "Five Years after the Liikanen Report: What Have We Learned?" (2017) Sustainable Architecture for Finance in Europe White Paper No 50 at 20–23, online: <http://safe-frankfurt.de/fileadmin/user_upload/editor_common/Policy_Center/SAFE_White_Paper_50.pdf>.

Minimum Requirements for Investors in Bail-in-able Debt

In general, PSI should not increase systemic risk. Therefore, a broad diversification across all market participants is generally desirable. Yet the identified perils suggest important restrictions. Ideally, an investor of bail-in-able debt exhibits the following properties:

- **Storm resilience:** If PSI occurs, an investor does not face the threat of a run on their liabilities. This implies that the investor is not a provider of liquidity (i.e., does not have a significant amount of runnable, short-term liabilities). Storm resilience is satisfied for life insurance companies, pension funds and other long-term-oriented capital funds. Banks, on the other hand, are not suitable investors. Moreover, retail investors are also not suitable due to their fixed consumption needs.

- **Sufficient provisioning:** Over time, an investor in bail-in capital should build up sufficiently high levels of reserves from coupon payments on debt instruments subject to bail-in. These reserves would cushion losses without imperilling the investor's own viability.

- **Ultimate risk-bearer:** Only the ultimate bearer of the default risk should be seen as the investor in bail-in capital. Therefore, any risk transfer (for example, via credit insurance or credit default swaps) must be taken into account when assessing whether the aforementioned requirements are met.

Storm resilience and sufficient provisioning are two characteristics that a prudent supervisor should assess and continuously monitor. This ensures that market participants have rational expectations and can realistically assume that they may become liable in case of bank distress.

However, the supervisory and resolution framework currently does not recognize these key properties as requirements for purchasers of bail-in capital.[49] The implementation of the FSB's standard for total loss-absorbing capacity (TLAC)[50] will move into the right direction, as it will introduce rules that largely destroy incentives to build up positions in other banks' bail-in capital on the asset side of the balance sheet of banks.[51] Yet, since the TLAC standard is only binding for the largest banks in the world (and was implemented in pertinent respects only for Europe's globally significant institutions),[52] it does not ensure a system-wide rectification of incentives for financial institutions. Instead, the catalogue of the central tasks of supervisory authorities and/or of resolution authorities should include monitoring of the two requirements of storm resilience and sufficient provisioning.

49 For an in-depth analysis of the insufficient safeguards, see Tröger, "Too Complex to Work", *supra* note 7 at 68; Götz & Tröger, *supra* note 27 at 7.

50 FSB, *Principles on Loss-absorbing and Recapitalisation Capacity of G-SIBs in Resolution: Total Loss-absorbing Capacity (TLAC) and Term Sheet* (2015), s 15, online: <www.fsb.org/wp-content/uploads/TLAC-Principles-and-Term-Sheet-for-publication-final.pdf>; Basel Committee on Banking Supervision (BCBS), *Standard TLAC holdings* (Bank for International Settlements, 2016), online: <www.bis.org/bcbs/publ/d387.pdf>.

51 For a more granular discussion, see Tröger, "Too Complex to Work", *supra* note 7 at 20–21; Gleeson & Guynn, *supra* note 4 at paras 4.17, 4.56.

52 See Capital Requirements Regulation as amended by *Regulation (EU) 2019/876 of the European Parliament and of the Council of 20 May 2019 amending the Capital Requirements Regulation as regards the leverage ratio, the net stable funding ratio, requirements for own funds and eligible liabilities, counterparty credit risk, market risk, exposures to central counterparties, exposures to collective investment undertakings, large exposures, reporting and disclosure requirements (CRR II)*, [2014] OJ, L 150/1, arts 72(h), 72(i).

Maximum Requirements for an Effective Bail-in

The idea that bail-in may encompass all bank liabilities responds to the political sentiment that governments should never again bail out failing banks with taxpayer money. Although there are also efficiency grounds for minimizing government involvement (see section above entitled "Bailout Rationality and Defunct Debt Governance"), the relentless desire to treat financial firms equal to other business organizations — where creditors bear all the losses in bankruptcy — neglects a fundamental difference between (non-financial) companies and banks: the risk of a run on a bank's liabilities.

Banks are exposed to this risk because their essential function lies in term and liquidity transformation between assets and liabilities. For instance, the liabilities of internationally operating major banks represent, in large part, the cash reserves of large corporations and the liquid assets of institutional investors. These institutions also provide for other short-term refinancing of their assets. Therefore, they constantly face the threat of a sudden withdrawal of funds. Economic theory sometimes regards the possibility of a run by investors (i.e., the inherent fragility of banks) as a welcome source of self-discipline.[53] From this point of view, a high degree of short-term debt can even attract depositors and thus enhance the performance of the intermediation process. This positive, incentive-oriented interpretation, however, disregards the possibility of contagion effects and the role of systemic risks,[54] which is exacerbated by the possibility that runs on bank liabilities may occur without fundamental reason (panic-driven runs).[55]

Due to deposit insurance schemes, the run risk is no longer present for covered deposits, but in principle remains real for all other unsecured positions. From an investor's point of view, in a regime with unlimited PSI, liabilities with seniority above TLAC/Minimum Requirements for Own Funds and Eligible Liabilities (MREL) instruments[56] (but below covered deposits) are secure only insofar as they can be withdrawn very quickly, prior to a bail-in. This self-defence, however, can in fact undermine recapitalization efforts in resolution and may endanger the stability of the system as a whole, not only in the event of a panic-driven crisis, if investors cannot predict where PSI actually stops. Therefore, any mandatory bail-in may reinstill *desirable* market discipline only up to a certain point, beyond which unwanted anxiety-driven behaviour dominates. It is important to consider the extent to which the disciplining (positive) effect of the marginal run risk outweighs the negative effects from increased systemic risk, inefficient (panic-driven) bank failures and so forth. (For an illustration of the fundamental trade-offs, see Figure 1.)

53 Douglas W Diamond & Raghuram G Rajan, "A Theory of Bank Capital" (2000) 55 J Finance 2431.

54 Franklin Allen et al, "Government guarantees and financial stability" (2017) ECB Working Paper No 2032, online: <www.ecb.europa.eu/pub/pdf/scpwps/ecbwp2032.en.pdf>; Tito Cordella, Giovanni Dell'Ariccia & Robert Marquez, "Government Guarantees, Transparency, and Bank Risk-taking" (2016) World Bank Policy Research Working Paper No 7971, online: <www.imf.org/external/np/res/seminars/2016/arc/pdf/Cordella_Dellariccia_Marquez_Session4.pdf>.

55 See section above entitled "Run Risks."

56 The MREL represents the European sibling of the FSB's TLAC requirements and thus characterizes bank debt that is designated to absorb losses in case of the institution's failure; for a detailed analysis, see *BRRD*, *supra* note 4; Tröger, "Too Complex to Work", *supra* note 7 at 6–20.

Figure 1: Trade-offs between Market Discipline and Run Risk

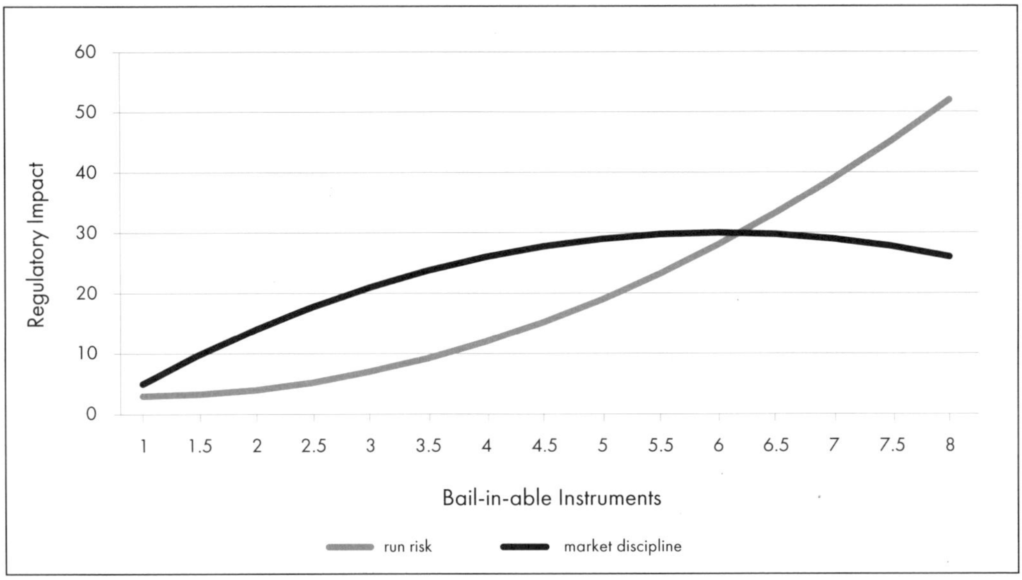

Source: Author.

Considering the negative effects, it is beneficial to restrict the bail-in threat to those investors who hold non-runnable positions of a bank's liabilities. Therefore, an upper limit should be set in addition to the minimum requirements for the amount of bail-in-able capital to be held available by banks (TLAC/MREL). To be sure, the a priori bailout guarantee for all other liabilities may trigger all the negative consequences associated with government guarantees (see section above entitled "Bailout Rationality and Defunct Debt Governance").

Hence, policy makers should aim at striking the right balance between the two countervailing objectives. The BRRD currently only provides for a highly discretionary and unspecified possibility to exclude certain liabilities from bail-in, in particular where "the exclusion is absolutely necessary and it is appropriate to ensure the continuity of the critical functions and core business areas, so that the ability of the institution that is in the process of liquidation is maintained to allow it to continue the main business, services and transactions."[57] Of course, this exception could be interpreted to facilitate an optimal trade-off, yet a rule that is clear *ex ante* would be preferable in order to shape market expectations and drive pricing without unnecessary ambiguities. If the liabilities subject to bail-in are of sufficiently high quality and potent backstops are available once (looming) losses exceed the available amount of liabilities designated for bail-in,[58] PSI should remain an idiosyncratic event of the failing institution even in a systemic crisis. An unconditional bail-in up to the maximum should therefore not increase fragility; on the other hand, PSI confined to a sufficiently thick layer of liabilities should provide adequate market discipline and prevent moral hazard.[59]

57 *BRRD, supra* note 4, art 44(3)(b).

58 It must be stressed that the concept proposed here at least partly relies on bailouts to achieve the stabilization objective of resolution after the generously upholstered capital cushion available for PSI is exhausted.

59 This is achieved by partly disentangling the conflicting resolution objectives of achieving *ex post* efficient outcomes without distorting *ex ante* incentives; see also *supra* note 24.

To arrive at such a rule, it may be helpful for analytical purposes to divide the liability side of a bank's balance sheet into three parts with diverging loss-bearing properties: a liable segment (TLAC/MREL instruments); a non-liable segment (covered deposits); and, between those two, a potentially liable segment. This mezzanine intermediate tier comprises a heterogeneous set of liabilities for which the regulatory risk-return profile (Figure 1) is somewhere between that of TLAC/MREL instruments and covered deposits. The *ex ante* designation of its treatment in resolution should be a primary task for regulators going forward. It is important to stress that the loss absorption in these mezzanine instruments can also be set at zero in individual resolution cases, depending on the inherent cost/benefit trade-off for the specific positions that appear on a particular bank's balance sheet. The added value from this proposition is that the key challenge can be grasped more lucidly and the need for *ex ante* transparency in pertinent respects is emphasized. The approach does not provide an off-the-rack, mechanically applicable formula to solve the difficulties. However, future research that looks at the regulatory risk-return profile just sketched for specific debt instruments can provide important guidance for regulators' case-specific determinations.

At first glance, this approach is more sophisticated than a straightforward bail-in tool that potentially encompasses all liabilities junior to covered deposits. However, it only anticipates the determinations that resolution authorities and other agencies otherwise have to make on an ad hoc basis on the resolution weekend. In fact, the front-loaded regulatory approach not only minimizes the negative impact of looming runs, but also enhances predictability and therefore improves market discipline emanating from PSI.

Conclusion

PSI through the bail-in tool is geared toward restoring private liability as a correlate to private property and to private profits. However, under the conditions of today's globally integrated, deeply intertwined financial markets, implementing the policy prescript of reinstilled market discipline requires an artificially created framework that goes beyond the imposition of losses by regulatory fiat. Market discipline in the banking sector can only emerge and function if there is a responsible gardener who closely observes and supports the development and stability of a greenhouse microclimate in which PSI can flourish.

The first conclusion from the analysis presented here is to expand the list of tasks of resolution authorities and/or banking supervisors: these agencies should focus also on the holders of bail-in-able liabilities and their behaviour.

The second conclusion also follows from the idea that a more holistic approach is required when reintroducing private investor liability in the banking sector. In order to reach an efficient trade-off between enhanced market discipline and heightened run-risks, regulators should also enhance their efforts to define what was called the mezzanine segment of banks' liabilities and determine its treatment.

Author's Note

This chapter has benefited tremendously from comments and critiques that colleagues and friends made on earlier drafts. Those of Alexander Friedrich, Martin R. Götz, Christos Hadjiemmanuil and Jan Pieter Krahnen were particularly beneficial. The author gratefully acknowledges financial support from the *Landes-Offensive zur Entwicklung wissenschaftlich-ökonomischer Exzellenz* (State Initiative for the Development of Scientific and Economic Excellence) Research Center Sustainable Architecture for Finance in Europe.

12

Pitfalls of Global Harmonization of Systemic Risk Regulation in a World of Financial Innovation

ROBERTA ROMANO

A working hypothesis of international financial regulation, whether it be capital requirements or, as is the focus of this book, systemic risk — "the risk that instability in the financial system will cause a recession or otherwise significantly impair the real economy"[1] — is that regulation should be globally harmonized. This chapter contends instead that we should be wary about mechanically assuming the efficacy of global harmonization and, in particular, harmonization of systemic risk measurement and regulation. My argument is informed by what I consider two key lessons from the recent global financial crisis. The first lesson is that, when internationally harmonized regulation incentivizes banks to follow similar business strategies that go seriously awry, the adverse consequences spread globally and are not limited to one regulator's domain. In other words, harmonization can amplify, rather than dampen, systemic risk, which is particularly troubling when we are operating more or less in the dark.

1 Steven L Schwarcz, "Securing Financial Stability: Systemic Regulation of Systemic Risk", 1 Wis L Rev [forthcoming in 2019] at 2, online: <https://ssrn.com/abstract=3233666>.

The second lesson cautioning against harmonization of systemic risk regulation stems from the relation between crises and financial innovation. Innovations in financial technology (fintech) that have been engines of prosperity across the globe also contain the seeds of financial calamity with imprudent use. This double-edged phenomenon poses an acute threat to regulatory efficacy. First, regulation that may have been effective when adopted can become counterproductive, if not toxic, as the economic environment changes with, for example, the introduction of new financial products.[2] Second, and relatedly, regulation must be attentively updated to retain its efficacy in light of the dynamism in financial markets, yet the necessary updating is exceedingly challenging when regulation has been harmonized worldwide, as it requires the participation of numerous nations. I illustrate this by discussing the cumbersome process for revising the Basel Accords, which set the international standards for financial regulation.

These lessons indicate that it would have been beneficial to have had regulatory diversity in capital requirements during the recent financial crisis. These lessons, in my judgment, are equally applicable to systemic risk regulation, in particular, given the limits to our knowledge of how to measure systemic risk.

My contention is not that regulatory diversity in international financial regulation would eliminate all financial crises or be accompanied solely by advantages with no drawbacks. Rather, my contention is that these lessons suggest that the benefits of diversity could well outweigh the cost, and that efforts to achieve global harmonization in financial regulation — as opposed to cross-border coordination by regulators in the supervision, support or sanctioning of multinational banks — should proceed with humility and caution. Financial regulation need not be harmonized for regulators to coordinate supervisory or enforcement efforts. The absence of global harmonization of securities regulation has not, for instance, prevented regulators from implementing numerous memoranda of understanding, facilitating cross-border coordination.

The Global Financial Crisis of 2008-2009

The case for introducing diversity into global systemic risk regulation is best conveyed by the lessons that should have been learned from the recent global financial crisis and its relation to globally harmonized capital requirements. In order to provide a context for understanding what happened and how it relates to regulatory harmonization, the analysis begins with a thumbnail sketch of Gary Gorton's canonical explanation of the trigger of the recent crisis, which, in subsequent co-authored work, he has maintained is true of past financial crises in the United States as well: a run in short-term funding markets.[3]

A core function of the banking sector is maturity transformation, by which financial institutions borrow short term through issuing retail deposits and lend long term to corporations or individuals for business investment or acquisition of property. Starting in the decades before

2 *Cf* Steven L Schwarcz, "Regulating Financial Change: A Functional Approach" (2016) 100 Minn L Rev 1441 (observing that "the pre-crisis financial regulatory network, which assumed the dominance of bank-intermediated funding, failed to adequately address a collapsing financial system in which the majority of funding had become non-bank intermediated" at 1443–44).

3 See Gary B Gorton, *Slapped by the Invisible Hand: The Panic of 2007* (New York: Oxford University Press, 2010) (trigger of recent global financial crisis); Gary B Gorton & Ellis W Tallman, *Fighting Financial Crises: Learning from the Past* (Chicago: University of Chicago Press, 2018) (characterizing panics in short-term debt markets as a trigger for all financial crises, from examination of crises in the United States in the nineteenth and twentieth centuries).

the global financial crisis, many financial institutions met their short-term funding needs by borrowing in wholesale or institutional markets, referred to as the shadow banking sector, as they perform the identical intermediation function as the regulated banking sector but are not subject to banking regulation. Accordingly, the shadow banking system was largely under the radar of regulators. Given shadow banking's unregulated status, the Federal Reserve did not collect information on the sector prior to the crisis (apart from the segment related to dealers in US Treasury securities), and we therefore cannot generate an accurate estimate of its pre-crisis size. It was, however, quite large: for example, traditional banking liabilities were $14 trillion[4] in 2007, while the gross size of shadow banking liabilities at its peak in June 2007 was approximately $22 trillion (although the appropriate comparison would be to net shadow banking liabilities, which cannot be estimated).[5]

Banking, in a nutshell, evolved dramatically over the last decades of the twentieth century as banks encountered increasing competition by non-banks on both the asset and liability sides: businesses were able to raise debt financing more cheaply by issuing junk bonds in capital markets than by borrowing from a bank; and depositors could earn a higher return without increasing their risk by shifting savings from bank accounts into money market funds.[6] Banks responded to the deterioration in their competitive position by entering into new lines of business, the most important of which was securitization, by which banks moved assets (corporate loans) off their balance sheets by selling interests in portfolios of the assets to investors. A further factor in the evolution of banking was deregulation, whose objective was, at least in part, to enable banks to compete more easily.[7] As Gorton notes, we do not know "for sure" why securitization arose,[8] but one factor in its increasing use was that it enabled banks to avoid costly capital requirements that were geared to assets that were retained on balance sheets.[9] This use of securitization correspondingly increased banks' leverage and thereby increased risk in the banking system.

My more specific point, however, concerns securitization and regulatory harmonization. The capital requirements set by the Basel Accords made securitized assets an advantageous form of capital for banks to hold. The worldwide harmonization of those requirements greatly increased both domestic and foreign bank demand for those assets, which in turn increased risk in the global banking system.[10] Furthermore, as next explained, that increased demand stimulated the growth of the even riskier subprime securitization market.

There are two primary funding mechanisms in the shadow banking sector: repos (sale and repurchase agreements) and asset-backed commercial paper (ABCP). Both of these mechanisms

4 All dollar figures in US dollars.

5 Zoltan Pozsar et al, "Shadow Banking" (2013) 19:2 Federal Reserve Bank of New York Economic Policy Rev 1 at 6.

6 Gorton, *supra* note 3 at 38.

7 *Ibid.*

8 *Ibid* at 40.

9 See sections below entitled "First Lesson: Harmonized International Financial Regulation and the Global Financial Crisis" and "Second Lesson: Financial Innovation, International Financial Regulation and the Global Financial Crisis."

10 For example, close to half of the sponsors of the $1.2 trillion worth of asset-backed commercial paper (ABCP) conduits outstanding as of January 2007, just prior to the global financial crisis, were non-US financial institutions, and of the $714 billion (74 percent) of ABCP funded in US dollars and sponsored by commercial banks, more than half ($412 billion) was sponsored by non-US banks. Viral V Acharya & Philipp Schnabl, "Do Global Banks Spread Global Imbalances? Asset-Backed Commercial Paper during the Financial Crisis of 2007-09" (2010) 1:1 IMF Economic Rev 37 at 48, 55 (tables 3, 4).

are secured by collateral and depend on maturity transformation. They are the markets whose collapse triggered the global financial crisis.

In a repo transaction, a financial institution, such as a commercial or investment bank that seeks to borrow funds, sells a security and agrees to repurchase it from the buyer at a later date at a higher price, which reflects interest charged for the use of the cash. If the borrowing financial institution cannot repay the loan (i.e., cannot repurchase the security at the agreed-upon price), then the lender keeps the security. Although these transactions are short-term contracts in which the repurchase is often set to take place the next day, the expectation is that the agreement will be rolled over indefinitely.

In the repo market's initial years, transactions were collateralized by US Treasury securities; but as the market grew in the mid-2000s, the range of acceptable collateral expanded to include residential mortgage-backed securities (RMBSs), a type of securitized asset whose payout is a function of the interest and principal collected on an underlying pool of mortgage loans.[11] By the mid-2000s, these underlying mortgage loans included subprime mortgages. Although the subprime borrowers had poor credit, the expectation was that increases in housing prices would enable the borrowers to refinance to be able to make payment. Furthermore, only the more senior-priority RMBSs were deemed acceptable, and the securities were structured to be oversecured (i.e., the projected income stream from the underlying mortgages was greater than the promised payouts to investors).

Gorton's analysis of the operation of the shadow banking system has two key insights that are central for understanding the financial crisis. First, institutional investors' transactions in repos can be characterized as paralleling retail investors' bank deposits: the investment-grade designation of the RMBS collateral functioned as a substitute for deposit insurance, while the feature of repo agreements that did not require contracts to roll over was the functional equivalent to the ability to withdraw bank deposits on demand.[12] Accordingly, the shadow banking system can be characterized as "resembl[ing] the pre-FDIC [Federal Deposit Insurance Corporation] U.S. banking system."[13]

Second, Gorton emphasizes that a critical feature of the short-term fixed income securities that financial institutions issue as debt (RMBSs used as collateral in the repo market and demand deposits in the commercial banking sector) is their "information-insensitivity," that is, the repo collateral's AAA rating (or deposit insurance) enables a lender to not have to investigate the creditworthiness of the financial institution that is its counterparty.[14] The purchaser of an information-insensitive security does not need to be concerned about asymmetric information (the issuer knows more about the value of the security than the buyer), in contrast to the purchaser of equity securities, which are information-sensitive. Although RMBSs are not riskless compared to federally insured bank deposits, the securities are designed so that, just like bank depositors, institutional investors can avoid expending time and effort on due diligence, with investment-grade collateral paralleling the deposit insurance fund as a guarantee of exit without loss of investment.

11 Gorton, *supra* note 3 at 43.

12 *Ibid* at 45.

13 *Ibid.*

14 *Ibid* at 19–23.

The ABCP market functioned similarly to the repo market. Financial institutions issued short-term commercial paper, which was rated investment-grade, and used the proceeds to purchase long-term assets, typically RMBSs. The maturing commercial paper either would be rolled over or repaid from collections on the RMBSs.

Following an uptick in the default rate of US subprime mortgage loans, a panic ensued in the shadow banking sector, preventing the rollover of repos[15] and commercial paper.[16] The drying up of these markets was due to asymmetric information regarding the quality of the assets securing the debt: investors were unable to ascertain the extent of defaulting subprime mortgages held by borrowing institutions (i.e., their counterparties) and comprising their collateral. What had been information-insensitive assets almost overnight became information-sensitive, transforming liquid claims into illiquid ones, and creating a panic as institutional investors — increasingly apprehensive over the quality of their collateral (whose value they were not equipped to determine) — began refusing to roll over the debt. As a consequence, financial institutions that had borrowed in the repo and ABCP markets were unable to replace the withdrawn capital and were forced to delever on a massive scale, selling assets at fire-sale prices.

Caught in a downward spiral of selling assets into a market with collapsing prices, even banks not selling assets had to mark down their value to fire-sale market prices under mark-to-market accounting rules, and that resulted in banks further having either to increase capital or sell assets. The fire sales fed back into investors' reluctance to lend at any price, as they could no longer be assured of the value of the collateral, and what began as a liquidity crisis morphed into a solvency one. As panic set in, investor apprehension over subprime mortgages spilled over into other securitized asset markets that had experienced no similar signs of borrower distress, such as automobile loans and credit card receivables.[17] Outside of the shadow banking sector, banks also financed themselves by borrowing in the interbank market, that is, from each other. That short-term funding market froze as well in the panic because banks were as uncertain as repo investors of their counterparty banks' exposure and, hence, of their creditworthiness.

As Gorton explains, the run on repo was similar to the frequent bank runs of the prior century in the period known as the National Banking Era, in which a shock to the system regarding adverse economic information caused investors to panic.[18] The analogue in the recent crisis was a shock to the system that indicated that housing prices had declined, rather than risen, in 2007, which led investors to no longer roll over repos and ABCP, the functional equivalent of depositors' withdrawals in historical bank runs following shocks indicating a spike in the liabilities of failed businesses.[19] And the source of investor panic was analogous: a lack of knowledge of which financial institutions had significant exposure to subprime in 2007-2008 parallels lack of knowledge of which banks would fail in the National Banking Era panics. As former Governor of the Bank of England Mervyn King put it, economic shocks (i.e., new

15 *Ibid* at 45–51.

16 Daniel Covitz, Nellie Liang & Gustavo A Suarez, "The Evolution of a Financial Crisis: Collapse of the Asset-Backed Commercial Paper Market" (2013) 68:3 J Finance 81.

17 Gorton, *supra* note 3 at 47, 51.

18 *Ibid* at 47.

19 *Ibid* at 32, 52.

information about economic conditions) change the narratives by which individuals make sense of an uncertain economic reality, which creates abrupt shifts in behaviour.[20]

While the panic Gorton describes began in the US subprime mortgage market, it was transmitted worldwide both because domestic and foreign banks were incentivized to hold RMBSs written on those subprime assets by Basel capital requirements and because investors feared that nations that had experienced housing bubbles similar to that of the United States would encounter similar banking system failures.[21]

Financial Crises in Relation to Financial Innovation

William Goetzmann's masterly history of finance provides the second key insight for situating the lessons to be learned from the recent crisis for international financial regulation: the dynamism of financial products and markets.[22] Defining finance as the means by which economic value is shifted over time, Goetzmann illustrates the importance of finance's dynamism in which innovations in fintech, from simple loans to more complex lending agreements and shares of stock or partnerships, led to the development of civilization and economic progress by enabling urbanization, industrialization and the democratization of enterprise (as financial contracts enable individuals with ideas but without resources to implement their ideas). It is a glorious history. But Goetzmann also emphasizes that throughout recorded history, there is a recurring cycle in finance: the bursts of innovation spurring entrepreneurial advances and prosperity are often followed by financial collapse.

Financial innovations often disrupt settled social and economic arrangements, creating new winners and losers. What precipitates financial crises from such disruptive innovations, in Goetzmann's narrative, however, is innovations being taken beyond the bounds of prudence. Human nature, as we know it, often leads individuals to embrace with an overabundance of enthusiasm new financial products, generating pricing bubbles that can burst with severe economic consequences. That is because pricing bubbles go hand in glove with increasing

20 Mervyn King, *The End of Alchemy: Money, Banking, and the Future of the Global Economy* (New York: WW Norton, 2016) at 135–36, 316–17. Nicola Gennaioli and Andrei Shleifer provide an explanation of the financial crisis that may seem similar to King's, as they contend that investors had been overly optimistic and neglectful of the possibility of a significant decline in housing prices (i.e., neglectful of "tail risk"), and when these "errors in beliefs" were eventually corrected, the financial system exploded. Nicola Gennaioli & Andrei Shleifer, *A Crisis of Beliefs* (Princeton, NJ: Princeton University Press, 2018). But King's analysis does not require, and indeed rejects, irrational beliefs to explain the sudden shift in investor behaviour, explaining it instead as "attempts to behave rationally in a world of radical uncertainty." King, *supra* note 20 at 308. Gennaioli and Shleifer further contend that their analysis differs from Gorton's, by explaining the collapse of short-term funding markets as a fire sale rather than a bank run, because the drop in housing prices and hence RMBSs' value could have been predicted well before the crisis began, yet were not. Gennaioli & Shleifer, *supra* note 20 at 72–73, 76–77. The distinction does not affect this chapter's analysis, as it focuses on the shadow banking sector being the locus of ignition of the financial crisis, a fact upon which Gorton, and Gennaioli and Shleifer agree.

21 Beyond the global crisis related to the use of RMBSs as collateral in short-term debt markets, the European Union experienced a further financial crisis in sovereign debt surrounding fears of a Greek default, a situation also affected importantly by incentives created by Basel requirements. See *infra* note 31.

22 William N Goetzmann, *Money Changes Everything: How Finance Made Civilization Possible* (Princeton, NJ: Princeton University Press, 2016).

systemic leverage, which is a precursor of financial crises.[23] Goetzmann's thesis is not that all financial crises are caused by imprudent uses of novel financial technologies, nor that such excesses are the sole cause of a crisis, but the more modest proposition that financial innovations contain the seeds of potential financial crises.

Goetzmann refers to the pattern that he describes as a "duality in the nature of finance."[24] Financial innovation creates a fragile equilibrium in which fintech can lead to some of humankind's greatest achievements as well as its severest failures. Implicit in his perspective is the suggestion that fragility in a financial system cannot be eliminated as it is inherent in the means by which civilizations achieve economic growth and, hence, improve social welfare. It would therefore be reckless for regulators to take elimination of fragility in the financial system as a sole objective.[25] Rather, the duality in finance would seem to be better served by a more measured and efficacious goal of crafting a regulatory regime that has the capacity both to recognize and react when a new financial technology is veering toward perilous rather than beneficial use — characteristics that, as the recent financial crisis made apparent, are not features of the international regulatory system that we currently have.

First Lesson: Harmonized International Financial Regulation and the Global Financial Crisis

The first lesson from the recent global financial crisis involves the relation, which is not often fully acknowledged in accounts of the crisis, between the crisis and international financial regulation. Namely, because international financial regulation is premised on harmonizing capital requirements across internationally active banks, when such regulation goes wrong, banks worldwide will have been incentivized to follow correlated business strategies, and as a consequence, their actions increase systemic risk. In other words, financial difficulties that start in a few banks could spark contagion that crosses borders, setting off a global conflagration. In the most recent crisis, international regulation incentivized banks to invest heavily in the

23 Carmen M Reinhart & Kenneth S Rogoff, *This Time Is Different: Eight Centuries of Financial Folly* (Princeton, NJ: Princeton University Press, 2009) at xxxiii, 217–20. John Geanakoplos makes a further contribution, identifying as key to understanding the pattern of financial crises, a "leverage cycle": a boom and bust in the availability of credit, measured by the amount of collateral lenders require, and corresponding rising and falling asset prices. See e.g. John Geanakoplos, "The Leverage Cycle" in Daron Acemoglu, Kenneth Rogoff & Michael Woodford, eds, *NBER Macroeconomics Annual 2009*, vol 24 (Chicago: University of Chicago Press, 2010) 1 at 2–3. The tightening of credit, forcing deleveraging at the tail end of the leverage cycle that Geanakoplos elucidates, leads to asset price declines and the collapse of highly leveraged institutions, whether or not the assets at issue were financial innovations. Geanakoplos does associate financial innovation with boom and bust cycles, but in his narrative, the innovation responsible for the boom is different from the innovation responsible for the bust (for example, he identifies RMBSs and credit default swaps as the innovations affecting the boom and bust sides, respectively, of the 2008-2009 global financial crisis). In Goetzmann's narrative, the innovation sparking the boom is also responsible for the bust (for example, securitized subprime mortgages in the recent crisis).

24 Goetzmann, *supra* note 22 at 519.

25 *Cf* Iman Anabtawi & Steven L Schwarcz, "Regulating *Ex Post*: How Law Can Address the Inevitability of Financial Failure" (2013) 92 Tex L Rev 75 (arguing that as a result of the inevitability of financial change and our failure to fully understand human behaviour, systemic collapses may be inevitable; therefore, financial regulation should be designed to work not only *ex ante* to try to prevent those collapses, but also *ex post* to try to mitigate their harmful consequences). The fragility inherent in a financial system due to innovation differs from fragility due to interconnections among financial institutions that transmit shocks across firms (i.e., contagion) because that type of fragility could presumably be reduced, albeit not entirely eliminated, by altering those institutional relationships, whereas the fragility Goetzmann analyzes cannot be eliminated because it is intrinsic to finance. See e.g. Andrew Haldane, "Rethinking the Financial Network" (Speech delivered at the Financial Student Association, Amsterdam, 28 April 2009), online: <www.bis.org/review/r090505e.pdf> (advocating altering the organization of firms and markets to reduce transmission shocks that create fragility in a financial network).

financial products at the fore of the shadow banking markets that, in Gorton's analysis, triggered the crisis.

Global capital standards were established in 1988 by the Basel Committee on Banking Supervision, a unit of the Bank for International Settlements, currently consisting of central bankers and supervisors of 28 jurisdictions, including the Group of Twenty nations. The key feature of the Basel Accords is the imposition of risk-weighted capital requirements, by which banks must have more equity capital the greater the credit risk of the assets they hold. The rationale for establishing the international regime was to promote the stability of the international banking system and to equalize international banks' competitive positions by "leveling the playing field." While in the abstract an internationally harmonized regime of risk-weighted capital requirements might seem sensible for realizing the committee's goals — it sets a minimum capital amount that takes into account a bank's risk and is thought thereby to foster stability and create a level playing field — in practice, it has turned out to be anything but straightforward, no doubt, in no small part because in establishing the standards, influential nations have not sought simply to devise the most economically efficient rules, but have sought to advance their own social and political objectives. For instance, the definition of core capital includes intangible assets that featured prominently in the balance sheets of some nations' banks, with otherwise little justification for being so included as they are not as robust a measure of capital as equity — deferred tax assets (Japanese banks), mortgage servicing rights (US banks) and minority interests in other financial institutions (French and German banks).[26]

Prior to the global financial crisis, the Basel capital requirement was set at eight percent. Under the standardized risk weights system of the first accord, corporate loans, deemed the riskiest asset, were assessed at the highest weight of 100 percent, whereas government bonds were characterized as risk-free with a weight of zero percent.[27] Accordingly, if a bank were to make a $1,000 loan to a business, it had to hold $80 in capital assets (at least half of which were to be common stock), but no capital was needed if it were to invest the $1,000 in a US Treasury note. The key feature of the system of risk weights for appreciating the financial crisis is that residential mortgages were preferenced over corporate loans, being assigned a risk weight of only 50 percent, so that $1,000 loaned to a homeowner required only $40 in capital. More important, mortgage-backed securities of investment grade were assigned an even lower risk weight, as the Basel Accords incorporated credit ratings into the weights, such that a bank

26 When Basel III sought to tighten the definition, the three items were retained but limited to the identical percentage of capital, so that those nations could protect their "national champions" from having to hold higher capital. Roberta Romano, "For Diversity in the International Regulation of Financial Institutions: Critiquing and Recalibrating the Basel Architecture" (2014) 31:1 Yale J Reg 1 at 22 [Romano, "Diversity in International Regulation"].

27 In addition, under Basel I, ABCP issuances were not subject to any capital requirements, given the structure that removed the mortgages from banks' balance sheets, while the banks' guarantees of those issuances required less than 20 percent of capital, compared to what would be required if the loans were held on the banks' balance sheets. Viral V Acharya & Philipp Schnabl, "How Banks Played the Leverage Game" in Viral V Acharya & Matthew Richardson, eds, *Restoring Financial Stability: How to Repair a Failed System* (New York: John Wiley & Sons, 2009) 83. A second accord (Basel II, adopted in 2005) replaced the standardized risk weights for the largest banks with an internal model approach to risk weights, under which banks computed capital by engaging in a value-at-risk (VaR) analysis of their assets, subject to parameters set by Basel and regulators' approval. That approach did not alter the assessed relative riskiness of assets (i.e., banks' internal models assessed corporate loans as riskier than residential mortgages or government securities), nor did it eliminate the preference for ABCP and related guarantees. But the internal models approach resulted in banks needing less capital than required under standardized risk weights as, for example, VaR models take account of correlations across assets. In the aftermath of the global financial crisis, the accords were further revised (in Basel 2.5 and Basel III), but the revisions, which increased the capital required, did not alter the centrality of risk-weighted capital, nor the preferential weighting of residential mortgages.

holding $1,000 in investment-grade RMBSs needed to hold only $16 in capital.[28] To illustrate the preference more starkly, a bank could use the $40 in capital required for a directly held mortgage of $1,000 to invest in $2,500 worth of securitized mortgages.

It should not, then, come as a surprise that banks held securitized mortgages, whose purchases they financed through repos and ABCP. These assets ended up on banks' balance sheets in two ways: warehousing in a dealer function or as investments. Commercial and investment banks that sponsored securitizations would buy mortgages, create securitized assets and hold them until they could be sold to investors. The purchases and consequently expanded balance sheets required financing, which the banks obtained in the repo market. Banks also bought the securitized assets for investment purposes.

What is most critical to observe (albeit surprisingly often omitted from analyses of the crisis) is that, although some of the large US firms that failed, such as Bear Stearns and Lehman Brothers, were not commercial banks, banks, on average, not only held more RMBSs, but their holdings were also more concentrated in those assets than any other financial sector, be it insurance companies, pension funds, mutual funds or hedge funds.[29] In addition, the large non-US financial institutions that failed were Basel-regulated banks.[30] The most plausible explanation of this pattern is that institutions that were not incentivized by Basel capital requirements to hold RMBSs did not consider them a good investment, given their risk/return characteristics and the alternatives. In short, financial institutions operating under Basel were incentivized to hold the assets whose implosion set the global financial crisis in motion.[31]

Moreover, global banks' standard use of VaR analysis as mandated or encouraged by regulators to manage risk further exacerbated the crisis: as securitized asset prices fell, the VaR analyses led banks that had been incentivized to hold similar assets simultaneously to sell them, compounding the frenzied fire sales in the repo and ABCP markets.[32] And because the regulatory regime was internationally harmonized, the collapse of those US markets had devastating global repercussions. This is not to say that all globally harmonized regulation is likely to magnify systemic risk. Capital regulation that is independent of banks' business strategies, such as a simple leverage ratio, might not incentivize banks to engage in similar activity and asset-holding;

---

28 Permitting the incorporation of credit ratings to determine risk under Basel II in both internal models and the standardized approach was intended to align risk weights more closely with credit risk. Although the United States was only transitioning to Basel II at the onset of the financial crisis, it had separately promulgated a rule allowing banks to rely on credit ratings for the capital required against securitized assets. See Romano, "Diversity in International Regulation", *supra* note 26 at 15, n 38. The examples in the text simplify Basel's structure of two tiers of capital to facilitate the exposition.

29 See e.g. Jeffrey Friedman, "Capitalism and the Crisis: Bankers, Bonuses, Ideology and Ignorance" in Jeffrey Friedman, ed, *What Caused the Financial Crisis?* (Philadelphia: University of Pennsylvania Press, 2011) 1 at 48.

30 See e.g. Tamim Bayoumi, *Unfinished Business: The Unexplored Causes of the Financial Crisis and the Lessons Yet to be Learned* (New Haven, CT: Yale University Press, 2017) at 186.

31 A similar phenomenon contributed to the European Union's sovereign debt crisis, given Basel's preferencing of such debt. See e.g. Romano, "Diversity in International Regulation", *supra* note 26 at 18–19. Ashoka Mody adds that contributing to the European Union's sovereign debt crisis was the weak condition of EU banks following the subprime mortgage financial crisis because neither the European Central Bank nor national governments acted decisively to shore up their banks, as did the Federal Reserve. Yet EU banks were in worse condition, having been more leveraged pre-crisis than US banks, given limited opportunities for profitable investing due to low euro-zone productivity leading to greater risk-taking; and operating under the lower capital requirements of Basel II while US banks were still operating under Basel I and subject to a (non-risk-weighted) leverage ratio. Ashoka Mody, *EuroTragedy: A Drama in Nine Acts* (New York: Oxford University Press, 2018) at 166–72, 226–27, 231.

32 See Charles K Whitehead, "Destructive Coordination" (2011) 96:2 Cornell L Rev 323 at 343–50.

hence, if a specific strategy or asset class were to fail under such regulation, it would be less likely that institutions worldwide would fail, as occurred in the global financial crisis.

Accordingly, a financial crisis that might have been largely contained locally to US banks operating in subprime markets instead became global in scope as banks worldwide were incentivized by Basel requirements to hold similar investments. The contention is not that banks would have followed totally dissimilar business strategies had there not been globally harmonized capital requirements favouring RMBSs. There may well be herding in financial markets independent of regulatory inducement. For instance, managers may have an incentive to imitate the strategy of others, on the rationale that if the strategy turns out to be mistaken, then all firms will do poorly simultaneously and that will shield a manager from being penalized by investors for underperformance, as poor performance cannot be readily attributed to a particular individual when all banks perform similarly poorly. Furthermore, the incentive to herd is said to be even more powerful for bank managers, for it is thought to increase the probability that a bank will be bailed out. The rationale is that although the government might be willing to let one bank fail, it would certainly not permit all or most banks to go under, given the perceived dire consequences.[33] But even if banks' pre-crisis behaviour were to fit into such a framework, the Basel Accords' preferencing of particular assets would have facilitated herding by providing banks with a focal point upon which assets to coordinate strategies. And as such focal points for herding will be on assets requiring the least capital, if those assets' value declines sharply, the financial system can swerve toward illiquidity followed by insolvency, as occurred in the global financial crisis.[34]

Second Lesson: Financial Innovation, International Financial Regulation and the Global Financial Crisis

The interaction of the Basel Accords with the financial crisis trigger as characterized by Gorton can be linked to Goetzmann's comprehensive historical narrative of the dual role of financial innovation throughout recorded history. Although the decision to assign low-risk weights to residential mortgages has a political dimension, to support government policies encouraging home ownership of influential Basel Committee members who feared that otherwise their large domestic banks would reduce their mortgage financing to what might be politically unacceptable levels,[35] there was at the outset a plausible economic rationale for treating those mortgages as less risky than loans to corporations. When Basel I was drafted in the 1980s, residential mortgages were available to individuals with prime credit ratings and had high value-to-loan ratios. Although mortgages were favoured in the assignment of risk weights to ensure government policies encouraging homeownership would not be adversely affected by capital requirements,[36] at the time, the probability of residential mortgages' repayment would have been

33 For the contention that herding allows banks to increase the probability that they will be bailed out, see e.g. Viral V Acharya & Tanjo Yorulmazer, "Too many to fail — An analysis of time-inconsistency in bank closure policies" (2007) 16:1 J Financial Intermediation 1.

34 *Cf* Daniel Schwarcz & Steven L Schwarcz, "Regulating Systemic Risk in Insurance" (2014) 81:4 U Chicago L Rev 1569 at 1602 [footnotes omitted] (discussing how harmonized regulation could prompt insurance companies to engage in widespread coordinated forced selling of downgraded [or about-to-be-downgraded] corporate bonds, creating fire sales in the bond market that could trigger systemic risk).

35 See e.g. Richard J Herring & Robert E Litan, *Financial Regulation in the Global Economy* (Washington, DC: Brookings Institution, 1995) at 109.

36 *Ibid.*

appropriately perceived as higher than that of loans made to small businesses, justifying a lower risk weight.

But by the mid-2000s, the financial innovation of securitization, which permitted the creation of RMBSs, facilitated a further financial innovation — subprime mortgages — which enabled low-credit individuals to borrow to buy residences, through a loan structure built not upon the borrower's ability to pay but upon the appreciation in the home's value over a short period of time, that would then become collateral for a new mortgage (with the low-credit borrower now having equity in the house), or cash extracted for consumption.[37] Subprime mortgages were not only made to individuals who were poor credit risks, but they also had extremely high loan-to-value ratios. These were therefore inherently high-risk securities. And this innovation facilitated a buildup of leverage in the financial system, with a predictable soaring of housing prices.

Despite the increased risk, RMBSs issued on pools containing subprime mortgages received the identical investment grade rating from credit rating agencies as did those written on pools of prime mortgages, for they replicated the same waterfall structure of priorities of payment and over-secured collateral. As a consequence, Basel's risk-weighting of the residential mortgage and investment-grade RMBS asset classes was creating a dangerous buildup of risk in the banking sector. For, as earlier noted, lower risk weights provided banks with an incentive to hold subprime mortgages and securities issued upon pools containing such mortgages, because they produced a higher return, given the greater risk, while requiring no more capital than what would be required for holding lower-yielding prime mortgages. And as the earlier numerical example illustrated, the lower risk weights accorded securitized assets over direct mortgages facilitated banks' increasing leverage. Embracing the innovation of the securitized subprime mortgages, which factor crucially in Gorton's analysis of the recent financial crisis, dovetails with Goetzmann's thesis that enthusiasm over a financial innovation can fuel a crisis.

These financial innovations did not spur regulators to re-evaluate the capital requirements for subprime mortgages and the securitized assets derived from them, perhaps because they were lulled by the experience from 1998 to 2006 when subprime mortgages worked as expected, as housing prices rose and borrowers repaid mortgages rapidly and refinanced their debt.[38] This regulatory attitude might have been compounded by knowledge of how cumbersome it would be to revise international standards, given the need for consensus among numerous nations. That is not to say that US regulators could not have acted on their own to increase the capital required for US banks to hold subprime mortgages or RMBSs, as they had always imposed a leverage ratio in addition to the international requirements. But reining in bank lending would have been contrary to government policy, supported across the political spectrum, of expanding home ownership to lower-income individuals,[39] and a large number of mortgages were made by non-banks (specialized mortgage companies regulated by states). In addition, there was no consensus among central bankers and economists over whether a central bank should take

37 For a comprehensive explanation of the extent of innovation in the structure of subprime mortgages and the RMBSs written on those mortgages, see Gorton, *supra* note 3 at 63, 74ff.

38 *Ibid* at 81.

39 See e.g. Ben S Bernanke, *The Courage to Act: A Memoir of a Crisis and Its Aftermath* (New York: WW Norton, 2015) at 102 [Bernanke, *The Courage to Act*] (regulators were concerned about restricting subprime mortgages, even though they were aware of trends of deteriorating credit, because they were viewed as an "antidote to redlining," that is, as a means of democratizing credit so that low-income minorities would be able to buy homes). Gennaioli and Shleifer, *supra* note 20, characterize this as an example of the behavioural phenomenon known as neglect of tail risk.

action to "lean against the wind" so as to proactively burst bubbles as opposed to mopping up the damage after they burst (in particular given the daunting difficulty of identifying bubbles), and the legacy of the Federal Reserve under Greenspan was a "mopping-up" approach that was perceived to have been successful.[40]

Even when the Federal Reserve took note of the rise in the rate of subprime mortgage defaults, it did not perceive this to be a source of concern because those mortgages comprised an extremely small piece of the housing market and overall economy.[41] As former Federal Reserve Chairman Ben Bernanke reflected post-crisis, while regulators were aware of "pieces of the puzzle," no one could "imagine" the full picture, and so they did not want to take any precipitous action.[42] With hindsight, that was a catastrophic error as subprime mortgages, which were a socially beneficial innovation by providing low-credit individuals the opportunity to become homebuyers, led to an economic fiasco. The increasing enthusiasm of borrowers, banks, government agencies and investors, respectively, to take up and issue such mortgages and purchase securities on them, fed into a housing bubble, which, as it burst, sparked a panic in the shadow banking markets with massive spillover effects for the broader global economy.

Gorton's analysis of financial crises, focused on bank runs in short-term funding markets, provides an account of the triggering event in the recent crisis of subprime mortgage-backed securities' loss of their information insensitivity. Goetzmann's broad historical perspective regarding the possible impact of financial innovation suggests that securitized subprime mortgages would appear to be a poster child for his theme of duality in the nature of finance, and the propensity of investors to become overly enthusiastic with a new financial product. Linking the two analyses makes plain the economic perils when regulators fail to attend to how markets in innovative financial technologies, in particular short-term debt products, are evolving and whether existing regulations are contributing to a buildup of potentially unsustainable levels of leverage in the financial system.

40 For instance, in the late 1990s, Federal Reserve Chairman Alan Greenspan favoured a "clean-up" approach, and thus the internet stock bubble burst on his watch, a subject of criticism for not having acted pre-emptively. See e.g. Alan Greenspan, "Testimony of Chairman Alan Greenspan" (Testimony delivered before the Committee on Banking and Financial Services, US House of Representatives, 22 July 1999), online: <www.federalreserve.gov/boarddocs/hh/1999/July/testimony.htm> (commenting on bubble bursting: "job of economic policymakers [is] to mitigate the fallout when it occurs"); "Monetary Myopia", *The Economist* (12 January 2006) (criticizing Greenspan's approach in relation to the bursting of the internet stock bubble in the early 2000s). Prior to the financial crisis, positive assessments were offered of Greenspan's approach, and it no doubt had a legacy effect within the Federal Reserve years later. See e.g. Alan S Blinder & Ricardo Reis, "Understanding the Greenspan Standard" in Federal Reserve Bank of Kansas City (FRBKC), *The Greenspan Era: Lessons for the Future, Proceedings of the 2005 Jackson Hole Symposium* (Kansas City, MO: FRBKC, 2005) at 11. The jury is still out, so to speak, on the issue, as the Swedish central bank "leaned against the wind" in the 2010s, and the experience was mixed. See e.g. "Tactic of 'lean against the wind' has failed Sweden", *Financial Times* (29 October 2014), online: <www.ft.com/content/9dfad56a-5f64-11e4-986c-00144feabdc0>; "Riksbank's Jansson changes his mind on leaning against wind", *Central Banking Newsdesk* (6 December 2017), online: <www.centralbanking.com/central-banks/monetary-policy/communication/3333181/riksbanks-jansson-changes-his-mind-on-leaning-against-wind> (the deputy governor of Sweden's central bank says with "benefit of hindsight," the "leaning against the wind" policy was "not entirely successful").

41 Ben S Bernanke, "The Subprime Mortgage Market" (Speech delivered at the Federal Reserve Bank of Chicago's 43rd Annual Conference on Bank Structure and Competition, Chicago, Illinois, 17 May 2007), online: <www.federalreserve.gov/newsevents/speech/bernanke20070517a.htm> ("[t]he effect of the troubles in the subprime sector on the broader housing market will likely be limited, and we do not expect significant spillovers from the subprime market to the rest of the economy or to the financial system").

42 Bernanke, *The Courage to Act*, *supra* note 39 at 82. He also subscribed to former Chairman Greenspan's view that monetary policy should not be used to burst bubbles, and in defending that view in his memoir, notes the failure of the approach taken in Sweden (*ibid* at 90).

Applying the Lessons to Systemic Risk Regulation

The lessons from the global financial crisis regarding the cost of regulatory error and the impact of financial innovation highlight the need to be wary about mechanically assuming the efficacy of harmonizing systemic risk measurement and regulation. There was much that smart, honest and diligent individuals at banks and regulatory agencies and in the academy did not know or understand regarding financial markets and products, and the interconnections across markets, institutions and products, such as the extent of the shadow banking sector and the workings of complex synthetic instruments derived from RMBSs, that affected the scope of the recent crisis. No doubt there is still much that is not known, and not knowable, as a fundamental characteristic of capitalist economies is what Mervyn King terms "radical uncertainty," unknowable unknowns (future states for which we cannot assign a probability as we cannot imagine them in advance), that limit the ability of financial markets and products to manage uncertainty and, correspondingly, regulators' ability to oversee them.[43] Moreover, systemic risk regulation is a far dicier proposition than capital regulation, the harmonization of which contributed to the global financial crisis, because there is no straightforward, generally accepted definition of systemic risk, nor method of measuring it. Accordingly, methods proposed to measure systemic risk vary with the definition employed (as proponents emphasize different aspects of systemic risk), and definitions are at times contradictory. This makes it extremely challenging to identify the measure or set of measures on which regulators ought to focus attention.

For instance, a survey of systemic risk measures by the Office of Financial Research, co-authored by prominent finance scholars, identified 10 definitions of systemic risk and 31 quantitative measures that had been advanced in the economics and finance literature.[44] And the list of proposed measures of systemic risk, which became an object of considerable research effort in the wake of the global financial crisis, is still mushrooming. Browsing the Social Science Research Network website for more recent research on "systemic risk measure" generated more than 250 papers posted after the year of the survey's publication (2012), including 15 in the first half of 2018 alone. The survey's authors put it well when they noted: "even if an exhaustive overview of the systemic risk literature were possible, it would likely be out of date as soon as it was written."[45] In addition, with almost every new systemic risk measure, the creators provide data to support their contention that it is a more accurate predictor of crises than other measures.[46] Further, given the uncertainty inherent in financial markets, to fix one measure of systemic risk for regulatory purposes in a point of time would be foolhardy, for even if we could identify an optimal measure, no measure would remain optimal over time.

In particular, the introduction of new financial products can alter the correlations across institutions and products and, correspondingly, the efficacy of extant measures of systemic risk. This is because proposed measures are derived from data regarding correlations between assets and institutional losses from the most recent financial crisis, and there is scant reason to

43 King, *supra* note 20 at 9, 143–45.

44 Dimitrios Bisias et al, "A Survey of Systemic Risk Analytics" (2012) 4 Annual Rev Financial Economics 255. Moreover, the authors note that their list of systemic risk measures was not exhaustive, as they focused on measures that could be most easily estimated from available data (at 257).

45 *Ibid* at 259.

46 See e.g. Stefano Giglio, Bryan T Kelly & Seth Pruitt, "Systemic Risk and the Macroeconomy: An Empirical Evaluation" (2016) 119:3 J Financial Economics 457 (constructing an aggregate systemic risk index from 19 previously proposed measures that predicts macroeconomic shocks whereas none of the individual measures do so).

have confidence that they will be effective in predicting where systemic risk might emerge out of sample (i.e., in the next crisis).[47] Systemic risk measures, in short, are subject to the same intractable difficulties that King ascribes to the Basel risk weights setting capital requirements: "it is extremely difficult, if not impossible, to judge how the riskiness of different assets will change in the future. The appropriate risk weights can change abruptly and suddenly, especially in a crisis."[48] Finally, setting capital requirements in terms of a specific measure of how much a bank contributes to systemic risk, to the extent that experience can be a guide, would have a similar effect as did the setting of relative risk weights: banks will be incentivized to develop methods of avoiding or reducing the effect through more clever and more complex products. Even if the new products have salutary economic effects, they will also create novel and largely unanticipated risk in the system, confounding the efficacy of measures of systemic risk developed for markets without such products and creating radical uncertainty, with a possible outcome that regulation will mistake where systemic risk truly lies and once again contribute to a financial crisis.

The behavioural phenomenon of institutions' responses confounding financial regulation has been characterized over the years in various ways by economists and social scientists. One version is known as Goodhart's law, described in a well-known paraphrasing as "when a measure becomes a target, it ceases to be a good measure."[49] The rational expectations approach to macroeconomics, most prominently expounded in the Lucas critique, provides a similar insight into the feedback loop between regulation and the regulated: in response to regulation, individuals take actions that enable them to continue to pursue their objectives, circumnavigating regulations intended to prevent that pursuit, thereby frustrating the implementation of regulatory policy.[50]

The terrorism literature provides a still further gloss on the implementation conundrum of financial regulation: regulation directed at tail risk is confounded by what this literature terms "dynamic uncertainty."[51] It analyzes dynamic uncertainty as follows: although the occurrence of a natural disaster, such as an earthquake, is as remotely possible as a terrorist attack, because humans adapt their behaviour in response to regulation, they can alter the risk of an event's occurrence in unanticipated ways, making it far more challenging, if not impossible, to predict the impact of regulation on terrorist attacks than in the natural disaster context. For instance, regulation of housing codes to reduce the damage to property from an earthquake will not affect the probability of an earthquake occurring, but regulation regarding the carrying of potential weapons, such as box cutters, aboard airplanes will surely reduce the probability of that threat recurring and instead increase the probability of an alternative, unanticipated future attack.

47 Bisias et al, *supra* note 44 at 259. This contention is supported by the experience of the Basel risk weights, for as King notes, in the crisis, mortgages ascribed low risk weights due to past data were anything but safe. King, *supra* note 20 at 138.

48 *Ibid.*

49 Marilyn Strahern, "'Improving Ratings': Audit in the British University System" (1997) 5:3 European Rev 305. Another expression of the phenomenon described by Goodhart's law is known as Campbell's law: "The more any quantitative social indicator is used for social decision-making, the more subject it will be to corruption pressures and the more apt it will be to distort and corrupt the social processes it is intended to monitor." Donald T Campbell, "Assessing the impact of planned social change" (1979) 2:1 Evaluation & Program Planning 67 at 85.

50 Robert Lucas, "Econometric Policy Evaluation: A Critique" in Karl Brunner & Allan H Meltzer, eds, *The Phillips Curve and Labor Markets* (New York: American Elsevier Publishing Company, 1976) 19.

51 Philip Auerswald et al, "The Challenge of Protecting Critical Infrastructure" (2005) 22:1 Issues in Science & Technology 77 at 80.

While regulators can anticipate that regulated entities will respond in ways to minimize a regulation's impact, they will likely not be able to predict the specificity of response to be able to devise their regulations at the outset to prevent all responses that limit the regulation's reach. The infinite range of responses that is a function of human inventiveness and resourcefulness works to sap the effectiveness of much regulatory effort.

A global financial crisis is the quintessential tail risk that is characterized by dynamic uncertainty, for shocks to the financial system tend to be endogenous. Even if they were exogenous, such shocks would be amplified by human responses. Yet prevention of tail-risk realization is the objective of systemic risk regulation. While dynamic uncertainty renders predicting the effect of regulation perplexing, it is especially so for systemic risk regulation, as there is no regulatory experience that could suggest even a base case from which to attempt to predict institutional responses, however foolhardy a Lucas-type critique might imply that such a task might be. We are in the realm of King's radical uncertainty of not knowing the possible states of the world, let alone being able to assign probabilities to states.

The fact that global financial crises occur rarely is not the only challenge to devising effective systemic risk regulation. Prior to the recent crisis, regulatory attention focused on ensuring the safety of individual institutions rather than overall system risk. That conventional approach to banking regulation deems it desirable for banks to hold diversified portfolios, so, for example, limits are placed on how much exposure a bank could have to one borrower. But when the risk of concern is to the system as a whole, rather than to a single bank, it is problematic for all banks to be similarly diversified as then a large shock to a subset of assets in their portfolios would undermine all banks, yet globally harmonized regulation is likely to result in similar patterns of diversification across banks, magnifying systemic risk. If banks' holdings are undiversified and varied across institutions, then a shock to a subset of assets would undermine only some banks, that is, there would be a lower probability of the shock having a systemic impact.

It cannot reasonably be expected that a large bank would voluntarily concentrate its holdings in one type of asset, as prudent management would counsel diversification. Small banks, by contrast, might develop a niche specialization, such as specializing in making agricultural loans.[52] However, the issue of concern with regard to diversification and systemic risk regulation is large, interconnected multinational banks, whose business strategies would not profitably be so delimited. Regulators have not required such banks to undiversify for, notwithstanding the benefit to system resilience of such an approach, it would be difficult to justify to the public — or to bank investors — a policy that increases the probability of individual bank failures, and that in the end might well increase, rather than decrease, the number of government bailouts. Still, the conflict between individual bank and financial system stability is no doubt real and presents a regulatory conundrum not present for microprudential regulation.

I have been emphasizing the challenge of systemic risk regulation stemming from definitional and measurement issues in a context of dynamic and radical uncertainty, and the conflict between individual bank and system-wide financial stability, with the lessons of the global financial crisis regarding the impact of innovation on harmonized rules in the background. Is the import of this dismal narrative that regulators should pack up their marbles and go home, so to speak? Hardly.

52 I thank Jon Macey for this example.

The radical uncertainty characterizing the markets that are subject to financial regulation does not imply that regulators can and should do nothing. Rather, it suggests that there would be value added from a regulatory framework that facilitates flexible adaptation to new financial technologies and economic shocks as they emerge. In conjunction with the two lessons from the global financial crisis regarding financial innovation and Basel's contribution to the panic, such uncertainty suggests a need for regulators to be highly attentive to the impact of new financial technologies and for efforts at global harmonization to proceed with humility and caution.

How might the lesson regarding the dual nature of financial innovation be addressed? First, regulators should attend to developments in short-term debt financing — both by ongoing monitoring of existing short-term financing markets and by scouting for new ones. This is a straightforward application of Gorton's identification of those markets as the source of financial crises. Second, monitoring leverage in the economy to identify increased risk generated by new products should be a prime focus of regulatory attention, along with monitoring financial innovations and their impact on economic behaviour more generally.[53] However, in doing so, regulators would need to take care that the monitored indicator(s) do not morph into capital regulation, in order to avoid Goodhart's law, that banks' responses would, in due course, undermine the indicators' ability to provide an accurate measure of systemic risk. Furthermore, when implementing a leverage-monitoring system or, indeed, any regulation calibrated to systemic risk measures, regulators must beware that the monitoring and regulation do not overly impede the development of new financial technologies. This formidable balancing of concerns follows straightforwardly from Goetzmann's narrative, which suggests that over time, the benefits of innovation have overwhelmed the cost, including the fallout of periods of sustained economic distress and even calamity.

How can we adapt the international regulatory architecture to take account of the lesson regarding the peril of global harmonization, that if regulation were to go awry, it would magnify systemic risk? It is my contention that a central focus of international efforts at systemic risk regulation should be the fostering of meaningful regulatory diversity along with periodic regulatory updating. The objective of such a policy is twofold: to reduce the probability that financial institutions across the globe follow correlated business strategies, as their incentives would differ if they were subject to different systemic risk measures, and thereby diminish the likelihood of a regulatory misstep leading to a global crisis; and to increase the probability that if financial innovation were to undermine the effectiveness of a chosen risk measure, the regulation would be revised.

As Simon Levin's work with a number of co-authors has emphasized, in studying the financial system, we can learn from the literature on biological ecosystems because, like financial markets, they evolve over time in a highly uncertain environment that experiences perturbations from unknown risks.[54] That literature indicates that biodiversity is one of a small number of properties

53 For such a policy suggestion, see e.g. John Geanakoplos, "Solving the Present Crisis and Managing the Leverage Cycle" (2010) 16:1 Federal Reserve Bank of New York Economic Policy Rev 101; John Geanakoplos & Lasse Heje Pedersen, "Monitoring Leverage" in Markus Brunnermeier & Arvind Krishnamurthy, eds, *Risk Topography: Systemic Risk and Macro Modeling* (Chicago: University of Chicago Press, 2014) 113. Geanakoplos's policy proposal is not conditioned on leverage related to new products but considers leverage on all products and in all sectors. Given the connection between leverage and financial crises, see *supra* note 21, his broader application makes much sense.

54 Simon A Levin & Andrew W Lo, "Opinion: A New Approach to Financial Regulation" (2015) 112 PNAS 12543; Robert M May, Simon A Levin & George Sugihara, "Ecology for Bankers" (2008) 451 Nature 893.

that enhance the robustness of ecological biosystems, and introducing diversity into financial regulation would operate analogously to enhance the resiliency of the global financial system.[55] Introducing meaningful diversity into the global regulatory architecture could also improve the quality of regulatory decision making, as regulators could learn from the experience of banks operating under differing regulatory arrangements which ones work more effectively.

There is a further rationale for advocating diversity in international financial regulation, as well as diffidence when regulating: the one-size-fits-all approach of harmonized requirements is likely to be inappropriate, given the heterogeneity in financial institutions and the level of financial and legal development across the many nations following the regulatory standards set out in the Basel Accords.[56] The desirability of tailoring systemic risk regulation is supported by the findings of an intriguing study suggesting that there are countervailing considerations regarding financial crises with respect to economic growth, questioning the very core of the effort to restrict systemic risk. Examining 83 nations over the period from 1960 to 2000, Romain Rancière and colleagues found that among nations with weak institutions (that is, developing economies), those experiencing financial crises have, on average, grown faster than those with stable financial conditions, despite the distress occasioned by crises.[57] They interpret the finding, which is robust to alternative specifications, as indicating "a positive effect of systemic risk on growth."[58] The channel for how systemic risk affects growth would appear to be its positive effect on investment (by reducing borrowing constraints, it permits firms to invest more, which fosters growth).[59] Hence, it would seem that, at least for such nations, it might not be wise to advance regulation focused on minimizing systemic risk.

How could the international regulatory framework premised on harmonization be reshaped to incorporate the benefits of regulatory diversity? In prior work, I have elaborated a procedural mechanism through which a modicum of diversity could be introduced into the Basel Accords by permitting voluntary national deviations from its approach to capital requirements.[60] Without rehearsing all of the procedural requisites for successfully implementing such an approach, the gist of the proposal is the establishment of a peer-review apparatus within the Basel framework that would approve a nation's proposed departure from Basel requirements, subject to ongoing monitoring to ensure that a departure was not increasing global systemic risk, with an illustration of a departure of replacing Basel's risk-weighted capital requirement with a simple leverage ratio and subordinated debt requirement.[61] I have further advocated the use of regulatory experimentation in domestic regulation as a mechanism for ascertaining which

55 Levin & Lo, *supra* note 54 at 12544.

56 For a discussion of empirical research indicating a need for differential financial regulations across nations, in particular for distinguishing between advanced and emerging economies, see Romano, "Diversity in International Regulation", *supra* note 26 at 29.

57 Romain Rancière, Aaron Tornell & Frank Westermann, "Systemic Crises and Growth" (2008) 123:1 QJ Economics 359.

58 *Ibid* at 360.

59 *Ibid* at 395, 399.

60 Romano, "Diversity in International Regulation", *supra* note 26 at 26–42. The focus of that work was the introduction of diversity into Basel's risk-weighted capital regime. Calling for diversity in systemic risk regulation is not as out of the norm as doing so for capital regulation. Although Basel III introduced a number of macroprudential capital requirements that are intended to reduce systemic risk, as opposed to microprudential policies that are intended to reduce the risk of individual banks, prior to the financial crisis many nations, in particular emerging economies, had adopted a variety of macroprudential policies, such as placing limits on borrowers and lenders, matters not regulated by Basel. See Eugenio Cerutti, Stijn Claessens & Luc Laeven, "The Use and Effectiveness of Macroprudential Policies: New Evidence" (2017) 28 J Financial Stability 203 (analyzing 12 macroprudential policies used across 119 countries from 2000 to 2013).

61 Romano, "Diversity in International Regulation", *supra* note 26 at 26–41, 46–48.

regulatory strategies might work best.[62] Such an approach has an equal, if not more important, purpose in the context of systemic risk regulation: if systemic risk measures were varied across banks, along with the method by which additional capital is calculated to account for banks' contribution to systemic risk, then banks' behavioural responses will diverge as well, and that should reduce the likelihood of increased systemic risk by discouraging what would otherwise be uniformity in banks' activities circumventing regulation.

Regulatory updating due to information gleaned from experiments concerning risks that arise from, and firms' responses to, regulation has commonalities with what has been a keystone of conservation efforts in natural resource management for decades: the strategy of adaptive management, which refers to "management as a learning process or continuous experiment where incorporating the results of previous actions allows managers to remain flexible and adapt to uncertainty."[63] Indeed, in adaptive environmental management, it is maintained that "even when current strategies seem to be working adequately," alternative strategies should be continually explored (referred to as "adaptive probing"), given the need for information to be able to adjust for unanticipated environmental changes.[64] Financial systems have the same need for flexible adaptability.

The gold standard of regulatory experimentation in a domestic setting would randomize across firms different approaches to systemic risk measurement and corresponding capital assessment, enabling regulators to explore which regulations were more difficult to game and, hence, more likely to reduce institutions' contribution to systemic risk. Randomized experiments might seem to be impractical because banks can be expected to lobby legislators vigorously to prohibit regulatory experimentation, contending that being subject to differing rules would place them at a severe competitive disadvantage. But there has been at least one successful randomized experiment addressed at financial regulation, which suggests that the use of such experiments in this context is in the realm of the possible. In 2004, the US Securities and Exchange Commission undertook a randomized experiment that varied the applicability of the uptick rule, which restricted short sales, to investigate the effect of relaxing the restrictions, and finding that the relaxation did not have the adverse effects managers had predicted, altered the rule.[65] In addition, a number of regulators around the globe have created "regulatory sandboxes" in the fintech area to permit experimentation with new products and services outside of existing regulation.[66] While these regulatory spaces are not random experiments, they are in the spirit of the experimentation that I am advocating, as they are directed at fostering the development of diverse business models for the provision of financial goods and services.

62 Roberta Romano, "Regulating in the Dark" in Cary Coglianese, ed, *Regulatory Breakdown: The Crisis of Confidence in U.S. Regulation* (Philadelphia: University of Pennsylvania Press, 2012) 86.

63 R Edward Grumbine, "What Is Ecosystem Management?" (1994) 8 Conservation Biology 27 at 31.

64 Simon A Levin, *Fragile Dominion* (Cambridge, MA: Helix Books, 1999) at 199–200.

65 US Securities and Exchange Commission (SEC), Office of Economic Analysis, *Economic Analysis of the Short Sale Price Restrictions under the Regulation SHO Pilot* (2007), online: <www.sec.gov/news/studies/2007/regshopilot020607.pdf>; SEC, Press Release, 2007-114, "SEC Votes on Regulation SHO Amendments and Proposals; Also Votes to Eliminate 'Tick' Test", online: <www.sec.gov/news/press/2007/2007-114.htm>.

66 The first regulatory sandbox was launched by the United Kingdom's Financial Conduct Authority in 2015, followed by regulators in Abu Dhabi, Australia, Canada, Denmark, Hong Kong, Indonesia, Malaysia, the Netherlands, Singapore, Thailand and, most recently, Arizona. See "The Role of Regulatory Sandboxes in Fintech Innovation" (10 September 2018), *Finextra* (blog), online: <www.finextra.com/blogposting/15759/the-role-of-regulatory-sandboxes-in-fintech-innovation>. The latest, and first, announcement by a US federal agency proposing to create a sandbox is the Bureau of Consumer Financial Protection; see *Policy on No-Action Letters and the BCFP Product Sandbox*, 83 Fed Reg 64036 (2018).

Where randomized experiments within a nation are infeasible due to domestic firms' intra-industry competitive concerns, if there is cross-border regulatory diversity, then there is another, albeit second-best regulatory approach consisting of observational studies, in which regulators compare outcomes across differing national regimes. For example, regulators could investigate whether there is a difference in systemic risk, calculated using a variety of measures, for banks operating under the US Volcker Rule compared to banks operating under the UK ring-fencing approach. In my judgment, devising how to implement such a policy effectively, and thereby generate information for policy evaluation, is a critical issue on which global efforts addressing systemic risk regulation should focus.

Conclusion

The contribution of the Basel capital requirements to the global financial crisis is a cautionary tale for systemic risk regulation. Basel's harmonization of capital requirements incentivized banks across the globe to hold large amounts of Basel-preferenced assets — securitized subprime mortgages — whose risk turned out to be far greater than the risk assigned by Basel, and when the default rate of the underlying mortgages increased, it triggered a panic in financial institutions' short-term funding markets that spread rapidly across borders as the collapse of highly leveraged banks wrought economic calamity worldwide. This is an oft-observed pattern throughout history, as financial innovations, such as securitized subprime mortgages, that can create tremendous social benefits also contain the seeds for potential collapse if enthusiasm produces pricing bubbles that generate unsustainable leverage.

The historical pattern, accordingly, argues for exercising caution in seeking to harmonize the regulation of systemic risk. For three types of uncertainty combine in this context to make fixed and uniform regulation problematic, in particular given the difficulty in nimbly revising globally harmonized requirements: the issue-specific uncertainty regarding how to measure systemic risk; the radical uncertainty of the financial system in which we do not know the possible future states and therefore cannot compute the probabilities of outcomes that would be necessary for formulating helpful rules regarding the use of a specific measure of systemic risk; and dynamic uncertainty (the fact that financial institutions respond to regulation in ways that cannot be predicted but that tend to undermine regulation's effectiveness).

The interaction of the different types of uncertainty suggests that a value-added international regulatory strategy would foster diversity across national regimes and periodic updating of global standards. This approach would reduce the probability of regulatory error contributing to a global catastrophe, for the number of banks that fail would be spatially delimited, as the probability of all banks following similar strategies would be reduced, thereby lowering the likelihood of a crisis spreading worldwide. In addition, as uncertainty unfolds, we could glean from the actions of banks operating under different systemic risk regulations information regarding which regimes are more or less effective in reducing risk. Finally, continuous assessment and periodic updating of international regulation would focus attention on the effectiveness of regulation as financial markets evolve over time. Informed by the learning gathered from the operation of diverse regulatory regimes, such updating would facilitate a nimbler revision of international regulation that is not functioning well and could thereby decrease the likelihood of a global crisis.

Author's Note

I have benefited from helpful comments from Ryan Bubb, Calvin Johnson, Jonathan Macey, Eric Orts, Frank Partnoy, Steven L. Schwarcz, David Zaring and participants at faculty workshops at the University of Texas, University of California Berkeley and Yale University law schools and the Wharton School of the University of Pennsylvania, the Duke Law and Economics Colloquium, and the Hong Kong Securities and Futures Commission.

13

Bank Leverage, Welfare and Regulation

ANAT R. ADMATI AND MARTIN F. HELLWIG

Banks tend to rely much more heavily on debt for their funding, i.e., to have significantly more financial leverage than other firms. Moreover, much of their debt involves short-term loans or deposits that must be paid on demand. This funding mix makes banks fragile. If there is a lot of debt, even small losses can cause insolvency. Moreover, if much of the debt is short term, there is a significant risk that creditors will become concerned about potential default and the bank will lose funding. These two problems are linked, because concerns about insolvency are a major reason that creditors might lose trust and withdraw their funds.

The financial system has also become increasingly complex in recent decades, with the advent of derivatives, securitization and globalization. Financial institutions are much more interconnected and systemic risks have increased. Through various contagion mechanisms, distress or insolvency are likely to affect many institutions at the same time, and even a single default can create a cascade of distress and affect the entire economy.

In the aftermath of the financial crisis of 2007–2009, bank regulators moved to reform the rules meant to restrain banks' leverage and the extent of the mismatch between the maturities of their assets and their liabilities. Basel III,[1] the international accord on banking regulation signed in 2010, imposed new rules concerning the maturity structure of banks' liabilities in relation to their assets.

Basel III still allows banks to fund 97 percent of their assets with debt. Yet the banking industry lobbies strongly to reduce equity requirements even today. The mantras often used are "equity is expensive" and "credit and growth will suffer," suggesting that safety in banking comes at a cost and that society would have to sacrifice some of the benefits of the banking system if regulations require more equity in the funding mix.

Many of the arguments and warnings made by industry lobbies and others in this discussion are flawed. In particular, those who oppose equity regulation often refer to the private costs of the regulation to banks and their loan customers without considering the benefits of the regulation to the banks' creditors, taxpayers and the rest of the economy.

Some researchers have suggested that banks' choice of extremely fragile funding mixes is efficient. For example, bank debt is said to provide its holders with special benefits because it is liquid and can be used for payments at any time. Given these benefits, the more debt the bank issues, the better the outcomes are said to be.[2]

However, the conclusion that high leverage of banks is desirable depends critically on very special and unrealistic assumptions in the makeup of the models used to support the argument. If these assumptions are modified to make them more realistic, the conclusions are overturned. In fact, the banks' choices are much better explained by their incentives to act in ways that harm others and by their inability to commit to behaviour that avoids such harm.

When managers and shareholders take actions that benefit themselves, the costs and risks are often borne by creditors or taxpayers. Managers might be motivated to use debt and avoid equity because compensation structures reward risk and leverage or because tax subsidies and explicit or implicit government guarantees make debt more attractive than equity funding.[3] If excessive borrowing cannot be prevented by commitments to existing lenders or by regulation, the outcome can be very inefficient — a far cry from the standard view that laissez-faire yields efficient outcomes.

1 Basel Committee on Banking Supervision, *Basel III: A global regulatory framework for more resilient banks and banking systems* (Basel, Switzerland: Bank for International Settlements, 2010).

2 See, in particular, Gary Gorton, *Slapped by the Invisible Hand: The Panic of 2007* (Oxford, UK: Oxford University Press, 2010); Gary Gorton & Andrew Winton, "Liquidity Provision, Bank Capital, and the Macroeconomy" (2017) 49:1 J Money, Credit & Banking 5; Harry DeAngelo & René M Stulz, "Liquid-claim production, risk management, and bank capital structure: Why high leverage is optimal for banks" (2015) 116:2 J Financial Economics 219.

3 Bank managers and executives are often compensated on the basis of return on equity. As we explain in Anat R Admati & Martin F Hellwig, *The Bankers' New Clothes: What's Wrong with Banking and What to Do About It* (Princeton, NJ: Princeton University Press, 2013), ch 8 [Admati & Hellwig, *The Bankers' New Clothes*], such a compensation structure encourages excessive risk-taking and borrowing. Tax subsidies and explicit and implicit guarantees and subsidies also encourage, enable and reward borrowing, and discourage the use of equity. See Admati et al, "Fallacies, Irrelevant Facts, and Myths in the Discussion of Capital Regulation: Why Bank Equity Is Not Expensive" (2013) Rock Center for Corporate Governance at Stanford University Working Paper No 161, s 4 [Admati et al, "Fallacies"]; Admati & Hellwig, *The Bankers' New Clothes* (*ibid*, ch 9); Anat R Admati, "Examining the GAO Report on Expectations of Government Support for Bank Holding Companies" (Testimony for hearing of Senate Committee on Banking, Housing and Urban Affairs Subcommittee on Financial Institutions and Consumer Protection, 31 July 2014) [Admati, "Examining the GAO Report"]; Admati et al, "The Leverage Ratchet Effect" (2018) 73:1 J Finance 146 [Admati et al, "Leverage Ratchet"].

The conclusion that the funding mix under laissez-faire in banking involves excessive borrowing holds, even if we consider only the interests of the banks' investors (shareholders and creditors) and if we ignore the risks and potential harm to the rest of the financial system and the overall economy. Effective regulation that limits bank leverage is beneficial because it counters incentive distortions and effectively commits banks to avoiding excessive borrowing. If, in addition, the regulation reduces systemic risk, the benefits are even larger.

Full commitment would require that explicit or implicit contracts specify decisions and actions, including actions concerning additional funding, for every possible future situation. Moreover, the covenants detailing these decisions and actions must be enforceable. Enforceability, in turn, presumes that the decisions and actions and the situations in which they are to be taken can be observed by creditors and, in the case of recourse to the legal system, verified by the courts. These presumptions may hold if covenants are simple and specific enough, but then they may be too rigid to allow borrowers to respond efficiently to changes in the economic environment.[4] More complex covenants that allow for flexible responses to changes in the environment may be difficult and costly to enforce, either because creditors must devote significant resources to monitoring and controlling the borrower's ongoing behaviour or because the courts are not able to verify whether the conditions for which the contracts stipulate a certain behaviour are actually met. When there are many creditors, any one of them may not have any strong incentives to invest in monitoring, and the scope for any one creditor to influence the borrower's behaviour may be small.

The problem of how to assure creditors that their trust will not be abused affects all firms, but this problem is particularly challenging for financial institutions, especially banks. Whereas a typical non-financial company has only a few lenders with relatively large positions, a typical bank obtains funding from thousands or even millions of lenders, each of whom is small relative to the bank. Because their number is small, the lenders to a non-financial company are better able to coordinate on pursuing their common interest in monitoring and control. Such coordination is all but impossible for the lenders to a bank.

The fragmentation of lenders and the implied coordination problem are a major reason why banks can and do borrow excessively, beyond the level they would choose with an effective *ex ante* commitment. Suppose that an already indebted bank negotiates with a new lender, unbeknownst to the other lenders. The additional debt harms the other lenders because they face a higher default risk and possibly lower returns in the event of default. The new lender, however, may be willing to provide the additional loan anyway, if given special terms with a sufficiently high interest rate and collateral securing the loan. But then the other lenders are hurt by the increase in default risk and the separation of collateral from the set of assets available to creditors in default. If the damage to the other lenders exceeds the benefits to the bank and the new lender, the total social cost of the additional loan is larger than its benefits. If, in addition, the new loan imposes risks and costs on the rest of the financial system and on taxpayers, the inefficiency is even greater.

4 The observation that this requirement is unrealistic is the starting point of the so-called theory of incomplete contracts; see e.g. Oliver Hart, *Firms, Contracts, and Financial Structure* (Oxford, UK: Oxford University Press, 1995).

Effective leverage regulation can improve on laissez-faire outcomes by providing a mechanism of commitment. If supervision enforces the regulation, banks are effectively prevented from borrowing as much as they would under laissez-faire when they cannot commit to a limit on their overall borrowing. Leverage regulation, in effect, serves as a substitute for the debt covenants that depositors and other lenders are unable to put in place and enforce in order to commit the bank to be sufficiently safe. The need for regulation as a substitute commitment device is even greater if the creditors' incentives to monitor are weakened by the prospect of government or central bank support.

The Inefficiency of Laissez-faire in Banking

We start our discussion of the welfare implications of banks' funding by considering an important and special function of banks' debt, namely that it provides *liquidity* to banks' creditors. In addition to the monetary returns that deposits and other short-term debt provide to their holders, the depositors and short-term creditors of banks attach a special value to their ability to convert their claims into cash quickly and to use them for payments.

The word "liquidity" requires an explanation. In the classical formulation of Keynes, an asset is said to be more liquid than another if it is "more certainly realizable at short notice without loss."[5] An asset that is surely and immediately realizable without loss may thus be called "perfectly liquid."[6] For assets that are not perfectly liquid, there may be tradeoffs between the different dimensions inherent in Keynes's formulation, the size of the expected loss in a sale, the degree of uncertainty about this loss and the duration of the sales procedure.[7]

Under this definition, in the absence of hyperinflation, cash is perfectly liquid because it can immediately be used in every transaction without any discount. In the absence of concerns about bank solvency, bank deposits are close to being perfectly liquid because, through cheques, credit cards or bank transfers, in most transactions, they can also be used for immediate payments without discounts. The same is true of holdings in money market funds that can be used for transactions. In contrast, listed securities cannot be used in arbitrary transactions, but if the markets for these securities work well (are liquid), they can easily be converted into cash.

Among the different assets, cash stands out in that it is not a claim to anything. The liquidity of cash is due to its being the means of payment, which is generally accepted as long as participants have confidence in the currency. In contrast, bank deposits are claims on the banks, and their liquidity depends on investor confidence that the banks can make good on these claims.[8] If this confidence vanishes, bank depositors may find that their holdings are not so liquid after all.

5 John Maynard Keynes, *A Treatise on Money*, vol 2 (London, UK: Macmillan, 1930) at 67.

6 For an extensive discussion, see John R Hicks, "Liquidity" (1962) 72:288 Economic J 787.

7 Even so, Keynes used the definition to assert unambiguously that "bills and call loans are more liquid than investments" and "investments are more liquid than advances." See Keynes, *supra* note 5 at 67.

8 Whereas holdings in money market funds are officially treated as shares, promises of "stable net asset value" of one dollar per share give the appearance that these shares also provide their holders with fixed claims. This is why the Reserve Primary Fund's "breaking the buck" after the Lehman Brothers' bankruptcy came as a big surprise and induced a panic among investors in money market funds. See Admati & Hellwig, *The Bankers' New Clothes*, *supra* note 3, ch 5.

The literature on banking mostly focuses on how a bank — whose own investments consist of highly illiquid loans — can make good on promises of paying depositors whenever they ask for it. Typical answers are:

- First, if there are many small depositors with payment needs that are statistically independent, then, by the law of large numbers, only a fairly determinate fraction of depositors will ask for their money at any one date, so it suffices to have a cash reserve for servicing these depositors; the remaining funds can be invested in illiquid loans.[9]
- Second, if customer payments result in a net outflow of funds from a bank, the bulk of the payments will go into accounts with other banks, and the banks that lose funding can use interbank borrowing to substitute for the lost deposits.[10]
- Third, if the bank's loans could somehow be made liquid, the bank might sell them in order to meet its obligations to depositors; this is one of the putative advantages of securitization, which involves packaging large numbers of loans together and creating different "tranches" of claims to the packages, with different levels of priority, so that the most senior tranches may have little default risk and may be tradable in liquid markets.[11]

Apart from concerns about bank runs and about potential incentive distortions in securitization, this literature tends to take the view that the extent of liquidity creation by banks is efficient. After all, investors cherish the liquidity of the assets that banks provide. Little attention is paid to the fact that deposits are a form of debt, i.e., that they are liabilities of the bank and thus may pose a risk to the solvency of a bank. To the extent that the issue is considered at all, the fact that the claims of a debt holder do not depend on the borrower's asset returns is praised as making these claims "information insensitive" and thereby enhance their liquidity, for example, by making bank notes and cheques acceptable means of payment or by making super-senior mortgage-backed securities tradable.[12]

In contrast, we consider the implications of solvency risks for liquidity provision by banks. If the bank is heavily indebted and its asset returns are uncertain, insolvency is a real risk. If the bank becomes insolvent and if it does not receive outside support, for example, from the government, it will end up in default or in bankruptcy. At that point, if not earlier, the liquidity benefits on which depositors count will no longer be available.

The risk of the bank's becoming insolvent is greatly reduced when the bank funds with a substantial amount of equity in addition to deposits and other forms of debt. If the bank issues additional equity and uses the proceeds to buy more assets, these assets can be used to pay the debt and avoid default or insolvency. Because depositors and other debt holders have priority

9 See e.g. Douglas W Diamond & Phil Dybvig, "Bank Runs, Deposit Insurance, and Liquidity" (1983) 91:3 J Political Economy 401.

10 This idea plays a crucial role in the theory that banks do not use deposits to fund their lending, but banks create deposits by lending. For the individual bank, the latter statement is correct at the level of flows of new lending, but problematic at the level of stocks of loans (and other assets) whose counterparts in the balance sheet include stocks of outstanding deposits. Even for the individual bank, however, this funding problem at the level of stock variables is unimportant if any outflow of deposits can be neutralized by interbank borrowing. See e.g. Zoltan Jakab & Michael Kumhof, "Banks are not intermediaries of loanable funds — and why this matters" (2015) Bank of England Working Paper No 529.

11 See Gorton, *supra* note 2, ch 3.

12 *Ibid.*

over shareholders, the additional equity and the assets it funds enhance the safety of deposits, and other debt, and help secure the liquidity benefits provided by deposits.[13] In the absence of government support, prospective depositors and other market participants who are aware of these issues might therefore insist that banks have substantial equity funding, and the banks might actually want to use substantial equity funding as a means of attracting deposits.

The question, then, is whether arrangements under laissez-faire are likely to be efficient. We study this question in the remainder of this section. We do not go into the specifics of how banks "create liquidity" through funding with deposits, but merely assume that, because of the liquidity benefits they expect, investors attach value to deposits (or other short-term debt) over and above the monetary returns they offer. We also assume that in the event of a bank default, under laissez-faire, i.e., in the absence of government support, there are no liquidity benefits from deposits. From an *ex ante* perspective, therefore, the value investors attach to deposits depends on their assessments of the bank's default probability.

We will argue that, in this setting, market outcomes under laissez-faire will actually involve inefficiently high levels of bank indebtedness. The inefficiency is likely to arise even if bank failures impose no collateral damage to third parties, such as taxpayers. Equity regulation can therefore improve on market outcomes. The inefficiencies provide an additional rationale for regulation on top of the harms banks can inflict on the economy.

The Impact of Creditor Fragmentation

The terms under which the bank can raise debt and equity are, in part, determined by "expected returns" that must be offered to compensate these claimholders for their foregoing other investment opportunities and for agreeing to bear the risks of the claims they acquire. For depositors and short-term debt holders, the terms are also based, in part, on the liquidity benefits they receive as long as the bank does not go into default. Because of these liquidity benefits, depositors and short-term lenders are willing to accept lower interest rates than they would if they only considered the promised debt payment. *Prima facie*, therefore, as long as the bank does not default, funding by debt that provides liquidity may seem like a particularly cheap source of funding.[14]

However, if the bank funds itself almost entirely with debt, its default probability will be very high. For a given value of asset holdings, the greater the bank's obligation to debt holders, the greater its default probability. With a greater probability of default, the liquidity benefits are less likely to materialize, and investors will ask for higher interest to compensate for this loss. The bank's initial owners thus face a tradeoff: whereas debt funding appears to be a cheap source of funding for fixed liquidity benefits, the per-dollar cost of debt funding itself may be lower if the bank has issued more equity, because the increase in expected liquidity benefits provides additional compensation to the bank's creditors.

13 For a thorough discussion of this point, see Admati & Hellwig, *The Bankers' New Clothes*, *supra* note 3, ch 10.

14 This consideration leads Harry DeAngelo and René M Stulz to claim that "high leverage is optimal for banks." See DeAngelo & Stulz, *supra* note 2 at 219. Liquidity provision may involve costs for branches, automated teller machines and payment services. However, the bank can also charge fees for its services. Provision of these services is a productive activity, generating producers' surplus from the difference between revenues received over the costs. In one form or another, depositors are willing to pay a premium for the liquidity benefits and associated services that the bank provides. See Admati et al, "Fallacies", *supra* note 3 at 17.

What funding mix will arise under laissez-faire? The answer depends on the way the bank and its investors arrive at the terms of funding. Suppose, first, that a bank is able to fully commit *ex ante* to an investment policy and to a funding policy, i.e., to make a binding announcement concerning the investments it will undertake, the riskiness of these investments, the fraction of the investments that it will fund by borrowing and the payments it will promise to debt holders. On the basis of this announcement, investors then form an opinion about the bank's default probability and about the prospects for monetary returns to debt and equity and the liquidity benefits of debt. Investors will provide funding if the offered terms are attractive enough.

The bank's commitment to a funding policy and an investment policy is similar to the announcement of a quality specification for a car or any other good that can be provided in different qualities. The funding and asset policies are effectively quality parameters that determine the bank's default probability and the prospect that liquidity benefits will be enjoyed. If *ex ante* commitments of banks are, in fact, binding and if there is no additional collateral harm from bank defaults, then market outcomes under laissez-faire may be presumed to be efficient, or at least no less efficient than outcomes in any other market in which suppliers must choose the quality as well as the price of objects put on the market. In such markets, suppliers find that, although higher quality is more expensive to provide, it may still be worthwhile to do so if buyers are willing to pay for it.

Will market outcomes under laissez-faire and binding commitments involve the use of equity by banks? Of course, in the very special case where the bank's assets are entirely safe, with no risk of losses and thus of default, there would be no point in issuing equity. In that special case, creditors would enjoy the liquidity benefit from bank debt for certain and equity does not enhance the quality of the debt. If the banks' assets are risky, however, we can expect banks to issue some equity as well as debt, thus enhancing the likelihood that creditors enjoy the liquidity benefits.

However, the assumption that banks make effectively binding commitments about their funding and investment policies is highly unrealistic. For commitments to be binding, they must be enforceable, by legal means or otherwise. Legal enforceability presumes that the stipulated behaviours can be observed and verified. If such behaviours can be made to depend on extraneous developments, the relevant conditions must also be observable and verifiable by the enforcing authorities. This latter condition is unlikely to be met in practice. Legally enforceable commitments may therefore be too rigid, i.e., they allow too little conditioning of behaviours on ongoing developments to be worthwhile. If such promises are nevertheless made, the banks will at some point want to break them; when they do so, the depositors and short-term creditors are not likely to be in a position to enforce the promises and control the banks' behaviour.

To see this point, note that bank debt funding generally comes from numerous small investors. The number of bank depositors ranges between thousands for small banks and millions for large banks. When it comes to bank funding through money market funds and other wholesale investors, matters are not very different. Reserve Primary, the money market fund that was effectively destroyed by the Lehman Brothers bankruptcy, provides an example. Reserve Primary had provided only between one and two thousandths of Lehman Brothers' total funding, some US$800 million out of more than US$600 billion; the rest was held by many other creditors with similarly small positions. The fragmentation of creditors makes it hard or even impossible for creditors to coordinate their actions. Any one creditor acting in his or her own interest is unlikely to take account of the collective interests of creditors as a whole. Instead of endeavouring to control the bank's overall risk and leverage, each creditor will then ask for substantial collateral and for a high interest rate.

To understand the implications of fragmentation, suppose that a bank has issued equity and debt in accordance with some previously announced funding policy. Consider a negotiation that a bank might have with a prospective new lender, which is not observed by other investors. If the bank proposes to borrow more without also raising additional equity, the prospective creditor will say yes if the bank provides the creditor with compensation or protection for the extra risk. Compensation may take the form of a higher interest rate and protection may take the form of collateral for this particular loan that is separated out from the other assets.[15]

Can the bank and the prospective new creditor find terms to which they both agree? The answer is typically yes. If the new loan is small relative to the total amount the bank borrows, the increase in indebtedness has only a small effect on the bank's default risk. From the lender's perspective, the risk of losing liquidity benefits because of a default is hardly different than it is for the other lenders. However, the benefit the creditor obtains from the higher interest rate or from the collateral protecting the loan can be made large enough to make the loan attractive. From the bank's perspective, the additional debt funding increases the returns to shareholders in the event there is no default.

The underlying reason that the new loan can benefit both the bank's shareholders and be attractive to the prospective new lender is that the costs of the agreement are largely borne by the bank's *other* lenders, whose interests neither the new lender nor the bank's shareholders or managers internalize.[16] Other lenders suffer because the bank is more likely to go into default and because their returns in the event of default are diluted by the new debt.

Lenders may anticipate such behaviour from the beginning. Each lender will form expectations about what may be going on in the negotiations with other lenders and what the overall debt ratio and the default probability will be. However, if the lenders cannot coordinate their behaviours, each negotiation will proceed on the pattern just described. The problem arises regardless of whether negotiations take place sequentially, at different times or at the same time, with different lenders in different places.[17] Relative to the outcomes that would be achieved in a world in which banks can make binding commitments, the overall laissez-faire outcome with fragmented negotiations will involve more borrowing, higher interest promises, higher default probabilities and lower levels of welfare, due in particular to a lower expectation of liquidity benefits from bank debt.

Because of the fragmentation of lenders and the banks' inability to commit fully to their overall investment and funding policies, there is an additional conflict of interest between the banks and their lenders, which harms the efficiency of the market outcome. Statutory regulations that substitute for the missing ability to commit can therefore improve on the laissez-faire outcome. For example, statutory equity requirements place an upper bound on bank borrowing. If this

15 Admati & Hellwig, *The Bankers' New Clothes*, *supra* note 3, ch 10.

16 Admati et al, "Leverage Ratchet", *supra* note 3.

17 Markus Brunnermeier & Martin Oehmke, "The Maturity Rat Race" (2013) 68:2 J Finance 483.

regulation is reliably enforced by the supervisors, it can raise welfare by effectively committing the bank to a safer funding mix that enables more reliable liquidity provision and prevents the harm of excessive borrowing and risk of default. The increase in the share of equity in the funding mix also reduces incentives to pursue excessively risky investment policies, which further mitigates the distortions and efficiency losses from the lack of commitment.

Leverage Dynamics

If banks engage with lenders sequentially over time (as actual banks do), the fragmentation of lenders is unavoidable. In this case, there is an obvious conflict of interest between lenders in earlier debt contracts and lenders in subsequent debt contracts. Prior coordination between these different lenders is not possible if later lenders are not yet present at the time that earlier contracts are concluded.

In this setting, at any one time, debt holders whose claims from past lending have not yet matured may be like sitting ducks that can be taken advantage of by the borrower and new lenders. Debt covenants meant to create some commitment may provide little protection because they are costly to enforce. If new lenders are not concerned about being themselves negatively affected by subsequent funding choices, then the bank would prefer to increase the amount of debt and harm these creditors later. If potential new lenders are concerned about being negatively affected by subsequent funding choices, they will try to protect themselves as best they can, for example, by insisting on higher interest rates.

Elsewhere, with our co-authors Peter DeMarzo and Paul Pfleiderer, we have explored the forces that affect the choice of funding mix once debt is in place.[18] In particular, we show that, if a firm with a significant amount of outstanding debt has a one-time opportunity to adjust its funding mix while terms under which it previously obtained funding remain the same, then it is *never* in the shareholders' interest to use this opportunity to reduce indebtedness, for example, by raising new equity and buying back debt. By contrast, it is *always* in the shareholders' interest to increase the amount of debt in the funding mix, for example, by issuing new debt that is senior to or *pari passu* with existing debt. If there is a tax advantage to additional debt, it is in the shareholders' interest to increase indebtedness even if new debt must be junior to all existing debt and even if the current debt level is the result of previous optimization. These conclusions hold no matter how heavily the corporation is already indebted, and they are independent of the costs associated with bankruptcy, which shareholders do not bear because of limited liability. They also apply to corporate decisions on retentions and distributions; the shareholders of a firm with a significant amount of debt outstanding have a strict preference for payouts over retentions and reinvestments.

We also show that what we call the "leverage ratchet effect" creates corporate funding dynamics in which shareholders choose to increase indebtedness when exogenous changes make borrowing more attractive, but never choose to reduce indebtedness.[19] If creditors are apprehensive about subsequent increases in leverage and charge higher interest to the borrower, initial indebtedness

18 Admati et al, "Leverage Ratchet", *supra* note 3.

19 *Ibid.*

may be relatively low, but even then, indebtedness will eventually become inefficiently high when the ratchet dynamics play out.[20]

Creditors might try to protect themselves by writing covenants, but unless additional borrowing is precluded altogether, such covenants may end up shifting the problem elsewhere rather than solving it. For example, if covenants preclude the issuance of new debt with the same priority or with higher priority than outstanding debt, incumbent creditors can still be diluted through the issuance of new debt with shorter maturities. Even if this new debt is junior, it becomes effectively senior to all debt with longer remaining maturities because it matures earlier. To avoid becoming victims of this effect, lenders might themselves want to insist on short maturities from the beginning. Markus Brunnermeier and Martin Oehmke have shown that, under laissez-faire, the resulting "maturity rat race" leads to outcomes with most debt having extremely short maturities even though welfare might be higher if maturities were longer and banks less fragile.[21] We also have shown that, even when maturities are very short, the leverage ratchet dynamics tend to drive debt to inefficiently high levels.[22] As mentioned above, even if any newly issued debt must be junior to all existing debt, the leverage ratchet dynamics come in as long as an increase in debt generates additional tax benefits.

The Weakness of Creditor-imposed Discipline

It has been suggested by some that the prominence of short-term funding of banks is useful because the fear of withdrawals by creditors imposes discipline on bank managers.[23] In fact, fragmented creditors, especially those who can withdraw their funds easily, have little incentive to invest in monitoring banks' risks from additional borrowing or from their investments. Moreover, in virtually all jurisdictions, depositors are currently protected by deposit insurance, which eliminates any incentives for them to monitor at all.

Money market funds and other wholesale lenders are not protected by deposit insurance, but they usually ask for collateral as a means of protection. When banks use collateral to obtain funding, the lender is not concerned about the bank's overall leverage but is instead focused on the "haircut" that is imposed, which is the difference between the value of the collateral and the size of the loan they are making. If lending takes the form of a so-called repo contract, with the fiction that the collateral is "sold" to the lender and "repurchased" by the borrowing institution on the following day or week, lenders are even exempt from a stay in bankruptcy through "safe harbour" rules, so they feel even safer than other secured lenders.[24]

20 For an illustration of the argument, including the game-theoretic analysis of borrower-lender interactions in randomly changing environments, see Admati et al, "Leverage Ratchet", *supra* note 3, s 3.

21 Brunnermeier & Oehmke, *supra* note 17.

22 Admati et al, "Leverage Ratchet", *supra* note 3 at 175.

23 Douglas W Diamond & Raghuram G Rajan, "Liquidity Risk, Liquidity Creation and Financial Fragility" (2001) 109:2 J Political Economy 287; Kenneth French et al, *The Squam Lake Report: Fixing the Financial System* (Princeton, NJ: Princeton University Press, 2010).

24 The insulation of collateral from the effects of bankruptcy comes at the expense of those lenders whose claims are settled in bankruptcy proceedings. It is thus another example of the possibility that the borrower and a new lender can write contracts at the expense of other lenders. The effect is particularly strong when, in the run-up to a possible bankruptcy, repo lenders insist on leveraging larger haircuts. Edward Morrison et al argue that the safe harbour exemption of repos contributes to the fragility of the financial system. See Edward R Morrison et al, "Rolling Back the Repo Safe Harbors" (2014) 69 The Business Lawyer 1015; see also Admati & Hellwig, *The Bankers' New Clothes*, *supra* note 3, ch 10.

Monitoring incentives would be stronger if there were no deposit insurance and if there were no exemption of collateral from bankruptcy proceedings. But even then, it is unlikely that monitoring would work well. Given the fragmentation of lenders, coordination is very difficult, and free-rider problems are important. Why should any lender with a small loan make any non-trivial investment in monitoring to impose discipline on management when the benefits of such discipline will be small to that lender? The benefits to all lenders may be large, but any individual lender would rather have others make that monitoring investment and free-ride on the results. The free-rider problem might be overcome by the consideration that lenders who are active in monitoring might be the first to hear of an impending default and therefore also first in line to get their money back. But the desire to be first in line when things go wrong also creates a risk of an inefficient run that can take down even a healthy bank.[25]

In any case, an investment in monitoring is only worthwhile if there is a significant chance of things going wrong so that the potential gains are large enough to cover the cost. However, the idea that bank debt provides liquidity is predicated on the likelihood of default being very small so that deposits are "informationally insensitive" and can reliably be used for making payments.[26]

If the bank's shares are listed on a public exchange, lenders might actually free-ride on the information contained in stock prices. Since shareholders' returns are very sensitive to the returns on the banks' assets, shareholders and other investors in the stock market have much stronger incentives to invest in information, and this information is potentially valuable at all times, not just when things go badly. The information that these investors gather affects stock prices, so stock prices provide a free source of information on how the bank is doing. For lenders, it makes sense to look at the borrower's stock prices and not invest in monitoring at all if stock prices indicate that all is well. In such a situation, there is no reason to expect uninsured depositors and short-term bank lenders to impose discipline on bank managers and prevent the managers from increasing the bank's leverage.[27]

The experience of the decade before the financial crisis of 2007–2009 accords with our analysis of leverage dynamics without creditor discipline. During this decade, the leverage of large banks went up significantly, without any imposition of discipline by debt holders. Share prices went up until the crisis broke. In the case of Lehman Brothers, the final run by money market lenders was triggered by a stock market fund manager selling the stock short and announcing that Lehman Brothers had large hidden losses — monitoring by stock market investors rather than debt holders.[28]

25 See Diamond & Dybvig, *supra* note 9.

26 See Gorton, *supra* note 2, ch 3. In Anat R Admati & Martin F Hellwig, "Does Debt Discipline Bankers? An Academic Myth About Bank Indebtedness" (2013) Rock Center for Corporate Governance at Stanford University Working Paper No 132 at 20 [Admati & Hellwig, "Does Debt Discipline Bankers?"], we give an extensive discussion of the tension between the "liquidity explanation" of bank funding by short-term debt, which requires this debt to be information insensitive, and the "discipline explanation," which requires debt holders to take an interest in constant monitoring.

27 The resulting dependence of creditor behaviour, in particular the laxness of lending standards, on stock prices may play a role in the mechanisms underlying so-called leverage cycles. See John Geanakoplos, "The Leverage Cycle" in Daron Acemoglu, Kenneth Rogoff & Michael Woodford, eds, *NBER Macroeconomic Annual 2009* (Chicago: University of Chicago Press, 2009) 1.

28 See Admati & Hellwig, "Does Debt Discipline Bankers?", *supra* note 26; Admati et al, "Fallacies", *supra* note 3, s 5.

The Social Costs and Benefits of Leverage Regulation

The discussion above suggests that laissez-faire markets lead to excessive levels of leverage for banks — levels that are excessive even in the absence of systemic effects and potential damage from bank failures to the rest of the financial system and the overall economy. If the possibility of bank failures creates systemic risk and harms unrelated third parties, this collateral harm provides an additional compelling reason for considering laissez-faire to be inefficient.

Regulation that constrains banks' use of debt can address these market failures. If such regulation is enforced effectively, it can provide a substitute for the missing commitment powers of banks in their interactions with their creditors. The commitment created by equity regulation enables banks to provide liquidity and make loans more reliably to their creditors by being safer.

Equity regulation also serves to constrain systemic risk and harms to third parties that are caused by bank failures and bank distress. In particular, if the government uses deposit insurance and other guarantees to contain such damage and to ensure the liquidity of deposits, there is a *prima facie* case for regulation to reduce the expected costs of such protection and counter the incentives banks have to take more risk and engage in more borrowing in order to increase the value of the insurance relative to its cost. As discussed above, deposit insurance eliminates incentives for depositors to engage in monitoring or to impose covenants that would restrict banks' risk-taking and borrowing, thus exacerbating the other effects. As before, regulation can provide a mechanism of commitment, thus providing a substitute for missing or ineffective debt covenants. Constraining the extent of bank borrowing thus helps banks perform all their usual functions, including liquidity creation and lending. Of course, for regulation to work, regulators must have the authority, the political will and ability to monitor banks and to enforce the regulation effectively.

Regulation to reduce banks' indebtedness and increase their reliance on equity produces another benefit by reducing the distortions of investment decisions that are caused by heavy borrowing. It is well known that, if corporations are heavily indebted, the conflict of interest between shareholders and creditors causes inefficient investment decisions that reduce the overall value of the heavily indebted firm. First, heavily indebted firms may choose to shift risk to creditors by making risky investments that benefit shareholders while reducing the value of creditors' claims, because shareholders benefit fully from the upside while sharing the downside with creditors. Second, the shareholders of heavily indebted corporations may avoid taking worthy investments that are relatively safe. This avoidance occurs because some of the value created by the investment may accrue to the creditors because their claims become less risky and more likely to be paid in full. When banks are distressed, they frequently stop lending, which creates a credit crunch that also motivates bailouts and other forms of support. With more equity, this problem, too, would be alleviated.

Finally, when banks incur losses and face trouble in rolling over their short-term funding, they may engage in selling assets even at distressed, fire-sale prices. The less equity the bank employs, the larger the fraction of the equity that disappears when asset values decline. Generally, for a given level of losses, a bank with high leverage and little equity must sell much more of its assets to become safer again than does a bank with less leverage and more equity. If many institutions sell assets at the same time and these assets are opaque, asset price declines exacerbate the weakness and make the situation worse. It is thus more likely that lending to businesses and households might freeze and, again, bailouts and supports might have to be provided, as they were in October 2008. With more equity, the fire-sale dynamics would be much weaker and bailouts might not be needed.[29]

Since the benefits of regulation that require banks to use much more equity are so substantial, are there significant social costs associated with such regulations? If regulations prevented banks from taking on *any* debt, it would preclude their taking deposits and providing liquidity, since deposits are a form of debt. However, the equity requirements that we now have are very far from such an extreme. Basel III still requires banks to fund at least *three percent* of their (non-risk-weighted) assets with equity, thus allowing them to fund up to 97 percent with debt. An increase in the required ratio for equity relative to assets can be realized by raising more equity, without any change in the amount of borrowing. The additional equity makes banks safer and thereby enhances the liquidity benefits that investors obtain from their deposits and other forms of short-term debt.

As we have shown in detail in many writings,[30] the costs associated with significantly higher equity requirements are entirely private to the banks' managers and shareholders, because with more equity, they are less able to benefit from tax and other subsidies and are less able to shift risks and costs to taxpayers and the public. These subsidies are provided to banks only when they borrow. Reducing subsidies by using more equity entails no social cost. While elimination of these subsidies has often been stated as an objective of the reforms undertaken after the crisis, and many bankers and policy makers claim that implicit subsidies are no longer present, empirical studies show that the subsidies are still substantial.[31] The persisting implicit and explicit guarantees continue to weaken investor monitoring and create moral hazard and distortions.

An increase in equity requirements does not actually force banks to reduce their funding by deposits or other short-term liabilities and the liquidity benefits that investors love. Banks could also raise additional equity in the market or, over time, increase their equity internally by retaining profits without reducing their deposit funding. They might use the additional funds for additional lending or for buying additional assets in the open market. As was shown by Admati et al. in "Fallacies, Irrelevant Facts, and Myths in the Discussion of Capital Regulation:

29 As shown in Admati et al, "Leverage Ratchet", *supra* note 3, the incentive distortions that cause the leverage ratchet dynamics also tend to generate a preference for asset sales rather than equity issues as a form of deleveraging when required.

30 Admati et al, "Fallacies," *supra* note 3; Admati & Hellwig, *The Bankers' New Clothes, supra* note 3; Admati & Hellwig, "Does Debt Discipline Bankers?", *supra* note 26; Anat R Admati & Martin F Hellwig, "The Parade of Bankers' New Clothes Continues: 31 Flawed Claims Debunked" (2015), Rock Center for Corporate Governance at Stanford University Working Paper No 143 [Admati & Hellwig, "Parade"].

31 See e.g. Bryan Kelly, Hanno N Lustig & Stijn Van Nieuwerburgh, "Too-Systemic-to-Fail: What Option Markets Imply about Sector-Wide Government Guarantees" (2016) 106:6 American Economic Rev, 1278–1319; Tryggvi Gudmundsson, "Whose Credit Line is it Anyway: An Update on Banks' Implicit Subsidies" (2016) IMF Working Paper No 16/224. For a discussion of the challenge of estimating the subsidies, see Admati, "Examining the GAO Report", *supra* note 3.

Why Bank Equity Is Not Expensive," the latter can be done without adverse incentive effects on bank managers.[32]

In the political debate, banks often claim that equity is expensive, so that if equity requirements were tightened, the rates they charge for their loans would have to increase and some loans might not be made at all. However, from the perspective of society as a whole, low interest rates on bank loans are not necessarily desirable. Loans should be made at interest rates that reflect the actual social costs of the funds being lent. If loan rates are low because of tax benefits and government subsidies through guarantees, bank lending to households and businesses may actually be excessive and wasteful. The expansion of mortgage lending in the years 2002 to 2007 in Ireland, Spain, the United States and elsewhere provides an example. The ultimate social costs were enormous.[33]

If policy makers determine that bank loans are too expensive or that too few are made in a particular area (for example, to small and medium enterprises), the proper remedy would be to intervene and target this problem directly, for example, by subsidizing specific forms of bank lending in certain circumstances. There may also be ways to support desired activities without relying on financial intermediaries to deliver the support (for example, by giving tax credit to first-time homeowners to be used for down payment instead of subsidizing mortgage debt to fund home ownership). Such targeted support is better than blanket subsidies to bank borrowing. Subsidies to bank borrowing often have little effect on bank lending because banks have significant discretion in how to use their funds, and they may prefer to gamble in risky securities rather than make socially desirable but "boring" loans.

There have been many attempts to support the "equity is expensive" mantra in banking. In past writings, we classified the claims and arguments that are put forward as "fallacies, irrelevant facts, and myths," where "irrelevant facts" involved claims referring to private, rather than social, costs and benefits of equity funding and "myths" involved theoretical models explaining why "banks have to fund with short-term debt."[34] Most of the myths appear to represent an exercise in "reverse engineering" as discussed by Paul Pfleiderer.[35] They also reflect the presumption that laissez-faire outcomes are efficient. As we have argued here, this presumption is unwarranted.

32 Anat R Admati, Peter Conti-Brown & Paul C Pfleiderer, "Liability Holding Companies" (2012) 59 UCLA L Rev 852–913; see also Admati et al, "Fallacies", *supra* note 3, s 7. Note that if the funds raised by issuing equity are invested in the open markets for shares and debt securities of other firms, the operation need not involve any net inflow of cash into banks. The question of where all the new equity funding would come from would be moot because the cash raised would be given back to the market right away. The only thing that changes is the structure of ownership of claims to returns from the different firms in the markets.

33 For more general treatments of excessive borrowing by the "real economy," see Atif Mian & Amir Sufi, *House of Debt: How They (and You) Caused the Great Recession, and How We Can Prevent It from Happening Again* (Chicago: University of Chicago Press, 2015); Moritz Schularick & Alan M Taylor, "Credit Booms Gone Bust: Monetary Policy, Leverage Cycles and Financial Crises, 1870–2008" (2012) 102:2 American Economic Rev 1029–61.

34 Admati et al, "Fallacies", *supra* note 3. In Admati & Hellwig, *The Bankers' New Clothes*, *supra* note 3, we called the flawed claims "the bankers' new clothes," arguments that lack valid substance. In Admati & Hellwig, "Parade", *supra* note 30, we inspected the continuing "parade of bankers' new clothes" and debunked 31 flawed claims.

35 Paul Pfleiderer, "Chameleons: The Misuse of Theoretical Models in Finance and Economics" (2018) Working Paper No 3020.

Conclusion

At a conference at a central bank some time ago, Martin Hellwig was asked why he was dissatisfied with the regulatory reforms that had been implemented since 2008. In his reply, he asked, in turn, whether the crisis would have been avoided if all the reforms introduced since 2008 had already been implemented in 2000. A former central bank governor who was listening immediately said, "No!" More than 10 years after the Lehman Brothers bankruptcy, many of the key drivers of the crisis are still present, and the financial system has changed too little and is still unsafe. The repeated claim by policy makers that the system is safer now is akin to claiming that roads would be safer if the speed limit for trucks loaded with explosives were lowered from 100 mph to 95 mph — perhaps a tiny bit safer, but still extremely unsafe, especially if authorities relied on the truckers' own speedometers to measure speed and these speedometers could be manipulated.[36]

The massive support that governments and central banks provided to banks and many other financial institutions in the crisis succeeded in preventing the implosion of the financial system and staving off another Great Depression. One consequence of the success was that the industry and its lobbyists lost little, if any, of their ability to influence policy in ways that benefit the industry but harm the public. They continued to advise governments, parliaments and regulators on the path of reform, almost as if the crisis had never happened. Their warnings about the impact of equity requirements on lending and growth contributed significantly to the weakness of Basel III, even though most of the warnings involved fallacies, irrelevant facts and myths.[37]

The reform of equity regulation, which in our view is the most powerful tool for supporting financial stability and reducing systemic risk as well as distorted decisions, did not receive much public attention. Negotiations for Basel III took place behind closed doors in the Basel Committee for Banking Supervision and were effectively completed before the public in most countries had even become aware of the matter. These negotiations were not based on any deep scrutiny of the causes of the crisis; in fact, the new Basel Accord was concluded before any of the official inquiries into the causes of the crises had been completed.[38]

Major weaknesses of previous regulation (Basel II) were left in place, for example, the excessive reliance on the banks' own models for risk assessments and the determination of required equity, and the failure to take account of certain risks altogether, such as default risks of sovereigns in their own currency or the risks attached to short-term funding of long-term assets in the bank

36 The speedometer analogy refers to the calibration of equity requirements on the basis of the banks' own risk models; see Admati & Hellwig, *The Bankers' New Clothes*, *supra* note 3, ch 11; Markus Behn, Rainer Haselmann & Vikrant Vig, "The limits of model-based regulation" (2016) European Central Bank Working Paper No 1928, doi:10.2866/906624.

37 In May 2010, a particularly outrageous statement from the British Bankers Association asserted that the Basel proposals would require British banks to "hold" more equity (amounting to £700 billion), and that this amount would not be available for lending. Since equity is a mode of funding rather than a cash reserve, this claim was outright nonsense. The lobby's willingness to use such nonsense was witness to their sense of mastery of the proceedings. Paul Volcker, former chair of the Federal Reserve, told Senator Ted Kaufman in January 2010, "just about whatever anyone proposes, no matter what it is, the banks will come out and claim that it will restrict credit and harm the economy....It's all bullshit," as quoted in Jeff Connaughton, *The Payoff: Why Wall Street Always Wins* (Westport, CT: Prospecta Press, 2012).

38 For example, the report of the commission that the US Congress appointed to study the causes and the course of the financial crisis only came out after Basel III had been agreed upon and after the Dodd-Frank Act had been signed into law. See Financial Crisis Inquiry Commission, *The Financial Crisis Inquiry Report* (Washington, DC: US Government Printing Office, 2011).

book.[39] Basel III did introduce a "leverage ratio requirement" so that, regardless of how safe the bank might proclaim itself to be, equity must not be less than three percent of total assets — the ratio Lehman Brothers had in its last balance sheet before it went bankrupt. In November 2010, a letter to the *Financial Times* from 20 leading academics in the area of banking and finance, including (by now) two Nobel laureates, protested the inadequacy of Basel III and called for requiring equity to be at least 15 percent of total assets (compared to three percent in Basel III), but by then the new Basel Accord had been concluded.[40]

Reluctance to impose tougher regulation is often justified by fears that such regulation would make it difficult for banks to compete with unregulated institutions and that a shift of risky activities from banks to these unregulated institutions would be very dangerous. Unregulated institutions, the so-called shadow banks, serve as a bugbear to warn against any regulation. However, the argument raises the question whether shadow banks are actually so dangerous and, if they are, why they remain unregulated.

In fact, some kinds of shadow banks, namely hedge funds and private equity firms, have so far not caused much of a danger to financial stability. In the financial crisis, the most harmful shadow banks were actually the creations of regulated banks, special purpose vehicles that the banks used to circumvent regulations by holding assets outside their balance sheets and funding them through the market, with explicit or implicit guarantees. When market funding broke down, in the summer of 2007, the sponsoring banks had to make good on their guarantees, and their balance sheets were much the worse for it, raising immediate doubts about capital adequacy and solvency.[41] If the supervisors had not tolerated these practices, the expansion of subprime securitization would have been much less extensive, and the impact of the subprime crisis would have been much smaller.[42] Yet even today, these practices continue; according to Manmohan Singh and Zohair Alam, off-balance-sheet funding of financial institutions — and hidden leverage — is higher now than in 2007, before the crisis.[43]

Money market funds are another set of shadow banks that played a detrimental role in the crisis. Whereas some authors consider the funding of banks and special purpose vehicles of banks by money market funds to be an example of socially useful liquidity creation through complex financial arrangements, the run by customers on these funds, and the run by these funds on

39 Behn, Haselmann & Vig, *supra* note 36, provide strong empirical evidence that internal risk assessments of loans are more optimistic and, in fact, too optimistic when they are also used to determine the equity needed to back the loans.

40 See Admati et al, "Healthy banking system is the goal, not profitable banks", *Financial Times* (9 November 2010). In an op-ed the next day in the same paper, Citigroup CEO Vikram Pandit argued that "we must rethink Basel or growth will suffer," illustrating the uphill battle of anyone trying to take on the industry. See Vikram Pandit, "We must rethink Basel, or growth will suffer", *Financial Times* (10 November 2010).

41 See Martin F Hellwig, "Systemic Risk in the Financial Sector: An Analysis of the Subprime-Mortgage Crisis" (2009) 157:2 De Economist 129–207; Viral V Acharya, Philipp Schnabl & Gustavo Suarez, "Securitization without Risk Transfer" (2013) 107:3 J Financial Economics 515–36; Admati & Hellwig, *The Bankers' New Clothes*, *supra* note 3, ch 5, 13.

42 Matthias Thiemann provides an extensive account of the politics behind this toleration: see Matthias Thiemann, *The Growth of Shadow Banking: A Comparative Institutional Analysis* (Cambridge, UK: Cambridge University Press, 2018). See also Martin Hellwig, "Germany and the Financial Crises 2007–2017" (2018) Max Planck Institute for Research on Collective Goods, Bonn (preliminary draft) (for the regulatory treatment of German banks using special purpose vehicles to invest in "toxic" securities in the United States).

43 Manmohan Singh & Zohair Alam, "Leverage—A Broader View" (2018) IMF Working Paper No 18/62.

banks, were crucial in the collapse of money markets after the Lehman Brothers bankruptcy;[44] the government even had to provide the money market funds with a kind of deposit insurance to end the runs. Even so, the regulation of money market funds has not changed much. The dependence of banks on the funds is still a source of substantial systemic risk.

Confusion, willful blindness and conflicted interests on the part of many have combined to maintain a financial system in which incentives to harm and to take risks at the expense of others are insufficiently disciplined by either regulation or market forces. The enablers of this system include individuals from across the private sector and government institutions, as well as some economists and media.[45] The claim most frequently made is that equity is expensive.

Whereas the enablers argue that equity is expensive, it is actually the inefficiently high leverage and the inadequate levels of equity in banking that are expensive for society. Properly designed equity requirements are needed to deal with this problem.[46] The industry is strongly opposed to such requirements because they restrict the banks' ability to borrow and take risks at the expense of creditors and taxpayers. When economists suggest that laissez-faire in banking is efficient and imply or state that equity regulation is harmful or expensive, they echo some of the flawed claims of the lobby. As we have shown, claims that laissez-faire in banking is efficient rest on special and unrealistic modelling assumptions. Once these assumptions are brought closer to reality and the implications of creditor fragmentation and weak commitment powers are considered, high leverage in banking is seen to reflect distortions rather than the mandate of efficiency.

Authors' Note

We are grateful to Emilios Avgouleas, Stefanie Egidy, Paul Schempp, Steven L. Schwarcz, an anonymous referee and especially Paul Pfleiderer for their helpful comments.

44 See Gorton, *supra* note 2, ch 2, 3, for the claim that "liquidity creation" through complex financial arrangements is useful. For critical assessments, see the empirical studies of Acharya, Schnabl & Suarez, *supra* note 41, and Arvind Krishnamurthy, Stefan Nagel & Dmitry Orlov, "Sizing up Repo" (2014) 69:6 J Finance 2381 (the former on distortions in the formation and funding of special purpose vehicles to hold mortgage-backed securities; the latter on the nature of the "run on repo" in September 2008, which was concentrated on the dealer banks). Both papers emphasize solvency concerns for the relevant issuers.

45 As described by Anat R Admati, "It Takes a Village to Maintain a Dangerous Financial System" in Lisa Herzog, ed, *Just Financial Markets? Finance in a Just Society* (Oxford, UK: Oxford University Press, 2017), online: <https://admati.people.stanford.edu/publications/it-takes-village-maintain-dangerous-financial-system>. After discussing the action and inaction of the enablers and their moral disengagement, she concluded that "change is possible, but it will take a village to repair a financial system" (*ibid* at 20). A major challenge comes from the use of confusing jargon to exclude much of the public, and the politics of banking, in which politicians tend to view banks as a source of funding and do not have enough incentives to care about risk.

46 For a discussion of the flaws in the existing design of capital regulations under Basel III, specific steps that can be taken immediately and related policy recommendations, see Admati & Hellwig, *The Bankers' New Clothes*, *supra* note 3, ch 11; Anat R Admati, "The Missed Opportunity and Challenge of Capital Regulation" (2016) 235:1 National Institute Economic Rev R4.

14

Leverage Caused the 2007-2009 Crisis

John Geanakoplos

The Leverage Cycle

There are two standard explanations of the cause of the 2007–2009 crisis. The first is greed, greed that overtook the banks, then the mortgage brokers, then the rating agencies, then the bondholders and then the borrowers. One can see these forces at work in the movie *The Big Short*.

A second explanation is that a panic exploded in 2008 and 2009, causing a run on banks, on money markets and on collateral. According to the second theory, the only way to stem the panic was to restore confidence, as former Federal Reserve Chairman Ben Bernanke explained in his book *The Courage to Act*, and as Treasury Secretary Timothy Geithner argued in his book *Stress Test*.

Greed and panic cannot be legislated away, or prevented by macroprudential policy.

At the World Econometric Society Congress of 2000, long before the crisis of 2007–2009, I proposed another theory of booms and crashes: the leverage cycle, caused by a buildup of too much leverage and then a faster de-leveraging.[1] Rising leverage leads to rising asset prices, making the economy progressively more vulnerable, so that eventually a little bit of "scary bad news" can trigger a great crash. If the asset prices end up far enough below the debts, then a failure to partially forgive underwater debtors can create more losses.[2]

Between 2000 and the 2007–2009 crisis, leverage did indeed rise in the banks and in households, and so did housing and mortgage-backed securities prices. Then leverage and asset prices collapsed. Eventually leverage and asset prices recovered. The failure to forgive a non-negligible amount of mortgage debt did, in my opinion, delay the recovery, and stirred resentment that lingers today. Unlike greed and panic, the leverage cycle crash can be prevented by wise public policy.

The conventional view in macroeconomics had long been that cycles are caused by fluctuations in aggregate demand. These can be smoothed over by raising the interest rate when demand is too high, and lowering the interest rate when demand is too low. The trouble with this interest rate-centric view of macroeconomics is that it leaves unanswered what we mean by tight credit, if not just a high interest rate. When business people talk about tight credit, they don't mean that the riskless interest rate set by the Fed is too high. They mean that at the going riskless interest rate, or anything close to it, they cannot get a loan, because lenders are afraid they might default. Default is what is missing in the traditional macroeconomics theory.

Once default is recognized as a possibility, we should expect lenders to require additional terms for a loan, such as a maximum debt to income (DTI), or a minimum credit score (FICO). The most important requirement is usually collateral, and I concentrate on collateral here.

If an \$80 loan requires collateral of \$100, then we say that the collateral rate is 125 percent, the loan to value (LTV) is 80 percent, the margin or down payment is 20 percent, and the leverage is five, since \$20 cash can allow for the purchase of an asset worth \$100. All of these amount to the same thing. It has been known for centuries that more leverage leads to more risk. If the collateral falls in value to \$99, and the \$80 loan is paid off, the borrower is left with \$19 out of his original \$20. A one percent fall in the collateral price leads to a five percent fall in investor capital, which are in the same ratio as the leverage.

The new idea in the leverage cycle is that more leverage causes higher collateral prices. The only precedents for this seem to be in the work of Hyman Minsky[3] and the economic historian Charles Kindleberger.[4] Neither of these authors used a mathematical model to express his

1 John Geanakoplos, "Liquidity, Default and Crashes: Endogenous Contracts in General Equilibrium" in Mathias Dewatripont, Lars Peter Hansen & Stephen J Turnovsky, eds, *Advances in Economics and Econometrics: Theory and Applications, Eighth World Congress*, vol 2 (Cambridge, UK: Cambridge University Press, 2003) 170 [Geanakoplos, "Liquidity, Default and Crashes"]. See also John Geanakoplos, "The Leverage Cycle" in Daron Acemoglu, Kenneth Rogoff & Michael Woodford, eds, *NBER Macroeconomics Annual 2009*, vol 24 (Chicago: University of Chicago Press, 2010) 1:65 [Geanakoplos, "The Leverage Cycle"].

2 I added the forgiveness dimension to the leverage cycle in 2008. See John Geanakoplos & Susan Koniak, "Mortgage Justice is Blind", *The New York Times* (20 October 2008); John Geanakoplos & Susan Koniak, "Matters of Principal", *The New York Times* (4 March 2009).

3 Hyman Minsky, "A Theory of Systemic Fragility" in Edward Altman & Arnold W Sametz, eds, *Financial Crises: Institutions and Markets in a Fragile Environment* (New York: John Wiley and Sons, 1977) 138.

4 Charles P Kindleberger, *Manias, Panics, and Crashes: A History of Financial Crises* (New York: Basic Books, 1978).

Figure 1: Credit Surface

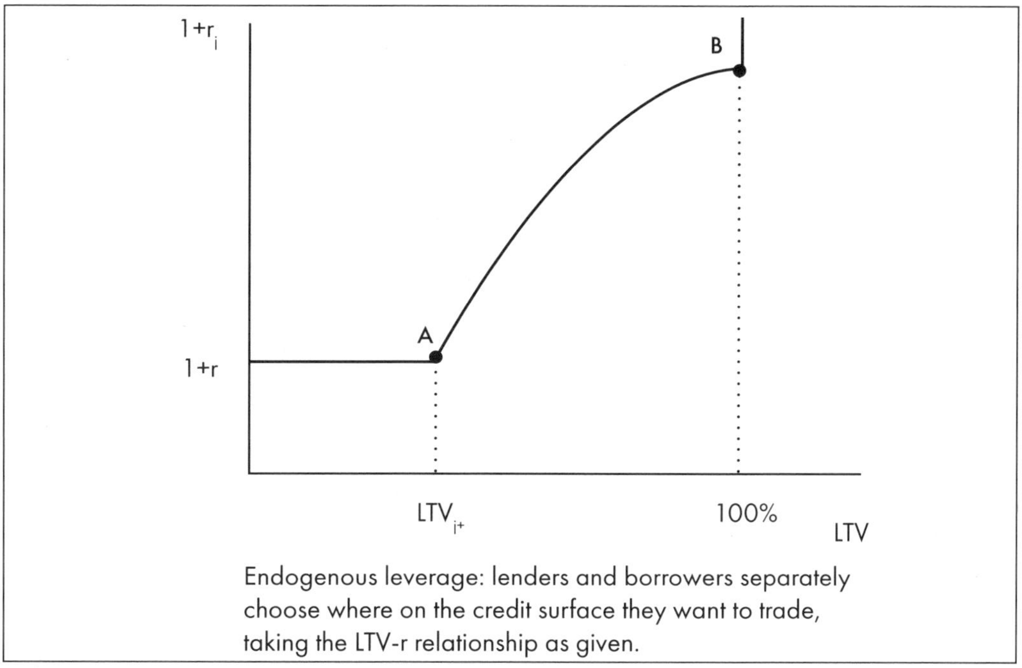

Source: Author.

ideas, and neither had collateral explicitly in mind (Minsky was talking about a firm borrowing money, and by leverage he meant a ratio of debt payments to income). Both of them made the extrapolative (irrational) expectations of borrowers the linchpin of their theories.[5]

There are four mathematical concepts behind the leverage cycle. The first is that leverage can be made endogenous via the credit surface. Second, that leverage increases when volatility, or more precisely, down risk, decreases. The third is that higher leverage makes for higher asset prices, all else being equal. Fourth, a highly leveraged economy is vulnerable to crashes stemming from small shocks that create more uncertainty, which I call "scary bad news." A little bit of scary bad news can topple a highly indebted economy through two kinds of margin calls: one caused by the bad news reducing collateral prices, and the other caused by the scary part of the news reducing leverage. Each concept corresponds to a precise mathematical theorem in the case of binomial economies. If the leverage cycle theory of crashes had to be stated in one or two words, it would not be panic; it would be margin call.

5 Collateral appears in formal macroeconomic models first in Ben Bernanke & Mark Gertler, "Agency costs, collateral, and business fluctuations" (1986) Proceedings, Federal Reserve Bank of San Francisco, and then simultaneously in 1997 in Nobuhiro Kiyotaki & John Moore, "Credit Cycles" (1997) 105:2 J Political Economy 211; Bengt Holmstrom & Jean Tirole, "Financial Intermediation, Loanable Funds, and the Real Sector" (1997) QJ Economics 112, and my own work, John Geanakoplos, "Promises, Promises" in W Brian Arthur, Steven N Durlauf & David A Lane, eds, *The Economy as an Evolving Complex System*, vol 2 (Reading, MA: Addison-Wesley, 1997) 285 [Geanakoplos, "Promises"]. One difference between my approach to leverage and the rest is that I emphasized the endogeneity of leverage and changes in leverage, while they did not.

Figure 2: Looser and Tighter Credit Surfaces

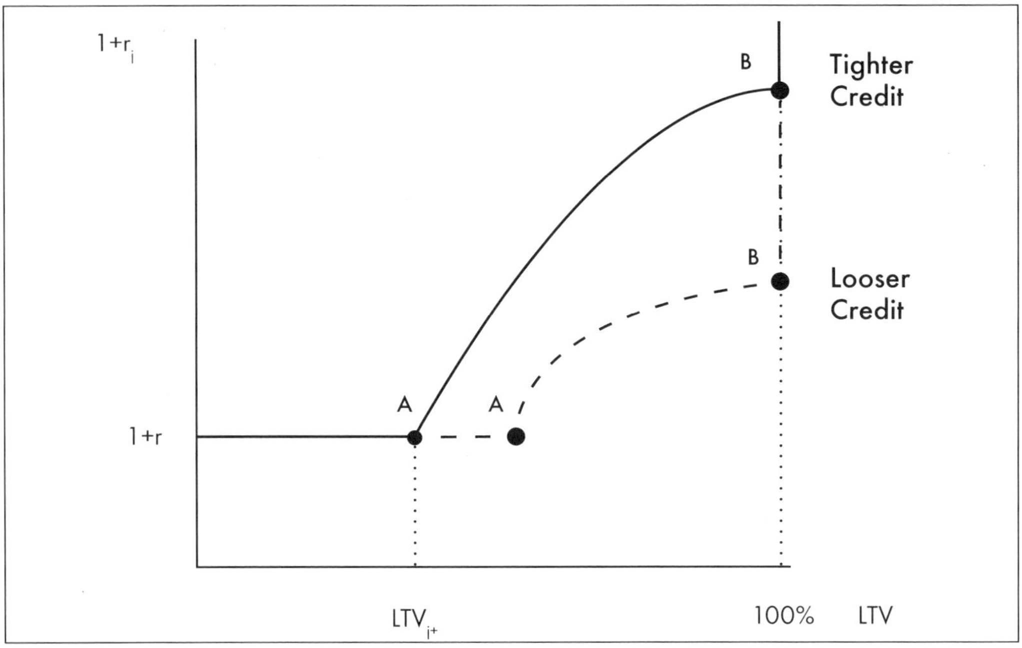

Source: Author.

As a graduate student, I never heard the word "collateral" mentioned in any course I took, even in macroeconomics and finance. But when I worked in the fixed income department at Kidder Peabody in the late 1980s and early 1990s, collateral came up in almost every conversation. I began to think about collateral as a theorist, and was immediately struck by a puzzle. How can a single supply-equals-demand equation for a loan determine the price (or interest rate) on the loan and also the collateral rate or leverage or LTV on the loan? It seemed impossible that one equation could determine two variables. This same problem becomes even worse when one considers all the other terms of a loan, such as FICO and DTI.

I resolved this puzzle for collateral when I realized that I should be thinking about a different price for each level of leverage. A loan should be defined by a pair (promise, collateral), not just by the promise, and each pair must have its own separate price. Fixing the collateral, bigger and bigger promises give rise to higher and higher leverage. At first the loans are so small that the collateral fully protects the lender. But after a certain point, the loans are not fully protected and might default. They get riskier and riskier and the interest rises. The surface generated by the interest rate corresponding to each level of leverage is what I called the credit surface.[6] See Figure 1. More generally, one could imagine a credit surface with independent axes including LTV, DTI and FICO, and a vertical axis giving the corresponding interest rate charged to a loan

6 See Geanakoplos, "Promises", *supra* note 5.

with any combination of those three characteristics.[7] I discuss only the collateral credit surface in this chapter, although I return to the more general case in the last section.

Borrowers and lenders each choose where they want to be on the credit surface. In equilibrium, for each level of leverage there is a separate supply-equals-demand equation and a separate price. At many leverage levels there may be zero supply and zero demand. The most interesting borrowers are not the ones on the flat part of the credit surface, who are able to borrow unconstrained quantities at the riskless interest rate as in the old style of macroeconomics. The agents who are at point A and beyond are often the pivotal drivers of fluctuations in economic activity, and they are constrained, because each time they try to borrow more (on the same collateral), they face a higher interest rate.

The credit surface also clarifies the meaning of tight credit. It is not the height of the riskless rate per se, but also the steepness of the credit surface that renders credit tight. Thus, in Figure 2, the bottom credit surface line is looser than the top credit surface line, even though the riskless interest rate is the same.

For binomial economies with financial assets, Ana Fostel and I proved that the only leverage level that would be positively traded in equilibrium is the maxmin loan, which promises the maximum without any risk of default. This is point A in Figure 1.[8] The theorem guarantees that, in equilibrium, the credit surface rises sufficiently fast beyond point A that nobody will choose to trade there. Leverage is completely endogenous, chosen freely by borrowers and lenders at any point, but the theory predicts exactly where it will end up. Of course the binomial assumption, that only two things can happen, is very unrealistic. (It approximates reality best with very short-term loans, such as repurchase agreements [repos].) But the conclusion does not depend on the preferences of the agents or their endowments, or their probability assessments of the future states.[9]

The binomial no-default theorem has an immediate consequence for leverage, which Fostel and I called the binomial leverage theorem. Geometrically, it is clear that point A is defined by the worst-case scenario. With a little bit of algebra, we showed that in binomial models with financial assets, equilibrium LTV is equal to the worst-case gross return, divided by the gross riskless rate of interest:

$$\text{LTV} = \frac{1}{1+r} \; \frac{\text{worst collateral payoff}}{\text{price of collateral}}$$

7 See John Geanakoplos, "The Credit Surface and Monetary Policy" in Olivier J Blanchard et al, eds, *Progress and Confusion: The State of Macroeconomic Policy* (Cambridge, MA: MIT Press, 2016) 143 [Geanakoplos, "The Credit Surface"]. One could also imagine different axes corresponding to different kinds of collateral, depending on the precise legal rights for the confiscation of the collateral.

8 See Ana Fostel & John Geanakoplos, "Leverage and Default in Binomial Economies: A Complete Characterization" (2015) 83:6 Econometrica 2191. Financial assets give no direct utility for holding them (like a painting would), and their future dividends do not depend on who holds them. Think of a share of GE stock, or of a mortgage-backed security. Thus, in binomial economies with financial assets, leverage to the right of point A will never be observed. This is not true for trinomial economies, where the most interesting borrowers might indeed be to the right of point A. Loans to the left of point A are overcollateralized. If we ignore the irrelevant extra collateral, we could say those loans are maxmin loans on a smaller collateral base.

9 In Geanakoplos, "Liquidity, Default and Crashes", *supra* note 1, I proved the same theorem, but only under the additional hypothesis that agents are risk neutral.

We emphasize that leverage rises when the down risk abates, that is, when the world gets safer. Of course, if expectations become so optimistic that returns on the collateral (relative to the riskless rate) are anticipated to be higher in every future state, then leverage will rise.

Feeling optimistic and feeling safe often go hand in hand. But sometimes they can be quite different. If agents think there is more upside in just the best state, leverage will not rise.

When risks are symmetric, the worst case is worse if volatility is higher. Expected volatility is easy to measure via options markets, whereas expected returns are hard to measure. It has been known among Wall Street traders that margins (in, say, the commodities markets) go up when volatility goes up. There is no comparable empirical correlation between expected returns and leverage. The binomial leverage theorem asserts that leverage is determined by volatility, or more generally, down risk, and it does not depend on utilities, endowments, the number of traders or the type of financial asset.

The third key mathematical idea is that all else being equal, more leverage increases asset prices. The reason is almost self-evident, yet it had not really been examined in the literature. With a smaller required down payment, more buyers can express their demand for the collateral (houses or mortgage-backed securities, for example), and the same buyers can buy more units, leading to greater demand and a higher price, provided there is heterogeneity in the valuations agents place on the asset.[10] We proved that in any binomial model with financial assets, constraining leverage below the equilibrium maxmin value always lowers the value of an asset, assuming that the risk-free interest rate does not change.[11]

The link between leverage and asset prices contradicts the famous Modigliani-Miller (M-M) Theorem, which asserts that prices should be unaffected by leverage. One difference is that Modigliani and Miller did not explicitly discuss collateral. They did have in mind a firm, which certainly might be thought of as collateral for its bond issuances. But they overlooked that their argument depends on the reliability of non-firm debt as well. Their argument, as clarified by Joseph Stiglitz,[12] is essentially the following. Suppose a firm issues a debt promise of D and raises the rest of its money-issuing equity of value E. Suppose it does not default on D in any state of nature. If the firm were restricted to sell a promise $D^I < D$, then it would have to issue more equity E^I. The bondholders who had previously purchased the promises $(D - D^I)$ would be disappointed at losing access to riskless debt, and the equity holders would be forced to absorb more equity, and tamer (less leveraged) equity, possibly reducing their expected returns. The M-M Theorem is proved by noting that the equity holders could themselves issue the missing debt $D^{II} = D - D^I$, thereby giving the market the same debt it had before, and at the same time releveraging the equity E^I so it becomes just like E. In essence, the reduced leverage at the firm level is compensated by increased leverage at the investor level.

10 Imagine all the buyers arrayed on a vertical corresponding to their valuation of the asset. The marginal buyer is the agent whose valuation is equal to the price. The higher valuation agents will be buyers, and the lower valuation agents will sell the asset. As the natural buyers get access to more borrowing, a smaller number of them can buy all the assets, creating a higher marginal buyer, and thus a higher price.

11 If the interest rate rose as agents leveraged more, agents would discount the cash flows from the asset more harshly, and so their lower valuations would partly offset their gain in purchasing power, leaving the final collateral price ambiguous.

12 Joseph Stiglitz, "A Re-Examination of the Modigliani-Miller Theorem" (1969) 59 American Economic Rev 784.

One flaw in this M-M proof is that collateral is not generally transferable: just because the firm can be used as collateral does not necessarily mean the equity can be used as collateral. The equity holder might have a different propensity to repay, perhaps not as reliably as the original firm, so D^{II} would not be treated by the market as a perfect substitute for D. When leverage goes down for the economy as a whole, there are real consequences.

For example, consider a new homeowner who is limited (say, by regulation or by a worse down risk in housing prices) to taking out a mortgage at smaller LTV. They would simply have to come up with a bigger down payment, since taking out a second loan would not be permitted by the regulation, or by the worse down risk. There is no outside agent who could use her increased equity to increase his leverage. The drop in debt will necessarily have real consequences for the economy and for the price of the houses. This same argument applies word for word to the purchaser of any asset, such as a mortgage-backed security. The only situation in which the M-M logic partially applies is the one they had in mind. The buyer of firm equity could indeed use the equity as collateral for a further loan, thus compensating for the lower debt-to-equity ratio at the firm level. But the flaw emerges here as well if we go one step deeper. If a regulation limits the leverage that can be used by agents using firm equity as collateral, or if the equity returns from firms have greater down risk, then leverage will go down at the agent level as well as at the firm level, and collateral prices will fall.

The fourth mathematical concept consists of three mechanisms that can combine to cause a crash. The first two involve a margin call: a situation in which a leveraged holder of an asset has to repay her debt and would like to reborrow it (i.e., to "roll it over") but finds that she can reborrow less than she must repay.

The first mechanism involves abrupt changes in anticipations of down risk. An awareness that the down risk is worse, even if unlikely, may cause expected cash flows to decline. But more importantly, it causes leverage to go down, which will also cause asset prices to go down. We express this in Figure 3, where we illustrate the effect of scary news (news that increases uncertainty, or more precisely, down risk).

The second margin call mechanism arises from high leverage, and the debt coming due, even if there is no change in leverage, and even if the leveraged buyer does not intend to sell the collateral. This kicks in when bad news leads to a fall in the asset price and a loss of equity for the leveraged holder. Normally, if a commodity declines in price by $1, an owner who is not planning to sell or buy it faces no loss of purchasing power. A leveraged owner whose debt is coming due and who plans to roll over the debt at the same LTV without trading the asset, on the other hand, faces a margin call of LTV*1. This loss in liquid wealth gives them a countervailing incentive to sell the asset, despite its drop in price.

In fact, they have a wealth effect incentive to sell a great deal of the asset. If their marginal propensity to spend on the (downpayment for the) asset out of each liquid dollar is m, and if they are leveraging the asset at λ, then they will want to sell $LTV^*m^*\lambda = m^*(\lambda\text{-}1)$ dollars worth of the asset on account of the liquid wealth loss of LTV*1 dollars. If $m = 1$ and $\lambda = 4$, the wealth effect is for her to sell $3 worth of each asset she owns for every $1 fall in the asset price. By contrast, the unleveraged owner of the asset, who has $\lambda = 1$, has no wealth incentive to sell.

Figure 3: Volatility-Leverage-Price Mechanism

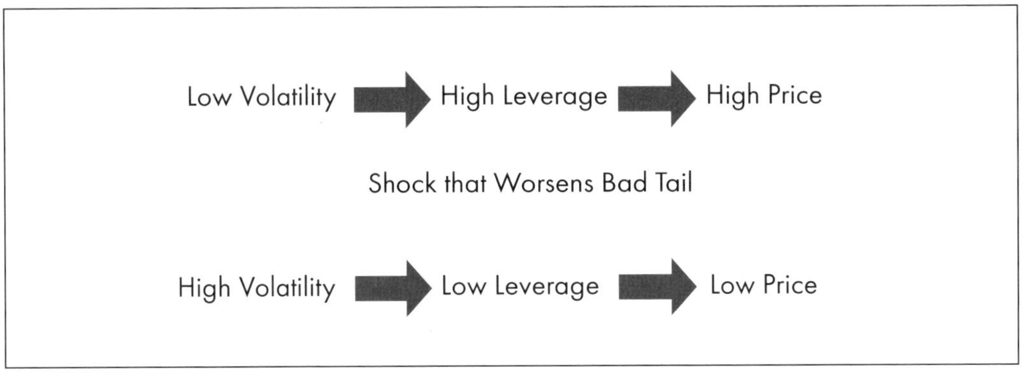

Source: Author.

The substitution effect stabilizes the price by propping it up when it falls by inducing bigger demand. By contrast, the wealth effect for the leveraged owner of the asset is to sell after the price falls, causing the price to fall further. This destabilizing effect makes for a more fragile economy.

The third mechanism arises from high levels of debt. I call it the income redistribution effect. Debt crises have always been linked to fragile economies. Historically, in times of debt troubles, politicians often make speeches about restoring confidence. Franklin Delano Roosevelt said you have nothing to fear but fear itself. Bernanke and Geithner said similar things about restoring confidence, as did Prime Minister Alexis Tsipras of Greece. All of them seemed to believe that by changing expectations, they could move the outcome a long way. In other words, they thought the economy was fragile: a small push could cause a big shift. So why does high debt make for fragile economies?

The answer comes from an old microeconomic dichotomy called the income and substitution effect. When the price of a good (Y) goes down, the substitution effect is that agents will try to buy more of it, because, all else being equal, it is more attractive by virtue of being cheaper. This tends to stabilize prices. But if an agent is already selling Y, then all else is not equal. There is an additional income effect. The lower price makes the seller poorer, which means they might want less of everything, including Y. In more dramatic terms, the further the price goes down, the more they might have to sell. The usual stabilizing effect of lower prices raising demand can be reversed for sellers. In the language of demand theory, the income effect counteracts the substitution effect for the sellers. On the other hand, the income effect reinforces the substitution effect for the buyers. As the price goes down, they effectively get richer and for that reason they want to buy more, beyond their pure substitution effect. The crucial observation is that if the marginal propensity to buy Y (out of an additional dollar of wealth) is higher for the sellers than for the buyers, then the sellers' income effect will be stronger.[13] A drop in the price of Y effectively redistributes income from the sellers to the buyers, in proportion to how much is

13 The famous Slutsky equation says that the income effect is the product of the marginal propensity to consume and excess demand. Since in equilibrium the excess demand of the sellers of Y must be the negative of the excess demand of the buyers, the aggregate income effect on Y is the product of the difference between the sellers' and the buyers' marginal propensities to consume Y and the excess demand of the sellers for Y.

sold. If the marginal propensity to spend on Y out of income is higher for the sellers, then their income-induced drop in consumption of Y will be greater than the buyers' income-induced increase in consumption. In aggregate, the income effect will tend to reverse the substitution effect. Unlike the income effect, the substitution effect is invariant to the quantity sold. Hence for bigger sales, the aggregate income effect diminishes the stabilizing aggregate substitution effects more. With big enough sales, the aggregate demand curve for Y will be close to flat.[14] But a flat demand curve means that equilibrium prices will have to move dramatically to restore equilibrium after a small shock. The economy is fragile. Thus, a little bit of bad news can have a big effect on prices in an economy with high sales of some good.[15]

See Figure 4, which illustrates how the same vertical shock down will produce a small change in the equilibrium price of an economy with steep demand (i.e., with a dominant substitution effect), but produce a large change in the equilibrium price of an economy with flat demand (i.e., with a dominant income effect).

When there is a large debt that is coming due, then there must be a large sale, either of some good or of more promises, to pay the debt. Economies that have large short-term debts are perpetually in a vulnerable situation, because they perpetually have enormous sales. The borrowers who accumulated the large stock of that asset presumably did so because they had a high marginal propensity to hold it. If the marginal propensities to consume are markedly higher for sellers than buyers, then the economy is fragile.

When leverage rises, asset prices rise, so borrowers are borrowing a higher percentage of a higher number. With higher leverage, borrowing is doubly boosted, so debt can skyrocket. Thus, by increasing debt, leverage can also make the economy fragile through the income redistribution mechanism. See Figure 5.

Thus, the leverage cycle I described in 2003 is shown in Figure 6 and goes like this. A long period of low volatility leads to a flatter credit surface and thus increased leverage, and laxer credit standards generally (for the same reasons). That raises asset prices and increases activity. But it also makes the economy more vulnerable, because of the double boost to new debt of higher asset prices and higher leverage. A little bit of bad news decreases everybody's valuations, and lowers prices a little. But as we saw at the outset, the most leveraged buyers will lose the highest fraction of their wealth from the price drop. They are likely to be the highest valuation/ highest marginal propensity to spend buyers, and their disappearance (or reduced purchasing power) further reduces asset prices, from the income effect discussed earlier. If the news is scary, as well as bad, the increased uncertainty steepens the credit surface and lowers leverage. Thus, asset prices drop for three reasons: the bad news; the wealth transfer away from high leverage/high valuation/high marginal propensity to spend agents; and the final drop in leverage reducing old and new buyers' demand for assets.[16] Asset prices and activity will stay low as long

14 With still greater sales, the income effect will reverse the substitution effect, and demand will be increasing. But that means there are multiple equilibria.

15 This is worked out in Yaniv Ben-Ami & John Geanakoplos, "Debt, Fragility, and Multiplicity: Thinking Outside the Edgeworth Box" (2017) Yale Working Paper.

16 Another driver of the crash is the sudden emergence of the credit default swap (CDS). CDS is a way for pessimists to leverage their short selling of the asset. For the same reason that leverage increases asset prices when buyers can leverage more, so too does increased access to leverage by the short sellers of the asset lower its price. I had not anticipated CDS in 2003, but added them to the story in 2010. See the third section of this chapter entitled "The Financial Innovation Cycle."

Figure 4: Fragile Equilibrium

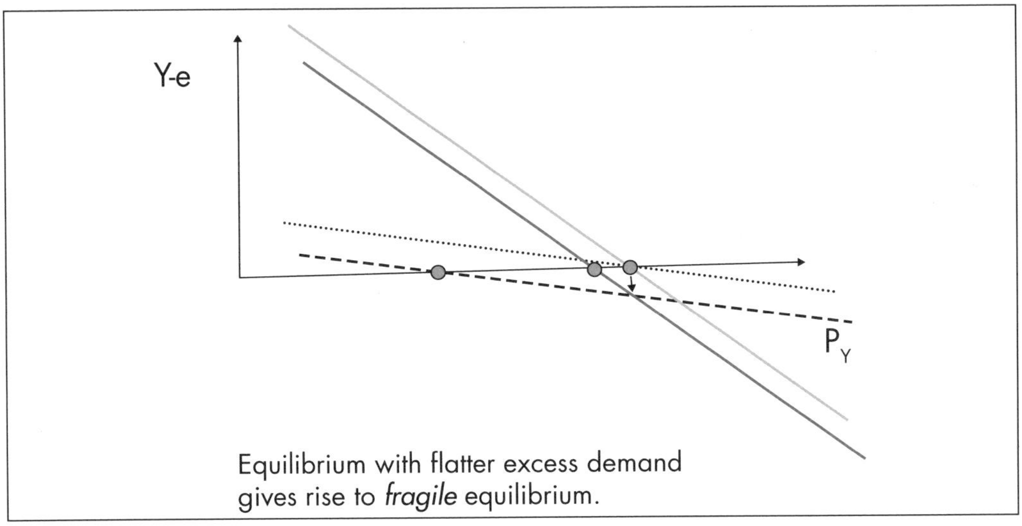

Source: Author.

Figure 5: Leverage-Debt-Fragility Mechanism

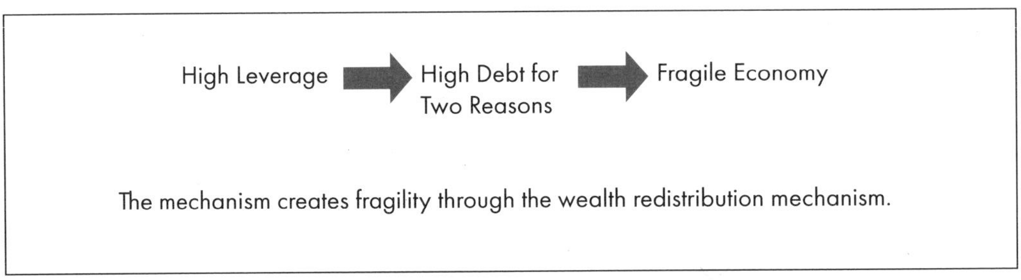

Source: Author.

Figure 6: Leverage Cycle

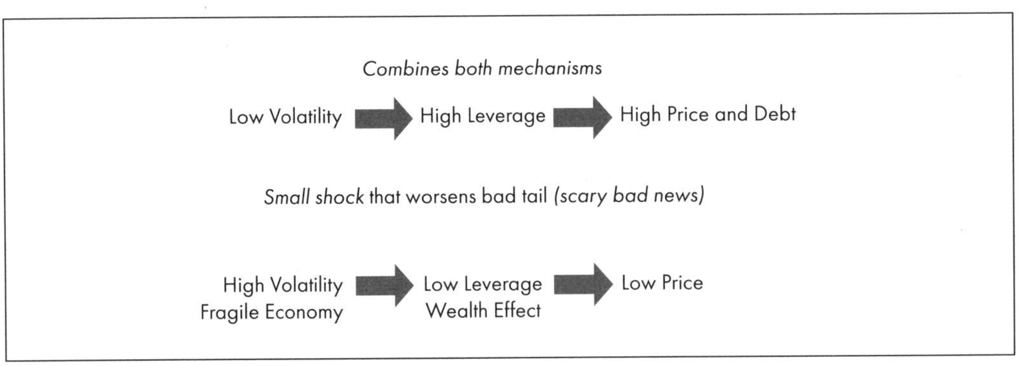

Source: Author.

Figure 7: Marginal Buyer Theory of Price

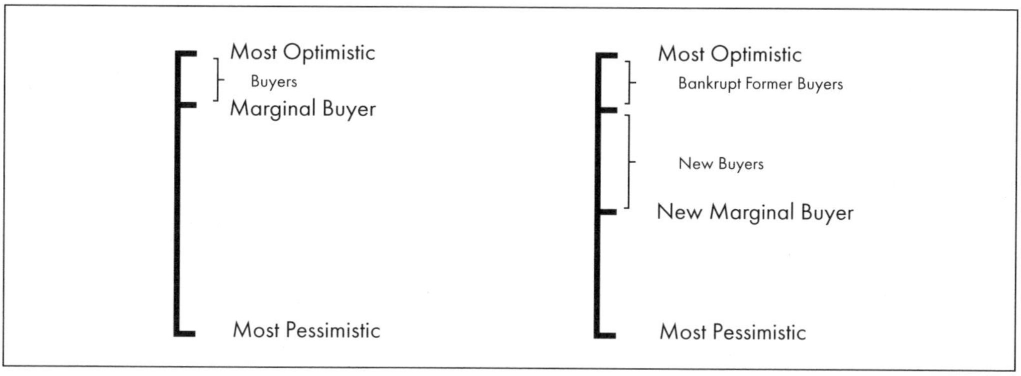

Source: Author.

as uncertainty remains high and the credit surface remains steep. And as I added in 2008, if the debt is too high relative to the lower asset prices, full repayment may become impossible. With a big enough disparity, partial forgiveness may be the only way out of the recession.

The leverage cycle can be described in another diagram that uses the idea of the marginal buyer. Suppose that we array all the agents in the economy in a vertical line according to their valuations of an asset, with the highest valuation at the top and the lowest valuation at the bottom. (For simplicity, think of a continuum of agents, each valuing the asset at a level independent of how much he buys.) The valuation heterogeneity could have many causes. Some agents might be more risk tolerant. Some might get higher utility out of holding the asset, or could use it more productively. Some might be more optimistic about the future value of the asset. The heterogeneity is important, not the source. In my 2003 paper, I assumed differences in optimism.

Whatever the asset price, some agent, whom I call the marginal buyer, will think it is fair. More optimistic agents will buy the asset and less optimistic agents will sell it. In the expansionary part of the leverage cycle, when volatility is low, leverage will be high. Fewer agents will be needed to buy the asset, since each one can buy more using borrowed funds. With fewer buyers, the marginal buyer will therefore be higher up the line, and since their valuation is equal to the price, the price will be high, as indicated in the left side of Figure 7.

When bad news comes, every agent, including the marginal buyer, will value the asset less, so the asset must fall at least a little in price. But the old buyers will be forced to sell the asset in order to pay back their loans. The initial fall in the asset price causes them to lose more wealth, especially because they are so leveraged. On the right side of Figure 7, we take an extreme case where the old buyers lose so much wealth that they can no longer buy any assets. The new marginal buyer is necessarily further down the line and more pessimistic. So the asset price falls for a second reason, caused by the loss in wealth of the original buyers.

If the news is scary, anticipated volatility will be high and leverage will drop. The new buyers will not have access to as much borrowed funds. Thus, even at a lower price, there will need to be many more buyers than previously, and the gap down from the original marginal buyer to the new marginal buyer will be very large, and bigger than the gap from the top to the original marginal buyer. The price will then reflect the valuation of a much more pessimistic buyer. The fall in price is due more to the change in marginal buyer, occasioned by the wealth losses of the optimists and the curtailment of leverage, than it is to the bad news itself.

Heterogeneity in asset valuations plays a crucial role in the leverage cycle. That is why some people leverage, and others lend, and why the price falls so much when the leveraged buyers are forced to sell.

The leverage cycle also relies critically on expectations. At the beginning, agents do not fear down risk in the near future, and so lenders extend loose collateral terms on short-term loans. Later, agents become much more worried about short-term down risk, and the collateral terms dramatically tighten.

In my 2003 and 2010 papers,[17] the heterogeneity is represented by different priors, thus infusing expectations throughout the leverage cycle. What characterizes the run-up in the model is that the risk of falling prices is low, and recognized as low by everyone, so that even the pessimistic agents can participate in the bubble stage by lending so much, while the more optimistic agents exercise disproportionate influence over prices by borrowing so much. When bad news hits and down risk increases in everyone's reckoning at the same time (scary bad news), leverage falls and after the ensuing forced sales, prices fall to reflect the views of a different and more pessimistic class of agents.

Although expectations drive the model, they need not be irrational expectations. Indeed, all the agents in my papers[18] are completely rational Bayesians, always aware of all the possible states of nature, always Bayesian updating, although they begin with different priors. There are other ways besides different priors to explain the heterogeneity, including differences in risk aversion or differences in utility for the assets, as has been demonstrated in later work.[19] Those models preserve the leverage cycle with completely rational expectations. In those models, expectations are also playing a driving role because, at the beginning, everyone rationally thinks the world is pretty safe, and then in the middle of the crisis, they think the world is very dangerous.

The leverage cycle model gets even more dramatic with extrapolative expectations.[20] Because the mathematics is simpler without the rationality hypothesis (a fixed point is replaced by a dynamical system), dropping rationality allows one to analyze a far richer environment, getting endogenous clustered volatility and so on. The essence of the leverage cycle is not rationality, but a focus on lending terms. It is the idea that in the upswing, lending terms get easier, and at the peak, and during the crisis, lending terms get more difficult. Irrational or extrapolative expectations do not contradict the leverage cycle; they can reinforce it. But they are not indispensable.

17 Geanakoplos, "Liquidity, Default and Crashes", *supra* note 1; Geanakoplos, "The Leverage Cycle", *supra* note 1.

18 *Ibid.*

19 See e.g. John Geanakoplos & Felix Kubler, "Why is Too Much Leverage Bad for the Economy?" [forthcoming Yale Working Paper].

20 See Stefan Thurner, J Doyne Farmer & John Geanakoplos, "Leverage Causes Fat Tails and Clustered Volatility" (2012) 12:5 Quantitative Finance 695.

After the crisis, a number of authors sought to explain the 2000–2006 price surge as a bubble stemming from optimistic expectations, which were then followed by pessimistic expectations. According to this view, in 2000, everybody began to think that future demand for housing was going to be high, and this persisted until 2007, when everybody began to think future demand would be low.[21] Iman Anabtawi and Steven L. Schwarcz, and Christopher L. Foote, Lara Loewenstein and Paul S. Willen pointed out that optimistic expectations would not only lead buyers to push up prices, but would also lead lenders to give out loans with more leverage, which would push prices further up.[22] By connecting (irrational) exuberance to lending, the irrational exuberance story and the leverage cycle become similar. Robert Shiller, who famously recognized the housing bubble as it was beginning,[23] advised me to interpret the leverage cycle as irrational exuberance by lenders. I am grateful to him for saying so simply what he took to be the innovation of the leverage cycle, that cycles can be driven by the changing beliefs of lenders, in addition to the animal spirits of investors.

The leverage cycle is, in spirit, the same as the irrational exuberance of lenders. But I find the leverage cycle story, with its reliance on changing expectations about volatility or uncertainty, more convincing and more aesthetically pleasing, than the irrational exuberance story about directional change (even if it includes lenders), although both could be right. There is a lot of evidence on expectations about volatility, from the volatility index and from past volatility, which is a good predictor of future volatility. There is very little evidence about directional expectations. It is just too easy to say, after the fact, that prices went up from 2000–2006 because expectations were optimisitc, and went down from 2007–2010 because expectations turned pessimistic. That applies in particular to those who think lending standards had nothing to do with either the boom or bust.[24]

---

21 See e.g. Greg Kaplan, Kurt Mitman & Giovanni L Violante, "The Housing Boom and Bust: Model Meets Evidence" (2017) National Bureau of Economic Research Working Paper No 23694.

22 Iman Anabtawi & Steven L Schwarcz, "Regulating Systemic Risk: Towards an Analytical Framework" (2011) 86:4 Notre Dame L Rev; Christopher L Foote, Lara Loewenstein & Paul S Willen, "Cross-Sectional Patterns of Mortgage Debt during the Housing Boom: Evidence and Implications" (2016) Federal Reserve Bank of Boston Working Paper No 16-12.

23 Robert Shiller, *Irrational Exuberance* (Princeton, NJ: Princeton University Press, 2000).

24 Kaplan, Mitman & Violante, *supra* note 21, take a more extreme view that changing expectations from 2000 to 2007 about future housing demand caused the boom and the crash, and yet that changing lending standards played absolutely no role in moving housing prices. The reason they give for the latter is that homeowners could always rent instead. In their view, borrowing constraints do not affect the total demand for housing, but merely redirect it from owning, which requires borrowing, to renting, which does not. Although Kaplan, Mitman and Violante's story is very interesting, I find it far-fetched. First, it takes an unprecedented shift in expectations alone to justify a 90 percent increase in housing prices in six and a half years from 2000 to 2006, as measured in the Corelogic Case-Shiller housing index. From where did this change in outlook come? Interest rates are fixed in Kaplan, Mitman and Violante's model, so those don't explain the change. At the same time, they must assume a simultaneous and completely exogenous shift in credit standards. How convenient that these two happened at exactly the right time, and together. By contrast, there had been years of stability leading up to the 2000s — which not even a foreign attack on American soil could shake — that led people to call it the Great Moderation. There is no mystery as to why people might have rationally believed in the 2000s that down risk was lower (without thinking that things were going to rapidly improve). In the leverage cycle, the volatility assumption endogenously leads to laxer credit conditions, which in turn endogenously produce price appreciation. Shiller might argue that the Greenspan-Fed drop in interest rates in the early 2000s caused housing prices to go up, and that extrapolative expectations kept pushing them further. That could also happen in a more sophisticated model of dynamic expectation revision, as in Pedro Bordalo, Nicola Gennaioli & Andrei Shleifer, "Diagnostic Expectations and Credit Cycles" (2018) 73:1 J Finance 199. But they recognize the importance of expectations on credit conditions as a channel for affecting asset prices. Second, although Kaplan, Mitman and Violante incorporate changing credit conditions into their model, their "proof" that credit terms do not influence housing prices depends on the ability of entrepreneurs to convert owner-occupied housing to rental housing at low cost. It also requires the use value of home ownership to be not much greater than the use value of home rentals. Finally, and most importantly, their paper ignores, by assumption, the obvious heterogeneity in the population. If some agents are more optimistic than others, they will prefer to buy rather than rent, and as credit conditions ease, they will want to spend still more on buying. Their total demand for housing will depend very much on credit conditions.

The leverage cycle crash is related to so-called fire sales. For a good account of the important literature on fire sales, see Andrei Shleifer and Robert Vishny.[25] There are, however, several differences. The most important is that the leverage cycle injects the critical element of varying and endogenous leverage. The fire sale literature misses the over-valuation and buildup of debt due to the soaring leverage, and the sudden transition from high leverage to low leverage, which play a vital role in all crashes. It also misses the aftermath, during which the credit surface is still steep and new borrowing remains low. The fire sales literature addresses part of the middle game, without discussing the opening or the endgame. The more recent fire sales literature uses terms such as "deleveraging," without actually endogenizing asset leverage. It does, however, include the idea of heterogeneous buyers and the loss in price when high-valuation buyers are forced to sell to low-valuation buyers.[26]

The 2007–2009 Crisis

The crisis of 2007–2009 did not happen out of the blue. There was a long period of increasing leverage and rising asset prices. Moreover, the crisis itself was not an overnight panic, like one sees in bank runs.[27] It lasted for at least three years,[28] and the aftermath carried on for many years after that, despite the most extraordinary central bank interventions in history.

Figure 8 illustrates the rise and fall in LTV over time on a portfolio of AAA floating rate MBS that Ellington Capital Management has followed since 1998, superimposed on an index of prices for similar securities kept by Morgan Stanley. As can be seen, LTV was around 90 percent in the late 1990s, then jumped down to 60 percent for a few months in the 1998 crisis, then returned to its previous level for seven years. Around 2005, it went up to 95 percent. But as scary bad news came out about subprime securities in 2007, leverage came down and the asset prices came down. And then they both went up together. This diagram first appeared in my 2010 paper, with data through 2009.[29]

At the end of 2007 and all through 2008, mortgage securities holders were going bankrupt every month. A website called ml-implode.com posted the names of the casualties as they happened. The biggest names were Countrywide, Bear Stearns, Merrill and Lehman Brothers, who were each leveraged more than 30 to one, but the list includes dozens of other names. As these companies failed, the mortgage securities inevitably ended up in the hands of agents who had not valued them as highly, consistent with the marginal buyer version of the leverage cycle.

A similar leverage story can be seen in the housing market. Figure 9 shows the Case-Shiller housing index, which rises by 90 percent from 2000 to the third quarter of 2006, then drops 30 percent after the crisis begins. Superimposed is the graph of average LTV for the top half

25 Andrei Shleifer & Robert W Vishny, "Fire Sales in Finance and Microeconomics" (2011) 25:1 J Economic Perspectives 29.

26 More subtly, the fire sales literature conflates valuation with marginal propensity to spend out of income, although to be sure the two often go hand in hand, as when there are linear utilities.

27 To be sure, the collapse of Lehman Brothers almost a year and a half into the crisis, in September 2008, made things a lot worse. But the crisis was vastly more than the Lehman story. And even the Lehman collapse itself was not obviously a panic rather than a margin call. Ben Bernanke excused himself from not bailing out Lehman by testifying that Lehman was insolvent, and not in a bank run.

28 The stock market was 33 percent lower in June 2010 than it had been in May 2005, and unemployment was up to 9.4 percent in June 2010 compared to 4.4 percent in May 2007.

29 Gary Gorton & Andrew Metrick, "Securitized Banking and the Run on Repo" (2012) 104:3 J Financial Economics 425 also documented the rise in repo margins during the crisis; Geanakoplos, "The Leverage Cycle", *supra* note 1.

Figure 8: Leverage and Mortgage Securities Pricing

Source: Ellington Management Group.

Figure 9: Housing Leverage Cycle

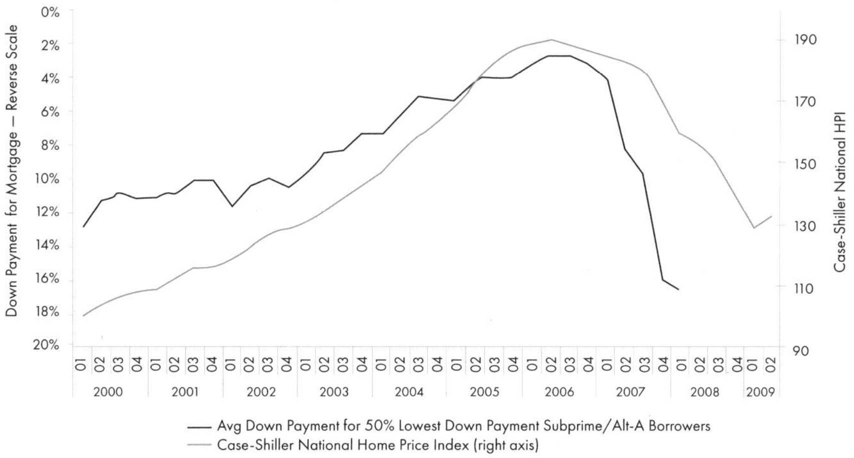

Observe that the down payment axis has been reversed, because lower down payment requirements are correlated with higher home prices.

Note: For every Alt-A or subprime first loan originated from Q1 2000 to Q1 2008, down payment percentage was calculated as appraised value (or sale price if available) minus total mortgage debt, divided by appraised value. For each quarter, the down payment percentages were ranked from highest to lowest, and the average of the bottom half of the list is shown in the diagram. This number is an indicator of down payment required: clearly many homeowners put down more than they had to, and that is why the top half is dropped from the average.
A 13 percent down payment in Q1 2000 corresponds to leverage of about 7.7, and a 2.7 percent down payment in Q2 2006 corresponds to leverage of about 37.

Note subprime/Alt-A issuance stopped in Q1 2008.

Source: Ellington Management Group.

(ranked in order of leverage) of all Alt-A and subprime non-government loans. It starts with margins at 14 percent in 2000, and goes to margins of 2.7 percent in the same quarter as housing markets hit their peak. Afterward, housing and leverage fall together.[30]

By any measure, volatility was low in the period preceding the crisis of 2007–2009. Indeed, Ben Bernanke dubbed the period "The Great Moderation."[31] Volatility soared during the crisis, and then eventually subsided, all in parallel to the changes in leverage and asset prices. All that remains is to describe the scary bad news that triggered the crisis.

Many people suggest the drop in housing prices caused the crisis. But that raises the question of what caused the drop in housing prices. It is easy to see why housing prices might have stopped going up in 2006. Leverage stopped going up because it could not go higher. LTV has a natural upper bound at 100 percent if there is little penalty for default. (Subprime borrowers have low ratings, and so the credit score loss of defaulting is not as high.) By 2006, the average LTV for the top half was already 97.3 percent, meaning that a lot of them were close to 100 percent. And many of these were negative amortizing loans that really should be counted as higher LTVs. But even if housing prices couldn't go higher, that still leaves the question: why did they fall?

In my opinion, the trigger to the crisis was the increase in subprime delinquencies. For many consecutive vintages of Countrywide loans, the percentage of original balance that were currently delinquent would slowly rise from zero percent at origination to about two percent and stay there. But in Figure 10 we see that by the beginning of 2007 the delinquency rate for

30 In Manuel Adelino, Antoinette Schoar & Felipe Severino, "The Role of Housing and Mortgage Markets in the Financial Crisis" (2018) 10 Annual Rev Economics 25, the authors argued that housing mortgage leverage did not rise leading up to the crisis, or fall afterward. They announce the surprising nature of their findings as "contrary to popular beliefs," including of most of Wall Street. Let me mention several ways in which their interpretation of the data strikes me as wrong. First, Adelino, Schoar and Severino acknowledge that DTI rose dramatically leading up to the crisis, as emphasized by Daniel Greenwald, "The Mortgage Credit Channel of Macroeconomic Transmission" (2018) MIT Sloan Working Paper No 5184-16. So credit terms manifestly became looser. The credit surface is multidimensional, as I mentioned at the outset, and as I shall emphasize more in the next section. LTV is not a standalone variable. Inverting the credit surface and writing LTV as a function of interest rate and other credit terms, such as DTI and FICO, the LTV surface got looser according to their own analysis. Second, LTV is a subtler measure when talking about a long-term loan (such as a mortgage) as opposed to a short-term loan (such as a repo). With a more appropriate measure of LTV, they would have found a big rise during the mid-2000s. Laurie Goodman, "Housing Credit Availability Index" (2019) Urban Institute, online: <www.urban.org/policy-centers/housing-finance-policy-center/projects/housing-credit-availability-index> constructs a risk index of mortgages and finds that it rose substantially in the mid 2000s. The mid-2000s were famous for introducing riskier mortgages, such as interest-only mortgages, negative amortizing mortgages and floating rate mortgages (whose initial interest is lower, especially with teaser rates for the first two or three years). These became 30 to 40 percent of all the originations in that time period. They defaulted much more frequently in the crisis than conventional mortgages with comparable borrowers. The reason these mortgages are regarded as riskier is that the borrowers pay less over the early years of the mortgage. Mortgage default is much more likely on a day in the third year than on the very first day. The mortgage payments through the third year are a smaller fraction of the original debt with the riskier mortgage. A measure of LTV that corresponds to the scheduled LTV in the third year (assuming stable housing prices) would have risen in the mid-2000s. Third, Adelino, Schoar and Severino focus their attention on new mortgages. But of course mortgage refinancing, especially cash-out refinancing, was notorious for higher LTVs during the mid-2000s, in part because the appraisal value used in the LTV calculation was widely viewed, even at the time, as inflated. It is simply not true that LTV on refinanced loans does not affect housing prices. Homeowners in need of cash can sell their homes, but if they can borrow more without selling, then the homes do not go on the market. An important reason housing prices fell rapidly during the crisis is that homeowners could not refinance their loans and were forced to sell. Fourth, and most importantly, by their own measures, Adelino, Schoar and Severino show that private lending standards, including LTV, did indeed get looser in the run-up to the crisis of 2007–2009, consistent with the diagram in Figure 9 ("Housing Leverage Cycle"). Adelino, Schoar and Severino say that the looser private standards were compensated by stricter government lending during the same time. (By "government," they do not mean Fannie and Freddie, who themselves were delving for the first time into subprime-like loans, but rather Federal Housing Administration loans.) They lose track of this distinction when later they emphatically declare that lenders did not change their LTV standards. The economy is much more vulnerable when the private sector is holding high LTV loans and the government is holding low LTV loans than it is in the reverse situation.

31 Ben Bernanke, "The Great Moderation" (Speech delivered at the meetings of the Eastern Economic Association, Washington, DC, 20 February 2004), online: <www.federalreserve.gov/boarddocs/speeches/2004/20040220/>.

Figure 10: Scary Bad News

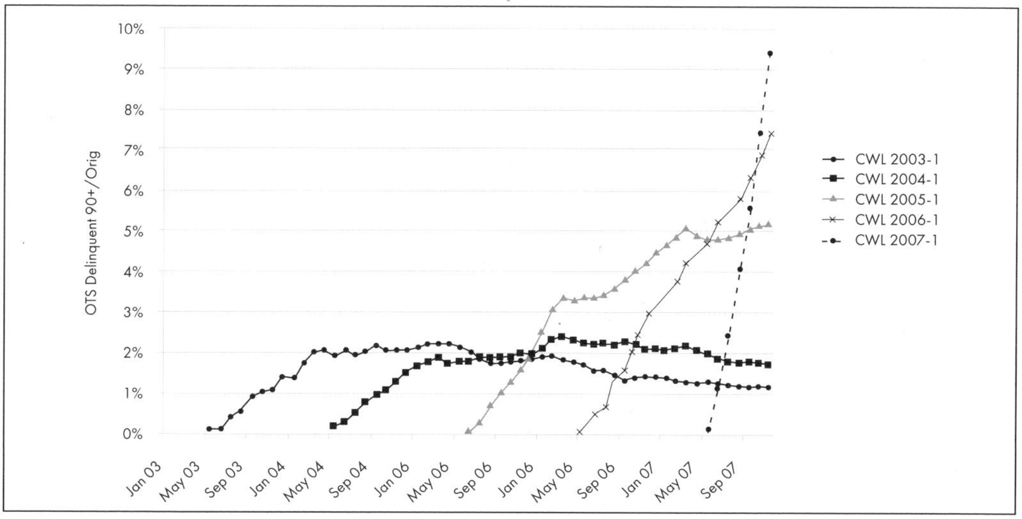

Source: Ellington Management Group.

2005 vintage loans had already reached four percent, and the delinquency rate for 2006 vintage loans had already reached three percent.

These are tiny numbers, but the fact they had broken through the old two percent threshold caused investors to worry that the number might go much higher. The down risk was much greater. Traditional macroeconomists would expect the prices of these loans to go down, and indeed the BBB subprime bond index collapsed in early 2007. I identified that, at the time, as the beginning of the down phase of the leverage cycle.[32]

But more importantly, lenders did not just increase the interest rate they charged on new subprime loans. They increased the margins, as can be seen in Figure 9. These higher down payments closed a large number of potential buyers out of the housing market, and (in my opinion) that led to the fall in housing prices.

The global financial crisis of 2007–2009 was the culmination of a double leverage cycle, in mortgages and in mortgage securities. George Soros's principle of reflexivity includes the proposition that historical crashes invariably involve disasters in two separate but interrelated markets.[33] Although Soros didn't apply this insight to housing and mortgage securities, the mortgage crisis fits. Leverage rose in housing and in mortgage securities together. Trouble with mortgage delinquencies depressed mortgage securities prices, which led to cutbacks in housing leverage, which depressed housing prices, which indicated future default losses, which reduced mortgage security prices.

32 See video of Geanakoplos talk on the Leverage Cycle at Santa Fe Institute, March 2007.

33 George Soros, *The Crash of 2008 and What it Means: The New Paradigm for Financial Markets* (New York: Public Affairs, 2009).

The Financial Innovation Cycle

Half a century ago, more and more goods became usable as collateral for leveraging. Thirty years ago, securitization and tranching, especially of mortgage-backed securities, emerged and grew dramatically. Finally, over the last 10 to 15 years, the credit default swap (CDS) mortgage market suddenly blossomed at the end of the securitization boom. After the crisis of 2007–2009, the complexity of these instruments declined, but is now on the rise again.

In Fostel-Geanakoplos,[34] we argued that there is a financial innovation cycle that follows and boosts the leverage cycle. The financial innovation cycle made the crash of 2007–2009 bigger than it would have been otherwise.

In periods of quiet, financiers innovate to stretch the available collateral. When a single asset can be used to collateralize multiple loans, it is stretched. When collateral backs promises that are in turn used as collateral to back further promises, which I call pyramiding, the original collateral is effectively reused and thus stretched. Leverage can be thought of as buying an asset while simultaneously borrowing. But it can equally be thought of as a way of cutting the collateral into two pieces: a bond and a risky junior piece. Cutting the bond into still more pieces, which involves pyramiding and tranching, is a more advanced financial innovation, requiring more complex record keeping, a more sophisticated court system and accomodating tax laws. By skillfully cutting the collateral into appropriate pieces, entrepreneurs can sell the pieces for more than the original collateral. Competition then bids the whole collateral price up to the sum of its parts. The search for profits from scarce collateral through financial innovation makes collateral more valuable, over and above its payoff value. Leverage raises the prices of assets, and tranching raises their prices still more. And they rise higher because the financial innovation comes in stages, not all at once. Once the prices get high enough — which, unfortunately, is the moment when the indebted economy is becoming especially vulnerable — another financial innovation, the CDS, is introduced. It enables the pessimists to bet against the asset. This tends to lower asset prices. A little bit of bad news can then lead to a great crash.

CDSs tend to lower asset prices because they lure optimists, who would have bought the assets on leverage, into selling the CDS insurance instead, where they are making a similar bet that assets can only go up in price. They make the crash just as bad because when prices do fall, the optimists must pay out on the insurance and the wealth effect kicks in, just as they would have lost money as forced sellers of the assets had they bought them on leverage.

The run-up to the crisis of 2007–2009 fits the pattern of the financial innovation cycle perfectly. Throughout the later 1990s and 2000s, higher LTV loans, known as subprime loans, began to be initiated by the private sector. These, in turn, were collected into pools, which were then tranched. The subprime market grew from almost nothing in 1990 to more than $1 trillion in 2006. Housing prices skyrocketed from 2000 to 2006. At the end of 2005, a small group of investors who thought housing prices and mortgages were overvalued pushed to get the indexed subprime mortgage CDS market established so they could bet against the subprime mortgages. The CDS/collateralized debt obligation market got even bigger than the subprime

34 Ana Fostel & John Geanakoplos, "Endogenous Collateral Constraints and the Leverage Cycle" (2014) 6:1 Annual Rev Economics 771.

market (although they were betting on subprime loans). The indices stayed high for about 11 months, but then cracked at the end of 2006 on the release of delinquency reports for subprime mortgages. The housing market tumbled soon afterward. Had the CDS been trading robustly from the beginning, prices might not have gotten so high.[35]

Multiple Leverage Cycles

Many kinds of collateral exist at the same time, hence there can be many simultaneous leverage cycles. Each one has its own credit surface. Collateral equilibrium theory not only explains how one leverage cycle might evolve over time, but also explains some commonly observed cross-sectional differences and linkages between cycles in different asset classes, like flight to collateral and contagion.[36]

It is commonly observed that in times of crisis some assets retain their value (or even rise in value) while the others lose value. This situation is often called a flight to safety. Another way to describe the situation is a flight to collateral. The safe assets, those with low volatility, turn out to be the assets that can be leveraged more.[37]

A second commonly observed phenomenon is that when bad news hits one asset class, the resulting fall in its price seems to migrate to other assets, even if their payoffs are statistically independent from the original crashing asset. There are two reasons for this contagion. As we saw in the first section of this chapter, the leverage cycle in one asset amplifies the bad news and creates wealth distribution away from the most optimistic buyers of the asset. If these buyers are also crossover holders of a second asset, their losses in the first asset might force them to raise money by selling the second asset. Moreover, the leverage cycle price decline in the first asset will make these buyers feel there is a special opportunity there, leading them to withdraw even more money from the second asset to take advantage. These two reasons to withdraw demand for the second asset lead to price declines there.

The Credit Terms Cycle and Central Bank Policy

The policy implications of the leverage cycle are that central banks should smooth the cycle, restraining leverage in booms, and in the acute stage of the crisis, propping up leverage. If, in the aftermath, depressed asset prices are too low relative to debts, debt must be partially forgiven.

As I mentioned at the outset, leverage is just one of many terms that come with loans, beside the interest rate. In boom times, many credit terms get relaxed, not just leverage. It is important to keep track of all of them. The general credit surface is the loan interest rate as a function of

35 A similar story unfolded with Greek sovereign debt. After Greece gained entry into the European Monetary Union in 2000, it was able to borrow more money. Eventually Greek banks were buying Greek sovereign bonds, at very high LTV, since the capital requirements for sovereign debt were so low. As the ratio of debt to Greek GDP rose, investors became more jittery. When the Greek crisis started just after the revision of Greek deficit numbers, Prime Minister George Papandreou blamed it all on the CDS market. In Galina Hale et al, "How Futures Trading Changed Bitcoin Prices" (2018) FRBSF Economic Letter, Federal Reserve Bank of San Francisco, the authors similarly describe the exponential rise of bitcoin prices and the subsequent crash as a result of financial innovation.

36 In this section, I follow Ana Fostel & John Geanakoplos, "Leverage Cycles and the Anxious Economy" (2008) 98:4 American Economics Rev 1211.

37 In the language of Fostel and Geanakoplos (*ibid*), they have more collateral value.

its various terms, including LTV, DTI, FICO (or credit score), and, of course, maturity. Not all of these terms can be displayed easily in the same picture. By picking any two credit terms, such as LTV and FICO, the Washington Federal Reserve has worked with me to produce credit surfaces such as the following.[38]

Figure 11 shows the average interest rate charged on all fixed rate mortgage loans from the Federal National Mortgage Assocation (Fannie Mae) and the Federal Home Loan Mortgage Corporation (Freddie Mac) in the second quarter of 2006 as a function of LTV and FICO. Loans with the highest FICO and lowest LTV, in the bottom left corner, are the safest loans. Loans with the highest LTV and lowest FICO, in the upper right corner, are the riskiest loans. Even for the conforming group of households who passed many hurdles to get into the government programs, there is a difference in interest rate depending on credit standards. But the curve is generally quite flat, indicating a loose credit surface.

Consider in Figure 12 the mortgage credit surface in the last quarter of 2008, after the crisis had started. It is much steeper, and the number of low FICO, high LTV loans is much lower.

In Figure 13 we see the corporate bond credit surface for 2007.[39] As it was for mortgages in 2006, the corporate bond credit surface is very flat.

As shown in Figure 14, in the fourth quarter of 2008, the credit surface became markedly steeper, making it much more difficult to borrow. The reader should be aware that the credit surfaces do not always move in tandem. Today, for example, the corporate credit surface has again become very flat, but the mortgage credit surface has not. These differences should be taken into account by the Fed in its deliberations.

In my opinion, the Fed should produce these credit surface images for the general public each quarter. They should also be produced for the unsecured consumer loan credit surface and other surfaces, including the mortgage credit surface and the corporate bond credit surface. This will give economists and business people a much better picture of credit conditions in the economy.

The Fed should also be aware of how its changes in the riskless rate (in the bottom left corner) affect the whole credit surface of each type. Perhaps they move every credit surface rigidly upward or downward, or perhaps the risky end of the credit surface moves less than the safer end, blunting much of the power of conventional monetary policy.[40] Do risky asset purchases (called quantitative easing) by the Federal Reserve have similar effects or are they better at tilting the credit surfaces? In my opinion, the Federal Reserve should use the language of the various credit surfaces to explain their policy aspirations. Do they hope to shift or steepen the mortgage credit surface or the corporate credit surface?

---

38 See Geanakoplos, "The Credit Surface", *supra* note 7. See also John Geanakoplos & David E Rappoport W, "Credit Surfaces, Economic Activity, and Monetary Policy" (2019) SSRN, online: <https://papers.ssrn.com/sol3/papers.cfm?abstract_id=3428729>.

39 There are complications in presenting simple interest rates for different bonds at different times if, for example, some of the bonds are callable and others are not. For corporate bonds, we replace the interest rate with something called the option adjusted spread, which adjusts for the option value of the bonds. I do not have space to go into these details here, but I refer the reader to Geanakoplos & Rappoport (*ibid*).

40 We analyze this question in Geanakoplos & Rappoport, *supra* note 38.

Figure 11: 2006Q2, 30-year Conventional Purchase Mortgages

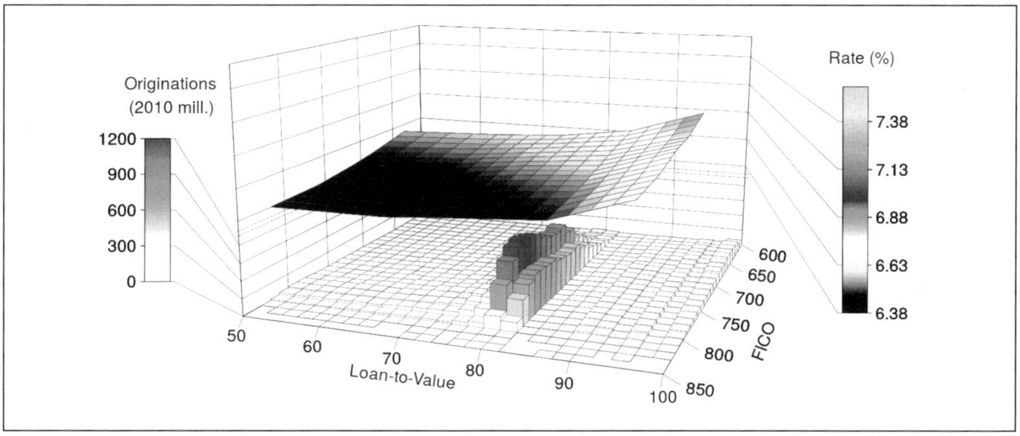

Source: Geanakoplos & Rappoport, *supra* note 38.

Figure 12: 2008Q4, 30-year Conventional Purchase Mortgages

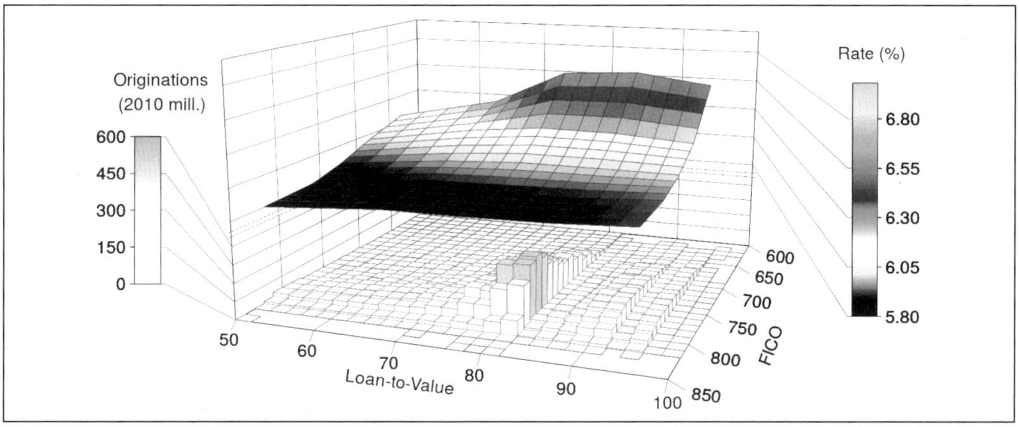

Source: Geanakoplos & Rappoport, *supra* note 38.

Figure 13: 2007Q2, 7- to 10-year Corporate Bonds

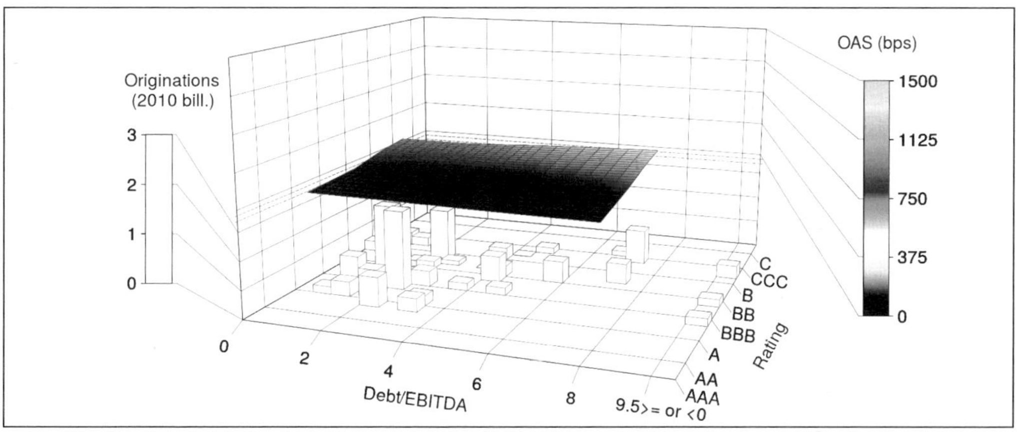

Source: Geanakoplos & Rappoport, *supra* note 38.

Figure 14: 2008Q4, 7- to 10-year Corporate Bonds

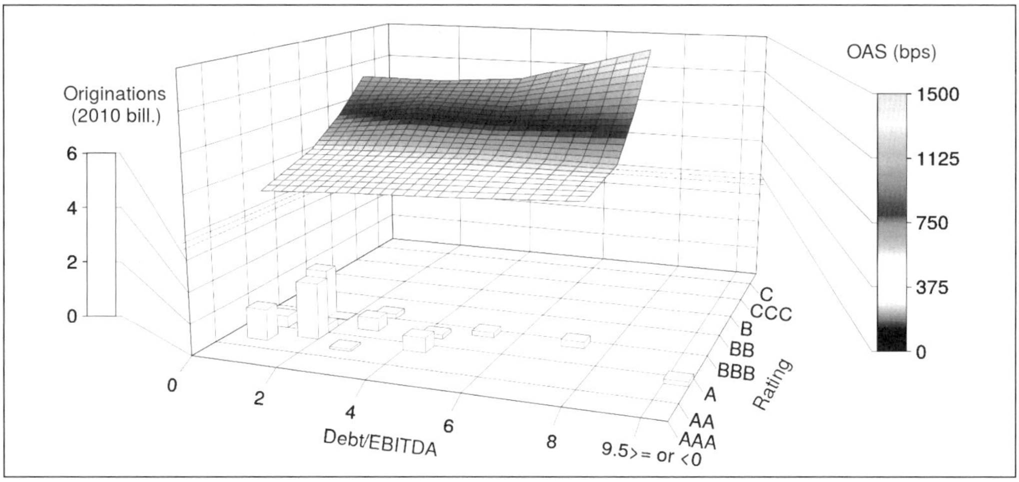

Source: Geanakoplos & Rappoport, *supra* note 38.

Finally, if there are parts of some credit surface they wish to affect, then they should use unconventional tools to target those areas. For example, at the current time, the mortgage credit surface is still very unkind to borrowers with a low to medium FICO. If the Fed wanted, it could purchase loans of that type, which would bring down their rates. If the Fed thought that housing prices were rising too rapidly, it might declare, as Stanley Fischer did in 2010 as head of the Bank of Israel, that no mortgage loans could be issued with more than 60 percent LTV.[41]

Forgiveness

In 2008 and 2009, Susan Koniak and I wrote two op-eds in *The New York Times* advocating partial forgiveness for subprime loans.[42] We argued that once homeowners with bad credit ratings fell far enough under water, they were likely to default on their loans, and that lenders who insisted on receiving full satisfaction would wind up with less money in the end than if they forgave some of the debt. We went on to predict that subprime debt would not be forgiven because the loans were all securitized in pools controlled by servicers who had no incentive to write down principal during a crisis. The bondholders, who ultimately receive all the cash flows and might have an incentive to forgive, did not know the names of the homeowners or the identities of the other bondholders, and did not have the legal right to modify the loans anyway. I testified two times in Congress about these matters, and 17 hedge funds also testified that they would like to partially forgive the subprime debt that paid their bonds.

The example Susan Koniak and I gave in favour of forgiveness was of a $160,000 subprime loan, backed by a house that had fallen in value to $100,000. Why should a homeowner, who did not

41 There is some doubt about whether the Federal Reserve has such powers, since it has not exercised them. It certainly does have the power to regulate margins on stocks.

42 Geanakoplos & Koniak, *supra* note 2. A fuller discussion appears in John Geanakoplos, "Solving the Present Crisis and Managing the Leverage Cycle" (2010) Federal Reserve Bank of New York Economic Policy Rev 101 [Geanakoplos, "Solving the Present Crisis"].

have a good credit rating to protect, pay 60 percent more than the house was worth, when he could walk away with no penalty? Foreclosing when the homeowner stopped paying turned out to be even worse than we predicted. The average subprime mortgage foreclosure recovered about 25 percent of the principal, which in our example would have been $40,000. The reason, as we argued, is that it can take two or three years to get the foreclosed homeowner out of his house, during which time he does not pay his mortgage, or pay his house taxes, or fix his house. And on the way out he might take all the copper. By partially forgiving the loan down to $90,000, the lender likely would have gotten the whole $90,000, either because the homeowner would keep paying his coupon (lowered by the principal reduction), or because he would sell the house for the profit of $10,000 and pay off the whole loan. On top of that, we added a clause that if housing values miraculously turned around and the homeowner sold the house for more than $100,000, then half the appreciation would be owed to the lenders, up to the point where the original loan was made whole.

Our recommendation was that all the significantly underwater loans in non-agency pools should be sent to community bankers hired by the government (so the New Haven loans would go to a New Haven banker, the Boston loans to a Boston banker, and so on). The banker's job would be to modify the loans they made in the way that would make the most money for the lender. We predicted that the community bankers, acting in the interest of the lender, would often choose principal reduction in cases like our example. The original servicer would continue to pass the modified homeowner payments on to the bondholders and continue to receive its fees. Of course the plan would have required an act of Congress to negate the original (failing) contracts that set up the pools. The plan was meant to solve the coordination problem of the bond holders who under the circumstances could not possibly negotiate their way into a Pareto improvement. Congress did not act.

There were many reasons given by the Obama administration and Treasury Secretary Geithner for not creating some kind of forgiveness plan for underwater homeowners. One argument was that it was too complicated. Another was a political concern that the prudent folks who didn't take large loans would resent a plan that "rewarded" reckless homeowners who took high LTV loans and subsequently found themselves under water. Finally there was a vague sense that principal forgiveness creates a moral hazard.

I have attempted elsewhere[43] to rebut each of these arguments, and there is not room here to repeat those rebuttals in detail. Let me mention simply that the burden of forgiveness was to be borne entirely by the (hedge fund) lenders who owned the loans, not by the government or taxpayers. It would have been up to the administration to explain that although your neighbour would receive a principal reduction and you would not, you would not personally lose anything. And the house next door would have stayed occupied and tended, rather than becoming a blight on your neighbourhood.

As for the moral hazard, the administration instead implemented coupon reductions for homeowners who stopped paying, once they proved that they had suffered some hardship, such as losing their jobs. The government coupon reduction plan created a direct moral hazard, since one had to stop payment in order to become eligible. The results of government programs to

43 Geanakoplos, "Solving the Present Crisis", *supra* note 42.

Figure 15: Subprime Cumulative Recidivism by Coupon and Months Since Modification

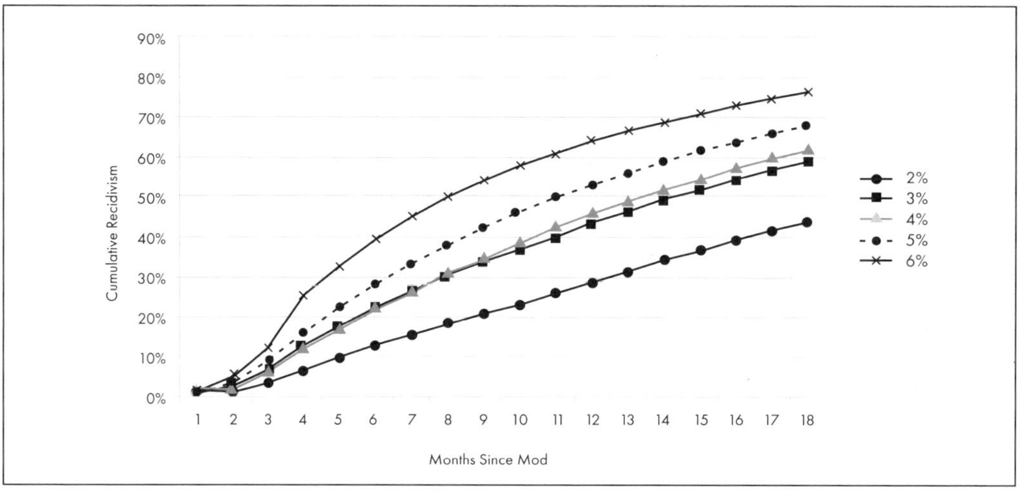

Source: Ellington Management Group.

Figure 16: Net Monthly Flow (Excluding Mods) from <60 Days to >60 Days DQ

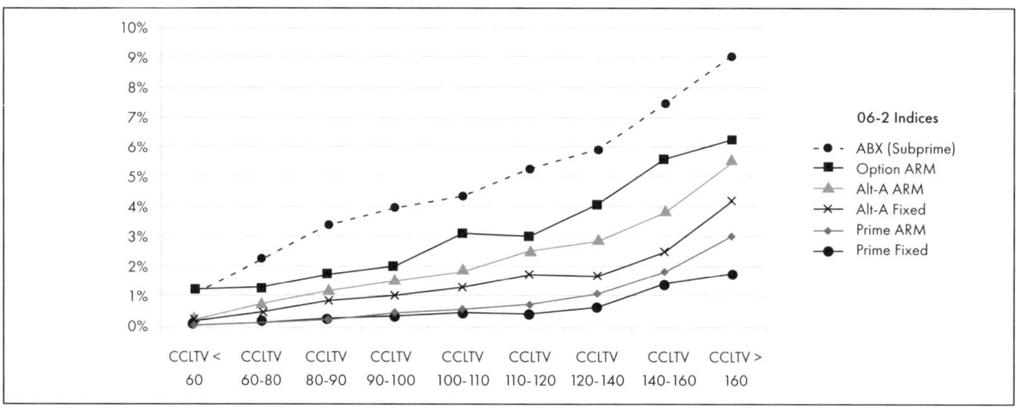

Source: Ellington Management Group.

reduce coupon rates were not good for subprime mortgages. Recidivism was high, as shown in Figure 15.

By contrast, we proposed principal forgiveness for subprime borrowers based on being far enough under water, especially if they were current, on the grounds that they would eventually default. At the time of the op-eds, it certainly seemed likely that most would eventually default. Figure 16 gives the monthly rates of new delinquencies. Subprime loans with combined current LTV of 140 to 160 percent were defaulting at six percent per *month*.

Reducing principal for seriously underwater homeowners, independent of whether they are delinquent, creates no moral hazard incentive to stop coupon payments.[44] Our plan was

44 It might create an incentive to take out bigger loans. To the extent that higher leverage raises home prices and makes the economy more vulnerable, the practice of writing down principal makes leverage constraints more important.

analogous to Robert Shiller's proposal that mortgage principal be written down automatically, as a matter of contract, depending on how far the local housing index falls. Since no homeowner can control the housing index, there is no moral hazard. The biggest difference is that we targeted the forgiveness to subprime borrowers and others who had bad credit ratings.

The most serious objection to principal writedowns was articulated by Lawrence Summers, former Secretary of the Treasury, at the time, and repeated often since the crisis. He felt that by writing down grossly underwater mortgages before they defaulted, the lenders might lose money on borrowers who would have paid back the entire principal in the end, even though they were underwater. Of course, such a concern could be raised at any time, not just in the middle of a crisis when the servicers are confronted with unusual incentives not to write down loans. If lenders were often willing to write down principal before and after the crisis, but not during the crisis, it suggests that principal reduction is, after all, an important tool, and that a great opportunity might have been missed during the crisis because of the perverse incentives of servicers in the crisis.[45] Figure 17 shows that principal reductions were indeed a much smaller portion of modifications during the crisis than they were before and after.[46]

Ten years later, scholars are trying to assess whether forgiveness might have worked. A consensus is emerging that, because of the enormous costs to foreclosures during a crisis, timely interventions starting in 2008 could have helped homeowners and lenders, but too little was done, too late.

On the more specific question of whether payment reductions or principal reductions would have been better, the preliminary assessments appear to be coming down on the side of Summers against principal forgiveness.[47] But I am skeptical. The forgiveness plans contemplated in these studies are not targeted. They casually suggest that because only eight percent of homeowners ultimately stopped paying, while a lot more were delinquent or underwater, principal forgiveness would have lost too much money from those who were ultimately going to pay. None of these scholars makes a loan-by-loan analysis of all the affected loans. None asks: what if we just targeted deeply underwater loans, or deeply underwater loans of people who have poor credit ratings, as Susan Koniak and I suggested in 2008.

Table 1 bears out what was suggested in Figure 16, that most deeply underwater subprime borrowers went into foreclosure. So losses from forgiving subprime borrowers who would

45 The crisis saw a flood of underwater homeowners, and the servicer staffs were too small to look into all of them at once. Hiring new staff would have been an enormous expense that would bring no return to the servicer (although it might have helped the bondholders). Second, after many bankruptcies, the servicers nearly all became owned by the biggest banks. These banks owned large amounts of second loans. If they reduced principal on large amounts of first loans (loans that they did not own), pressure would have built to start writing down second loans to zero, which would have represented a huge loss. Third, by doing nothing, the servicers ran less legal risk than they would have by taking radical steps. There is also a crucial reason why banks that directly owned loans virtually stopped writing down principal during the crisis. Writing down a loan requires taking an immediate loss. If the bank does not write down the principal, it may be able to hold the loan on its books at par (for example, if it has not yet defaulted), even though it knows that eventually the loan will default with some probability, at a higher expected loss than the forgiveness loss. In a crisis, banks near bankruptcy themselves are eager to avoid taking losses.

46 Some of the principal modifications after the crisis were forced on the banks by government penalties for the banks' handling of mortgages leading up to the crisis. The penalties were paid in principal forgiveness to underwater homeowners.

47 See e.g. Peter Ganong & Pascal Noel, "Liquidity vs. Wealth in Household Debt Obligations: Evidence from Housing Policy in the Great Recession" (2018) National Bureau of Economic Research Working Paper No 24964. For a summary of many of these studies, see Christopher L Foote & Paul S Willen, "Mortgage-Default Research and the Recent Foreclosure Crisis" (2018) 10:59-100 Annual Rev Financial Economics.

Figure 17: Non-Agency Modification Rates

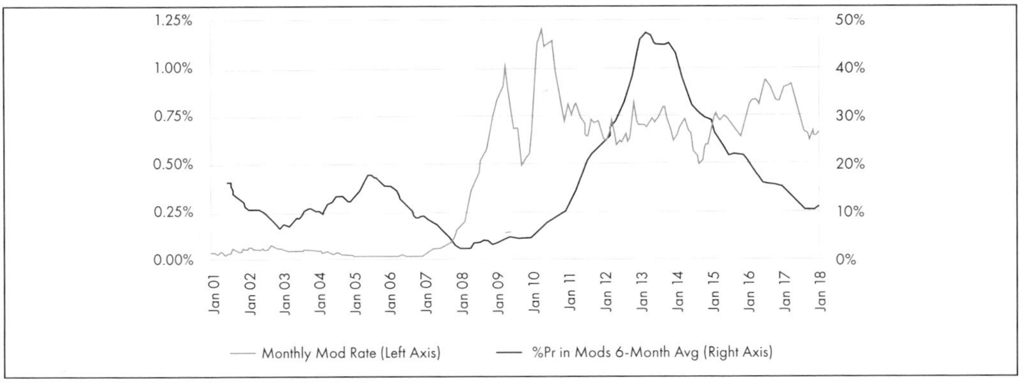

Source: Ellington analysis using data from Loan Performance and CoreLogic. Data as of August 2018.

Table 1: Defaults and Losses from Securitized Subprime Loans Active on January 1, 2008

LTV					Defaults as % of	
Subprime	Vintage	Bucket	# of Loans	Originated UPB	UPB	Losses
	2005	Total	1,279,159	193,851,423,927	60.11%	43.89%
	2005	<100%	431,239	48,801,419,674	41.08%	29.81%
	2005	100-120%	403,819	59,415,146,407	55.83%	40.69%
	2005	120-140%	214,185	39,502,695,654	68.13%	49.84%
	2005	140-160%	118,376	22,909,685,144	75.56%	55.23%
	2005	>160%	111,540	23,222,477,048	82.15%	60.38%
	2006	Total	1,974,792	297,597,342,221	67.93%	50.12%
	2006	<100%	332,379	32,860,245,805	44.49%	32.50%
	2006	100-120%	774,534	107,165,017,069	58.97%	43.17%
	2006	120-140%	305,899	53,614,399,261	72.12%	53.35%
	2006	140-160%	294,598	54,029,393,474	79.57%	58.82%
	2006	>160%	267,382	49,928,286,612	85.51%	63.74%
	2007	Total	439,628	75,977,800,805	66.94%	48.16%
	2007	<100%	41,552	4,487,639,121	45.26%	32.40%
	2007	100-120%	218,195	34,442,860,192	59.17%	42.30%
	2007	120-140%	69,664	14,292,865,051	71.00%	51.06%
	2007	140-160%	64,363	13,120,081,080	78.28%	56.59%
	2007	>160%	45,854	9,634,355,361	83.37%	60.62%
	Total	**Total**	3,693,579	567,426,566,953	65.13%	47.73%

Source: Ellington Management Group.

have eventually paid would not have been high.[48] For loans that reached 120 percent LTV or more, about 75 percent went into foreclosure, with losses on average of about 75 percent per foreclosure (giving total losses of about 56 percent of the unpaid balance of all active loans in 2008 that reached LTV above 120 percent). Many of these loans defaulted even though they got coupon payment reductions. By contrast, a policy that wrote down principal to just below 100 percent LTV would have cost about 35 percent of the unpaid principal balance, and might have eliminated almost all the foreclosure losses.[49] And some of the 35 percent would have been recouped from the borrowers who never defaulted, when their houses regained their value.

The recent debate on forgiveness versus temporary payment reduction revolves too much around a false classification of homeowners into one of two extremes. Either homeowners default because they run out of money (by losing their jobs, for instance), in which case reducing their coupon payments will keep them afloat until they can resume paying fully, or homeowners default strategically before they run out of money because they realize their house is never going to be worth as much as the loan, in which case principal reduction of the right size can be the innoculation against default. In fact, nobody ever waits to default on their mortgage until they are completely penniless. Everybody is strategic to some extent. And everybody has to worry about their future income when paying their mortgage. A correct analysis of the optimal mortgage modification policy must quantify, person by person, their willingness to default — that is, their sensitivity to how bad a deal their mortgage is.[50] One thing is clear: subprime borrowers will be, on average, more willing to default than prime borrowers, hence principal forgiveness will be, on average, more useful for them.[51] Another critical issue is to quantify the effect on housing prices on stopping the wave of foreclosures, and the feedback of higher prices on reducing defaults and increasing recoveries.[52] These topics need further work. Among the issues to be investigated is how the results might depend on the timing of the policy.

I close by noting that it is uncontroversial that more could have been done to help keep homeowners in their homes during the crisis, whether by forgiveness or payment extension — or, better, some combination of the two, tailored to individual circumstances. It is ironic that the government was hesitant to act for fear of enraging the population that did not get helped. By helping banks instead of homeowners, even if those homeowners were subprime homeowners, the government caused much more trauma to the psyche of the nation.

---

48 The statistics on so-called Alt-A loans are similar, although not quite so bad.

49 Writing down a 150 percent LTV loan by 35 percent would give a new LTV of 97.5 percent.

50 Another problem with some of the empirical studies is that they are based on a very small selection of loans. The authors do not quantify how important the selection bias might be. For example, Ganong and Pascal, *supra* note 47, study the Home Affordable Modifications Program (HAMP), which was a small, non-representative sample of loans, and then look at a tiny experimental subgroup of those that got principal reductions. They conclude that principal reductions lose money for the lender. To be eligible for HAMP, homeowners had to certify that they had suffered some special income hardship. The program was therefore biased toward agents who were going to default for income reasons. Second, the HAMP principal reductions were ill-advisedly set to 115 percent of LTV, large enough to lose money from the homeowners who would have paid anyway, but too small to convince a defaulter to change his mind. The principal reductions were biased toward failure. Third, the principal reductions were given very late, to people who had managed to stay more or less current on their loans despite being underwater for a long time. Again, a biased sample. Fourth, the program did not target subprime or Alt A homeowners. The vast majority of HAMP homeowners paid in the end, so of course principal reductions to all of them would have lost money.

51 Philip Kalikman is conducting a comprehensive person-by-person analysis of the income loss-strategic default calculation as part of his dissertation research at Yale.

52 Ahyan Panjawani is conducting a careful loan-by-loan analysis in the context of an agent-based housing model as part of his dissertation research at Yale.

Conclusion: Closing Perspectives on Regulating Systemic Risk

STEVEN L. SCHWARCZ

With a decade of hindsight since the financial crisis, this book[1] has examined the macroprudential regulations enacted to protect the stability of the financial system. It is still uncertain, however, whether that regulation is sufficient to prevent another crisis.[2]

The primary focus of that regulation is on banks and other systemically important financial institutions (SIFIs). Such an entity-based approach may be too narrow, however, because it largely ignores other critical elements of the system, such as financial markets. Furthermore, even the regulation that focuses on SIFIs is ad hoc[3] and, in response to political and media pressure to assign blame for the crisis, sometimes is punitive or seeks to correct non-existent wrongdoing.[4]

1 This chapter is based, in part, on Steven L Schwarcz, "Systematic Regulation of Systemic Risk" (2019) Wis L Rev 1 [Schwarcz, "Systematic Regulation"], online: <https://ssrn.com/abstract=3233666>.

2 *Cf infra* notes 31–33 and accompanying text (discussing concerns by regulators).

3 See *infra* notes 50–54 and accompanying text.

4 See *infra* notes 34–49 and accompanying text.

To more effectively protect financial stability, macroprudential regulation requires a more systematic framework. This chapter attempts to construct such a framework, first, by comparing current macroprudential regulation.

Current Macroprudential Regulation

As mentioned, this regulation is primarily entity-based. This targeted approach reflects concern that SIFIs engage in morally hazardous risk-taking because they deem themselves "too big to fail" (TBTF).[5] Capital requirements epitomize this approach, protecting SIFIs against losses by requiring them to hold minimum levels of capital.[6] Worldwide capital requirements are promulgated by the Basel Committee on Banking Supervision, composed of bank regulators from various industrialized nations.[7] The earliest requirements, referred to as Basel I and II, took a somewhat liberal approach.[8] Because those requirements did not prevent bank failures during the financial crisis, the Basel Committee promulgated a more stringent post-crisis version, known as Basel III.[9] However, the ability of capital requirements to control systemic risk is unclear.[10] The cost of capital requirements is also uncertain; some argue they impose no public costs,[11] while others argue to the contrary.[12]

The entity-based approach includes liquidity requirements,[13] which require certain SIFIs to have sufficient cash on hand to protect against the default risk of maturity transformation — the asset-liability mismatch that results from the short-term funding of long-term projects.[14] Although essential to providing funding,[15] maturity transformation can create a maturity gap — the risk that cash flows from long-term projects may be insufficient to pay maturing short-term

5 See e.g. John Glover & Ilya Arkhipov, "End of 'Too-Big-To-Fail' Banking Era Endorsed by World Leaders", *Bloomberg* (15 November 2015), online: <www.bloomberg.com/news/articles/2015-11-15/end-of-too-big-to-fail-banking-era-endorsed-by-world-leaders>. Even the preface to the Dodd-Frank Act states it is "[a]n Act…to end 'too big to fail.'"

6 Kern Alexander & Steven L Schwarcz, "The Macroprudential Quandary: Unsystematic Efforts to Reform Financial Regulation" in Ross P Buckley, Emilios Avgouleas & Douglas W Arner, eds, *Reconceptualising Global Finance and Its Regulation* (New York: Cambridge University Press, 2016) 127 at 136. In its most pristine form, capital consists of equity.

7 *Ibid.*

8 Steven L Schwarcz, "Banking and Financial Regulation" in Francesco Parisi, ed, *The Oxford Handbook of Law and Economics* (Oxford, UK: Oxford University Press, 2015) 11.

9 Hervé Hannoun, "The Basel III Capital Framework: A Decisive Breakthrough" (Speech delivered at the BoJ-BIS High Level Seminar on Financial Regulatory Reform: Implications for Asia and the Pacific, Hong Kong SAR, 22 November 2010) at 2–3, online: <www.bis.org/speeches/sp101125a.pdf>.

10 *Cf* Steven L Schwarcz, "Beyond Bankruptcy: Resolution as a Macroprudential Regulatory Tool" (2018) 94 Notre Dame L Rev 709 [Schwarcz, "Beyond Bankruptcy"], online: <https://scholarship.law.duke.edu/faculty_scholarship/3755/> (discussing the uncertainty of whether protecting SIFIs individually against unexpected losses will protect the financial system).

11 See e.g. Anat Admati & Martin Hellwig, *The Bankers' New Clothes: What's Wrong with Banking and What to Do about It* (Princeton, NJ: Princeton University Press, 2013) at 98.

12 See e.g. Jean Dermine, "Bank Regulations After the Global Financial Crisis: Good Intentions and Unintended Evil" (2013) 19:4 European Financial Management 658 (arguing that "excessive" capital "might lead to inefficiently higher interest rates on bank loans" and impose "social costs as banks reduce their supply of loans or securitize assets" at 662); Reint Gropp et al, "Bank Response to Higher Capital Requirements: Evidence from a Quasi-Natural Experiment" (2016) Halle Institute for Economic Research Discussion Paper No 33/2016, online: <www.econstor.eu/bitstream/10419/148361/1/874406994.pdf> (finding that higher bank capital requirements cause banks to reduce their credit supply, resulting in lower economic growth).

13 These requirements are also promulgated under Basel III. *Cf* Hannoun, *supra* note 9 and accompanying text (observing that Basel III requires liquidity reserves).

14 Jeanne Gobat, Mamoru Yanase & Joseph Maloney, "The Net Stable Funding Ratio: Impact and Issues for Consideration" (2014) IMF Working Paper WP/14/106, online: <www.imf.org/external/pubs/ft/wp/2014/wp14106.pdf>.

15 Douglas J Elliott, "Bank Liquidity Requirements: An Introduction and Overview" (2014) Brookings Institution, online: <www.brookings.edu/wp-content/uploads/2016/06/23_bank_liquidity_requirements_intro_overview_elliott.pdf>.

liabilities, leading to a default.[16] The liquidity requirements help to protect against the maturity gap, but they do not apply to all SIFIs.

Ring-fencing represents another form of entity-based regulation. It refers to steps taken to "protect a firm from becoming subject to liabilities and other risks associated with bankruptcy; to help ensure that a firm is able to operate on a standalone basis even if its affiliated firms fail; to protect a firm from being taken advantage of by affiliated firms, thereby preserving the firm's business and assets; and to limit a firm from engaging in risky activities."[17] UK law, for example, ring-fences "retail" banking services — those provided to individuals and small businesses — by requiring certain banks to segregate their deposit-taking activities from affiliate risks.[18] Stress tests represent yet another form of entity-based regulation. These tests examine a SIFI's response to hypothetical "stressed" adverse financial conditions.[19]

Finally, "resolution" refers to the entity-based regulation that seeks to mitigate the systemic impact of a SIFI's failure. For example, the Federal Deposit Insurance Corporation (FDIC) developed the single-point-of-entry approach to orderly resolution of troubled SIFIs, under which it would take control of the parent of a distressed SIFI and use the parent's resources to recapitalize the SIFI, thereby reducing systemic shocks.[20] To be successful, this approach depends on finding larger, healthy SIFIs to acquire troubled SIFIs.[21] If a SIFI becomes troubled, however, there may not always be a larger, healthy firm available to acquire it — especially if multiple SIFIs become troubled around the same time.[22]

Macroprudential regulation also focuses on regulating the transactions that are believed to be responsible for causing the financial crisis. Under the originate-to-distribute (OTD) model, for example, lenders make loans with the intention of selling them off in securitization transactions.[23] Because the lenders do not hold onto, and thus do not bear risk for the ultimate performance of, the loans, the OTD model is believed to encourage lenders to make riskier loans.[24] That riskier lending, in turn, is blamed for causing the high rate of residential mortgage-loan defaults that contributed to the financial crisis.[25] In an effort to align incentives and reduce moral hazard, macroprudential regulation typically requires originators of loans that are intended to be sold

16 Gobat, Yanase & Maloney, *supra* note 14 at 4–6, 10–12.

17 Steven L Schwarcz, "Ring-Fencing" (2013) 87 S Cal L Rev 69 at 81–82 [Schwarcz, "Ring-Fencing"].

18 Financial Conduct Authority, *Ring-fencing: Guidance on the FCA's approach to the implementation of ring-fencing and ring-fencing transfer schemes* (2015), online: <www.fca.org.uk/publication/guidance-consultation/gc15-05.pdf>.

19 Robert Weber, "A Theory for Deliberation-Oriented Stress Testing Regulation" (2014) 98 Minn L Rev 2236 at 2238–39.

20 Paul H Kupiec & Peter J Wallison, "Can the 'single point of entry' strategy be used to recapitalize a failing bank?" (2014) American Enterprise Institute Economic Working Paper 2014-08, online: <www.aei.org/wp-content/uploads/2014/11/SPOE-Working-paper-Nov-5.pdf>.

21 FDIC, *Managing the Crisis: The FDIC and RTC Experience* (1998) at 55–56.

22 *Cf* Stephen J Lubben, "Resolution, Orderly and Otherwise: B of A in OLA" (2013) 81:2 U Cin L Rev 485 (observing that "in times of systemic crisis there might well be no buyers large enough or confident enough to perform a similar function with regard to a large financial institution" at 509).

23 Vitaly M Bord & João AC Santos, "The Rise of the Originate-to-Distribute Model and the Role of Banks in Financial Intermediation" (2012) 18 Federal Reserve Bank of New York Economic Policy Rev 21 at 21.

24 Antje Berndt & Anurag Gupta, "Moral hazard and adverse selection in the originate-to-distribute model of bank credit" (2009) 56:5 J Monetary Economics 725 at 741–42.

25 *Ibid.*

off in securitization transactions to retain a minimum unhedged position (usually five percent) in the risk on those loans.[26]

Macroprudential regulation also focuses on regulating residential mortgage lending. A collapse in US housing prices led to the widespread mortgage-loan defaults that caused many mortgage loans to default.[27] This regulation seeks to strengthen the quality and integrity of mortgage lending.[28] Other macroprudential regulation focuses on rating agencies, which have been criticized for contributing to the financial crisis by giving unduly high ratings to complex and highly leveraged mortgage-backed securities (MBS).[29] This regulation seeks, among other things, to improve ratings quality by reducing potential conflicts of interest.[30]

Vulnerabilities Remain

These approaches to macroprudential regulation represent good faith and, in many cases, highly thoughtful efforts to control systemic risk. Nonetheless, regulators worry that vulnerabilities remain. They fear they have made "little progress in figuring out how they might actually" prevent another financial crisis.[31] Timothy Geithner, former US Secretary of the Treasury, has observed that "[a]lthough regulations [imposing specific requirements] have reined in banks' risk-taking behavior, they can go only so far."[32] Officials at the Bank of Spain believe that even well-calibrated macroprudential tools cannot "cope perfectly" with the "objective[s] for which they are designed."[33]

Some of this concern may reflect flaws in the macroprudential rule-making process itself. That process has been strongly influenced by political and media perceptions that wrongdoing and

26 See e.g. *Dodd-Frank Wall Street Reform and Protection Act,* 15 USC § 78o-11(c)(1)(B) [*Dodd-Frank Act*]; EC, *Proposal for a Regulation of the European Parliament and of the Council laying down common rules on securitisation and creating a European framework for simple, transparent and standardised securitisation,* COM(2015) 472 final, 2015/0226 (COD), art 4 [*STS Regulation*] (proposing a similar risk-retention requirement for securitizations in the European Union). The media often refers to risk-retention requirements as maintaining "skin in the game."

27 Richard A Posner, *A Failure of Capitalism: The Crisis of '08 and the Descent into Depression* (Cambridge, MA: Harvard University Press, 2009) at 75–76.

28 See Ryan Bubb & Prasad Krishnamurthy, "Regulating Against Bubbles: How Mortgage Regulation Can Keep Main Street and Wall Street Safe — From Themselves" (2015) 163 U Pa L Rev 1539.

29 See e.g. Amadou NR Sy, "The Systemic Regulation of Credit Rating Agencies and Rated Markets" (2009) IMF Working Paper No 09/129, online: <www.imf.org/en/Publications/WP/Issues/2016/12/31/The-Systemic-Regulation-of-Credit-Rating-Agencies-and-Rated-Markets-23030>.

30 See e.g. *Dodd-Frank Act*, *supra* note 26, § 932; *Regulation (EU) No 462/2013 of the European Parliament and of the Council of 21 May 2013 amending Regulation (EC) No 1060/2009 on credit rating agencies*, [2013] OJ, L 146/1 at 14–15 (addressing alleged conflicts of interest caused by the issuer-pays model). Macroprudential regulation also addresses monetary policy. Some central banks, for example, manage short-term interest rates to try to control asset-price bubbles. See e.g. Board of Governors of the Federal Reserve System, *The Federal Reserve System: Purposes & Functions*, 10th ed (2016) at 21. This use of monetary policy is subject to several criticisms, including that asset-price bubbles are difficult to identify before they burst; Neel Kashkari, "Monetary Policy and Bubbles", Federal Reserve Bank of Minneapolis (17 May 2017), online: <https://minneapolisfed.org/news-and-events/messages/monetary-policy-and-bubbles> and that "raising interest rates to prick asset bubbles can risk increasing unemployment"; Kern Alexander, *Regulating Financial Systems* [forthcoming in 2019] (calling this use of monetary policy a "blunt instrument").

31 Binyamin Appelbaum, "Policy Makers Skeptical on Preventing Financial Crisis", *The New York Times* (5 October 2015) at B1 (reporting the consensus view of an international conference of regulators at the Federal Reserve Bank of Boston). Donald Kohn, former vice chairman of the Federal Reserve Board, observed at that conference that the Federal Reserve "doesn't really have the tools" to prevent another crisis (*ibid* at B3).

32 Timothy F Geithner, "Are We Safe Yet? How to Manage Financial Crises", *Foreign Affairs* (12 December 2016).

33 Enrique Alberola, Carlos Trucharte & Juan Luis Vega, "Central Banks and Macroprudential Policy: Some Reflections from the Spanish Experience" (2011) Banco de España Occasional Paper No 1105 at 24, online: <www.bde.es/f/webbde/SES/Secciones/Publicaciones/PublicacionesSeriadas/DocumentosOcasionales/11/Fich/do1105e.pdf>.

wrongdoers caused the financial crisis.[34] These perceptions follow human intuition to assign blame for harm.[35] Politicians and the media have assumed, for example, that moral hazard caused SIFIs to engage in morally hazardous — and thus excessive — risk-taking.[36] In response, regulators have framed TBTF, moral hazard and associated wrongdoing as a central target of post-crisis macroprudential regulation.[37]

That framing, however, is questionable. Although SIFIs did take excessive risks,[38] there is no evidence that was caused by moral hazard.[39] Furthermore, there is evidence that it was not so caused[40] and that other factors may better explain that risk-taking.[41] Macroprudential regulation based on that questionable framing is sometimes problematic.[42] For example, the Dodd-Frank Act strips the Federal Reserve of much of its last-resort lending powers under section 13(3) of the Federal Reserve Act.[43] Although intended to quash SIFI expectations of a government bailout (thereby reducing TBTF-induced moral hazard), this virtually assures a crisis if a SIFI fails and the law's resolution mechanisms are inadequate.[44] Similarly, regulators are under great pressure to break up SIFIs into smaller firms that are not themselves TBTF. Any such breakups, however, might jeopardize economies of scale and scope, making firms less competitive in increasingly globalized financial markets, without necessarily correcting a real problem.[45]

That questionable framing has also produced macroprudential regulation that seeks to correct non-existent wrongs. Politicians and the media have assumed that the high rate of mortgage-loan defaults that contributed to the financial crisis resulted from moral hazard brought on by the OTD model of making and then selling off loans in securitizations.[46] In response, the Dodd-

34 See e.g. Financial Crisis Inquiry Commission, *The Financial Crisis Inquiry Report: Final Report of the National Commission on the Causes of the Financial and Economic Crisis in the United States* (2011) (stating that the "crisis was the result of human action and inaction, not of Mother Nature or models gone haywire" at xvii); Gretchen Morgenson & Louise Story, "Naming Culprits in the Financial Crisis", *The New York Times* (13 April 2011), online: <www.nytimes.com/2011/04/14/business/14crisis.html> (arguing that the financial crisis was caused by the "financial industry [choosing] profits over propriety").

35 *Cf* Elaine Walster, "Assignment of Responsibility for Accidents" (1966) 3 J Personality & Social Psychology 73 at 73 (observing the tendency to assign responsibility to someone when people hear about an accident).

36 *Cf* Glover & Arkhipov, *supra* note 5 and accompanying text (discussing the concern that SIFIs may engage in morally hazardous risk-taking because they deem themselves TBTF).

37 *Ibid.*

38 *Cf* Financial Crisis Inquiry Commission, *supra* note 34 at xviii–xix (identifying excessive risk-taking by systemically important banks as a primary cause of the financial crisis).

39 *Cf* Steven L Schwarcz, "Too Big to Fool: Moral Hazard, Bailouts, and Corporate Responsibility" (2017) 102 Minn L Rev 761 at 765–67 [Schwarcz, "Too Big to Fool"] (observing that the economic studies purporting to "prove" that TBTF causes firms to engage in morally hazardous behaviour merely show that SIFIs can borrow at lower-than-average cost; and that although economists presume this funding advantage derives from investor belief that these firms will be bailed out before they default, there are many other reasons besides the expectation of a bailout why SIFIs can borrow at lower-than-average cost).

40 *Cf ibid* at 768–69 (showing, among other things, that the idea that TBTF causes SIFIs to engage in morally hazardous behaviour is antithetical to managerial incentives).

41 See *infra* notes 108–111 and accompanying text.

42 If individual wrongdoing by SIFI managers in fact caused the financial crisis, the post-crisis prosecution of SIFIs in their institutional capacity, instead of prosecuting individuals, has also been flawed. *Cf* Steven L Schwarcz, "Excessive Corporate Risk-Taking and the Decline of Personal Blame" (2015) 65 Emory LJ 533 (making that argument and explaining why individuals were not prosecuted).

43 Schwarcz, "Beyond Bankruptcy", *supra* note 10.

44 *Ibid.* The current resolution mechanisms are almost certainly insufficient.

45 Schwarcz, "Too Big to Fool", *supra* note 39 at 774–76; *cf* Anna Kovner, James Vickery & Lily Zhou, "Do Big Banks Have Lower Operating Costs?" (2014) 20:2 Economic Policy Rev at 22 (concluding that imposing size limits on banks would increase costs).

46 See *supra* notes 23–26 and accompanying text.

Frank Act requires lenders to retain a minimum unhedged portion of the risk on the loans they securitize.[47] That response, however, ignores that it was always common practice for sponsors of securitizations to retain substantial risk on the underlying loans. They did this to signal the quality of the securities they were selling to investors.[48] We now understand that the signalling inadvertently created a novel information failure: not the typical asymmetric information but, instead, a mutual misinformation problem caused by *complexity*. Neither the sponsor of the securitization nor the investors fully understood the risks — especially those associated with highly leveraged re-securitizations of the underlying loans.[49]

Designing Future Macroprudential Regulation

As described, current macroprudential regulation is limited. A more systematic regulatory framework could improve the design of macroprudential regulation in at least three ways. On a basic level, it would help to increase the transparency, and hence the legitimacy, of macroprudential regulation.[50] The very existence of such a framework would also provide pushback to the political and media pressure that has left the post-crisis regulatory process flawed, resulting in overreactive, underreactive or otherwise misguided macroprudential regulation.[51]

A more systematic framework would also provide a coherent analytical approach to designing macroprudential regulation, in contrast to the current ad hoc approach. Regulators often view macroprudential regulatory measures as a loose assortment of "tools" in their "tool kit."[52] Even the theoretical scholarship on law and finance takes a somewhat similar ad hoc approach, yielding "propositions [that] can serve as a tool kit" for regulatory scrutiny.[53] The result is "unsystematic" macroprudential regulation that "almost certainly will not optimally reduce, and might even increase, systemic risk."[54]

47 See *Dodd-Frank Act*, *supra* note 26 and accompanying text.

48 Bubb & Krishnamurthy, *supra* note 28 at 1591. In fact, sponsors often invested in the most junior "equity" tranches of the deals they were arranging, believing that putting their own money at stake in a first-loss position would signal the quality of the deals and also would generate additional value. *Cf* Michael S Gibson, "Understanding the Risk of Synthetic CDOs" (2004) Federal Reserve (FEDS) Working Paper No 2004-36 at 17, online: <www.fdic.gov/bank/analytical/*cfr*/bank-research-conference/annual-4th/2004-14-gibson.pdf> (explaining that CDO sponsors often retain equity tranches for those reasons and also to limit informational asymmetry).

49 Steven L Schwarcz, "Regulating Complexity in Financial Markets" (2009) 87 Wash L Rev 211 at 241–42 [Schwarcz, "Regulating Complexity"].

50 *Cf* Robert F Weber, "New Governance, Financial Regulation, and Challenges to Legitimacy: The Example of Internal Models Approach to Capital Adequacy Regulation" (2010) 63 Admin L Rev 783 at 850–55 (discussing issues with legitimacy in the context of capital adequacy regulation).

51 *Cf* Henry N Butler & Larry E Ribstein, abstract to *The Sarbanes-Oxley Debacle: What We've Learned; How to Fix It* (Washington, DC: AEI Press, 2006) (describing the Sarbanes-Oxley Act of 2002, enacted in response to the Enron scandal, as "a colossal failure, poorly conceived and hastily enacted during a regulatory panic"); Larry E Ribstein, "Market vs. Regulatory Responses to Corporate Fraud: A Critique of the Sarbanes-Oxley Act of 2002" (2003) 28 J Corp L 1 (stating that the Sarbanes-Oxley Act was "passed in a hectic environment in which politicians played on public misperceptions of risk and eschewed careful balancing of costs and benefits" at 19).

52 See e.g. Robert C Hockett, "Implementing Macroprudential Finance-Oversight Policy: Legal Considerations" (2013) (Drafted for the IMF) at 12–13, online: <http://papers.ssrn.com/sol3/papers.*cfm*?abstract_id=2340316>.

53 Daniel Awrey et al, "An Overview of the Legal Theory of Finance 2" (2014) [unpublished, on file with author].

54 Alexander & Schwarcz, *supra* note 6 at 129. For example, Group of Twenty (G20) nations (as discussed) have been requiring most derivatives to be cleared and settled through central counterparty clearing houses (CCPs). This central clearing requirement, however, concentrates systemic risk in the CCP, and it is uncertain whether the net effect is to reduce, or inadvertently to increase, systemic risk. See Steven L Schwarcz, "Central Clearing of Financial Contracts: Theory and Regulatory Implications" [forthcoming in 2019] 167:6 U Pa L Rev at 7–8, online: <https://ssrn.com/abstract=3104079>. The extent to which derivatives themselves are inherently systemically risky is also uncertain (*ibid*).

A Normative Foundation

Constructing a more systematic framework for macroprudential regulation should start by engaging the normative justification for financial regulation: to correct market failures.[55] The justification for macroprudential regulation thus should be to correct market failures that could trigger and transmit systemic risk.[56] To accomplish this, we need to identify and better understand those triggers and transmission mechanisms. Consider how to accomplish this.

Economists and finance scholars have identified three categories of shocks that can trigger the collapse of the financial system:[57] bank runs; asset-price falls; and foreign exchange mismatches.[58] Current regulation addresses some of those categories of shocks, although not always perfectly.[59] Those scholars have not, however, tried to identify the market failures that could cause those shocks.[60] I have argued that at least five types of market failures could cause those shocks: complexity, conflicts, behavioural limitations, change and a type of tragedy of the commons.[61] Also, maturity transformation could cause a maturity gap, which in turn could lead to a default that triggers a systemic shock.[62] I will consider these in turn.

Identifying and Correcting Market Failures that Could Trigger Systemic Shocks

Complexity represents a market failure insofar as it can distort information and impair disclosure as a means to reduce asymmetric information.[63] Complexity can also, as mentioned, result in mutual misinformation.[64] Macroprudential regulation should be designed to reduce complexity, thereby correcting this market failure.[65]

55 *Cf* Paul A Samuelson & William D Nordhaus, *Economics*, 15th ed (New York: McGraw-Hill, 1995) at 756 (observing that the primary goal of financial regulation should be to correct market failures); David Gowland, *The Regulation of Financial Markets in the 1990s* (Cheltenham, UK: Edward Elgar, 1990) (characterizing regulating markets to correct market failure as the "public interest theory" at 21).

56 This chapter uses the term "market failure" loosely because the economic literature defines the term loosely.

57 The term "shock" refers to the event triggering the collapse of a system. *Cf supra* note 56 (noting that the event triggering the collapse of a system is called a "shock").

58 See e.g. Franklin Allen & Elena Carletti, "Systemic Risk from Real Estate and Macro-prudential Regulation" (2013) 5 Intl J Banking, Accounting & Finance 29; Milton Friedman & Anna Jacobson Schwartz, *A Monetary History of the United States, 1867–1960* (Princeton, NJ: Princeton University Press, 1963) (identifying bank runs as the most important systemic shock).

59 For example, regulation limits bank runs by providing government guarantees of bank deposits up to specified limits. Such government deposit insurance, however, allegedly creates moral hazard, which is itself a source of market failure. See e.g. Thomas M Hoenig, Vice Chairman of the FDIC, "Deposit Insurance: Addressing Its Moral Hazard Effect" (Speech delivered at the 16th Annual IADI General Meeting and Annual Conference, Quebec City, 11 October 2017), online: <www.fdic.gov/news/news/speeches/spoct1117.pdf>.

60 See Samuelson & Nordhaus, *supra* note 55 and accompanying text; Gowland, *supra* note 55 and accompanying text.

61 I have elsewhere referred to these market failures, collectively, as the "4Cs and the TOC", characterizing behavioural limitations as "complacency" in the expansive sense of that term. See *Merriam-Webster Dictionary*, s.v. "complacency", online: <www.merriam-webster.com/dictionary/complacency> (defining "complacency" as "self-satisfaction especially when unaccompanied by awareness of actual dangers or deficiencies").

62 See Elliott, *supra* note 15 and accompanying text; Gobat, Yanase & Maloney, *supra* note 14 and accompanying text.

63 See e.g. Steven L Schwarcz, "Disclosure's Failure in the Subprime Mortgage Crisis" (2008) Utah L Rev 1109 at 1111 (observing that even sophisticated institutional investors did not fully understand certain complex financings); Andrew G Haldane & Vasileios Madouros, "The Dog and the Frisbee" (2012) Proceedings – Economic Policy Symposium 109 (observing that "[c]omplexity has externality type properties, making risk more difficult to monitor and manage" at 149).

64 See *supra* notes 48–49 and accompanying text.

65 This chapter's analysis of how macroprudential regulation should be designed to correct market failures does not take into account potential costs and benefits.

Top-down approaches to try to reduce complexity would likely be costly and futile. For example, mandating more simplified finance could stifle innovation and interfere with the ability of parties to achieve the efficiencies that arise when firms tailor securities and other financial products to the particular needs and risk preferences of investors.[66] Standardizing securities and other financial products could also backfire, potentially increasing systemic risk by correlating investments.[67] Incentive-based approaches to try to control complexity would have greater flexibility and less downside risk. For example, the European Union is creating a regulatory framework favouring simple, transparent and standardized (STS) securitization transactions.[68] This framework incentivizes (rather than mandates) STS transactions by reducing regulatory capital requirements for investors therein, thereby allowing for potential innovation.[69]

Conflicts represent a market failure insofar as they can distort incentives. Scholars have long studied conflicts of interest between managers and owners of firms within the broader context of principal-agent problems and agency costs. Post-financial-crisis regulation attempts to fix this traditional type of conflict. Post-crisis regulation, however, overlooks the intra-firm problem of secondary-management conflicts, which are an intra-firm principal-agent failure.[70] The problem arises because secondary managers are almost always paid under short-term compensation schemes, misaligning their interests with the long-term interests of the firm.[71] Complexity exacerbates this problem by increasing information asymmetry between technically sophisticated secondary managers and the senior managers to whom they report.

Macroprudential regulation could be designed to correct, or at least mitigate, this market failure by requiring SIFIs to pay secondary managers under longer-term compensation schemes — for example, compensation subject to clawbacks or deferred compensation based on long-term results. In practice, that solution would confront a collective action problem: firms that offer their secondary managers longer-term compensation might be unable to hire as competitively as firms that offer more immediate compensation.[72] Regulation may be needed to help solve this collective action problem not only within nations, but also across nations, because good secondary managers can work in financial centres worldwide.[73]

Behavioural limitations represent a market failure because they can undermine two perfect-market assumptions that underlie financial regulation — that parties have full information and that they will act in their rational self-interest.[74] Although there is no generally accepted way to categorize these limitations, scholars often associate them with herd behaviour, cognitive

66 Steven L Schwarcz, "Controlling Financial Chaos: The Power and Limits of Law" (2012) 3 Wis L Rev 815 at 820.

67 *Cf infra* notes 140–42 and accompanying text (discussing how lack of investment diversity contributed to the financial crisis). But *cf* Saule T Omarova, "License to Deal: Mandatory Approval of Complex Financial Products" (2012) 90 Wash L Rev 63 (arguing for requiring approval of complex financial products: "adopting and operationalizing the *general concept of precaution* in the context of post-crisis financial systemic risk regulation may be a worthwhile, and even necessary, exercise" at 84).

68 See generally *STS Regulation*, *supra* note 26.

69 *Ibid.*

70 See Steven L Schwarcz, "Conflicts and Financial Collapse: The Problem of Secondary-Management Agency Costs" (2009) 26 Yale J Reg 457.

71 *Ibid* at 460.

72 *Ibid* at 468.

73 *Ibid.*

74 *Farlex Free Financial Dictionary*, s.v. "Perfect market assumptions", online: <http://financial-dictionary.thefreedictionary.com/Perfect+market+assumptions> (discussing perfect-market assumptions, including that market participants have equal access to information and are completely rational).

biases and overreliance on heuristics.[75] In the context of financial regulation, I have proposed a fourth category: the tendency to panic, which is strongly connected to the stability of financial markets.[76]

Herd behaviour refers to the human tendency to follow others. The frenzied worldwide demand to purchase certain highly leveraged MBS in the years prior to the financial crisis almost certainly represented herd behaviour of investors following misleading information about the value of that MBS.[77] Cognitive biases refer to implicit simplifications of our perceptions of reality.[78] The most prominent are availability bias[79] and optimism bias.[80] Availability bias is the tendency to over-emphasize a recent or especially vivid event and to under-emphasize a long-past event.[81] Optimism bias is the tendency to be unrealistically positive when thinking about negative events with which one has no recent experience.[82] By distorting the internalization of information,[83] cognitive biases violate the perfect-market assumption that parties have full information, which can trigger financial market failures.[84]

Overreliance on heuristics refers to undue reliance on explicitly adopted simplifications of reality. These simplifications can distort the perfect-market assumption that parties have full information. Without reliance on heuristics, financial markets could not operate.[85] Investors routinely use credit ratings, for example, to help estimate risks associated with securities.[86] Overreliance, however, can cause problems. Prior to the financial crisis, investors rarely questioned the accuracy of credit ratings because of their long record for reliably assessing the creditworthiness of relatively simple debt instruments, such as corporate bonds.[87] But that unquestioning faith continued even when ratings were extrapolated to much more complex and highly leveraged MBS.[88]

The tendency to panic refers to the flight reflex to run from a perceived danger.[89] A panicked person will rarely attempt to deal rationally with the threat, distorting the perfect-market

75 See Richard H Thaler & Cass R Sunstein, *Nudge: Improving Decisions About Health, Wealth, and Happiness* (London, UK: Penguin Books, 2009) at 23–31, 53–71.

76 Steven L Schwarcz, "Regulating Complacency: Human Limitations and Legal Efficacy" (2018) 93 Notre Dame L Rev 1073 at 1082–83 [Schwarcz, "Regulating Complacency"].

77 *Ibid* at 1078.

78 *Ibid* at 1079.

79 See e.g. Norbert Schwarz et al, "Ease of Retrieval as Information: Another Look at the Availability Heuristic" (1991) 61:2 J Personality & Social Psychology 195 at 195.

80 See e.g. Tali Sharot, "Optimism Bias: Why the Young and the Old Tend to Look on the Bright Side", *Washington Post* (31 December 2012), online: <www.washingtonpost.com/national/health-science/optimism-bias-why-the-young-and-the-old-tend-to-look-on-the-bright-side/2012/12/28/ac4147de-37f8-11e2-a263-f0ebffed2f15_story.html>.

81 Iman Anabtawi & Steven L Schwarcz, "Regulating Systemic Risk: Toward an Analytical Framework" (2018) 86 Notre Dame L Rev 1349 at 1366–67.

82 *Ibid* at 1366.

83 See Christine Jolls & Cass R Sunstein, "Debiasing Through Law" (2006) 35 J Leg Stud 199 at 204–05, 207.

84 *Cf* Schwarcz, "Regulating Complacency", *supra* note 76 at 1085 (discussing certain parallels between the Great Depression and the financial crisis that show how cognitive biases can combine to create a tendency to define future events by the recent past, causing shocks that can trigger a systemic economic collapse).

85 *Ibid* at 769. *Cf* Haldane & Madouros, *supra* note 63 (arguing that "heuristics may be the optimizing response to a complex environment" at 113).

86 Kathryn Judge, "Fragmentation Nodes: A Case Study in Financial Innovation, Complexity and Systemic Risk" (2012) 64 Stan L Rev 657 at 680.

87 Steven L Schwarcz & Lucy Chang, "The Custom-to-Failure Cycle" (2012) 62 Duke LJ 767 at 772–73.

88 *Ibid* at 774–75.

89 EL Quarantelli, "The Nature and Conditions of Panic" (1954) 60 American J Sociology 267 at 269.

assumptions that parties have full information and act in their rational self-interest. Prior to the financial crisis, the unexpected defaults on MBS caused uncertainty and investor loss of confidence in credit ratings as a gauge of risk.[90] Investors not only stopped buying MBS — which caused prices in the MBS market to collapse even further[91] — but also stopped buying even the most highly rated corporate debt securities, collapsing the credit market.[92]

I have separately examined how regulators could design macroprudential regulation to help control behavioural limitations.[93] For example, by studying how information cascades develop and requiring increased due diligence on market information, regulators could help to reduce herd behaviour.[94] Cognitive biases could be regulated by "debiasing through law."[95] Overreliance on heuristics could be regulated by trying to increase the accuracy of heuristics; society benefits when heuristics reasonably approximate reality.[96] Overreliance on heuristics could also be reduced by requiring firms to engage in more self-aware and transparent operational risk management and reporting.[97] The proclivity to panic could be regulated by trying to promote financial stability, even after an economic shock.[98] To try to prevent bank runs, for example, the FDIC guarantees deposit accounts up to specified limits.[99] Regulation might also create a market liquidity provider of last resort to try to stabilize securities prices after a market panic.[100]

Notwithstanding our best efforts, financial regulation will remain imperfect because we do not yet fully understand human behaviour.[101] As a result, future financial failures are inevitable.[102] Macroprudential regulation should therefore be designed not only to try to deter financial failures resulting from behavioural limitations, but also to mitigate their inevitable harm.[103]

Change represents a market failure insofar as it can cause regulation to become obsolete or insufficient. Although the financial system is constantly changing, regulation normally is tethered to the distinctive design and structure of firms, markets and products in existence when the regulation is promulgated.[104] Without continuous monitoring and updating — which rarely occurs because it is costly and subject to political interference — present-day regulation can quickly become outmoded.[105] Regulation cannot correct the market failures underlying

90 See e.g. Mortimer B Zuckerman, "Preventing a Panic", *US News & World Report* (1 February 2008), online: <www.usnews.com/opinion/mzuckerman/articles/2008/02/01/preventing-a-panic> (arguing that "the credit system has been virtually frozen" because "few people even know where the liabilities and losses are concentrated").

91 Schwarcz & Chang, *supra* note 87 at 778.

92 Steven L Schwarcz, "Keynote Address: The Financial Crisis and Credit Unavailability: Cause or Effect?" (2017) 72 Business Lawyer 409.

93 See Schwarcz, "Regulating Complacency", *supra* note 76.

94 *Ibid* at 1084–90.

95 Jolls & Sunstein, *supra* note 83 at 200.

96 Schwarcz & Chang, *supra* note 87 at 769.

97 Schwarcz, "Regulating Complacency", *supra* note 76 at 1094.

98 *Ibid.*

99 12 USC § 1811 (2012).

100 Schwarcz, "Regulating Complacency", *supra* note 76 at 1094 (arguing that such a liquidity provider should be at least partly privatized in order to reduce moral hazard, and comparing that to the FDIC's assessing deposit-taking banks to fund its deposit insurance guarantees).

101 *Ibid* at 1098–99.

102 *Ibid.*

103 *Ibid.*

104 Steven L Schwarcz, "Regulating Financial Change: A Functional Approach" (2016) 100 Minn L Rev 1441 at 1442.

105 *Ibid* at 1443.

change without stultifying innovation. These obstacles present yet another reason why, despite our best efforts, macroprudential financial regulation designed to deter financial crises will remain imperfect.[106] Macroprudential regulation should therefore also be designed to mitigate the inevitable harm of financial failures.[107]

The tragedy of the commons represents a market failure insofar as it causes externalities. The shareholder-primacy model of corporate governance causes this failure by encouraging firms to engage in risk-taking that has a positive expected value to the firm and its shareholders, regardless of harm to third parties — unless, of course, that harm is prohibited by other law or internalized through tort law.[108] This governance model is problematic for SIFIs because systemic harm is neither prohibited by other law nor internalized through tort law.[109] SIFIs therefore are motivated to engage in "excessive" risk-taking — effectively risk-taking that has a positive expected value to the firm and its shareholders, but a negative expected value to the public, who would suffer the externalized systemic harm if the firm were to fail.[110] This externalization of harm evidences a market failure.[111]

Correcting this market failure would require SIFIs to internalize systemic costs. In theory, resolution — which seeks to mitigate the systemic impact of a SIFI's failure — could help to "internalize" those costs by reducing them.[112] In practice, however, most resolution approaches are effectively microprudential,[113] focusing on protecting individual SIFIs. Correcting this market failure would require modifying the shareholder-primacy model of corporate governance, which encourages the excessive risk-taking.[114] The most direct way of doing that would be to impose some type of a public governance duty that requires SIFI managers to also consider the public

106 But *cf ibid* (arguing that a more functional regulatory approach could better address financial change).

107 *Cf supra* note 103 and accompanying text.

108 Steven L Schwarcz, "Misalignment: Corporate Risk-Taking and Public Duty" (2016) 92 Notre Dame L Rev 1 [Schwarcz, "Misalignment"].

109 *Ibid* at 18–21.

110 *Ibid* at 10.

111 *Cf* Paul Kiel & Dan Nguyen, "Bailout Tracker", *ProPublica* (20 July 2018) (reporting that as a result of the financial crisis, more than US$500 billion of public money was used to bail out financial institutions); John Kell, "U.S. Recovers All Jobs Lost in Financial Crisis", *Fortune* (6 June 2014) (observing that it took more than four years of recovery to regain the 8.7 million jobs lost as a result of the financial crisis).

112 *Cf* John Crawford, "Resolution Triggers for Systemically Important Financial Institutions", Neb L Rev [forthcoming in 2019] (discussing resolution as a mechanism to internalize the systemic costs of a SIFI's failure); email from Paul Tucker, Senior Fellow, Mossovar-Rachmani Center for Business and Government, John F. Kennedy School of Government, Harvard University, to the author (2 December 2016) (arguing that because "nothing, other than moving to an economy without debt, can crush the probability [of a systemically important firm's failure] to 0%," a "robust policy [should] include[] an effective/credible regime for resolution").

113 Schwarcz, "Beyond Bankruptcy", *supra* note 10.

114 *Cf* Daniel K Tarullo, "Corporate Governance and Prudential Regulation" (Remarks delivered at the Association of American Law Schools 2014 Midyear Meeting, Washington, DC, 9 June 2014) (arguing that "prudential regulation [should] need to involve itself with corporate governance" because "risk-taking" by systemically important financial intermediaries "carries substantial potential societal consequences"); Jonathan R Macey & Maureen O'Hara, "The Corporate Governance of Banks" (2003) 9 Federal Reserve Bank of New York Economic Policy Rev 91 at 97–98 (arguing that it may be economically efficient to modify the corporate governance of FDIC-insured banks to account for systemic risk); John Carney, "Big-Bank Board Game Puts Shareholders in Second Place", *The Wall Street Journal* (5 April 2015), online: <www.wsj.com/articles/big-bank-board-game-puts-shareholders-in-second-place-heard-on-the-street-1428255363> (noting a speech by US Federal Reserve Governor Daniel Tarullo suggesting that "corporate governance would need to change to broaden the scope of boards' fiduciary duties to reflect macroprudential [i.e., systemic] regulatory objectives").

consequences of their firm's actions.[115] Proposing such a duty would engage the longstanding debate as to whether corporate governance law should require a duty to the public.[116]

Finally, recall that maturity transformation refers to the asset-liability mismatch that results from the short-term funding of long-term projects.[117] Although not itself a market failure,[118] maturity transformation could cause a maturity gap that could lead to a default if cash flows from long-term projects are insufficient to pay maturing short-term liabilities.[119] Consider how macroprudential regulation should be designed to reduce the likelihood that maturity transformation will cause a maturity gap.

As discussed, the Basel III liquidity requirements already help to reduce the risk that maturity transformation will result in defaults that could trigger a systemic economic collapse.[120] Significant risk remains, however, because not all financial firms that engage in maturity transformation have been designated as SIFIs.[121] Furthermore, a recent policy trend might disfavour SIFI designation and regulation, substituting for it the regulation of financial activities that could create systemic risk.[122] That creates a new macroprudential regulatory challenge: how should maturity transformation be regulated as an activity?[123]

One possible approach would be to innovate on a low-transaction-cost approach, used for years in structured finance to control the risk of maturity transformation.[124] Financial firms, just like issuers of short-term structured finance securities, could carefully monitor and try to cover payment of their maturing securities with cash received from their long-term projects and from issuing new short-term securities. Financial firms, again like those issuers, could also enter into "liquidity" facilities with creditworthy banks that obligate the banks to purchase the newly

115 *Cf* Schwarcz, "Misalignment", *supra* note 108 at 21–29 (arguing for a SIFI public governance duty and explaining why it could be feasibly implemented). Although current regulation requires many SIFIs to establish risk committees, these committees need not consider systemic risk or public harm. For example, risk committees required under the Dodd-Frank Act are only required to focus on risks to the SIFI itself, not to the public. 12 CFR § 252.20–35 (2017). Even the guidelines of the Basel Committee merely require SIFI managers to "look after the interests of the bank as a whole" and do not require them to take into account the possibility of systemic externalities. See Basel Committee on Banking Supervision, *Guidelines: Corporate Governance Principles for Banks* (Basel, Switzerland: Bank for International Settlements [BIS], 2015), online: <www.bis.org/bcbs/publ/d328.pdf>.

116 The accepted wisdom is not to require such a duty because corporate profit maximization provides jobs and other public benefits that exceed any harm. The assumption underlying that wisdom is that any significant public harm would be prohibited by other law or internalized through tort law. That assumption fails, however, for systemic public harm. See *supra* note 109 and accompanying text (observing that systemic public harm is neither prohibited by other law nor internalized through tort law).

117 See Gobat, Yanase & Maloney, *supra* note 14 and accompanying text.

118 *Cf* Borys Grochulsky & Wendy Morrison, "Understanding Market Failure in the 2007-08 Crisis" (2014) Federal Reserve Bank of Richmond Economic Brief EB14-12 at 2 (observing that a potential market failure known as a "pecuniary externality" may be associated with maturity transformation).

119 See Elliott, *supra* note 15 and accompanying text; *supra* note 16 and accompanying text.

120 See *supra* notes 13–16 and accompanying text.

121 See Jeremy C Kress, Patricia A McCoy & Daniel Schwarcz, "Regulating Entities and Activities: Complementary Approach to Nonbank Systemic Risk" (draft on file with author).

122 *Cf ibid* (arguing that the Trump administration is driving that policy trend).

123 A threshold question is whether maturity transformation should always be regulated as an activity. All maturity transformation can result in defaults, but not all defaults — even defaults by financial firms — have systemic consequences. This suggests that maturity transformation as an activity should only be regulated for financial firms whose default could have systemic consequences. SIFI designation has provided a clear basis for identifying those firms. Absent SIFI designation, it is unclear how those firms should be identified. A middle ground might be to designate certain financial firms as SIFIs for limited purposes, such as regulating maturity transformation, in contrast to imposing capital and other substantive entity-based requirements.

124 See Schwarcz, "Systematic Regulation", *supra* note 1 (describing this approach in detail).

issued securities if the financial firm/issuer remains solvent but, due to market disruptions, it cannot otherwise sell those securities. Because the banks only take the timing risk of a cash-flow mismatch and do not bear any credit risk, these liquidity facilities have been — and, as applied to financial firms, should likewise be — low cost and practical.

The foregoing discussed the triggers of systemic risk. Next consider the mechanisms by which systemic risk, once triggered, can be transmitted. Although these mechanisms have not formally been identified, certain factors, discussed below, are associated with the transmission of systemic risk.[125]

Identifying and Controlling the Mechanisms that Could Transmit Systemic Risk

One of the most important factors is interconnectedness. Historically, this was thought to increase financial system resilience by dispersing risk and liabilities among many parties, who could better absorb them.[126] The financial crisis revealed, however, that interconnectedness can also propagate an economic shock throughout the financial system.[127] Consider how macroprudential regulation could be designed to help control the tendency of interconnectedness to propagate economic shocks.

It is the very nature of a financial system to be interconnected. Financial firms routinely do business with each other. Restricting that interconnectedness would restrict finance. Current macroprudential regulation implicitly recognizes this by indirectly regulating interconnectedness. For example, it identifies interconnectedness as an important factor for designating a financial firm as a SIFI[128] and requiring SIFIs to be financially robust or, in the event of their failure, to be

125 Financial Stability Board (FSB), IMF & BIS, *Guidance to Assess the Systemic Importance of Financial Institutions, Markets and Instruments: Initial Considerations* (2009) at 13; Basel Committee on Banking Supervision, *Global systemically important banks: Assessment methodology and the additional loss absorbency requirement* (Basel, Switzerland: BIS, 2011) at 1.

126 See e.g. Franklin Allen & Douglas Gale, "Financial Contagion" (1998) 108 J Political Economy 1 at 4 (finding that an interbank market can increase resilience of the financial system).

127 *Cf* Carlos León et al, "Too-connected-to-fail institutions and payment system's stability: assessing challenges for financial authorities" (Paper prepared for the second BIS CCA Conference on "Monetary policy, financial stability and the business cycle", Ottawa, 12–13 May 2011) at 39 (arguing that interconnectedness is as serious a potential threat to financial stability as size).

128 FSB, IMF & BIS, *supra* note 125.

resolved in ways that have minimum systemic impact. Regulation could also indirectly address interconnectedness by strengthening the resilience of the financial system, as a "system."[129]

Size is also associated with the transmission of systemic risk. Other things being equal, the larger the size of a financial firm, the greater the impact of its failure. Indeed, the very concern over TBTF assumes that the bigger a financial firm, the greater the capacity of its failure to transmit systemic risk. Consider how macroprudential regulation could be designed to help control size.

Current macroprudential regulation addresses size by focusing on ending the TBTF problem.[130] To try to accomplish that, regulators have been advocating massively increasing capital requirements for TBTF firms in order to prevent them from failing and also breaking up such firms so they are no longer TBTF.[131] If (as this chapter argues) the TBTF problem is exaggerated,[132] such measures could be inefficient or even harmful.[133] There may be a less intrusive regulatory approach. Size is a transmission mechanism, not a trigger, of systemic risk. Regulation could therefore focus on trying to protect large SIFIs from systemic risk triggers.

Finally, lack of substitutability is also associated with the transmission of systemic risk. Certain financial firms provide essential services that few other firms provide. For example, CCPs help to ensure the ongoing operation of the financial system by clearing and settling derivatives and other securities contracts.[134] There are few CCPs, and they have few, if any, substitutes.[135]

129 Regulation could accomplish this by reducing the financial system's tight coupling and interactive complexity. Iman Anabtawi & Steven L Schwarcz, "Regulating *Ex Post*: How Law Can Address the Inevitability of Financial Failure" (2013) 92 Tex L Rev 75 at 112 [Anabtawi & Schwarcz, "Regulating *Ex Post*"]. Regulation could reduce the financial system's tight coupling by providing liquidity to a SIFI to prevent its default, thereby helping to prevent a disturbance (a SIFI default) to one part of the financial system from spreading rapidly to other parts of the system, including the SIFI's counterparties. As discussed, however, the Dodd-Frank Act strips the Federal Reserve of much of its last-resort lending powers, in order to try to reduce moral hazard. See *supra* notes 43–45 and accompanying text. The importance of reducing tight coupling provides yet another reason why stripping the Fed of those powers is misguided. Regulation could also reduce the financial system's tight coupling by controlling marking-to-market. See Anabtawi & Schwarcz, "Regulating *Ex Post*" (*ibid* at 129) (discussing in detail how regulation could accomplish that). Regulation could reduce the financial system's interactive complexity by requiring SIFIs to disclose more detailed information about their securities holdings and contractual obligations. SIFIs cause at least two sources of interactive complexity in the financial system, both resulting from information failures. The first source is that market participants do not know what securities other firms hold; they therefore assume that distressed securities owned by a given firm are also held by similarly situated firms (*ibid* at 95). Regulation could help to reduce this source of interactive complexity by requiring SIFIs to disclose — at least periodically, if not also on demand — the amount and identity of their securities holdings. Another source of interactive complexity is that market participants do not know the contractual obligations of other firms (*ibid* at 114). Market participants may refuse to extend credit to firms whose contractual obligations appear similar to a defaulting firm but, in fact, are financially healthy. See *ibid* at 95–96. Regulation could help to reduce this source of interactive complexity by again requiring SIFIs to disclose the amount and nature of their contractual obligations. *Cf* Schwarcz, "Regulating Complexity", *supra* note 49 at 203–07, 246 (discussing disclosure as an option to help avoid a "crisis of confidence").

130 See Glover & Arkhipov, *supra* note 5 and accompanying text; *supra* note 37 and accompanying text.

131 See *supra* notes 44–45 and accompanying text.

132 See *supra* notes 38–42 and accompanying text.

133 See *supra* notes 42–45 and accompanying text.

134 *Cf* Richard Squire, "Clearinghouses as Liquidity Partitioning" (2014) 99 Cornell L Rev 857 ("The [CCP] clearinghouse interposes itself between the parties, serving as the counterparty to each. Instead of selling the cattle future to Buyer, Seller sells it to the clearinghouse, which sells an identical future to Buyer" at 862).

135 Robert T Cox & Robert S Steigerwald, "A CCP is a CCP is a CCP" (2017) Federal Reserve Bank of Chicago Working Paper No PDP 2017-01 (observing that "there are few substitutes for most systemically important CCPs" at 14).

Macroprudential regulation could be designed to help control the lack of substitutability by protecting non-substitutable firms that provide essential financial services through ring-fencing.[136] Ring-fencing is already an essential part of macroprudential regulation.[137]

Cross-border Regulatory Considerations

Being normative, this chapter's analysis should be applicable to lawmaking in any jurisdiction. Except in discussing worldwide capital requirements[138] and secondary-management conflicts,[139] however, this chapter has not addressed how macroprudential regulation should adapt to the cross-border nature of finance. At the very least, it is important to globally coordinate that regulation. US regulators, for example, have been studying a more coordinated regulatory framework for swaps.[140] The Basel Committee on Banking Supervision has also proposed new global liquidity standards to "introduce more consistency."[141]

Although global coordination is important, regulators should be circumspect about globally correlating macroprudential rules. Regulatory correlation could exacerbate systemic risk by decreasing the flexibility and resilience of the financial system.[142] Some argue, for example, that the Basel II capital requirements actually contributed to the financial crisis by globally correlating faulty rules.[143]

Conclusion

Although regulators have accomplished much in the past decade to help stabilize the financial system, much remains to be done. We need a more systematic regulatory framework in order to correct market failures that could trigger and transmit systemic risk.

One such market failure, for example, is excessive SIFI risk-taking. Politicians and the media often claim, without evidence, that SIFIs take excessive risks because they are "too big to fail." The shareholder-primacy model of corporate governance more likely causes that risk-taking, however, by favouring shareholder profits and largely ignoring systemically harmful externalities. To help control that risk-taking, SIFI directors should also consider the public consequences of their firm's actions.

Similarly, maturity transformation is essential to finance, but it creates the default risk that long-term cash flows may be insufficient to pay short-term liabilities. To reduce that risk, regulators might consider innovating on a low-cost and practical approach used for years to control similar risk in structured finance.

136 For a discussion of ring-fencing, see Schwarcz, "Ring-Fencing", *supra* note 17 and accompanying text; Financial Conduct Authority, *supra* note 18 and accompanying text.

137 See *ibid* (discussing current macroprudential ring-fencing regulation).

138 See *supra* note 7 and accompanying text.

139 *Cf supra* note 73 and accompanying text (observing the need for global regulation because good secondary managers can work in financial centres worldwide).

140 *Cf Dodd-Frank Act*, *supra* note 26, § 719(c) (directing regulators to engage in that study).

141 Basel Committee on Banking Supervision, *The Basel Committee's response to the financial crisis: report to the G20* (Basel, Switzerland: BIS, 2015) at 5, online: <www.bis.org/publ/bcbs179.pdf>.

142 Roberta Romano, "For Diversity in the International Regulation of Financial Institutions: Critiquing and Recalibrating the Basel Architecture" (2014) 31 Yale J Reg 1 at 5–7.

143 *Ibid* at 13–20.

Ultimately, this chapter's identification of triggers or transmission mechanisms of systemic risk, or their underlying market failures, is less important than its proposed methodology: to try to secure financial stability by identifying market failures that could trigger and transmit systemic risk, and then to analyze how regulation could help to correct those market failures.

Author's Note

The author thanks Tom Yu, Duke Law School Class of 2020, for excellent research assistance.

Contributors

Anat R. Admati is the George G. C. Parker Professor of Finance and Economics at the Graduate School of Business at Stanford University, faculty director of the Corporations and Society Initiative, and a senior fellow at the Stanford Institute for Economic Policy Research. She has written on information in financial markets, trading mechanism, financial contracting, corporate governance and banking. She is co-author (with Martin Hellwig) of the highly acclaimed book *The Bankers' New Clothes: What's Wrong with Banking and What to Do About It* (Princeton University Press, 2013). Her current research, teaching and advocacy efforts focus on governance issues in the nexus of business, law, political economy and policy. Anat is a member of the Systemic Resolution Advisory Committee of the Federal Deposit Insurance Corporation and has served on the Market Risk Advisory Committee of the Commodities and Futures Trading Commission in the United States. She has also been on a number of editorial boards, served on the board of the American Finance Association, and is a fellow of the Econometric Society and the recipient of multiple awards. Anat holds a B.Sc. from Hebrew University; an M.A., M.Phil. and Ph.D. from Yale University; and an honorary doctorate from the University of Zurich.

Anita Anand is a professor of law and the J. R. Kimber Chair in Investor Protection and Corporate Governance in the Faculty of Law, University of Toronto. She served as associate dean from 2007 to 2009, and since 2010 has served as the academic director of the Centre for the Legal Profession and its Program on Ethics in Law and Business. She is a senior fellow and member of the Governing Board, Massey College, and is cross-appointed to the Rotman School of Management and the School of Public Policy and Governance. During the 2009-2010 academic year, Anita was a visiting scholar at the Bank of Canada and a Herbert Smith Visitor at the University of Cambridge.

Douglas W. Arner is the Kerry Holdings Professor in Law at the University of Hong Kong (HKU) and one of the world's leading experts on financial regulation, in particular the intersection between law, finance and technology. At HKU, he is faculty director of the Faculty of Law's LLM in Compliance and Regulation, LLM in Corporate and Financial Law and Law, Innovation, Technology and Entrepreneurship program. He is a member of the Hong Kong Financial Services Development Council, an executive committee member of the Asia-Pacific Structured Finance Association and a senior visiting fellow of Melbourne Law School, University of Melbourne. He led the development of the world's largest massive open online course, "Introduction to FinTech," launched on edX in May 2018, now with more than 30,000 learners from every country in the world. Douglas served as head of the HKU Department of Law from 2011 to 2014 and as co-director of the Duke University-HKU Asia-America Institute in Transnational Law from 2005 to 2016. From 2006 to 2011, he was the director of HKU's Asian Institute of International Financial Law, which he co-founded in 1999, and from 2012 to 2018, he led a major research project on Hong Kong's future as a leading international financial centre. He has published 15 books and more than 150 articles, chapters and reports on international financial law and regulation, including most recently (with Ross Buckley and Emilios Avgouleas), *Reconceptualising Global Finance and its Regulation* (Cambridge University Press, 2016).

Emilios Avgouleas is the International Banking Law and Finance Chair at the University of Edinburgh and the founding director of the Edinburgh LLM in International Banking Law and Finance. He is also a senior research fellow at Edinburgh University's blockchain lab. He is a member of the Stakeholder Group of the European Banking Authority, elected in the "top-ranking" academics section, and an independent member of the Eurogroup Select Panel of the Hellenic Financial Stability Fund, the major shareholder of the Greek banking sector. Emilios is currently a visiting research professor in the Faculty of Law, University of Hong Kong, and a senior fellow and visiting professor in the Department of European Political Economy at the Libera Università Internazionale degli Studi Sociali Guido Carli. He has served, at different times, as a distinguished visiting professor, visiting professor, visiting professorial fellow and senior research scholar at Yale Law School, Harvard Law School, National University of Singapore, Hong Kong University, Duke Law School and the China-Europe School of Law. Emilios has published extensively in the wider field of finance law and economics, banking theory and regulatory policy, systemic risk and leverage, blockchain derivatives markets and systemic risk distribution, and behavioural economics and financial markets regulation. He is the author of many scholarly articles and acclaimed research monographs, including *Governance of Global Financial Markets: The Law, the Economics, the Politics* (Cambridge University Press, 2012) and *The Mechanics and Regulation of Market Abuse: A Legal and Economic Analysis* (Oxford

University Press, 2005). He co-authored the *Principles of Banking Law*, 3rd edition (Oxford University Press, 2018), and recently co-authored and co-edited three research volumes: *Reconceptualising Global Finance and its Regulation* (Cambridge University Press, 2016), *Capital Markets Union in Europe* (Oxford University Press, 2018) and *The Political Economy of Financial Regulation* (Cambridge University Press, 2019).

Richard Berner is executive-in-residence at the Center for Global Economy and Business at the New York University Stern School of Business, and adjunct professor in the Department of Economics. Dick teaches risk management and financial stability, as well as fintech regulation. He is an adviser to FinRegLab and to HData, Inc., a member of the Milken Fintech Advisory Committee, and a senior adviser to MacroPolicy Perspectives. He served as the first director of the Office of Financial Research, and was counselor to the Secretary of the Treasury. He was co-head of Global Economics and chief US economist at Morgan Stanley, held similar positions at Mellon Bank, Salomon Brothers and Morgan Guaranty Trust Company, and served on the research staff of the Federal Reserve. Dick has been a member of the Economic Advisory Panel of the Federal Reserve Bank of New York, a member of the Panel of Economic Advisers of the Congressional Budget Office, and has served on the Executive Committee of the Board of Directors of the National Bureau of Economic Research. He is a past president and fellow of the National Association for Business Economics.

Ross P. Buckley is the KPMG Law and King & Wood Mallesons Professor of Disruptive Innovation and Law, and a Scientia Professor, at the University of New South Wales in Sydney. His research focus is fintech, regtech and blockchain. His research on these topics has been downloaded more often from the Social Science Research Network than that of any other social scientist. His joint world-first research has developed the generally accepted timeline for the evolution of fintech; reconceptualized the true potential of regtech; undertaken the first comprehensive analysis of the liabilities of blockchain; and, in a forthcoming article in the *Harvard Journal of International Law*, analyzed the rise and regulation of initial coin offerings. Ross chairs the Digital Finance Advisory Panel of the Australian Securities and Investments Commission, and has consulted to government departments in 10 countries, including Australia and the United States. He consults regularly to the Asian Development Bank, and has twice been a Fulbright Scholar, at Yale University and Duke University.

Danny Busch is Chair in Financial Law and director of the Institute for Financial Law at Radboud University, Netherlands. He is a research fellow of Harris Manchester College and a fellow of the Commercial Law Centre at the University of Oxford. He is also visiting professor at Université de Nice Côte d'Azur, Università Cattolica del Sacro Cuore di Milano and Università degli studi di Genova; member of the Dutch Banking Disciplinary Committee (Tuchtcommissie Banken) in Amsterdam; and member of the Appeal Committee of the Dutch Financial Services Complaints Institute (Klachteninstituut Financiële Dienstverlening) in The Hague. Danny is a general editor of the *Oxford EU Financial Regulation Series* and an editor of the *Capital Markets Law Journal* (both published by Oxford University Press). He has published widely in the field of banking and capital markets law, including *Governance of Financial Institutions* (with Guido Ferrarini and Gerard van Solinge) (Oxford University Press, 2019) and *European Banking Union* (with Guido Ferrarini) (Oxford University Press, 2015). He is extensively engaged in providing training to attorneys-at-law, financial regulators and financial professionals. In 1998, he was awarded the degree of magister juris in European and comparative law by the University of Oxford. From 2002 until 2010, he was an attorney-at-law with the leading Dutch international law firm De Brauw Blackstone Westbroek in Amsterdam.

Ron Feldman is first vice president and chief operating officer at the Federal Reserve Bank of Minneapolis, where he leads bank operations, including finance and budgeting, strategic planning, workforce and talent development, and performance against strategic objectives. Ron is also a primary adviser on monetary policy, playing a leadership role in preparing for Federal Open Market Committee meetings and in the development and communication of positions on monetary policy. An expert on financial institutions and related government policies, Ron has authored more than 50 articles on topics related to banking, finance and monetary policy. He is one of the foremost authorities on the too-big-to-fail problem, co-authoring *Too Big to Fail: The Hazards of Bank Bailouts,* published by the Brookings Institution (2004). Ron has a B.A. with distinction from the University of Wisconsin and an M.P.A. from the Maxwell School, Syracuse University, where he was a university fellow. He is a fellow of the National Academy of Public Administration.

Guido Ferrarini is emeritus professor of business law in the Department of Law at the University of Genoa, director of the Centre for Law and Finance, and visiting professor at Radboud University. He holds a J.D. from the University of Genoa (1972), an LL.M. from Yale Law School (1978) and a Dr. jur. h.c. from Ghent University (2009). He is founder and fellow of the European Corporate Governance Institute in Brussels. He was a member of the board of trustees of the International Accounting Standards Committee and an independent director at several Italian blue-chip companies. He was an adviser to the Draghi Commission on Financial Markets Law Reform, to Consob (the Italian Securities Commission) and to the Corporate Governance Committee of the Italian Stock Exchange. Guido has held visiting professor positions at several universities in Europe and the United States. He is the author of many articles in the fields of financial law, corporate law and business law, and the editor of several books, including *European Banking Union* (with Danny Busch) (Oxford University Press, 2015); *Regulation of the EU Financial Markets: MiFID II & MiFIR* (with Danny Busch) (Oxford University Press, 2017); *Capital Markets Union in Europe* (with Emilios Avgouleas and Danny Busch) (Oxford University Press, 2018); and *Governance of Financial Institutions* (with Danny Busch and Gerard van Solinge) (Oxford University Press, 2019).

John Geanakoplos is the James Tobin Professor of Economics at Yale University. He received his B.A. in mathematics from Yale in 1975 (summa cum laude) and his M.A. in mathematics and Ph.D. in economics from Harvard University in 1980. He was the director of the Cowles Foundation for Research in Economics from 1996 to 2005. He co-founded and is currently the director of the Hellenic Studies Program at Yale. He was elected as a fellow of the Econometric Society in 1990, the American Academy of Arts and Sciences in 1999, and the Yale Faculty of Arts and Sciences Senate in 2015 (and chair in 2019-2020). John was awarded the Samuelson Prize in 1999 and was awarded the first Bodossaki Prize in economics in 1994 (for the best economist of Greek heritage under 40). He has directed the economics program at the Santa Fe Institute, and from 2007 to 2014, chaired its science steering committee. He has spent terms as a visiting professor at the Mathematical Sciences Research Institute at the

University of California, Berkeley; Churchill College, University of Cambridge; the University of Pennsylvania; Harvard University; Stanford University; and the Massachusetts Institute of Technology. From 1990 to 1994, he was a managing director and head of fixed income research at Kidder, Peabody & Co. He was one of the founding partners in 1995 of Ellington Capital Management, where he remains a partner. In 1970, John won the United States Junior (under 20) Open Chess Championship. His current research is on the leverage cycle.

Charles Goodhart was trained as an economist at Cambridge and Harvard. His career has alternated between academia (Cambridge, 1963–1965; London School of Economics, 1967-1968; 1985 until today), and work in the official sector, mostly in the Bank of England (Department of Economic Affairs, 1965-1966; Bank of England, 1968–1985; Monetary Policy Committee, 1997–2000). He is now the Norman Sosnow Professor Emeritus at the London School of Economics. He has worked throughout as a specialist monetary economist, focussing on policy issues and on financial regulation, both as an academic and in the Bank. He devised "the Corset" in 1974, advised HK on "the Link" in 1983, and RBNZ on inflation targetry in 1988. He has written more books and articles on these subjects throughout the last 60 years than any sane person would want to read.

Martin F. Hellwig is director emeritus at the Max Planck Institute for Research on Collective Goods in Bonn, Germany. After completing a doctorate in economics at the Massachusetts Institute of Technology, he went on to university positions at Stanford, Princeton, the University of Bonn, the University of Basel, Harvard and the University of Mannheim. Martin has published extensively in many areas of economics and finance, in particular the economics of information and incentives, public economic theory, financial markets and financial institutions. His publications in the 1990s on systemic risk and financial regulation were the first to expose some of the mechanisms that would be detrimental in the crisis of 2007–2009. For his work on international financial regulation, Martin was awarded the 2012 Max Planck Research Award. He is co-author (with Anat Admati) of the highly acclaimed book *The Bankers' New Clothes: What's Wrong with Banking and What to Do About It* (Princeton University Press, 2013). He is past president of the European Economic Association and the Verein für Socialpolitik, a fellow of the Econometric Society and an Honorary Foreign Member of the American Economic Association. He has also been active in policy work as president of the German Monopolkommission and as the first chair of the Advisory Scientific Committee of the European Systemic Risk Board.

Paul Hiebert heads the Systemic Risk and Financial Institutions Division of the European Central Bank (ECB). In this role, he leads systemic risk analysis for the euro area, feeding into the ECB's flagship Financial Stability Review, as well as macroprudential policy for the largest euro-area banks. His current role builds on more than 20 years of experience within the ECB, the International Monetary Fund, the Reserve Bank of Australia and the Canadian Department of Finance in various capacities, spanning economic, financial and policy functions for a wide range of countries. He has published on a diverse set of topics, including financial cycles, global banking, macroprudential policy, housing markets and fiscal policy. He holds an M.A. in economics from McGill University in Montreal.

Howell E. Jackson is the James S. Reid, Jr., Professor of Law at Harvard Law School. His research interests include financial regulation, consumer protection, international finance and federal budget policy. He is the author of numerous scholarly articles and has co-authored three books: *Financial Regulation: Law and Policy*, 2nd edition (Foundation Press, 2018); *Analytical Methods for Lawyers*, 3rd edition (Foundation Press, 2017); and *Fiscal Challenges: An Interdisciplinary Approach to Budget Policy* (Cambridge University Press, 2008). Howell frequently consults with public officials and regulatory agencies on financial regulation. He is also trustee of College Retirement Equities Fund (CREF) and affiliated Teachers Insurance and Annuity Association of America-CREF investment companies. Before joining the Harvard Law School faculty in 1989, Howell practised law in Washington, DC, and was a law clerk for Associate Justice Thurgood Marshall. He received his J.D. and M.B.A. from Harvard University in 1982 and a B.A. from Brown University in 1976.

Kathryn Judge is a professor of law at Columbia Law School. She is an editor of the *Journal of Financial Regulation,* a research member of the European Corporate Governance Institute, and a member of the Financial Research Advisory Council of the Office of Financial Research. She is an expert on financial markets and regulation, including banking, regulatory architecture, central bank governance and regulatory accountability. Her scholarship has been published in numerous leading journals, including *Stanford Law Review, Harvard Law Review, University of Chicago Law Review, Virginia Law Review* and *Columbia Law Review.* She has had two articles selected by peers as among the top business law articles of the year. Prior to joining Columbia, Kathryn clerked for Judge Richard Posner of the 7th Circuit Court of Appeals and Justice Stephen Breyer of the Supreme Court. She also worked as a corporate associate with Latham & Watkins. She is a graduate of Stanford Law School, where she earned the Urban A. Sontheimer Honor (second in class), and Wesleyan University.

Jeremy C. Kress is assistant professor of business law at the University of Michigan Ross School of Business. He researches macroprudential financial regulation, with an emphasis on financial institution corporate governance. Before entering academia, Jeremy was an attorney at the Federal Reserve Board of Governors in Washington, DC. In that capacity, he drafted rules to implement the Dodd-Frank Act and Basel III. He is a senior research fellow at the University of Michigan Center on Finance, Law and Policy, where he previously served as assistant executive director. He has testified before Congress about financial stability oversight and frequently comments on financial regulatory matters in the press.

Donato Masciandaro has been professor of economics since 2001 at Bocconi University, Milan, and Chair in the Economics of Financial Regulation since 2005. Since 2018 he has been director of the Baffi Carefin Centre for Applied Research on International Markets, Banking, Finance and Regulation. Since 2011, he has been a member of the Management Board and honorary treasurer of the Société Universitaire Européenne de Recherches Financières. He has been associate editor of the *Journal of Financial Stability* since 2010 and of the *Italian Economic Journal* since 2016. His research focuses on monetary policy, financial regulation and illegal financial markets.

Patricia A. McCoy is the Liberty Mutual Insurance Professor at Boston College Law School. Her research interests focus on the nexus between financial services, consumer welfare and systemic risk. In 2010-2011, she was the inaugural assistant director of mortgage markets at the newly formed Consumer Financial Protection Bureau in Washington, DC, where she oversaw all of the bureau's mortgage policy initiatives. She has also served on the Consumer Advisory Council of the Federal Reserve Board and the Advisory Council on Economic Inclusion of the Federal Deposit Insurance Corporation. Patricia has been a visiting professor at the University of California, Berkeley, School of Law and a visiting scholar at the Massachusetts Institute of Technology Department of Economics.

Maziar Peihani holds the Lawson Lundell UBC Professorship in Business Law at the Peter A. Allard School of Law, University of British Columbia. His teaching and research focus on banking and financial law. Prior to joining UBC, Maziar was a research fellow with the Centre for International Governance Innovation's (CIGI's) International Law Research Program, as well as a senior fellow with the Hennick Centre for Business and Law at Osgoode Hall Law School, York University.

Roberta Romano is the Sterling Professor of Law at Yale Law School and director of the Yale Law School Center for the Study of Corporate Law. Her research has focused on state competition for corporate charters, the political economy of takeover regulation, shareholder litigation, institutional investor activism, and the regulation of securities markets and financial instruments and institutions. Roberta is a fellow of the American Academy of Arts and Sciences and the European Corporate Governance Institute, a research associate of the National Bureau for Economic Research, a past president of the American Law and Economics Association and the Society for Empirical Legal Studies, and a past co-editor of the *Journal of Law, Economics and Organization*. She is a recipient of the William & Mary Law School's Marshall-Wythe Medallion, which recognizes exceptional accomplishment in law. Roberta has received the Yale Law Women teaching award three times and is the author of *The Genius of American Corporate Law* (AEI Press, 1993) and *The Advantage of Competitive Federalism for Securities Regulation* (AEI Press, 2002), and editor of *Foundations of Corporate Law*, 2nd edition (Foundation Press, 2010).

Paolo Saguato is assistant professor of law at Antonin Scalia Law School, George Mason University (GMU), where he specializes in financial regulation. His research interests encompass the intersection of banking, securities and derivatives regulation and the international and comparative dynamics of financial markets. His recent scholarship has been published in the *Yale Journal on Regulation*; *Stanford Journal of Law, Business and Finance*; *Journal of Corporate Law Studies*; and *The Oxford Handbook of Financial Regulation*. Before joining GMU Law, Paolo was a research fellow at Georgetown Law Center and the London School of Economics and Political Science, and a Global Hauser Fellow at New York University School of Law. He holds an LL.M. from Yale Law School, which he attended as a Fulbright Scholar. He graduated *summa cum laude* from the University of Genoa and received a Ph.D. in private, business and international law from the same institution.

Daniel Schwarcz is the Fredrikson & Byron Professor of Law at the University of Minnesota Law School. His research focuses on a broad range of issues in insurance law and regulation, spanning systemic risk, regulatory federalism, consumer protection, employer-sponsored health insurance and insurance coverage litigation. Daniel's research has won numerous awards, including the American Law Institute's Early Career Scholars Medal and the Liberty Mutual Prize. He is co-author (with Kenneth S. Abraham) of the leading insurance law casebook in the United States, *Insurance Law and Regulation*, 6th edition, which has been used as the principal text in courses on insurance law in more than 100 American law schools. Media outlets such as *The New York Times*, *The Wall Street Journal* and National Public Radio have covered Daniel's scholarship. He regularly testifies to US congressional committees on insurance matters, and has served as an expert witness in a wide range of insurance disputes.

Steven L. Schwarcz is a CIGI senior fellow with the International Law Research Program, and the Stanley A. Star Professor of Law and Business at Duke University School of Law, where he is the founding director of the interdisciplinary Global Financial Markets Center. His areas of research and scholarship include insolvency and bankruptcy law; international finance, capital markets and systemic risk; and commercial law. He is a fellow of the American College of Bankruptcy, a founding member of the International Insolvency Institute, a fellow of the American College of Commercial Finance Lawyers and business law adviser to the American Bar Association Business Law Section.

Tobias H. Tröger has been Chair of Private Law, Trade and Business Law, Jurisprudence at Goethe University Frankfurt since 2011. He has a Ph.D. from the Eberhard Karls University of Tübingen, where he received the qualification of post-doctoral lecturer, and a master of laws from Harvard Law School. His research interests include contract law and contract theory, corporate law (in particular comparative corporate governance and corporate finance), banking law and the economic analysis of law. Tobias is program director of Corporate Finance and Corporate Governance at the Research Center Sustainable Architecture for Finance in Europe and co-director of the Center for Advanced Studies on the Foundations of Law and Finance. He is an adviser to the European Parliament on matters regarding the Single Supervisory Mechanism responsible for the euro area's largest banks. In recent years, he has been a visiting professor at various universities, including Stanford Law School and the University of Pennsylvania Law School.

Mirik van Rijn is a Ph.D. researcher and financial law lecturer at the Institute for Financial Law at Radboud University. His doctoral dissertation analyzes whether the right to effective judicial protection for banks regulated and supervised under the first pillar of the European Banking Union (the Single Supervisory Mechanism) is sufficiently safeguarded. Together with Danny Busch, Mirik has also conducted research, commissioned by the European Central Bank, on the feasibility of cross-sectoral supervision and resolution for systemically important financial institutions. He previously worked as a junior lecturer in EU law at Utrecht University.

Dirk Zetzsche is a full professor and holds the ADA Chair in Financial Law (Inclusive Finance) at the University of Luxembourg, as well as a non-executive directorship at the Center for Business and Corporate Law at the University of Düsseldorf. He holds a doctoral degree from the University of Düsseldorf, an LL.M. from the University of Toronto and a habilitation from the University of Düsseldorf. His main interest lies in international and comparative aspects of banking, financial, corporate, securities and private law. He has published extensively in German and English and advised various European, global and national regulators on the subject. Dirk is a member of the European Banking Institute.